GUNNAR

GARFORS

198

D1335011

HOW I RAN

OUT OF

COUNTRIES*

* By Visiting Random People on Incredible Travels to Every Country in the Whole Wide World

910·4

What you'll get

P.S.

This book is based on factual events, as I remember them. Dialogues have been reconstructed to the best of my ability. Some given names have been changed. Full names are real, unless otherwise stated.

There are some 90 photographs in the Norwegian version of this book. You can see most of them online by visiting garfors.com

THE END?

"Thank you for flying with us!" the captain said over the crackling speakers of the aging Boeing 737, representing a less than famous European airline.

He could have said whatever. I wouldn't have cared less. I had been to 197 countries. This was to be my last. I would soon have visited *every* country in the world. All 198. With a story to tell from each and every one of them.

The instant the plane touched down I felt goose bumps all over my body. I was about to finish my project. Every country. The madness. My life's work. I felt empty. What now? I felt despair. Never another new country to visit? Never that peculiar sensation when you are about to venture into unknown territory? Never any more forced thoughts about travels, impossible visas or erratic route combinations?

But I was happy, more than anything. Joyful, ecstatic, upbeat. And my legs carried my body at a very high speed from the plane across the tarmac, and I was among the first five people in the queue.

I soon reached into the air in a celebratory stretch just as my passport was to be stamped by a policeman, in the grim airport of a remote African country. This was it. The venue didn't quite match the occasion. The concrete walls were cold, white and ugly. I noticed some lapis blue graffiti in a couple of spots near the floor - bored queueing passengers were to blame, I guessed.

The air conditioners made unhealthy sounds, so did the impatient people in the queue behind me. They wanted to get through passport control ASAP. So did I.

I was virtually inside! Although it looked like my bizarre behavior made the grey haired policeman think twice. Should he not stamp the passport after all? Would he order me to return on the same flight? Could he?

Shit!

HOW IT ALL CAME ABOUT

The beer bet

Most of the fuss had started as a bet with my good friend, Ola Akselberg. My Muslim friends joke that I don't need to marry as long as I have him, because he nags me more than four wives ever could. It's a good thing he lives on the outskirts of Oslo - I can barely hear him downtown where I live, on the shortest street in Norway.

I was hosting a party at my place when I told him, "Ola, I will visit every country in the world."

"Every country? How many countries are there?" he asked.

"197," I replied. This was 2009, two years before South Sudan was welcomed as a member of the United Nations and the number increased to 198.

"Ha! There is no chance in hell that you will make it!" he assured me.

"Oh, no?" I asked, offering him my hand. "You wanna bet?"

"OK, but you have to finish by the time you are forty," he stipulated.

My hand was still there. Ola grabbed it and we shared a long handshake. The bet was official. We even had witnesses. There wasn't too much at stake, though. Only honor, glory, and beer. One beer for every country. I had 112 countries left at the time, and I had to visit them within six years to win.

Months passed, and the odds of me actually managing to visit every country before I turned forty were rapidly diminishing. Ola even agreed to add a bottle of rum to our bet when South Sudan became independent. Ola is a fair guy.

Fair, with one exception. He organizes his annual sheep head-eating party every January, something he has done since the '90's. If you miss two of his parties, for whatever reason, you are banned from future participation. You will also be punished for not finishing your head; for not drinking enough aquavit (a strong liqueur flavored with caraway seeds); or, for refusing to eat at least one sheep eye.

The problem is that Ola's sheepheads are too good, so we will accept pretty much any rule. Unfortunately, Ola has realized this. Our little revenge is his nickname, which came about during the height of the "Seinfeld" sitcom fame: *The Sheep Nazi*.

But, being a fair person myself, I can't really blame Ola for the predicament I found myself in. My fate as a traveler was sealed long before that bet, and long before I had ever met Ola. I developed itchy feet at a very early age.

I was four years old, and lived in Naustdal with my mother and little brother, Øystein. Naustdal is a village on the West Coast of Norway, tiny but beautiful, with fjords, mountains, glaciers, rivers, waterfalls, forests, and islands.

Mom had taken us on a walk down the road to the mailboxes. The envelope hunt was on. It was always exciting. Would the envelope from Dad be there today?

The envelope was unmistakable. It was white and thick, with a blue and red dotted line around the front. A blue box in the bottom left corner said, "Par avion," and the stamps had strange characters on them. Even I could tell.

We ran back home with our prize, and I got to open it. Øystein wanted to, but he was just two. Only four-year-olds got to open special envelopes.

There were several sheets of paper inside. They were boring. They were for Mom. She had to read them later - we insisted on being read to aloud first by Dad.

I inserted the audiocassette into the little stereo on the kitchen table and quickly pressed the "play" button.

Øystein smiled in awe. Dad's voice was loud and clear on the tape. He worked as a medical doctor on Royal Viking Sea, a cruise ship that was sailing on the other side of the world. I didn't quite understand how. Mom had told us that the world was round, so didn't that mean Dad and the ship would be sailing upside down? Never mind, that wasn't important. Dad worked there, and he spoke to us, so it couldn't be too bad or too dangerous.

It was like a walkie-talkie, except that it took forever to get a reply. We did of course insist on replying to our dad in the same manner. We recorded stories about our lives in Naustdal, Mom wrote a letter to Dad, and we put all of it into an envelope and sent it back to the other side of the world. For it to travel that far, we had to put a lot of stamps on it. Most of them had the head of our king on them, King Olav. He looked like a nice man.

It must have been amazing for our dad to hear his two sons tell stories from far afield, with Mom inspiring us in the background. It wasn't always easy to keep telling him stuff for many minutes on end. Our mom is frequently heard asking us questions to make sure we didn't forget anything.

Dad, on the other hand, always knew what to tell us. He shared stories about the Forbidden City, the Great Wall, and about boats that had to be maneuvered by long sticks. I remember wondering why they didn't have oars in China. He also told stories about grizzly bears in Alaska, about police officers riding on horses in Canada, and kids riding on boards with wheels in California.

They were fantastic stories from countries far, far away. Lasting impressions were created. I didn't really have a choice. I was destined to become a traveler - a traveler to every country in the world.

The inspiration from my childhood combined with extreme curiosity and more energy than most didn't hurt either. And I eventually ended up traveling to every country in the world. As the youngest amateur in the world. A few people have been younger. They have been full-time travelers, i.e., professional ones. I did it with a full time job and only 5 weeks of holiday each year.

Madness? Maybe, but an interesting form of it. Or so I have been told.

It has also helped that I have a strong desire to discover things or solve problems myself. To my mom's despair. Not only did she have seven kids to raise, but the oldest always nagged her. Two minutes rarely went by without me asking "*koffor*", the West Coast dialect for "why". And I didn't stop at that. Any answer lead to a follow-up question. That I would turn into an extreme traveler probably didn't surprise her much. And she was sufficiently foresighted to raise us to want to explore for ourselves, to try and to fail. To not go for the easy way out, the safe choice, the solutions that never become memorable ones.

"Mom, we do not want to stay in a tent. It's wet and cold!" we could complain.

"Then you will remember this, it will be a memory for life. Just imagine how boring it would be if everything was normal, always."

Probably the wisest words I have ever heard.

I played football from I was the size of a fist. A lot of training eliminated my restlessness and kept my energy levels relatively stable. But I never made it past Norwegian Division 2 and a trial with Plymouth Argyle in England. When I finally quit team sports, I exchanged the football for planes. A lot of them. And in 2004 I discovered the stans. The seven countries in the world ending with –stan.

The trips contributed to an understanding that impulsiveness is key to the best way to travel. Too much planning has killed millions of holidays, as it removes both the urge to discover and curiosity overall. Planning everything is not possible. And if you plan too much you will only annoy your fellow travelers. Because things rarely go as planned. Whenever you make a plan it gets a name. Plan B. The medicine is called creativity and impulsiveness.

I decided to visit every country in the world in 2008. I had almost run out of stan countries, and I needed another goal. To be able to finish such a project in a relatively short amount of time, I was depending on having two passports. Two Norwegian ones, mind you. The government allows this if work demands it. And it does. If my main passport is with an embassy, waiting to be stamped with a visa, I require a second passport to take part in work related events abroad. At the busiest of times, I filled both passports with stamps in 18 months. And popped by the police station in Oslo to pick up two new ones.

To travel to every country in the world may seem like the ultimate ego trip. And it is. But it isn't arrogant or decadent.

Not necessarily.

I have decided to travel, to spend all my money and most of my spare time on it. You need a hobby, after all. Other people collect stamps and use a lot of time and effort to find that one particular stamp and buy it. Before it is put into a safety deposit box. It is so easy with a stamp. Either you have it or you do not. It is different with traveling. Journeys result in various experiences. And they last forever and will always be mine. Even without a box in a bank.

The radio breakfast show

In May, 2012, I was interviewed by celebrity DJ and journalist Ronny Brede Aase on Norwegian Broadcasting Corporation's NRK P3, the national radio station with the best music. Their popular breakfast show had picked up that I had been to 197 countries and planned to visit the last one too. It was way too early for me, but Ronny was all smiles. He must consume a fair amount of coffee to manage. I assume all breakfast hosts do. The interview started rather normal.

"Which country will be your final one?"

"What is the best country in the world?" (I am asked this question 10-20 times a week).

"And which travel story have you told most often?"

I told Ronny and the radio listeners about Oleg from Turkmenistan. Our guide god. You will meet him later.

Before a little bit of music, before Ola. That beer betting mate of mine. In the middle of the interview he suddenly came into the studio with 8 cases of beer and a bottle of rum. On a trolley he had borrowed from NRKs transport department. He acknowledged that the bet was lost, a few days before I was scheduled to land in the last country. At least he was PR savvy enough to lose it in style, on live radio. Having conspired with P3 and gone behind my back, and all.

"*Ryggstikkar!*" I told Ola on NRK P3. It means "back stabber", and is not in the Norwegian dictionary. I was reminded of the term from a lot of people that summer.

Ola is a great guy and an amazing friend. He even loses bets with a smile. A little one.

Before pushing the cases of beer to the lot where he had parked his car. We barely managed to fit them all in. I don't have my own car. I am rarely at home anyway, and I would rather spend my money on airplane fuel. Not on 95 octane. He drove the 198 bottles all the way to my door. That's what I call a good loser of a bet.

I was in the air again only three days later. To finish my count to 198.

The start

Long before all of this, I was just a traveler. By the time I was thirty-four - the beginning of the bet - I had visited eighty-five countries.

My mom and dad are both well-educated and well-traveled. They saw the value of showing their kids large parts of Norway and foreign countries, to open our eyes to the diversity of the world.

Mom, in particular, also believed in letting us find things out for ourselves. Her attitude was, "If you fall down from that tree, you might learn to be more careful next time."

I might be slightly biased, but I'd say that was great parenting - and much better than just telling curious kids what to do and what not to do. Essentially, my parents were teaching us the importance of both theory and practice. I like both, but only if theory can be verified through experimentation. Or travel.

So, we traveled a lot within Norway when I was a kid, but also to Greece, Ireland, Sweden, and the UK. There were nine of us (eventually my brother Øystein and I were followed by five more siblings), so to be able to afford it, my parents bought a huge caravan that was pulled by our minibus.

Yeah, of course we had a minibus - to the amusement of the rest of the village. The other kids would say, "There are three buses in Naustdal. One says Førde, one says Bergen, and one says Garfors," before laughing their heads off.

I didn't really get the purpose of the English language until we traveled to England when I was about fourteen. We stayed in our caravan parked outside Newquay, Cornwall, for three weeks. We met loads of English kids there. To communicate we had to speak English, and I suddenly realized that English was useful. Fun, even.

Back home in Norway, studying English in school suddenly became interesting, too, now that I understood that through that language I could explore and communicate with more of the world.

When I was seventeen, my friend Tor Egil Hovland and I got European train passes and traveled through as many countries as possible. We had no money, so we slept on benches, on trains, in train stations, and in the occasional youth hostel. It was upon arrival back home that I discovered I was infected by the travel bug.

I would get even more inspiration just a few weeks later, when I traveled to Lawrenceburg, Indiana, as an exchange student for a year.

After my year in the land of the free, I returned to Norway to finish high school. Two years later I discovered that the chance for me to continue my studies at university in Norway was slim because the grade point average to get into journalism - my chosen major - was sky high.

But why worry? The world was at my feet. I returned to Cornwall and enrolled at Falmouth College of the Arts.

I continued to travel, usually now with friends or girlfriends, and even managed to join the legendary "Mile-High Club," which turned out to be a dubious distinction in retrospect. We snuck into the tiny toilet of the Eastern European aircraft rather discreetly. Or so we thought. And we somehow managed to perform in the cramped space. Afterward, I left the toilet first.

A male cabin crew member stood just outside.

"Was that good for you?" he sneered.

I have rarely been more red-faced. But neither that nor other mishaps could stop me from travel. I was hooked.

The travel rules

Why I count 198 countries? There are many ways of counting countries. FIFA does for instance count 209 member countries. The world's football association doesn't count the UK as one, but as four (Northern Ireland, Scotland, England and Wales) and the Vatican is not a member, while American Samoa, Tahiti and Faroe Islands are. Other examples include IOC, the International Olympic Committee, with 204 members and the UN with 193 members and 2 observer states.

I count all 193 UN countries.

I also count the 2 observer states, the Vatican and Palestine.

Yet another 3 countries are acknowledged by a number of the 195 above. I do therefore also count Kosovo, Western Sahara and Taiwan.

That gives a total of 198.

A lot of people ask me how I count a country. The answer is short, I must have done something there and have a story to tell. And no, I do not count transit stops in airports. It should also be needless to say that I prefer to stay for a while. To have time to explore, time to meet people.

I don't count driving through a country by car or train either. I must have had my feet on the ground. Some people even count an airport transit without having left the plane. Others demand a passport stamp or having had a toe merely across the border. That makes at least 11 countries a day possible by private plane. And four friends from the Netherlands, Sweden and Australia managed 17 countries in 24 hours by car in 2012. I challenged that world record together with my friends Øystein Djupvik and Tay-young Pak two years later. We equalled the feat. But sharing world records isn't quite my cup of tea. The three of us would try again.

Counting in such a manner is pushing it, in my opinion, but I suppose everything is allowed in love and war and world record attempts. The most important thing is to have your own consistent rules.

The next question thrown at me is usually whether I need to stay overnight to count a country. Of course not. I may have visited a country 10 or 15 times in a year without having spent the night there. That is easily achievable by taking a morning train or plane, spending all day in meetings, having breakfast, lunch and dinner, running a marathon, meeting friends, drinking a dozen umbrella drinks, shopping to the limit of the Platinum Am Ex or having amazing sex with that special one. Or a combination of the above. And still manage to leave the country by midnight. Should I ignore the examples above, including a possible conception of a potential first born daughter?

I can alternatively have landed at 23:40, taken a taxi to the airport hotel, gone to bed, raised six hours later for a continental breakfast with burned toast, a very soft boiled egg and a slice of Edamer, returned to the airport, cleared security and been safely in seat 8A to another country by 06:40 the following morning. I have indeed spent the night, but experienced next to nothing. Do you still insist that staying the night is required?

Yes? Then, how do you count the Vatican?

Why I hate guide books

Did I mention that I have an aversion against travel guide books? I hate them. Like garden owners hate smelly little brats that steal their apples. Guide books reduce your creativity and destroy impulsiveness. A lot of people use guide books to plan their holidays to death. All I know is that such plans must, shall and have to be changed.

I write the best guide books myself. On paper or in my head. And I do appreciate not to be charged with plagiarizing other people's works. Or holidays. That soon happens if I base everything I do on well-meaning advice of others. Stay in the same room as travel writer X when he visited country Y and found the service amazing and the value of money much better than at home. A lunch in her favorite coffee shop where Wi-Fi is free and the coffee was made exactly according to her taste. Or a trip to the statue park, a visit to the concert hall, a little bit of haggling in that local market or a pint of that must-have dark beer in the particular pub by the park. A travel writer often tries to cover all audiences. Everyone will get something. I am not everyone.

When I arrive in a new place I want to do so with an uncorrupted mind. If I start out with a stress creating list of what I have to see, I have lost as a traveler. Not because planning is all bad. But because I base my holiday on what a random contributor to a guide book coincidentally ended up doing before me. During the 12 or 24 hours he was in town. Seven months or two years ago. Or in the previous millennium. What she wrote has since helped create queues of backpackers between all the places we just *have to see*. The owners of the bars, cafés and restaurants have therefore hiked their prices. Of course! Wouldn't you? With brigades of well-off foreigners coming from nowhere into your business? I prefer meeting local people, asking them for advice on what to do and what not to. Even though I, as a shy Norwegian, usually need to drink myself into daring entering into such encounters. In the nearest bar with free WiFi.

That is why I never travel with guidebooks. Then again, where is the exception that proves the rule? The guide book series Inyourpocket.com is free for download online. But even better, it is written by locals and updated several times a year. Unfortunately it primarily covers European and some Asian cities.

I try, as far as possible, to ask local people of what to do wherever I am. Firstly, I might make a friend. They also know their area, sights, restaurants, cafés and nightlife much better than someone who passes through. There is of course one exception. People usually know nothing about hotels where they live.

To travel without being bombarded with impressions in advance works best for me. I want to come there with a free and open mind. But to read up on culture, history and political and religious matters is good. It provides background info. And might help me avoid making stupid mistakes or insults. Or go to jail.

Extensive planning is still overvalued, in my opinion. How can I really plan what to do in a place I don't know? All I risk doing is to rule out amazing possibilities. Possibilities I didn't know about until I met Oleg, Relebohile or Kaure.

How do I know so much about guide books, by the way? Well, I used them in the past. Until I actually realized that I was much better off without them.

"198" and how it was written

So, this is not a guide book.

I hope it can be a source of inspiration with stories from every country in the world. Please keep your tolerance of irony intact while reading. Each country has its own chapter. But they are not listed alphabetically, chronologically based on the time of my trips or by continent. Each country is listed under one of 21 umbrella chapters. Each covers a certain theme. Such as trouble, women or drinks.

Sometimes all of the above are combined.

To easier navigate your way through the book, there are lists in the back of the book where you can find an alphabetical list of the countries, divided by continent. There you can also tick off which countries you have visited. Or visit garfors.com to find a printable list, should you not wish to carry the book around in your luggage. There you will also find photos from many of my trips.

"198" starts with a chapter covering "the stan countries." That's where I decided to see more than the western world. Where the madness started.

Project: visit the entire world.

Prospect: running out of countries.

198.

THE STANS

In 2004, my brother Øystein and I decided to go to Kyrgyzstan. "The Stans" is a well-known expression among my friends, because that's really where it all started.

Øystein and I were at our mom's house in Naustdal. I was visiting for the weekend from Oslo, where I work. In the local newspaper, *Firda*, there was a story about a group of Kyrgyz engineers who had come to the region to learn about hydroelectricity. The story itself wasn't very exciting, but Kyrgyzstan certainly was. Øystein and I had already discussed going somewhere off the beaten track together. He's a teacher and gets time off for the autumn holidays, and I had some vacation days saved up.

I shouted to Øystein, and showed him the article. Neither of us had ever even heard of this former Soviet Union Republic until now. We quickly found the atlas and an encyclopaedia and looked it up. We even threw in a few Internet searches on Mom's awfully slow dial-up connection.

The biggest drawback, it turned out, was the high ticket prices to Bishkek, the capital. We decided to think about it.

I was back at work in Oslo the following Monday. And there, waiting for me, was an email from Sharad Sadhu, the technical director of the Asian-Pacific Broadcasting Union, headquartered in Kuala Lumpur. He wanted me to give a speech at ABU's General Assembly that autumn, which just happened to be taking place in Almaty, Kazakhstan - just kilometers away from neighboring Kyrgyzstan.

I immediately called Øystein. "You are not gonna believe this!" I told him before sharing my news.

Øystein's autumn holiday coincided with the trip, and since my travel would be covered by work, we each paid half for his ticket. It was fate. Or at least, I would have said that it was had I believed in such.

Kazakhstan

I took Lufthansa to Almaty, Kazakhstan. Øystein would follow a few days later. I knew the visit would be memorable, even before I got to passport control, when I saw a young man waiting for me with a sign that read "ABU delegate." My greeter, Vladimir, escorted me past the long passport control queue to a special designated policeman. My passport was inspected and stamped within a minute.

And the VIP treatment didn't stop there. Two soldiers armed with Russian machine guns guarded the exit from the baggage hall. They wanted to examine my luggage, but Vladimir shook his head and showed them his white plastic ID card. They didn't touch my luggage, and they even saluted me into their country.

I suppose I should've thought to smuggle something. I wonder if diplomats ponder about whether to smuggle something whenever they go through customs. Then again, they probably *do* smuggle various goodies every time. Where is my diplomatic passport?

Outside the airport, I was met by a private driver who took me to a luxurious hotel. Luxury, Soviet style, that is. The huge suite of rooms even came with Kazakh "champagne". And yes, Kazakh bubbles are very good.

I walked over to the conference venue before lunch the following day, a Tuesday, even though my presentation wasn't until Wednesday. I like to be prepared, so I handed over my PowerPoint presentation on a memory stick to the conference staff, and then stayed to watch a few other presentations.

It was all very formal. Everyone wore suits and ties, and I noticed the occasional bowtie, too. As usual, I was the youngest delegate at the conference.

During a coffee break, I was approached by a young Korean man. He was polite, but clearly on a mission.

"Can you please ask a question to my boss?" he asked. "He is a very high executive, and he will lose face if he gets no questions."

He seemed rather desperate, so I reluctantly agreed. He immediately produced a printed question on a little piece of paper, which he discreetly passed to me. The Korean had come prepared. I was not happy to ask a planted question, but I also felt sorry for the young assistant. If his boss lost face, so would he.

Luckily, someone else asked the Korean executive a question, which also may have been planted. In any event, I welcomed the opportunity to refrain from asking mine.

My presentation the next day started out OK, but soon went down the drain. I had included some short video clips of the world's first mobile news video and of a Norwegian comedian who laughed constantly while being flown on an F-16 fighter plane. But Kazakh hardware wasn't built to process videos, and they froze up several times. There's nothing worse than the demo effect when you're on stage. When what you want to show just won't work.

I've given hundreds of presentations since then, and I've always insisted on running through them in advance or using my own laptop, all the wiser for my mistake. Fortunately, several of the Asian delegates were still impressed, despite my technical difficulties, and asked quite a few questions.

I hadn't planted a single one.

We had been told to get up early the following day for a tour of some of Kazakhstan's most impressive sights. The 300 of us were transported by several buses, each with its own police escort. Two police cars each.

Raushana, our guide, told us we were going to see the capital city, Astana.

"What?" I asked. I had done my homework since reading about Kazakhstan and Kyrgyzstan for the first time. "But that is a thousand kilometers (621 miles) away!"

Raushana just nodded and smiled.

We were soon back at the airport. Two Boeings took us to Astana, where we landed ninety minutes later. New buses awaited us in the parking lot outside the airport, along with at least twenty police cars. I entered one of the green buses. We had one police car in front of us, one just behind us, and police cars were blocking every intersection from the airport to the city. Don't get the wrong idea. Astana is a safe city. This was more for show than anything else. But it sure worked. I have rarely felt more VIP.

We were shown around the presidential museum and the gigantic aquarium. Yes, the aquarium. In the middle of Central Asia, almost 3,000 kilometers from the nearest sea. If you aim to impress, do it properly. It's in the DNA of Central Asian dictators.

Lunch would be served in the banquet hall below the huge dome of the presidential museum. But not until after the mayor finished his speech in Russian, which was repeatedly stopped to allow for translations in English. It took a while.

Local vodka and whiskey were served when he finally finished, along with a four-course meal. A forty-member orchestra was playing. Not bad for a working lunch. I'm sure I could get used to it.

Before our return to Almaty, we had time to visit the 97-meter-high Baiterek tower. It looks like a lollipop and is the most famous landmark in what is one of the world's few "fake" cities. Kazakh politicians decided to build a new capital city from scratch, and billions of dollars have been spent to construct what is now a modern and rather impressive capital. There was virtually nothing there before.

The police cars guided us back to the airport. Upon our arrival in Almaty, we were offered fermented horse milk. I would only recommend it to anyone with a severe cold and inability to smell and taste.

My brother arrived that evening. I had registered him to attend the conference as my consort, which meant that he, too, was picked up by a private driver at the airport.

Øystein and twelve other consorts - all middle-aged wives - had their own agenda on the last day of the conference. They were taken on a sightseeing trip by minibus. They not only had a police escort, but their own in-bus giant of a bodyguard who spoke no English. The Kazakhs don't joke around when it comes to personal security. Or the impression thereof.

Our last night at the conference included a banquet at the Japanese Embassy. All delegates and their consorts were invited. It was stylish. Very stylish. Øystein experienced minor shock.

"So this is normal for all the conferences you attend?" he asked.

I said nothing and smiled, deciding to let him believe that was the case.
We stayed in Almaty for a few days after the conference. We wanted to
experience the local nightlife. We found a cellar bar with a bunch of people our
age - a relief after the embassy party where Øystein and I had been half the
average age. Tonight's party was much less formal. Beers were thirty cents apiece, and
beautiful women were plentiful. Advanced high heel walking is presumably a
subject in school there.

Two of the most beautiful girls suddenly started stripping. No one reacted.
Except for the two Garforses, who were not quite used to such things back
home. The girls clearly worked there - they were serving drinks in the bar later. I
imagine they were tipped a bit more than the other servers. The locals we spoke
to explained that stripping was normal and expected in Kazakh bars.

"We have worked hard all week, the least we deserve is some quality stripping,"
they told us.

Øystein and I didn't complain.

Kyrgyzstan

The bus ride from Almaty to Bishkek, Kyrgyzstan, was pretty nice. We drove in
between mountains, passing traditional green, yellow, blue and orange worn-
down brick houses partially covered in cement, with fruit sellers by the road, lined
with trees I had never seen before. But there was one exception to the niceness:
the ten-minute stop at a break area, complete with some sort of toilet. I have seen
more appealing shacks in the slums of Mumbai. Such so-called toilets, or holes in
the ground covered by a roof-like structure, are plentiful in Central Asia. Bring
your own toilet paper if you're into such luxuries - the substitute here is called
"left hand," and it contributes to widespread food poisoning.

Bishkek is a nice little town about the size of Austin, Texas but with a much
more rural feel to it. Øystein and I walked from the bus station into town, where
we met with the owner of our rented flat. He let us in, took our money, and gave
us keys. He didn't seem to know any English, but managed to communicate
rather effectively via a series of grunts.

As soon as he left, Øystein and I put down our bags and headed back out again
to explore the town on foot. We hadn't come to watch Soviet wall paper peel.

On the Ala-Too Square, in front of the presidential palace, various
photographers were trying to attract the attention of kids, and the wallets of their
parents. They did so by displaying various items for the kids to be photographed
with, such as a rocking horse, a miniature car, and someone dressed up as the
Cookie Monster from Sesame Street. One particularly clever guy had a Superman
outfit the kids could put on before having their picture taken. He had a long
queue full of little boys. The girls, on the other hand, preferred being

photographed sitting on top of a life-size My Little Pony doll. Somehow, I doubt that the rightful rights owners of Superman and My Little Pony got a share of the income.

We strolled on and entered a shopping center. You could buy almost anything there, as long as you didn't insist on authentic merchandise. Fake "Nokia" phones, "Sony" televisions, "Philips" DVD players and "Gucci" T-shirts were everywhere.

I bought a raincoat, presumably not a real Hermes. It still proved quite useful when hiking in the mountains later. Kyrgyzstan is fantastic mountain country, and boasts one of the easiest 7,000-meter (23,406 feet) climbs in the world - Lenin Peak. Hundreds of people make their way to its summit every year. Øystein insisted that we conquer a peak, although not necessarily one of Lenin's dimensions.

Through a travel agent we met Sergei, a 22-year-old mountain guide. He asked if his younger brother, Ivan, could join us on our climb.

"It won't cost you anything extra. He would just love to practice English," Sergei explained. We figured the more the merrier. Once a deal was struck, they called their driver, Idar, and the five of us headed for the mountains in a rather modern Audi 100.

We were going to be climbing higher than either Øystein or I had ever been before - 4,300 meters (14,107 feet), so our guides insisted that we stay one night at base camp to acclimate to the altitude.

They carried all the tents, sleeping bags, food and drinks. They wouldn't allow us to carry a thing. "You are our guests," we were told.

We got up early the next morning and practically ran up the mountain, the last hundred meters or so through snow and without any sign of altitude sickness along the way. The Kyrgyz brothers were impressed. We were awarded by amazing views of a small glacier on a distant peak, and the town of Bishkek down below us.

Back in town that evening, we invited Sergei and Ivan to a restaurant, where we ordered Russian caviar. That got us talking about fish and fishing in this landlocked country.

"You cannot leave without seeing Issyk-Kul Lake," Ivan insisted. "It is as close as we will ever get to see the ocean."

Issyk-Kul is the second largest mountain lake in the world, trailing only Lake Titicaca in Peru and Bolivia. Its depth of 668 meters (2,191 feet) makes it the seventh deepest lake in the world. Øystein and I were game to see it, and the decision was made to leave for Issyk-Kul early the next morning. Kyrgyz vodka would have to wait.

We were unceremoniously awakened the next morning by our driver Idar, who was vigorously honking the Audi's loud German horn. Idar was about forty-five, and sported a mustache that would make any male porn star green, yellow and purple with envy. He spoke no English, but Sergei told us that Idar had seventeen girlfriends in Bishkek and other nearby towns. He stayed with each of them for a night or two before moving on to the next. The goal was to decide which one would become his lucky future wife.

But according to Sergei, Idar's mom was not particularly impressed with this little scheme, and had demanded that her son choose. He had opted for Julia, one of the seventeen, and the wedding would take place in just a few weeks.

"It's a shame you are not here for that! Idar would love to have some special foreign guests for the occasion," Sergei told us. "He is currently saying goodbye to his other sixteen girlfriends, spending one last night with each and every one of them before picking up all the clothes and belongings he has left at their flats."

Øystein and I laughed. "What a sly man!" Øystein said in Norwegian. Their way of deciding on a wife was a bit different than we are used to at home.

We drove eastward down Lenin Street. The memory of Soviet times won't leave Kyrgyzstan any time soon. Vladimir Lenin may be seen as a crook and a killer in many parts of the world, but not to the same degree in all the fifteen former Soviet Republics.

The Audi was moving fast. We were keen for the day trip Sergei had arranged, but had made it clear that we wanted to get back to town by evening. After all, it was Saturday, and we had a city to conquer. So Idar was pushing it, in fourth gear. The speedometer showed 120 kilometers per hour. The speed limit was 80. Not surprisingly, we were soon stopped by police. Idar swore loudly in Russian, while braking and pulling over to the side of the road. He left the car to speak with the three officers, all of whom were wearing traditional big, tall, pointy old communist police hats.

"What will happen to him?" Øystein asked, sounding a bit nervous. We had heard a couple of stories about police brutality in this part of the world.

Sergei shrugged. All we could do was wait.

Idar was back in the car a few minutes later. He threw a piece of paper onto the dashboard, swearing, before immediately spinning the car back into motion. Probably not the best way to leave three police officers, but our driver had his ways. Sergei told us he had been given a fine of six dollars.

"Six dollars? Bloody hell, it's cheap to speed in the Stans," Øystein said.

Sergei laughed. "Rich Norwegians!"

Idar was still not too happy. Actually, he was furious. This mysteriously made his right foot rather heavy. Now we were doing 140 km/h in a 60 km/h zone.

Within minutes, Sergei shouted, "Shit!" We could see another police patrol car behind us. Idar cursed and hit his steering wheel before pulling over. Øystein and I held our breath in the back seat. Two violations within a matter of minutes. Now what?

Idar left the car and walked over to the two officers. He was back just two minutes later. He tossed another piece of paper onto the dashboard and muttered something to Sergei before he put the stick in gear and yet again continued on to Issyk-Kul - this time at a slightly more measured speed.

"What's the damage?" I asked.

"Only three dollars," Sergei said.

"But why so low? He drove faster this time, and inside a village," Øystein wondered.

"Yes, but this policeman knows his grandmother," Sergei replied, smiling. Long live the Stans.

Less than an hour later, we arrived at the little spa town of Cholpon-Ata, on the northern shore of Lake Issyk-Kul. The place was picture postcard perfect, with incredibly beautiful mountains surrounding the lake. Our race car driver parked the Audi and disappeared in an instant. The rest of us - Øystein and Sergei and Ivan and I - did the usual holiday stuff. We walked to the beach, stripped down to our trunks, and dove into the slightly salty water. It was a spectacular bathing experience, given the beautiful scenery and the pleasant temperature of the lake. Turns out Issyk-Kul means "hot lake" in Kyrgyz.

After an hour or so, we dressed and headed back to the village to try to find Idar. No luck. Sergei and Ivan started asking around, and eventually found him about fifteen minutes later. He was playing Counter-Strike - a shoot-'em-up computer game - with a friend in the friend's mother's living room. We witnessed a few computer killings before Sergei managed to get our reluctant driver to return to work. Idar had a rather psychotic look in his eyes.

Øystein and I were a little wary of the drive home, and with good reason. Idar was soon doing 170 km/h on leaded fuel and more than a little Counter-Strike inspiration. Luckily, the police officers had gone home for the day. Or perhaps we weren't so lucky after all. Pretty soon, a Mercedes with tinted windows came from behind and passed us. Idar was not having it! He was not going to be passed by a bloody black Merc.

The speedometer passed 200 km/h, and Øystein and I shuddered a bit in the back seat, where seat belts are optional - as in, there were none - in Kyrgyzstan. Idar managed to reclaim the lead, eventually passing the Mercedes on a curve. He laughed and shouted "Victory!" in English. I guess he had picked up more than road rage from Counter-Strike.

Øystein and I exchanged a look, both of us just happy that the race was over and we were still alive. We soon stopped at a yurt-like tent where a woman was selling fresh fish.

"Caught today in Issyk-Kul," Sergei promised, so we picked up a few.

"You are invited to dinner at our parents' home," Ivan told us.

Half an hour before reaching Bishkek, Idar turned off the main highway and onto a gravel road. We drove a few hundred meters before arriving at a small farm, where we were introduced to Sergei and Ivan's parents. They spoke no English, but greeted us warmly. Their dad was named Sergei, of course. To have the same name as your father is not unusual in Kyrgyzstan.

Sergei Sr. had gigantic hands. My hand drowned in his when he shook it. Good genes and hard work, I guessed. There didn't appear to be a tractor on the farm. Olga, his wife, accepted the fish we had brought, and we were asked to go to the garden to pick potatoes and tomatoes. A fresh dinner, indeed!

A six-year-old boy from the neighborhood also joined us for dinner. His name, too, was Sergei. Name creativity has some way to go in this country.

We were served local vodka with dinner. Not a huge surprise, seeing that we were in vodka country. Sergei Sr. poured generous drinks, and we all smiled and toasted. Well, all except Idar. He was clearly a drinking man, and was looking anything but happy with only water in his glass.

The oldest Sergei gave him a pointed look that said, "My sons will be driven downtown later by a sober Idar!" Øystein and I appreciated that. A Counter-Strike-influenced, wanna-be-racecar-driver with *any* amount of alcohol in his bloodstream was not high on our wish list.

When our delicious dinner came to an end, we were seen off by Sergei and Ivan's family, who waved as we drove back down the gravel road to the highway. Idar was smiling again, obviously anticipating his first drink of the day. And back in Bishkek, we found a small kiosk where we bought him a bottle of vodka to compensate for the inhumanely delayed drinking session. And another one as a much appreciated tip for not crashing the car and killing us. Idar smiled his biggest smile and shook our hands. He would presumably spend the night saying goodbye to a girlfriend or two.

It was quite late, but it was Saturday night, and Sergei and Ivan had plans to show us the town. It turned out to be a night I will not forget any time soon. They took us to the best club in Bishkek, with a big black and white sign out front that said "Face Control" in English. Which meant that only the rich, pretty and famous were allowed in. This sort of thing is being done in clubs all over the world on a daily basis, but I had never before seen it done so explicitly - or so honestly.

The practice was successful, judging by the dance floor view. We received a lot of smiles from girls, and vicious looks from guys. The U.S. has long had an Air Force base outside Bishkek, and the American soldiers are not well liked in the community. This is largely because they pick up a lot of beautiful girls and take them back to the U.S. after completing their service. Many Kyrgyz girls are attracted to their uniforms, the prospect of moving to the West, and the

American Dream. This is not surprising, really. There are a lot of American TV series, films, products and ads in Kyrgyzstan.

The local guys in the club obviously thought Øystein and I were Americans, and continued to look daggers at us as we went up to the bar and ordered drinks. It didn't help much when two pretty girls came over to join us and chat us up. About half an hour later, we heard angry shouting coming from a guy across the bar.

"We need to leave immediately," Sergei whispered to me. "He says you are fucking Americans, and that he will slice you up as soon as he finishes his beer."

A lot of guys in Kyrgyzstan carry knives on a regular basis, and we didn't particularly want to find out if he was joking or not. We threw some money to the bartender, left our drinks, and hurried off. The girls joined us, and the six of us flagged down a taxi. Edna, one of the girls, sat in the front passenger seat with me, and the other four crammed into the back.

"I told the driver to take us to a kiosk," Sergei told me, after rattling something off to him in Kyrgyz.

That sounded strange, given that it was the middle of the night. But the driver stopped only 400 meters later by a tiny small kiosk with windows on all sides. We got out of the cab and peered inside the windows. It was dark inside, and we couldn't see anything but bottles, primarily vodka.

"We need some drinks. Party continues at your flat," said Sergei.

"But it's closed," Øystein replied.

Sergei smiled. "Oh, yeah?"

He knocked four times on the glass of the shack. The light came on a few seconds later, and a middle-aged woman with dyed blond curly hair suddenly appeared. She had been sleeping on a mattress on the floor. The shop keeper swiftly produced two bottles of local booze, received three dollars in return, switched the light off again and returned to her mattress. Shopping, Kyrgyz-style.

The taxi driver took us back to the flat, where the six of us emptied the bottles. Øystein managed to make it to his bed, while Edna fell asleep on my arm on the carpet. Sergei and Ivan fell asleep with the other girl between them on the sofa. The flat looked like a war zone. It had been a good night.

The morning after was not.

Two days later, Øystein and I returned by bus to Almaty. Or at least we attempted to. We walked to the bus station and entered the right bus, right on schedule. But the driver had no intention of leaving until the bus was full.

An hour passed, and our fellow passengers were close to mutiny. Only two seats were empty, there was no sign of anyone else wanting to go to Almaty, but the driver still wouldn't budge. Finally, all of us chipped in to pay for the two remaining seats, and we were on our way.

When we arrived at the border, all the locals flew through passport control and customs. This was not the case for the two Norwegians in the queue.

A policeman wearing a blue shirt stained with red wine over his large beer belly waved us into a little painted brick house. He had a pistol in his belt. His English was non-existent, but he still managed to efficiently order us to sit on two metal chairs that were standing against the wall. He slammed the door shut and took a seat behind the big wooden desk that monopolized the room.

The policeman said something to us in Russian. "Sorry, only English," I told him. He was not impressed and put the gun down on the desk, with the barrel pointing at us. "Nice guy," I remember thinking to myself. The officer opened the desk drawer and produced a big red book, which he placed on the desk. He opened it and turned to one of the last pages.

"Straff!" he shouted, pointing a fat finger at us.

Norwegian has adopted a lot of English words, but apparently a few Russian ones as well. "Straff" means penalty or punishment in Norwegian. I didn't know it meant the same in Russian, too. I do now.

He waved us over to him, and gestured for us to look at the book. Everything was written in Russian, but despite the fact that we had no idea what it said, he made a circle around one word: "Наказание."

He shouted at us again. "Nakazaniye!"

By now, we sort of got the idea that he wanted money. But how much? No figures were mentioned in the book, but someone had written "$250", by pencil, next to the printed text. Very convincing!

But we were in a country that doesn't exactly score well on Transparency International's index of corruption, so this sort of thing was to be expected. And we had a bus full of impatient passengers waiting outside. We could feel the heat. The situation was probably thoroughly described in the training manual for all Kyrgyz border guards.

Fortunately, I had done enough traveling by now to have developed a "damage control" system that works well for getting out of situations like this without too much of a loss. I always carry money in at least two pockets. One of the pockets contains the big notes, while I keep smaller bills and change in a separate pocket. Because if I start counting money in front of a policeman or other corrupt fucker, I will most likely lose it all. But if I randomly pull a few creased bills out of my pocket, it seems like everything I've got.

My first five dollar bill didn't impress the officer, though.

"Straff!" he shouted again, pointing to his beloved book.

A twenty dollar bill later, Øystein and I were back on the bus with our passports stamped. Twenty-five dollars didn't feel too bad when the alternative was 250.

The bus driver was not impressed with our little delay, and drove as fast as the bus could go. We were soon back in Almaty.

The trip to the two "Stans" had been totally different than any place Øystein or I had ever been before. On the plane back, we decided to visit more Stans together. All of them, in fact. The country collection had begun.

Uzbekistan

If there is only one Silk Road country, Uzbekistan is it. With the arrogant camels, endless deserts, mosaic buildings and people who know how to trade. They learnt it while sipping warm camel milk as kids.

Øystein and I had often asked friends if they wanted to join us on our traditional autumn trips to unusual destinations, and some of them were always up for it until it was time to actually buy the tickets. Then, without exception, we experienced an abundance of excuses. If it wasn't a girlfriend who was having a boob job, then it was a neighbor's dog or a plant that needed tending. We have heard them all before, and we could take a hint. They were scared to travel with us, "the Slum Brothers Garfors."

The nickname was bestowed upon us after our first trips to countries unknown to our friends. To countries they would never include in a holiday-related sentence. To countries they presumed were war zones, playgrounds for terrorists and slums. It was their way of saying that we were mad. We liked it. We were never all that pretentious anyway.

However, a closer inspection of our friend base revealed one man who might not be afraid to travel with us, and that was Asbjørn Havnen. He and Øystein had been in the same class in high school, and I had played football with him. (Football, as in the real deal. The game also known as soccer in some parts of the world where the term "football" is ironically used for a game that consists mainly of ball throwing.) I had been a striker, and Asbjørn a goal keeper. Not a big surprise to those who have seen us together.

Fearless as ever on the football field, Asbjørn agreed to join us, and even accepted our nothing-but-hand-luggage policy. Good man.

We flew Norwegian to St. Petersburg, where Russian transit hell awaited. Pulkovo Airport, a relic from the 1970's, isn't much to get excited about unless you're the contractor who gets the job to renovate it. At least they have Baltika, a Russian beer that comes in a number of varieties - such as Baltika 1, 2, 3, 4, 5, 6, 7, 8 and 9. Plus Baltika 20, of course. The logic is Russian, but the beer is decent. Especially given the limited options for passing the time on an eight-hour layover in a terminal where the term "service" is unknown to employees and travelers alike.

Rossiya Airlines would take us to Samarkand, Uzbekistan, on a type of plane you have neither heard of nor would want to fly on. The galley was in the middle, and the overhead bins could only narrowly fit a laptop. The Uzbeks didn't seem to mind - they still squeezed in all sorts of exotic purchases from their trip to Russia. Automatic potato peelers, toy dolls, and electric blankets in creative colors were stuffed into the bins, under the seats, and inside jackets.

We even spotted a brand new double tape recorder. Out of date? Not in Uzbekistan. The proud owner was a woman in her thirties. She had two big gold teeth, and wore a very satisfied smile for most of the trip. The tape recorder remained on her lap throughout the flight. No one would ever take it away from her.

In Samarkand, the city of Silk Road fame, luggage was delivered by an old Soviet farm tractor to the little arrival hall, which was absolutely stuffed with people. The tractor pulled only one cart at a time, and had to make several trips to the plane to retrieve it all. (Asbjørn had been forced to check his luggage due to the small overhead bins, so we had to wait despite our hand luggage only policy.) We were further delayed by the customs officers, who opened and went through every piece of everyone's luggage manually. They clearly want to know what enters the country. We finally made it through all the queues and headed outside, where nearly a hundred people waited. The woman with the tape recorder was greeted by a man about her age who seemed thrilled by her purchase.

As the only westerners in the crowd, we soon attracted a number of taxi vultures eyeing easy prey. One of them necessarily hit the jackpot and drove us to our hotel, where we checked in and crashed. We were in dire need of some sleep before exploring the city.

When we woke up, we had lunch for breakfast before leaving the hotel to find a bank. A one hundred dollar bill was soon transformed into a huge pile of cash. Four hundred dollars would make you a millionaire in Uzbekistani *som*. The local currency took up so much space, we needed to bring a little backpack to carry it all. I have felt worse.

Samarkand's main tourist attraction is Registan, a public square surrounded by three madrasahs, or Islamic schools. They were built almost 600 years ago, and are truly breathtaking. But after millions of colorful tiles, even such architectural wonders become routine. We were headed for the more modern part of town.

At the Blues Bar Jazz Club we met two locals with four-day beards and thick jackets made of sheepskin. They were working on a sheep farm, but had taken a few days off to go drinking.

Asbjørn eyed an irresistible challenge, and about an hour later, the sheep farmers had given up trying to match him drink for drink. The former goalie had earned his first drinking scalp outside Western Europe - and in a former Soviet Republic, no less. He was thrilled. The sheep farmers, on the other hand, were severely beaten, and they knew it.

"How can you drink so much? You are not even from Uzbekistan," one of them asked.

Asbjørn grinned. He was used to far worse. Back in the day, most of us brought a six pack of beer to parties. He brought a case. And he always finished before the rest of us.

"It is all about the technique," he explained before paying his bill and theirs too. That must have eased their emerging hangovers a little bit.

While Asbjørn was busy beating the locals, Øystein and I were chatting with a group from Dushanbe in Tajikistan. They had needed a break from what they claimed was a violent capital, and had decided on a weekend trip to Samarkand. They told stories of wild mountain ranges, poor people, and a lot of vodka.

"It isn't fair. You should visit our country for *real* hospitality. We are much nicer than the Uzbeks," they joked. Before asking if we wanted to join them at a discotheque party. Discotheque. I hadn't heard the term since 9th grade. Posters around town were advertising the place, which was located in the nightclub of one of the hotels.

"Why not?" Øystein said. We didn't even consult Asbjørn. Some dancing would be a sensible option after his drinking competition.

Three Norwegians and five Tajiks easily fit into the first taxi that passed, a dark red Lada. Three in the front passenger seat, five in the back. The local taxi drivers didn't mind, as long as they got their fare.

We arrived at the hotel shortly after. Two policemen were standing outside chatting. Somehow we still managed to disembark from the tiny car without drawing any unwanted attention. Eight passengers in a Lada is presumably normal - or at least acceptable - there.

The disco hall looked as if it was taken from Overlook Hotel in *The Shining*. The DJ turned out to be a tall, skinny guy in his mid-twenties. He was in control of two cassette players, which were nowhere near as modern as the one we had seen on the plane. Between each song he quickly unplugged the 3.5 millimeter plug from the headphone jack of one of the cassette players and moved it to the other. The other end of the cable was connected to an amplifier and two big speakers.

He then changed cassettes and cued the new one up for the next song on the first deck.

We rocked the night away listening to Depeche Mode, ZZ Top, Elvis Presley and various local Uzbek artists we will never know the names of. About twenty people were dancing, most of them girls. Plus three Norwegians. Another fifty people, predominantly shy guys, were watching the dancers. They didn't hit the dance floor until after quite a few drinks. The beer was sold in half-liter glasses, after being poured from two-liter plastic bottles.

Øystein and I had had enough by around 2:30 AM. Asbjørn had not. He had his own hotel room, and was eyeing the possibility of getting company there with one of the girls he was dancing with. They seemed rather interested in the prospect of Norwegian love. We wished him luck, and walked home.

The next day, Asbjørn was awakened for a very late breakfast. There were no traces of a female companion in his room.

"What's going on? You didn't manage to bring home any of the girls you were dancing so wildly with?" Øystein was curious.

"Bloody hell! I was almost trashed by some drunk local hoodlums," he grumbled. "They weren't happy about my success with the girls, so four guys came after me when the club closed. They told me to stay away from their women, and then one of them picked up an iron rod from the trunk of a car. I left the girls and ran home."

We laughed. "Not too bad of a deal. Two of the girls you were dancing with had moustaches anyway," I said. A breakfast later, and we were bound for neighboring Tajikistan.

Tajikistan

I don't usually run into closed borders or closed countries. Tajikistan proved an exception this particular week. The presidents of the former Soviet Republics were having a meeting in Dushanbe. This naturally means that you seal off the entire country. For days. Understandable, of course. Terrorists disguised as tourists are commonplace in this part of the world.

So are kangaroos.

This unforeseen problem threatened to ruin our plan to visit Uzbekistan's eastern neighbor. When we arrived at the border, we saw that a couple of tourist buses were stopped on the Uzbek side. A short German was standing near one of the buses, cursing.

"The ztupid border is clozed. I hate it," he told us.

Helmut turned out to be a nice guy, despite his rather dubious appearance. Dirty white wife-beater shirts have never won fashion awards, not even in the Stans.

"You will not get in, the polize offizerz are nazty," he told us.

All we heard was a challenge.

"Everything burns with gas," Øystein said. "Let's try!"

The German produced a silly laugh, waved and wished us good luck before entering one of the tourist buses.

We had a multiple entry visa, which meant we would be able to return to Uzbekistan even if the police on the Tajik side a few hundred meters away refused entry. The Uzbek police officers stamped us out of the country and we walked across the border.

The little passport control shack soon appeared in sight on the other side of the border. We stepped up onto the patio and knocked on the door. No response. I opened the door, and we went inside. We had decided on an "I know nothing" strategy, despite knowing about the top meeting in the capital.

"Hello, sir! We would like to get visas on arrival, please," I said.

We handed our passports over. I did not have high hopes of success. Especially not after the person in charge pushed us outside, and pointed to a tree on the other side of the road.

"Wait there!"

A red Lada was parked in the shade. We followed its example - it was rather hot in the Central Asian sun. The next five minutes were spent preparing for visa denial. Then a sergeant came out of the shack. Or at least that's what Asbjørn claimed that he was. He has done national service, and should know. Neither Øystein or I have. Taxes in Norway are already high. Why give the government a year of free labor in addition?

The army guy was wearing a huge hat. He walked over to us, but without our passports in his hand, as we had expected.

"Get into the car!" he ordered, gesturing toward the Lada. Please is not a commonly used word in Tajikistan, but at least he spoke some English.

He drove us about twenty kilometers until we were in a little town called Panjakent. The military man stopped the car by a tall white wooden fence, and told us to get out. He did the same, and knocked on a gate.

A gray-haired man in his sixties with a thin, little moustache came out. They exchanged words, and the old guy was given our three red Norwegian passports, which the army guy produced from his inside jacket pocket. Then he got back into the car and drove off without another word to us.

"Welcome to Tajikistan! My name is George," the old man greeted us.

Apparently, we had been assigned a guide.

"The good news is that I will guide you. The bad news is that I have your passports, so it will not be cheap."

He laughed at his own joke before giving our passports back to us.

"I am only pulling your legs, my friends. I only charge you normal rate," he assured us. "You are from Viking country. I always appreciate a little bit of brutality. Where would you like to go?"

Before we could answer, he quickly added that Dushanbe was off-limits due to the big meeting there. "Too much bureaucracy and paperwork to go there," he said.

"Well, then, how about a mountain hike," Øystein suggested.

"Your wish is my command!" George replied.

He opened a garage and reversed a big four-wheeler out of it. We were at the food market a few minutes later, where we bought bread, cheese, honey, beer and vodka for the trip. Just as we were about to leave the market, a dark haired forty-year-old man appeared, seemingly out of nowhere.

"This is Mirek. He is a good guy. He will be your driver," George told us, before leaving us in his care.

Surprisingly, Mirek spoke rather good English. Then again, I guess you have to in order to read the repair manual of the old Land Rover that would take us up into the mountains. Not bad for Panjakent, though. We had hardly seen anything but Ladas, in a few different colors. We were told that it all comes down to the way Russian flagship cars are manufactured. A car model is mass produced for a couple of months, but only in one color. History repeats itself the following two months, but in a new color. That doesn't provide for a huge selection, although it's a slight improvement on the black-only Model-T Fords of a hundred years ago.

We arrived at the tiny village of Artush three hours later, including a much-needed stop halfway to cool down the engine. The village is located high up in the mountains, not too far from the border to Uzbekistan. For reasons unknown to mankind, 300 brave souls live there. The only accessible road there is closed all winter. In that part of the world, that means for five to seven months, depending on how harsh the winter is. There's just too much snow - and too many avalanches - for it to be kept open. Inhabitants there live there at their own risk. Entertainment options are limited.

We decided to go hiking the same day. Our goal was to reach 4,000 meters above sea level, something we just about managed to do before the sun disappeared. That meant a freezing but fast descent. We ran most of the way to avoid hypothermia.

While we had been hiking, Mirek had been organizing a thing or two. A local teacher named Dilshod had agreed to provide us with sleeping accommodations in a small outbuilding. It was not heated and contained only three big mattresses on the floor and an old wooden set of drawers. There were four thick blankets on top of each mattress. We guessed the night would be cold.

But first dinner. We had brought our own. The flatbreads we had picked up at the market when they were still warm had become rather dry and less than appealing pieces of food. But our host contributed to an upgraded dinner experience through his wife's homemade vegetable and lamb soup. It all took place on the roofed terrace just outside the small house we would sleep in. Over dinner, we told Dilshod and Mirek about our mountain trip. The views had been stunning.

"So, what do you all do for a living?" Dilshod asked, changing the subject. He was far more curious about us than about our travel experiences.

Øystein told him he was a teacher, too, something that clearly impressed Dilshod. A Norwegian teacher! In his house. They even discussed teaching techniques.

"How do you punish naughty students in Tajikistan?" Øystein asked jokingly, but his irony wasn't decoded.

"I usually hit them over the fingers with a ruler," Dilshod replied.

Øystein and I exchanged a look, and silently agreed not to comment any further.

It was then my turn. "I work with mobile services," I told Dilshod.

He shook his head in response. My occupation was clearly totally uninteresting to him. Then again, this was 2008, and mobile services weren't yet very advanced even in Norway.

"And what do you do?" Dilshod asked Asbjørn.

Asbjørn was a real estate agent at the time. I reckoned that if Director of Mobile Services was boring, a Real Estate Agent title would elicit the same response. There were less than a hundred houses in Artush. They had probably never even heard of real estate transactions. So before Asbjørn could answer, I did it for him.

"He's a doctor".

It took me less than a second to realize the impact of what I had just said. We were in the middle of nowhere. Literally. The nearest doctor was hours away, by four-wheel drive. And we had just seen a pregnant woman outside the shop. But Dilshod was satisfied and impressed by our answers. At least two out of three guests held prominent positions.

"If that woman is giving birth tonight or if there is a bloody heart attack, I know who will be my assistant. As in assistant in charge!" Asbjørn whispered loudly to me. There was no danger of them understanding Norwegian anyway. I smiled back nervously, and crossed my fingers for a calm and uneventful night. But we didn't get around to discussing the matter further, because Mirek interrupted our whispering.

"Fifty-fifty," he shouted, and held his glass high. It looked like a water glass, but contained vodka.

"Fifty-fifty?" Øystein asked. Neither of us understood what he meant.

It was clearly a toast, but what did fifty-fifty mean? Should we drink 50 percent of it, or should we add 50 percent of the peach juice from the shop and create an Artush Ice Tea?

"Fifty-fifty!" Mirek was getting impatient and annoyed. He soon realized that a demonstration was called for, and emptied his glass.

In Tajikistan, fifty-fifty simply means 50 percent plus 50 percent. Or "bottoms up," as it is known as in the western world. Asbjørn did not need to be asked twice, and downed his immediately. Mirek smiled.

"Ah, you are not only a doctor, you are also a very good drinker. You are Doctor Vodka!" he exclaimed.

The birth of a nickname.

Øystein emptied his glass next, in two big zips. Acceptable. He was after all a teacher, and therefore automatically a family friend of the host.

I, however, am not the best of vodka drinkers, and left half the vodka in my glass. It was like shouting, "Oh my God, fucking hell," in St. Paul's Cathedral. It is just something you don't do in Tajikistan. Period and full stop.

Mirek considered me *persona non grata* for the remainder of our stay. He probably still does after the experience of such a disgraceful manner. Øystein and Asbjørn both received hugs when he dropped us off outside George's house the following day. I would have considered myself lucky had he spat at me. Although that would have been to acknowledge my existence, so he didn't. The older man drove us to the border, and we crossed over to Uzbekistan again. The police officers on duty wanted our phones. Asbjørn's iPhone and my Nokia were particularly interesting. Luckily they were satisfied by brief demonstrations and abused neither powers nor guns to claim ownership.

Afghanistan

Afghanistan is the tenth least visited country in the world. Not because it lacks a fascinating history, impressive architecture and beautiful natural scenery, but because it has regular bombings, terrorist attacks, and the Taliban. War zone tourism never really did catch on.

I traveled there in 2009 with two friends, eventually. Getting visas wasn't the easiest of tasks. The friendly people at the Afghan embassy in Oslo made it very clear that tourists were not welcome. Full stop. In other words, we could only get in as journalists or military personnel. The most dangerous weapons I've ever had my hands on are a 5 mm homemade slingshot, a Zulu bow and arrow, and my dad's sledgehammer. So the army option to get in was quickly ruled out.

Luckily I am originally a journalist, and the owner of a legitimate press card. So is Marius Arnesen, one of the two fearless friends who tagged along. Dr. Vodka is not. He is also no longer a soldier, despite his physical strength and drinking abilities, so he ended up posing as our "fixer" to be able to get in with a press visa.

He should have known better. Signing up as the fixer for two spoiled journalists would give him more of a headache than a couple of bottles of Ukrainian vodka. He sure had to work for his fixer title.

"Asbjørn, can you fix me a beer?" Marius would ask.

"Yes, and don't forget to fix-shine my shoes, fix-iron my shirt, and fix-taste my food to see if it's been poisoned," I would add. Admittedly, I was even worse than Marius.

To get to Afghanistan, the three of us first flew into Mashad, Iran. Entering via an airport enabled us to get visas into Iran upon arrival. Single entry visas. Take note, traveling overland into Iran does *not* give you the same privilege. No visas are issued at land-based border posts. This meant that once we crossed over into Afghanistan, we wouldn't have visas to get back into Iran. The fact that we might end up being stuck in Afghanistan without visas out of there freaked Marius out. Sort of. Sort of, as in totally, completely, utterly, and then some. I have never seen a man closer to a severe fit.

Surprisingly enough, Marius is among the most adventurous of guys. He eats extreme sports equipment for breakfast. He kites on snow, ice and water. He downs a cocktail a minute, still managing to down a shot of whatever is on hand in between every one of them. He will laugh you under the table, and if his laughter doesn't make you smile or crack up, please cut down on the Botox. But he is not too keen on being stuck in a war-ridden country without the possibility of getting out.

He first refused to join us across the border, but soon realized he'd possibly miss out on the holiday of a lifetime. After some convincing involving how easy it would be to get another visa at the Iranian Consulate in Herat, he reluctantly joined us into unknown territory. Would he ever forgive the inhuman amounts of peer pressure from Asbjørn and me? I think he did. Afghanistan is a photographer's paradise. Marius is one. He shot hundreds of photos there.

After crossing the border we met two locals, Maroof and his brother, just outside Herat. They asked if we needed a ride. They even agreed to drive us around for our entire stay, and they took personal pride in our safety. Much appreciated, although that task must have taken its toll as we explored various neighborhoods as if there would be no tomorrow. They showed us several hotels, and we chose the only one that appeared to be semi-civilized. It even had decent Wi-Fi and good security. Of course, if you are a terrorist, that would be the hotel to blow up. The best and "safest" hotel in town usually is the main target, as we have seen all too many times.

We still felt pretty safe, despite the odd gunshot at night. After all, most of the other guests were hired guns. Or at least, that's what they looked like. In Afghanistan you don't ask other foreigners what they are doing there. It's a rule, we found out. Most of them were there on shady business, or so it seemed. Their heavily armored cars in the hotel parking lot didn't do anything to dispel that impression.

The third biggest city in Afghanistan has tales to tell. It dates back to ancient times, and feels in part like an old museum. The Herat Citadel is well worth a visit, so is the Friday Mosque of Herat, one of the oldest in the country. We were even given old tiles from the mosque as souvenirs by one of the guys restoring the mosque. He showed us around and told us about their massive workload.

They had to make sure that all the millions of tiles look as they did originally. A never-ending task, I imagine.

Herat also used to have many minarets, but most of them have fallen thanks to the unstable foundations of the ancient city. A lot of heavy traffic on the circle road around it certainly hasn't helped either, but at least the Fifth Minaret is still standing. It gives you a chance to see such a historic structure in relatively good shape. There are also some beautiful mountains outside town, but we were politely advised not to go there. Kidnappings had recently occurred. We listened - especially Marius - and we didn't go.

And of course, there was the market. It has amazing fruit – much tastier than at home, traditional carpets, cooking utensils, leather shoes, ornaments and burqas. One particular burqa shop, exhibiting nothing but blue burqas, somehow caught our attention. Both Marius and Asbjørn are bigger than I am. They both had girlfriends at the time. Both girlfriends were allegedly my size. For some kinky reason or another they wanted to buy burqas as presents for their girlfriends. Do not ask why. Needless to say, I had to try them on. I have ever since struggled with mental images of what the burqas I wore have later been used for.

As a bonus, Marius took a photo of me with the burqa on. It later appeared on the front page of a French newspaper with the photo caption, "Close up of Afghan woman. Photo: Marius Arnesen." Thanks, mate!

Entering Afghanistan from Iran had not been a problem, since we had procured our "journalist" visas back in Norway. Getting visas to re-enter Iran turned out to be a major obstacle. Maroof drove us to the Consulate our first morning in town. Standing next to the wall of it, there was a queue of thirty-six men with beards. At the end of the queue, toward the corner of the wall, there was a small window. The first guy in line was bent down in front of the window, negotiating with the Consulate staff inside.

We were in a hurry to get back into Iran, where we were to meet my brother four days later. I initially entered the queue in a very British manner, at the far back, nodding and smiling politely to everyone. Many of them smiled back.

After fifteen minutes without moving an inch, I realized the British way wasn't working for us. I decided to queue Norwegian style instead - rude, ignorant, and with active elbows. It worked. I was bending down to the little window in a matter of minutes. The smiles of my local queue colleagues had disappeared.

"I'm sorry, but this is an emergency," I told the clerk. "We must get visas to get back into Iran. My brother is there. It is urgent."

"How soon do you need the visas, sir?"

"Tomorrow. Or at most two days from now," I said.

"I am sorry, sir. That is impossible. It will take at least a week," he replied.

"A week?" I shouted. I could literally feel Marius panicking, even though he was a few meters away from me.

The dialogue continued, and I used the words "emergency", "disaster" and "urgent" a lot. In the end I got three forms to fill out.

"I really want to help you, sir. Come back when you have completed them, please. I will see what I can do."

We quickly filled out the forms, and I jumped the queue again. There were even fewer smiles this time around.

A fair amount of the next three days was spent near Herat's Iranian Consulate. They did among other things need two photographs apiece and a copy of the application form. Photographers and copy shops were conveniently located across the street - no discounts were offered.

The Consulate staff also demanded knowledge about our parents' religious backgrounds. And proof that we were HIV negative, so we had to find a clinic where we could have HIV tests taken. The hygiene level of the clinic seemed to be decent, and the needles used for the blood tests looked reasonably clean, but Asbjørn wasn't convinced.

"If we don't currently have HIV, I am sure that we'll get it here," he joked. Marius and I were not particularly amused.

There were not, surprisingly, fees to be paid too. I had cash, but our "friends" demanded that it be deposited into a bank account. Which could only be done through a specific bank in town, to obtain proof of payment in return.

I was soon a hated man in the Iranian-visa-seeking community of Herat. Rarely has one queue member pissed off so many others. Finally, after jumping the queue thirteen times, I received some good news.

"We have what we need. Please come to the entrance door," the clerk told me.

Wow, a breakthrough! No more back-busting correspondence through a tiny window in a wall. Marius looked particularly happy. I knocked and stated our names and nationality when asked to do so. A porter let us into a waiting room. There were nine people already there. It turned out to be interrogation time - on an individual basis. No chance to make sure our stories matched.

I was first up. I was taken into a big room. There was a desk. A big man was seated behind it. I tried to shake his hand, but he wasn't having it. He either knew what he was doing or had seen too many Russian cop shows.

He pointed at a little chair by the opposite wall and touched his well-trimmed moustache.

"What are you doing in Afghanistan?" he asked calmly.

We had entered on journalist visas, but I somehow didn't think this was the right time to reveal that particular technicality.

"We are here as tourists to see the beautiful city of Herat and the scenic surrounding areas. We have heard so much about it. Great place!" I said.

He hit his fist on the desk. Hard. The bang echoed through the sterile white room.

"There are no tourists in Afghanistan! What *are* you doing here?" he repeated. Then, after two long seconds of silence, he looked at me accusingly and said, "Are you a spy?"

I decided this was not the time for bad jokes, so I stuck to my story and explained that we wanted to explore for ourselves this country we heard only awful things about in the western media. As tourists. I told him that we had already traveled to a number of other unusual countries. He probably didn't believe a word of it. Then again, he had two others to interrogate.

Marius was next up. His grilling was a bit shorter than mine. I used the time to coordinate with Asbjørn. I explained that I had told the guy that we had already traveled together to Uzbekistan, Tajikistan, Belarus and other less-than-popular destinations for most tourists, as proof of our genuine interest in the road less traveled.

"And you think that will make us look like anything but spies?" he asked.

Just when Marius returned from his fifteen minutes of Iranian Consulate fame. He told us that he, too, had assured the Iranian official that we were only tourists. Now it was Asbjørn's turn.

He came back just a few moments later, laughing.

"What happened?" I asked, incredulous.

"Nothing," Asbjørn replied. "He asked me, 'Are you really here as tourists?' Then, before I could even answer, he shook his head and said, 'You crazy, crazy guys!'"

With our return sorted, we had time to properly act as tourists in Herat. We had seen the citadel and the mosque in between the Consulate action earlier, and we decided it was finally time to get postcards. But where do you get postcards in a country without tourists?

We struck gold in the fourth store, a bookshop. The first three shop owners didn't even know what postcards were. But here, a few cards were hidden under layers of ancient looking books. And some dust.

Good stuff, but of course the friendly shop owner didn't have stamps.

"Try the post office," he suggested.

A ground breaking idea. Maroof drove us there. We walked across a big courtyard and into the building. We found a counter in a dark room in the back. No one spoke English. We showed the postcards, and asked for stamps. Our request was met with lots of head shaking. Maroof started translating. He told us that we couldn't send anything without an envelope.

"But they are postcards. They are designed to be envelope independent," I tried to explain. Maroof translated again, and ten minutes later they reluctantly agreed to sell us stamps. The postcards arrived safe and sound in Europe six weeks later. You know you are in a tourist-deprived country when even the concept of postcards is unfamiliar. And that is Afghanistan today. It was one of the most modern countries in the world in the 1970's. Thanks, Taliban! Good job. May the war end soon and democracy return. A realistic possibility? Probably not, but the people there deserve it. So do future travelers. Afghanistan is a truly fantastic country. I will be back. In the short term, I hope.

And Marius? He has been back to Afghanistan half a dozen times, well protected by the Norwegian army while filming news reporters and making award-winning television documentaries about Norwegian military operations. On subsequent visits he made sure he had his return visas sorted out in advance. I don't blame him.

Turkmenistan

Øystein never made it to Afghanistan. Not because he didn't want to, but because Benedicte, his wife, refused his participation. The rumor of Afghanistan had reached her. He still met up with the rest of us in Iran after we finally managed to get visas back into that country, and from there the four of us crossed the border into Turkmenistan.

Yes, Turkmenistan. One of the strangest countries in the world. Not quite at the level of North Korea, but the countries compete in the same league. Not surprisingly, perhaps, they are the two only remaining Stalinist countries in the world. As in North Korea, you will only be allowed in with a guide.

The capital is called Ashgabad. Say it out loud. "Ash-ga-badd". It just so teasingly intrigues your mouth. I was, in fact, so fascinated by the mere name of the capital that I kept repeating it to myself for years before finally going there. Some people thought that I had Tourettes. I guess they were onto something. Why the fascination? I will give a few examples.

Weekdays and months have been named after the relatives of late dictator Saparmurat Nijazov. A man who took the name "Turkmenbashi". It means Father of all Turkmens. The personal glorification seemed to match rather well. One of his first decisions was to declare himself President for life. To better brainwash his citizens, streets, schools, a city and a 300 kilo meteor that crash landed in his country were all named after him. So was January. April was called Gurbansoltan edzhe, after his mom. But she was still not impressed. What was previously known as bread (chorek), also changed its name to gurbansoltan edzhe. Bizarre. Who wants to eat their own mother?

I can only imagine various interesting linguistic challenges. What if I were to travel with Turkmenbashi (the man) from Turkmenbashi (the airport) to Turkmenbashi (the city) in Turkmenbashi (the month) to visit Turkmenbashi (the school) in Turkmenbashi (the street) to drink Turkmenbashi (the vodka)? Probably not what you should do in a school, but you get my point.

In 2001, Turkmenbashi wrote a book he called *Ruhnama*. It means the book of the soul and contains a mixture of poems, poetry and the history of Turkmenistan. Not to forget moral guidelines to citizens, of course. The book had to be visible in all book shops and public offices. And in mosques, it had to be positioned next to the Koran. As an act of pure evil, or sadism, he demanded that anyone that was to be employed by the government or wanted a driver's license needed to know the entire book by heart. And for some time, all other books were even banned, even in libraries. At least it was easy to find the book you wanted. "Oh, so you are looking for *Ruhnama*? You can find it on book shelves 1-65."

Nijazov, or Turkmenbashi, commissioned a 15 meter tall gold plated statue of himself. It would later be erected on a 63 meter high platform. But, to make things more interesting, he also asked for the statue to automatically turn in such a manner that he would always face the sun. I might have commissioned such a statue myself, had I ever been in possession of unlimited power and money. The platform was actually torn down after our visit, only to be replaced by a 15 meter taller one.

Turkmenbashi even turned a health freak after he gave up smoking back in 1997. Smoking was immediately banned in public areas. Gold teeth were not approved of either, and banned. His citizens should rather avoid cavities, he demanded, and gave some advice while at it.

"Chew on a bone!" he proclaimed.

Before banning makeup too. He had watched a female news reader on television. She had way too much makeup on, in his opinion, and he became furious. Turkmen women were beautiful enough, and did not need paint on their faces, he decided. The law was immediately enforced.

At least he was not afraid of challenges. He once ordered a giant ice castle to be built in the Karakum desert, one of the hottest places in his country. A zoo was planned next door and penguins would be among the animals to be forcefully moved there. Circus and similar fun activities on the other hand were banned in Turkmenistan for nine years. Turkmenbashi claimed that circus clowns, cinemas, nor opera and ballet performances had any tradition here.

Ashgabad itself is also rather impressive. The city is full of huge and impressive marble buildings where almost no one works. They have been built primarily to impress and are of little use.

To stay in power, you cannot outlaw everything, and some incentives are needed. Electricity is free in Turkmenistan whereas gasoline is extremely cheap.

And believe it or not, but Turkmenbashi was really a very modest man. He was against seeing pictures and statues of himself everywhere, but he narrowly let it pass.

"Since it is the will of the people." He said.

Of course. It went without saying that we had to visit. The country was too surreal not to.

After the usual formalities on the Iran border, we were greeted by our guide, Oleg. He is one of the biggest guys I have ever seen. About six feet, nine inches tall, and almost as wide at the shoulders. He was wearing a military camouflage jacket, his trademark garment of choice, and showing off a gold tooth. Oleg is an occasional smiler.

"Welcome to Turkmenistan," he said.

He shook each of our hands in turn. More accurately, he dwarfed them. His Russian accent was very distinct, and he'd make a great James Bond villain.

"People from Iran consider this hell," Oleg told us. "They have no girls or alcohol. We have no shortage of girls or alcohol."

There was little doubt about his sincerity. "So, are you here for girls or drinks?" he asked.

"We'll have some drinks, of course. But we all have girlfriends or wives at home," I said, trying to be diplomatic.

This was a concept Oleg didn't seem to know existed. "So?" he replied.

"So," I began, searching for an explanation that would make sense to him. "But Oleg, do you not believe in love?"

He frowned and spat out this comeback without hesitation.

"Love was invented by the French. They were too cheap to pay for prostitutes."

We were going tenting in the middle of the desert, next to a huge crater that sports an "eternal" flame. Oleg drove us to one of the food markets in Ashgabat to get supplies. When we arrived, he told us to get whatever we wanted. Except alcohol.

"I already got vodka," he said.

Dr. Vodka was not convinced that our alcohol supplies were sufficient, so Oleg showed him the booze. Asbjørn balked at the sight of just two vodka bottles for the five of us. We left the market with enough food for a small army, and another five bottles of vodka.

Asbjørn was smiling as we sped off in Oleg's four-by-four. The driver was shaking his head.

A three-hour drive later, we were in the Karakum Desert, where we would camp next to the "Door to Hell," a crater 30 meters deep and 70 meters across. In it, gas sifting from the ground is constantly burning. That has been the case since a gas drilling operation gone wrong in 1971. The Soviet exploration team tapped into a cavern filled with natural gas - extracting it caused the ground to collapse and the engineers lit the gas to burn it off. They expected that would take a couple of weeks. The "Door to Hell" was opened, and that fire is still burning.

If you ask me, it's the most amazing tourist attraction in the world. Except that there are no tourists. Which is part of the point.

We had put up our tents and Oleg was cooking dinner on a couple of gas burners behind the car. The rest of us were sitting on an Afghan carpet placed directly on the sand and drinking beers. The crater was a few hundred yards away, and it lit up the night sky. The fire made a distinct sound in the background.

Asbjørn decided to put Oleg through a little test. He picked up two bottles of vodka and took them over to the Russian, a few yards away from where the rest of us were sitting. They came back about thirty minutes later. With two empty bottles.

Asbjørn was smiling. Oleg not so much. He looked pretty shabby, in fact. But he still managed somehow to finish preparing our meal, a delicious soup with cabbage, carrots, herbs, and large chunks of lamb. We started eating. Suddenly, Oleg jumped up and ran off out into the desert. He came back ten minutes later, looking even worse.

"I had to piss," he said, a little defensively. "And you are a monster. How can you drink so much?"

He pointed at Asbjørn, who just laughed back. Oleg was not amused.

I decided to change the subject. The trip had been organized by Stan Tours, a guide company, and I had been on the phone a few times with Natasha, our contact in the company. She had a sexy voice, and Asbjørn and Marius and Øystein and I had discussed what she might look like more than once before entering Turkmenistan.

"Oleg. You know Natasha with Stan Tours. Is she nice? She sounds nice," I asked with enthusiasm and a smile. There might also have been a slight undertone of sexual innuendo.

Oleg immediately stopped eating. There was silence for several seconds.

"Of course she is nice," he replied. "She is my wife!"

I had made the situation worse. Much worse. There was nothing I could say that would salvage the conversation. Asbjørn decided that more vodka was the only way to make Oleg happier. There was plenty in the car.

They drank more. Much more. Only half a bottle of vodka remained unfinished by the time we all went to bed.

We had to return to Ashgabat early the next morning, and Marius was given the task of waking Oleg up. He slept on his own in a little yellow tent, while Øystein and I had shared one and Marius and Asbjørn had shared another. It took Marius several minutes to wake the fallen giant up. I have never seen anyone with a worse hangover. He woke with a roar, opened the tent, stood up just outside it and gulped down a two-liter bottle of Coca-Cola in one go.

"My friend will drive you to town," he informed us.

And that was all he uttered during breakfast, which consisted of old Turkmen bread, cheese, and tea. When his friend arrived to drive us back to town, he stayed on in the desert, presumably to cure his hangover.

Asbjørn, Øystein, Marius and I spent the weekend in Ashgabat. We didn't see Oleg again until Monday morning, when he was waiting for us in the hotel lobby. My brother had been concerned about him, and asked, "How are you doing?" "Now? Fine," Oleg replied slowly and pointedly.

The poor bugger had been feeling the results of Dr. Vodka's vodka love for seventy-two hours!

Pakistan

Three or four months after Øystein, Asbjørn, Marius and I had survived Afghanistan and Turkmenistan, I was headed to Pakistan - this time on my own.

Pakistan and Afghanistan are the only two "Stans" that are not former Soviet Republics. That doesn't mean they're any easier to negotiate. Just being allowed to enter Pakistan was a challenge. I had to use my press card to get in, and invent a research mission. And that wasn't even my idea. The helpful man at the embassy strictly followed the rules, but he didn't mind telling me which loopholes I could use. What a problem solver! Then again, I should probably have been suspicious when it was the gatekeeper who told me how to get past him.

I traveled to Karachi in southern Pakistan via Istanbul. I had done virtually no research, except for finding a local, Nadia, who was happy to join me for a meal. She loved traveling too, she assured me. And she was proven right when we got to her flat in a high-rise near the beach. It was light and decorated in a contemporary European style. Except for the wooden masks she had picked up on trips to Kenya and Tanzania.

"Those countries are not far from us, but man are they different," she claimed. I agreed.

While Nadia made tea - local, quality tea. The radio was on while we drank. That's how we heard about the terrorist attack. A bombing during a Shi'ite procession commemorating the Day of Ashura, the holiest of days for followers of Shi'a Islam. Thirty people had been killed and hundreds more had been injured by the bomb blast.

"These things happen, but they never target foreigners," Nadia said, trying to reassure me.

I wasn't worried. If I were to worry about every incident around the world, I should have set out to collect Icelandic butterflies, not countries.

I said goodbye to Nadia and walked to town. I was curious about the attack, but I couldn't get to Muhammad Ali Jinnah Road where it had happened. The police were keeping people away, and my Norwegian press card didn't impress them a single bit.

The next day I decided to walk from my hotel to town, seemingly without a care in the world. Posing such an attitude is important. I believe that to appear uncomfortable or scared is a recipe for disaster, especially when in unknown territory. Tourists and travelers who act scared attract con men and thieves the way strawberry jam in the sun attracts flies. In unfamiliar or sketchy areas, I try to walk slightly arrogantly. And my dress code clearly shows that I am not a spoiled brat from the nice part of town. Or any town.

A kilometer from my hotel I was stopped by no less than fourteen police officers. Twelve of them were sitting on the back of a police lorry. One of the officers inside the truck was clearly the boss.

"What are you doing here?" The police boss screwed the formalities and went straight on to demand an answer.

"I am just walking to town, sir." I figured politeness wouldn't hurt.

"No, you are not. Not anymore. You cannot walk here. It is dangerous for a white kid like you! Where are you going? You will take a taxi!"

There was no use in protesting. Several of the other police officers were standing around me in half a circle, curiously listening in on our conversation. Lone Norwegians weren't stopped every day around Karachi. A few minutes later saw me inside a tiny banger of a black-and-yellow car. A Suzuki Alto taxi. Lovely!

The driver had been given clear orders, to get me to safety. But at the first red light I left the car, amid loud protests. Child safety doors do not come standard on Altos designed for the Pakistani market.

I paid through the open window and continued walking. I wasn't having it - being dictated into a taxi. Not even by an overprotective high level police officer.

HOME SWEET HOME

I am easily moved. As in physically. I live where my luggage is. Home can mean a hotel, a tent, my log cabin in northern Norway or anywhere else I might decide to spend the night. In this chapter I cover the six countries in which I have lived. Not all of them are equally home. Four places are in fact more home than others. Three of them are in my home country; Naustdal, my home village on the West Coast goes without saying. Henrik Klausens gate, where my apartment is located in Oslo cannot be left out either. I have lived there since 2000, when not on the road. And finally Skjomen, where my brother Håkon and I built my log cabin a few years ago. It's located next to the farm where my dad was born in 1940, and we spent every summer there as children.

I am unable and unwilling to leave out my home country number two, Great Britain. I studied in Falmouth in Cornwall in England for three years. The tiny town center, the rugged coastline, the pubs, the people. If too long time passes between visits, I feel the withdrawal symptoms knocking on my door. That usually means that I book a plane ticket within minutes. Long live impulsivity and readily available airplane fuel.

Norway

It's hard to come up with a short version of everything I have experienced in Norway. There still wasn't much doubt, really. It has to be something from Naustdal. I called it my home town. It never was. My home village, at best. Population: 1,200. Plus 1,500 more in rural parts of the municipality. I don't understand why so few, though. The beauty of the place will outdo anything your imagination can come up with. Ten times over. I am not usually into bragging, but my mom even has the best view in the village. From her terrace of the house in which I grew up you can see Heilefjellet, a characteristic mountain with several sharp peaks and the westernmost glacier in the country. Between the rock formations and my mom's house there is a fjord, complete with green islands and surrounded by smaller mountains, covered in evergreen trees. A river, one of the best for salmon in the country, runs into it from the valley, past my mom's house and many miles up into the unknown. Norway is a dream of a country, and the scenery in Naustdal and the rest of the west coast and in the north is simply incredible. The view from my mom's is just one picture perfect example of many. Many as in uncountable. Uncountable as in googolplex. Squared.

And anyone can enjoy nature. Thanks to "Right of Every Man", a law that guarantees people to access any part of Norway that isn't farmed or within meters from a residential house. You can even put your tent in fields and forests, pick berries or mushrooms on mountains and islands or paddle on fjords and rivers, all year around, all for free. Norway will take your breath away. If for no other reason than being the most expensive country in the world.

My brother Øystein and I lived in a little beige wooden house, only 20 meters from our family's residence. There is a road on one side, a forest and a mountain on the other. Our parents had built a smaller house that was to be used as an office and as sort of a flat for visitors. To be able to live there as late teenagers was amazing. Away from the mayhem of our five youngest siblings. Then again, that meant that our mother was left alone with it all. I should have helped out a bit more. In retrospect. I'll send her some roses. Or a greenhouse. Then again, she deserves a full field of flowers. The Netherlands, perhaps.

One evening, we watched TV 2 together with two friends. It was the first available commercial TV channel transmitting to rural parts of the country. Naustdal certainly qualified. Øystein Djupvik, or DJ as we often called him, was in high school, only one year above me. The creative, energetic and fast left wing soccer player of Naustdal's only team, Tambarskjelvar has since become a businessman, engaged in cosmic top secret material at the NATO base in High Wickham, fished salmon the size of a small car and eventually become a prominent local politician for Venstre (Left).

André Eilertsen was mate number two. He supports Tottenham Hotspur, the only real football team in England, and he rarely turns down any prospect of creating or engaging in mayhem. He looks like a calm and well balanced fella, but that only exemplifies the old saying. He is the exception that proves the rule.

There was a commercial break just before the main newscast at 7pm. It included a 20 second spot for McDonald's. We looked at each other. Øystein had an essay to write, due the next day. He had naturally not started it, and frenetically shook his head. The pressure from the rest of us proved immense, and we were all inside a black little Fiat Uno Turbo three minutes later. The nearest McDonald's joint was in Bergen, 180 kilometres away. The roads were in a state not known to American man. We had to drive around fjords, through mountain passes and even cross a fjord by a 20 minute ferry. The roads more often than not had one lane, occasionally one and a half. We used to dream about two lane roads. Good dreams, optimistic dreams. But bloody futuristic ones.

The trip would normally take four hours, but we were hungry. The fast little car helped us get to Bergen, Norway's second biggest city and one of the prettiest, in only two. André did a particularly good job as a map reader. The car's engine had to remain running on the ferry. To give the turbo well deserved cooling.

Four "quarter pounder with cheese" menus awaited in Bergen. Of course. Pulp Fiction was our first and foremost inspiration back then. Although we didn't shoot backseat passengers in the face. Not often, anyway.

We were back in Naustdal just after midnight. There was a welcome committee there. Our mom. She was not very impressed. Her lion's roar sort of gave that away. Øystein's essay was written on the school bus the next morning. It's a 15 minute ride. He still somehow avoided to flunk. I think his teacher liked him. The short trip to Bergen was very different to anything I had done up until then. I had arrived back in Norway only six months earlier, following a year as an exchange student in Indiana, USA. But the impulsive burger run made me want more. Impulsive traveling, not instant French fries. I already knew that there would be more trips without much planning.

USA

I lived in the US not only once, but twice, back in the 90's. The stays contributed to an ambivalent relationship. I have a lot of good friends there, but at the same time, I've met many superficial and arrogant people. The US has a lot going for it, but before a guy from Georgia or a woman from Wisconsin claim that it is the best country in the world, they might find it an advantage to have visited a few others. The US isn't the only central place in the world.

My first stay started when I traveled there as a 17 year old exchange student. I was hoping to go to California, Florida or New York. The only states I had heard anything good about. Or heard about, at all.

I ended up in the Midwest, in the residential area of Hidden Valley Lake outside Lawrenceburg, Indiana. My host parents were Jane and Jim, and my host siblings were Jeremy and Julie. Jeremy was my age, and we became good friends. He later married a girl named Jessi, with a "J," of course. Why the family of "Js" decided to "adopt someone with a G name, never seized to make me wonder. They still live in Indiana. Where guys drive pickup trucks and meet up to talk, parked side by side in the parking lots of gas stations. They carry shotguns in the back, sometimes accompanied with a dead deer in the cargo bed. The drivers typically have huge wads of chewing tobacco in their jaws. The most hard-core of them would add another wad half an hour later, still outside the same gas station. Nothing has been spat out. Little has been said. They don't talk much, or fast, in the Midwest.

The Links, my host family, took me to several states while I was living with them, further whetting my appetite for travel. And my year there changed me a lot. My perspective on life changed, and I truly understood that everything wasn't the same as back home in Naustdal.

Even though we have the occasional pickup truck there, too.

I found myself in the US, to use a cliché. I became more independent and humble. I understood that there was somewhere else outside tiny Naustdal. Where other kinds of people lived other kinds of lives, had other religions and faiths, ate other types of food and taught different things in school. Even their jokes were different. At first I reacted with quiet shock. I was as homesick as a polar bear in Rio, as a penguin in Puerto Rico. My solution? To not take part in anything I didn't have to, to just patiently wait for the evening, to fall asleep and to be able to tick one more day off the calendar. My host family, sports activities and friends helped me get out of my misery. Indirectly. I soon realized the destructiveness of my behavior. And changed tactic. Instead of not taking part in stuff, I over indulged and took part in everything. And suddenly I was having too much fun for my own good.

Why would I want to return home again?

And if the USA - which I had heard so much about, dreamed so much about and longed to for so long - could be so different to what I had expected, what then about Yemen, Paraguay, Bhutan or China? I spent a lot of time in 1992-93 pondering over big questions, the meaning of life. The American Dream had certainly affected me, made me move there for a year. Maybe I should give countries with fewer resources and languages not suited for cultural brainwash a chance too. Even without the massive marketing I had been subject to throughout my life in Norway. Norway, a country from which hundreds of thousands of people had emigrated to the United States of America.

What I had essentially picked up was the realization that participation is key. Try everything or miss out. I have lived by the rule ever since, on every journey, travel, excursion and trip. Well, except for drugs. I prefer to remember my experiences.

I have visited the States a lot of times since, both for work and fun. Once together with NRK colleagues Nicolai, Andreas and Marius who later joined me in Afghanistan. We were there for a conference in Las Vegas, Nevada. Where what had to happen happened. We hit town and got hammered. Some of us got drunk beyond reason. At least that is our official cover story. Should any photographs that show unmentionable things ever surface.

I know Nicolai Flesjø from when we worked together in P4, Norway's biggest commercial radio station. He was the visionary digital director there, with his head full of groundbreaking ideas.

To hire me was not among them.

History has since showed that he was too early with many of them, audiences weren't ready yet. But Nico still never lost sight of his ambitions, and he later changed employers to NRK. So did I. He has since been one of the brains behind NRK's success online. Both at work and at play he has a talent of asking the right questions. And he is an eminent wingman out on the town. Nico's presence makes even me seem like a tallish guy.

Andreas Munkelien, or Munk for short, started working for NRK ten years ago. I was director of mobile services and was asked to put the mobile genius, half a year my senior, to work. He solved every task to perfection, and we soon decided to get to know the well-dressed man from Kolbotn, a small wannabe town outside Oslo, a little better. We had gone to the pub after work, and phoned him to ask him to join us. It was a Tuesday, he was a little reluctant. There was no other way to get him there than to resolve to threats. He was told to show up immediately or to work with teletext services for the remainder of his career. It worked. Andreas proved himself in the bar too. He is now director of development at NRK, and still works closely with all of us. Extensive work travel means that I have only traveled to more countries with Øystein than with Andreas.

We had planned to go to Los Angeles, California the next day to visit a former colleague who had married and moved there. None of us felt great after a legendary Las Vegas night, but we eventually managed to pack and load the Chrysler by noon. A quick count proved that Andreas was missing. Not necessarily strange, he had singlehandedly finished six bottles of bubbly the night before. He did not answer his mobile, but the 24th ring to his hotel room proved successful. He uttered some strange sounds that may have meant "hello".

"Are you ready or what? We are fully packed and the car is good to go. Have a fast shower and come."

It was soon clear that Andreas was unable to speak, shower or pack anytime soon, and we had to leave to get to our dinner meeting in L.A. in time before a meeting with Facebook, YouTube and Google in Palo Alto the following day.

"Get some sleep and sort out a plane ticket to San Francisco. We'll pick you up there tomorrow." The order was clear. There was some form of a response, before we left. Martin and his wife took us to a laid back restaurant in L.A. before we drove to the sort of hip Cadillac Hotel on Venice Beach.

We next heard from Munk late at night. He had eventually woken up to hangover of the millennium, and developed an acute fear of flying. His option was to rent a Dodge and to drive after us. He had checked into a motel outside the city due to heavy traffic but would get up earlier than us the next morning to catch up.

Nico, Marius and I started the next day with breakfast on the beach and set our course northward. We had scheduled a meeting with YouTube the same afternoon at 3pm. Contact was established with Munk via the phone network, he was half an hour behind us. Marius had a GPS enabled navigator, which made him our designated map reader. We were a little late for the meeting, and I tried to compensate. The speedometer soon showed almost 115 miles per hour.

"Ehe....Gunnar, I think you should slow down a little," Nico suggested from the backseat.

"Screw that! The roads are nice and we are late," I replied.

"I think that our meeting is no more, we have blue lights behind us."

A fast glimpse in the mirror proved him right. And then the siren was turned on. I indicated, turned onto the shoulder of the road and stopped.

"Bloody hell, Garfors, I hope you brought a soap-on-a-rope!"

Marius has watched a few American prison films. He wasn't particularly optimistic on my behalf, but opened the passenger window. A big female police officer with short red hair and glasses stood outside.

"Licence and registration, please!" she shouted. The "please" in the end didn't seem sincere.

"I am sorry, officer. We are a little late for a meeting, and I got carried away." I gave her my driver's license and Marius found the car registration papers in the glove compartment. Nico kept quiet in the backseat. She inspected the papers and found nothing wrong. The officer was still not impressed. Who could understand that?

"You better slow down, sir. This is not how we drive in the State of California! Understand?"

That was the clearest and strictest message I had received since a teacher caught me drowning a class mate in snow during a school break in fourth grade.

"I do, officer. I am very sorry."

She gave me the license back. Via Marius. We were free to continue. With a slightly shaken driver.

"Should we warn Andreas?" Nico asked.

"No, he is way behind us. If he slows down, we will be late for sure," I responded.

"Yeah, and what are the odds of Munk being stopped by the same lady?" Marius quipped. We laughed.

Andreas called Marius 20 minutes later. Marius put the call on the loudspeaker.

"Were you guys just stopped by the police?" Andreas asked.

"Why do you think so?" Marius asked back with a disbelieving voice.

Had the unthinkable happened?

"I was doing over 100 miles per hour to catch up with you, when I was stopped by a big red-head with a male figure. When she saw my driver's license she totally flipped and asked me if I was here with anyone."

"Seriously?" Marius said. Nico was already applauding in the back.

"I told her that I was trying to catch up with some colleagues to get to a meeting on time. And then she exploded: 'This is not how we drive in the State of California. I just stopped someone with an identical driver's license. Please tell your friends to slow down. If any of my colleagues stop you or your friends ever again, you will not leave the State of California!'" she shouted before I got my driver's license back.

"That is not bloody possible!" Marius responded in a sceptic voice before telling Andreas about our experience. The combination would have led to a record pay-out from any betting company.

We stopped at a gas station a little later to wait for the second offender. The rally driver had already made a call back home. A mate had done a few web searches and found out that we had probably been saved by our Norwegian driver's licenses. We would normally have had to pay around 10,000 USD each in fines, but it would also have led to paperwork bonanza for the police officer. She should have confiscated our passports and taken us to court. In California, that could easily take 2-3 weeks.

We parked outside YouTube's office three minutes ahead of time. Nico and Marius did most of the talking. Andreas and I were still sort of shaky.

Ireland

Yes, I have lived in Ireland. No, I can't remember anything about it. I was three years old, Øystein was one and a half. Our dad was there to take a medicine course at Royal College of Surgeons, our mom had enough to do with two wild kids. Øystein still sat in the push wagon, I insisted on walking. It almost ended with disaster one beautiful day. I still hadn't accumulated much brain power, and I suddenly ran into the road without thinking. A woman driving a Ford Transit practically stood on the brakes. Young and promising Garfors was very close to never become anything more than that. I allegedly stood as if I had been hypnotized as the blue van came closer and closer. It stopped ten centimetres away. Mom screamed! The lady who drove the van did too. While she jumped out of the van and to the front of it in panic. I was so short that she couldn't see if she had run me over or not me from the driver's seat.

Mom then installed belts in the double push wagon, and I was grounded. No more walking as long as we were near a public road. The near death experience contributed to us moving back to Norway. There were some Transits there too, but they drove on roads far from our entrance door. Far enough for little kid legs, at least.

I was back in Ireland many years later. For work. But pleasure often follows business, we ended up in a reasonably good restaurant near the Liffey. The discussion topic ended up being, for reasons I cannot remember, swearing. People from Northern Norway are particularly infamous for their nasty, and sometimes very long swear sentences. Or should I say paragraphs. In which country are people the worst when it comes to slagging other people off?

I mentioned some northern examples, they included both genitalia and horse. The latter seems to be used quite a bit in swearing practices both in Norway and abroad. But Paul put any northerner to shame with what I called the ultimate offense.

"The next one is borderline bad, but it will either top anything you have heard from your opponent, or get you killed," he said.

"Yeah, you mean it tops Northern Norwegian language?"

He looked at me as I had multiple mental disorders. And fired from the hip.

"Fuck your mother. And the horse she rode in on."

Ireland-Norway 1-0.

United Kingdom

Ireland's only neighbor, United Kingdom, did in many ways become my second home country following three years of studies at Falmouth College of Arts in Cornwall. To see me in an art college was against all logic known to mankind, but there were both journalism and broadcasting courses there too. My grade point average in high school was pretty good, but not good enough to be accepted to any Norwegian journalism course which had the highest entry level demands in the country (even higher than medicine studies). The solution was to stay in Norway and try improve my grades while working part-time as an assistant to a pig farmer, church gardener or road painter. Instead, I decided to apply in the UK. In August 1995 I stood alone on The Moor, a little square in the harbor town of Falmouth, population 17,000.

"What the hell am I doing here?" I thought to myself.

But I soon discovered the culture, the people and their sense of humor, their irony, their sarcasm. I actually liked the Brits. The industrial revolution had started in Cornwall due to demands from its mining industry, but the country is now lagging a little bit behind the rest of the country. But the incredible nature, the mild climate, the great educational institution and world-class surfing spots aren't too bad. I never regretted it.

I was still in Falmouth in 1996 when three mates from back home joined me. Knut Øyvind Aasen, Oddleif Løset and Kai "the Kid" Kilnes, one of my best friends. He still retains his eternal youth kind of look, hence his nickname. We played football together on level three in Førde. Knut Øyvind, or Knuts among friends, was more of an outsider. I knew him briefly from when he sold petrol at the second biggest gas station in Førde. He was behind the counter most evenings, and I had purchased considerable amounts of gasoline from him for my run down Volkswagen Polo, the worse Honda Civic and the disastrous Toyota Corolla. My rapid change of cars was due to the sad state of them, I didn't have much of a choice. In England we really hit it off and became good friends, even sharing an apartment. His name was however on the difficult side for faculty. One of the professors, let me call him Barry, could not for his life pronounce Knut the right way. And he didn't even try to say Øyvind or Aasen. In English, a "k" before an "n" is silent, as in "knife". That is not the case in Norwegian where the "k" is pronounced is a very distinct manner. Knut was therefore firstly pronounced Nut, before my friend tried to correct the mispronunciation.

"The 'k' is not silent."

"Oh, so it is Key-Nut?"

A staring competition later led to a compromise between Knut and Barry; Nuut.

Oddleif isn't ideal in English either. "Hi, so you are Odd Life?" soon became a standard opening phrase, followed by a giggle. Oddleif wasn't impressed. We had played football against each other as kids, and we started off on a hating note representing different teams, but in Falmouth we soon discovered that we enjoyed each other's company. Oddleif turned out to be a maestro in the kitchen, I was anything but. I usually lived off spaghetti with something from a can on top. My most famous course turned out to be spaghetti with canned spaghetti on top. I had opened the wrong can.

One Tuesday night, the four of us walked to a graveyard in Falmouth. By an old grave, there was a dead eel. Falmouth is a beach town, so we reckoned that a seagull astray had dropped it. The nearest beach was only a kilometre away.

"We can certainly use that for something," I said, and picked it up with a stick and carried it home to the house shared by Knut, Oddleif and Kai. They stayed with Kevin, an old middleweight boxer who slept in his own living room, while renting out the rest of the house to students. The rest of the house included one bathroom. That meant that he shat in a plastic bucket in the living room. Tasteful. Then again, what do you not do to make a few extra pounds? Well, quite a lot except to shit in a bucket, but that's just my opinion.

We had gone to Knut's room to further develop the eel plan.

"Let's put it in an envelope and send it to Øystein. If we mail it on Thursday, he won't have it until Monday. By then it should smell pretty fucking disgusting."

Kai, Knut and Oddleif all knew Øystein from back home where they had gone to high school with him. He studied at a Business School in Bergen when we were in Falmouth, and he lived in a small flat in Laksevåg, a run-down suburb. We put down Jameel Wheeler, Eel Street 447, Eeltown as the sender's address. We should not be accused of a lack of hints.

Øystein told me about the result of our cunning plan a few days later. This was in the age before mobile phones, and I called him from a payphone outside college on the Tuesday.

As usual, in case of such practical jokes, it started with abuse and ended up with laughter.

"What the hell did you send? It smelled so incredibly fucking bad that I had to evacuate my flat and stay with a mate last night. In addition I had to cancel a date with a gorgeous girl, yesterday. You owe me, or else!"

And that wasn't the only practical joke committed in England. As students, we had to register with a medical doctor, undergo a mandatory check-up and have our urine tested. We usually relaxed in Knut's room, he had the biggest one. Once, when he was in the loo, we sabotaged the little glass that was meant for his urine sample. We added a little drop of duty free vodka. Knut Øyvind later had an interesting talk with his doctor.

We did too little schoolwork at Falmouth College of Arts. In retrospect. But the quality of the education was good, and I met friends from all over the world. I have visited quite a few of them since, another benefit of a lot of traveling. There is still one thing I hate with the British. Marmite. An awful spread that can be found on way too many breakfast tables. The company behind it, the food giant Unilever, employs some smart marketing people, and the marketing campaign takes advantage of people's feeling towards it. "Love it or hate it."

Let me introduce you to the Marmite loving Brit, Sera, who I met one spring in London.

"I love Marmite! Put it on a pancake with sugar and lemon. It's fantastic!" She said with real enthusiasm.

"What isn't, with pancakes?"

The dry and immediate response of a mate caused laughter around the table. Not even fresh pancakes can save the brown slime. But we kept in touch, despite our irreconcilable palate differences. We shared a sense of humor and curiosity and I asked her to go traveling with me, quite a few times. I liked that she is creative and always up for new ideas. Wherever they would be played out. She did however always ask me an essential question before agreeing to join.

"Will I get shot?"

My answer usually influenced her decision.

Denmark

I moved to Denmark in 1999 to work for LookSmart, a pre-Google search engine. Yet again I lived in a new, flat country. With very little rain. The transition from the wet Norwegian West Coast was stark. And the pay was better, although the Danish tax of 49% certainly took away a lot of what should have been extra cash.

LookSmart had gathered all the Nordic offices in one location. 35 employees from Norway, Sweden, Denmark and Finland all in one building. Iceland was too little to be of interest to the Australian American company. To work that close with people from neighboring countries was surely an experience. We learnt a lot of inter-Nordic cultural differences, and soon realized that there is a high level of truth in the myths about the Finns.

We worked a lot, but also found time for trips to town. A nightclub near our office stayed open until 10am the next day on Fridays and Saturdays. By paying 150 kroner (25USD), you'd get in and could also drink as much as you would like. Potentially life threatening for Norwegians. I was still sensible enough to go home by 3ish. Thomas was not. I didn't see him again until the following Monday. He had not stopped partying until he was kicked out, at 10am. To get home, he had to walk through the busiest shopping street in Denmark. He had woken up at 7pm on Saturday evening with 8-10 plastic bags around the bed. He had gone ape shit with his credit cards in various shops, yet without remembering anything. None of the shoes or clothes fitted him.

Thomas, or Psycho-Thomas among friends, has become a good mate. He needs to be experienced. His nickname is well deserved and is due to a relatively consistent unorthodox behavior. He did in other words fit in well with my other friends. Thomas is, needless to say, also a drinker, and does not fall far behind Doctor Vodka in consumption at parties.

"I hate blood in my alcohol stream," he claims.

Thomas has held more job titles than you can count on the hands of Siamese triplets. Following the LookSmart period, he has for instance done everything in the restaurant business. He started there following a rocket career in education. Rocket as in space shuttle. Space shuttle as in Challenger.

But a good and well-connected friend of his had noticed Thomas' talent with wine and food, and called him out of the blue.

"Thomas, I have the perfect job for you. You will start working for Cato."

Cato Pedersen is an eminent chef who has run a number of top-notch restaurants, including famous Bon Lío in Oslo. Thomas did not protest, and showed up at the job interview the following day. The guys shook hands and sat down at a table in the empty restaurant. It was 10am, and it didn't open until lunch.

"I've been told to start here."

"And I 've been told to hire you."

Silence occurred for five seconds. Uncomfortable silence. Cato eliminated it.

"What have you done before?"

"Does it really matter?" Thomas said outright, as usual. As he always did the six months we worked together in Denmark.

Taiwan

A decade passed until I decided to move out again. This time I decided to try to learn a new language. Easy is boring, Chinese is neither. The capital of Taiwan is one of the cities with the highest density of restaurants in the world. Barbie, Hello Kitty and A380, the world's biggest passenger plane, all have themed eating rooms. Not to forget Modern Toilet Restaurant where toilets are used for chairs and where you eat from soap dishes. You can guess what the chocolate ice cream comes shaped as.

I found a tiny flat in Shida, a three minute walk from NTNU, the university. Shida also comes with a night market where you can buy pretty much anything cheaply. Just don't expect quality goods.

At university I got along well with Darren from Britain. He is a nice guy, but we also developed a joint hate relationship against our tutor, a semi attractive girl our age. She had no educational skills and a temper from the darker areas of hell.

A poor combination given the difficulty Darren and I had in pronouncing Chinese correctly. Darren's revenge was a nickname. Satan. To blame our lack of learning capabilities on Satan was logical and made it easier to accept our limited progression.

Two of the weeks in Taiwan were made a lot better thanks to visits by Haenim, who I was going out with back then. She is from Seoul, South Korea, where we had met at a conference she helped organize. We had soon discovered that we had a lot in common. Probably too soon. We decided to marry a year and a half after Taiwan. More about that later.

My flat was one of several identical ones that was rented out by the same landlady. That meant that it was easy to complain in case of problems. Haenim and I were still very much in love, and we spent a lot of time in bed. One evening, I got a text message from the landlady.

"Please keep the noise down when you are happy. Your neighbors are jealously complaining."

In university, I also met Ken, a local student with the typical adopted English name. We often had coffee together. I got to practice Chinese, he improved his English. A win-win situation! Late on a Friday, he asked me if I wanted to join him at Club 7. I had never heard about the place, and I wasn't hard to convince. To try new nightclubs is rarely wrong. Ten minutes later saw us sitting on the step just outside a Seven-Eleven shop. I had a beer in my hand, he had a ready mixed vodka tonic in one hand and a hot-dog in the other. There were 8 or 10 other people sitting there as well. In Taipei, Club 7 means drinking outside one of the many Seven-Eleven shops in town. They come with cold and cheap drinks inside, and they are always open. Bargain! Just don't expect much dancing.

The mayor of Taipei used to be able to brag about having the highest skyscraper in the world on his turf. There is a gourmet restaurant on the top floor, although getting a table is a challenge. I decided to give it my best shot when Andreas announced his visit. In particular, because he has a fear of heights. He did not appreciate the window table, but put on a brave face and ordered a lot of bubbly. His theory is that it cures anything, in this case acrophobia. As well documented in the US, he can hold his bubbles.

MY HOME IS YOUR HOME

To visit new countries open eyes. But you will never get a closer encounter of new cultures as when you actually go to someone's home. To see how people live might be the very best way to get insight into a new culture, its people. Some places it is quite normal to be invited to your friend's home. Other places, this hardly ever happens. Do consider it a true honor should it still occur. South Koreans do for instance never invite anyone home unless you are related or a very close friend. A Korean delegation that visited Oslo therefore refused to pay me a visit in my flat. I persistently insisted, and they eventually showed up with a fine wine and grade A ginseng. Too late I realized that North Korean propaganda posters and a North Korean flag were draping my living room walls. I had no other option than to humbly apologize. Luckily, I knew the head of the delegation very well, my mistake could otherwise easily have been the start of the end of our work relationship.

Japan

The alleged homeland of the sun cannot compare with any other country. It is just different. Or in which other country is it seen as good thing for you to fall asleep at work, since your boss then assumes that you have worked real hard? Some employees even pretend to be sleeping to impress. Just do it sitting, if you lean forward on your desk, it is an offense. I have of course never really worked in Japan, despite writing a travel column for Mainichi, the biggest newspaper and despite having taken part in a lot of meetings there. But a Japanese friend whom I first met in a coffee bar in Tokyo gradually let me in on a few secrets on Japanese society. Kaoru had studied three years in New Zealand, something that really opened her eyes.

"Man, I had no idea that we are actually very, very different to probably any other citizens," she once enthusiastically explained to me over a beer. Her New Zealand drawl made no secret of where she had gone to school.

"You may be tempted by a soine-ya, some sort of a coffee shop where you can lie next to a beautiful woman or even sleep on her arm. It is not a brothel though, and you will have to pay extra to stare into her eyes, to stroke her hair, to watch her change or to have a foot massage by her."

There was no denying that I was fascinated by the weirdness. But there were more strange tales to tell. Many more. I could for instance go to the dentist and have my teeth shaped Dracula style. It is called *yaeba*, and is the latest fashion in order to come across as more sexy. I decided not to. Neither did I use a sun bed to the extreme. The result is called *ganguro*, and is yet another way of becoming "attractive". Women are known to use sunbeds daily, and also use darkening creams to get the "perfect" skin tone.

"Brown skin somehow make you look thinner. So everyone goes for it."

The next craziness might have been more tempting A fair amount of young girls wish to sleep with a foreigner before marrying. And we are not talking about soine-ya, but the full monty. Western men working in embassy areas occasionally experience that their pulling power has tripled over night. But it is allegedly all over after one night, when their mission has been completed and they are ready to marry a Japanese man.

Kaoru shared a few more kinky secrets. She told me that any thinkable kind of brothel exists. If a customer would like a girl dressed in a particular uniform or outfit, consider it done. In any kind of a context that is; On the metro, in a phone booth or on an office desk. I didn't look particularly impressed. Nor aroused.

"Still not tempted? How about a brothel where the 'prostitutes' are inflatable dolls?" Kaoru asked. I laughed out loud.

"And how exactly are they cleaned between customers?" I giggled. I was genuinely curious.

"My sources never said anything about that," she smiled.

The strange and extreme Japanese fetishes are renowned around the world. Why, is harder to pinpoint. And don't try to ask just any Japanese either. They will swiftly blush, change subject or pour you another drink. Usually a combination of the above.

Except for Kaoru. Although she had admittedly had a drink or three.

"Well, Japan is still pretty conservative when it comes to sex and no one really talks much about their sexual encounters. I feel like people here are sexually suppressed in a way and everyone has their own secret fetishes which probably explains the demand for different kinds of brothels. I think this is the case with both the cuddle cafés and the sex dolls. More and more people are withdrawn from society as they spend most of the time with online friends. They have almost lost connections with real people and have a hard time communicating face to face because they are afraid of rejection. And neither dolls nor girls at the cafe will reject them." She whispered the last sentence.

There are also huge differences between the US and Japan. In the latter country only two people are killed by guns every year. 4,000 are killed per annum in the US. But 100 people kill themselves in Japan. *Every day*. Most jump from high-rises or in front of locomotives. The phenomenon is inspired by harakiri, a ritual suicide where people take their own life by cutting themselves in the tummy. It was historically performed by samurais, and is extremely painful. Dying could take hours. It is much faster to jump from the 45th floor.

A lot of people do still live for a long time. There are over 50 000 people that are older than 100 years. No other country has higher life expectancy. Which explains why more diapers are sold for adults than for babies. The combination with low birth numbers also contribute.

My first trip to Japan was for work, I was on a delegation of Nordic broadcasters. We were there to find out why Japan was a world leader within mobile services. One of the nights proved more memorable than the others. We ended up in a bar. Closing time was not far away when the owner invited us to his penthouse suite on the 7th floor of the building. We had quadrupled his normal daily revenue. He offered us more booze. And access to a karaoke machine.

It is still a mystery why colleague Sindre Østgård later became Head of New Media at Norwegian Broadcasting Corporation, not tenor in The Norwegian Opera. Thanks to his musical abilities we were allowed to stay to drink, sing and dance until tomorrow came.

"Thank you so much for letting us use your apartment so late!" a Swedish colleague said.

"It is my highest pleasure. I would never throw out Pavarotti or his friends."

Papa New Guinea

It was dead early. The Air Niugini plane from Manila had just landed, and I was set to visit the capital of Papa New Guinea. I was due to meet Victoria, who I had found on sofa exchange website Hospitality Club. She was the only person who was willing to let me stay overnight in Port Moresby. There are very few visitors to the country, except business people and NGO workers. The hotels are priced accordingly.

She arrived 20 minutes late at the airport in her old banger of a Mazda. Port Moresby is known for high crime levels, and I had already started to consider alternative transport and accommodation options.

"I am sorry for being late! I slept through my alarm clock. Why the hell did you arrive so early, anyway? Jump in!"

Victoria talked a lot, and rarely waited for a response. She worked for the UN, and was clearly busy with a range of projects. We got to her two-bedroom flat, and she apologized for not having a room for me. A Swedish female colleague was staying in the spare room, she slept in her own room with her two kids.

"So you will have to sleep on the sofa."

The green couch seemed to have experienced a couple of wars and would certainly manage to carry me too for a couple of nights.

"I have to go to work. Do you want to join?" she offered.

Nice one, I thought, immediately accepting the offer. It is always ace to see how people work. Her office was only ten minutes away by car. She worked on heightening the knowledge of HIV and AIDS among the locals. Not an easy task.

"Less than 60 percent of people here can read and write. So I have to think outside the box."

Victoria never explained what that meant, and I didn't get time to ask before she ran to a different part of the ground floor office which only housed a handful of people. Every person had to cover a range of tasks. She soon headed downtown for a meeting, and offered me a ride. I was given a security speech before being let off.

"Port Moresby is not the safest of places. Don't walk outside the centre and don't talk to people. Here is my address, take registered taxis only." she commanded and sped off.

Victoria was always busy, always in a hurry. I ignored her warning immediately. What is the point of traveling if you can't talk to locals or walk about?

I soon attracted interest by a local guy in his 60's on the city beach who asked where I was from before continuing his interrogation.

"Why are you here?"

"I am a traveler."

"You shouldn't talk to me. I am dangerous," he said and touched his straw hat. As if that would emphasise what he just said.

"Well, you started it. And so am I." I smiled. So did he. After ten seconds. Before he started laughing out loud.

"I don't like many foreigners. They come here and take our resources. That's why we are a little rough with some of them."

"You trying to scare me?"

The tattooed and tanned tall man laughed heartedly. "Is it working?"

"Not really."

"I like you, Norwegian boy. Enjoy my country. And let me know if you get into trouble. I'm Kevin, by the way."

"Nice to meet you, Kevin. I'll send a letter pigeon if I find myself in trouble."

We shook hands and I returned to the town center to find somewhere to eat. I ended up in a local joint, full of local people of all ages. That is usually a good sign when it comes to food quality. Unless it is McDonald's or some other fast food joint.

I decided to walk to the yacht club. There were no local people of any ages there. Just wealthy and white middle-aged western people. As in white ones. Plus a few teenagers dressed in Polo gear. The price level was way above what I had just experienced in the local restaurant. I ordered a caffe latte from a tall table on the terrace only meters from the club house. Cabin cruisers, sailing boats, yachts of all types gave an indication of where the money from the vast natural resources of the country went. A new lucrative oil project was *the drop*, according to Victoria. She told me that Papa New Guinea had more or less given away the oil to western oil companies. The locals agreed that no one except the odd politician would benefit at all, and they openly talked about corruption.

No wonder that I was looked upon as one of them. One of the white exploiters. It made sense that three of four black workers sitting on the cargo bed of a pickup truck had showed me the finger when they passed me on my three kilometre long stroll to the yacht club.

I had another latte and walked home to Victoria. She arrived at the same time as I did.

"I have to pick up my kids from school. Do you wanna watch TV or come along?"

I'll watch TV when I am old.

We arrived at school, and I soon realized that we weren't only picking up her kids. It was the day of parental meetings. And she expected me to join. We first met daughter Sophia's teacher in her classroom. It was on the first floor of a non-insulated building that stood on piers. All windows had been opened and the fans in the ceiling tried to cool down the place. Unsuccessfully so. The walls were lined with various pupil productions. Drawings and poems in many colors. Sophie's teacher clearly believed that I was the stepfather. Victoria is originally from central parts of Africa, I was clearly not the biological dad.

"Your daughter is very bright. She is among the top three readers in her class. And she excels in math. You should be very proud!"

The female teacher said, and looked straight into my eyes. I just smiled in response.

"Philip's teacher is next. She's a little bit of a bitch," Victoria whispered the last sentence when walking down the stairs.

Another parental meeting? Well, why not. When in Papa, New Guinea, etc. We walked across the school yard to a similar building and up another set of stairs. Kids were playing football and basketball on a little sports field nearby. The atmosphere was somehow strange. I shook the hand of teacher number two. She didn't cut to the chase.

"Philip has not improved much. He is very talkative when he shouldn't be. And not paying much attention to what I teach. His reading is appalling."

Oops. I didn't really want to be part of *that*.

"Well, maybe he is not receiving the appropriate teaching!" Victoria barked back.

"Both myself and my colleagues have excellent credentials. You as a single parent better follow up more carefully on his homework. Although it seems like you have acquired some company, I hope it is more fruitful than the last."

The teacher hit back, using me as a weapon. And I had only looked for a couch. I had to bite my lower lip to not start laughing, something that would unlikely have helped the situation. I had not participated in a parental meeting since 1999 when I was at the other side of the table. As a temporary head teacher for grade 9 at Førde secondary school in Norway. I was rather certain that I had done a better job on the other side of the world back then than what this particular teacher achieved now. And I don't even have an educational degree. I sort of hoped this woman didn't either.

"Philip's reading is particularly poor. If it doesn't improve rapidly he will have to retake my second grade class. Neither of us want that. I will see you again in three months."

We were practically pushed out of the room. To say that Victoria was unhappy and mad would be a major understatement. Philip was given hell in the car, he consequently promised proper improvement. That resulted in fried chicken for dinner, clearly the children's favorite dish.

Back at Victoria's I got to meet Annika, the Swedish colleague who had occupied the guestroom. She had just returned from work, and told me that she hoped to be able to move into her own apartment within a week. Her husband would join her there by the end of the month.

Our host started preparing pasta for us, the kids were no longer hungry. Victoria asked if I could have a look at the VCR which had stopped working a few days earlier, so the kids could no longer watch their top cartoons. It seemed like the connection between the cable and the SCART plug was poor, and I asked for a soldering iron in order to fix it.

"The cable is destroyed? I am gonna kill Philip."

What had I done? Philip had clearly contributed to the state of the cable. The 8 year old was carried into the bedroom, the pasta was boiling heavily. He understood very well what was about to happened, and cried like a tortured pig. The sounds from the bedroom soon told the rest of us what was happening. He was beaten on his trouser-less bum. The boy screamed. The beats echoed in the artless room. Sophie had covered her ears with her hands and desperately watched the telly. Annika and I exchanged looks, but we didn't quite know what to do, what to say.

No one said much over dinner, spaghetti with delicious minced meat and a homemade tomato sauce. Sophie sat in the green sofa watching TV. Philip stood next to it. There would be no sitting for him in a while.

Palestine

There are six countries in the world without an airport, Palestine is by far the biggest of those. There are as many inhabitants there as in Kentucky, but there are more Palestinians outside its borders than inside. The country is divided into The West Bank and Gaza and totals just over 6,000 square kilometers. That is less than Delaware. 45 percent of the land is used to grow olives.

To enter Palestine is not easy. Israel controls all routes in, and you will be asked curt questions about where you are going, and why. It is as if the border patrols are trying to scare visitors from visiting the squeezed country. Sera from Britain had eventually volunteered to visit the country with me.

"Will I get shot?" she had asked.

"Of course not!"

And she was in. I had conveniently skipped telling her about well-trained rock hurlers. However, neither of us were in their target group. We had driven from Tel Aviv, and were refused entry at the first check point.

"Stone throwers are very active today," one of the soldiers said with a broad southern drawl. He had clearly lived in the US. The other soldier talked on the radio. They were polite, but very determined. Armed to their teeth, too. And then some. We did not protest. But neither did we give in, stone throwers or not. We found a back road with less anal gate keepers and drove into Ramallah. The small town has a little and very colorful fruit and vegetable market. Sera was in heaven, it was an unusual sight for a semi-posh London girl. A couple of hours of sightseeing later, and we drove into the village of Jifna. By the main road from Ramallah we met a man in his 50's. He rented out rooms in the house where he lived with his wife, and guided us to the big brick villa a kilometre from the road and invited us to tea. Jifna is 15 kilometres from Ramallah, which functions as the capital of Palestine. But it isn't. I soon understood that this was an issue we ought to discuss with care.

"You have a nice capital," Sera exclaimed to Issa before sipping the tea at their kitchen table. The couple was very hospitable.

"Oh, so you have been to Jerusalem?"

"No, Ramallah," she responded the moment I kicked her leg.

"Jerusalem is our capital," our host swiftly responded. His voice was dry as a desert.

Issa wasn't impressed with the history knowledge, or lack thereof. The Palestinians look at themselves as an occupied people, whom have had strict restrictions imposed on what they can do and what they cannot. Even on where they can travel. We promised to compensate for our historical ignorance by visiting Jerusalem the next day. Every time we came back to Palestine we had to go through the same procedure. Non-smiling Israeli border guards wanted to know what we were about to do. And why.

Neither Issa nor his wife were ill tempered for long. They showed us around the three-story house which came with a huge open kitchen. Big, expensive looking furniture lined the living room. They clearly had money, but it was all a little over the top for my taste. Bordering kitsch. The herb garden outside more than compensated, and the wife sold her home grown herbs from the kitchen. The thyme spice has presumably won awards. One of a kind!

Back in Ramallah we were surprised by the amount of good restaurants. The gourmet garden Orjuwan Lounge totally impressed us, especially when taken into account that goods don't exactly flow freely into Palestine from Israel. We finished with coffee in the chain Stars and Bucks. The logo, the cups and the selection of coffee drinks and food came with a very prominent Seattle inspiration.

Chile

The coffee interest in Chile is far less noticeable. Every person there only drinks half a kilo of coffee per year. Every Norwegian drinks 20 times more. The long and thin country is relatively free of corruption, compared to most continent colleagues, at least. I was told that Chile is the only country in South America where passing the police a few dollars may escalate a minor traffic violation to a serious corruption investigation. Luckily, I have not been in a position to test out the theory.

I visited Chile in 2003 when I was going out with Nicole Salazar who was born there. Her dad was not on Pinochet's side, he rather spoke out against the dictator. That was something you did not do unpunished in the 80's, and the entire family had to escape. Their choices were Australia and Norway. Nicole's dad has regretted his poor geographical research ever since. Bloody Norwegian climate.

Nicole arrived in Norway when she was 7, we met each other many years later. She was about to start studies at the University of Oslo. The intention was to become a teacher, and she later succeeded. Her parents didn't live in town and she needed a place to stay. I had an extra bedroom to rent out and saw the benefit of having an extra income to pay the bills. And travel expenses. There was a mutual attraction. And it ended as it had to end when a beautiful girl with a wide smile and a contagious laugh moves in. She didn't stay in my guestroom for a great number of months.

Nicole met me in the airport in Santiago. Together with dozens of relatives. They were curious to find out who this Norwegian boyfriend was, and they certainly needed some background material to the forthcoming evaluation later the same evening. Nicole's uncle drove us to Rancagua, a medium sized mining and tourist town, best known for a battle in 1814. Local soldiers fought for independence from Spain, but they lost overwhelmingly.

Hours and hours of family talk, cheese and mediocre red wine awaited in the living room of her uncle and aunt's house. Not that I understood much, but I apparently smiled at the right times. They lived in a simple but clean house in the center of town.

They had several bedrooms, but there was no chance in hell that Nicole and I would share one in the Catholic country, and I went to bed before the others. I had just flown in from New Zealand and I was tired. There also seemed to be a fair amount of anticipation among the others. They would clearly discuss me as soon as the door to the bedroom was closed. Poor Nicole. She's probably having to deliver numerous defense speeches for her choice. Imagine dragging a blond

Norwegian all the way to Chile. I was given a narrow wooden bed in a cream colored and nicely decorated room. A home-sown tablecloth covered the night stand, and a yellow homemade wooden chair in the corner was empty, awaiting my clothes. Nicole's uncle and aunt clearly knew how to use their hands. He worked in the copper mine, she was a housewife. A cross hung on one wall, there was a picture of the Virgin Mary on the other. Faithful people.

The evaluation seemed to have passed favorably. I was served an impressive breakfast consisting of newly baked bread, tasty cheese, fresh tomatoes and cucumber. Plus soft boiled eggs and coffee. Everyone was smiling. Nicole too.

"They like you," she said in Norwegian. Almost surprised.

"But not well enough to let us share a bed," I teased her.

"Come on! It is a tradition. And they are super religious! Give them a break."

Nicole and I later visited Santiago and Viña del Mar. I have never seen as many pharmacies before, and we entered one of them. I needed sunscreen due to the strong sun. I asked Nicole to ask which sun protection factor I would need.

"They claim that you need at least 50!" she laughed.

I purchased 20. And got a sunburn. They know what they do, these pharmacists.

To travel around Chile felt similar to doing the same back in Europe. Modern busses drove fast on good roads and took us where we wanted to go on time. Nicole acted as translator and guide, ensuring a problem-free trip. Except for all the looks I got from local women as I was holding hands with "one of them". I dare to claim that South American women, as a general rule, rates above average when it comes to jealousy. Nicole also knew that art, and threw some nasty phrases to those she deemed most insolent. Coincidentally that turned out to be 100 percent proportional to their beauty.

Cameroon

She would have been jealous in Cameroon too. It was in the big and dirty harbor city of Douala that I met Stella. The aspiring tour guide wondered if she could guide me. There isn't much I dislike as much as tour guides. And there is nothing personal. I simply prefer to explore new places on my own or with friends. That applied in Cameroon too. Stella got the point, and instead invited me to come visit her village, tiny Miliwe north of Douala, the next day.

"Not as a guide, but as a friend. I would like to cook for you."

She also recommended a local restaurant for that very evening. I responded by inviting her along, and we ended up eating goat meat in the shape of brochettes, some sort of a kebab. Stella told me that she had a teacher's degree, but that she was still unable to find work in a difficult job market. She now tried to start her own travel company that would offer guided tours for foreign visitors.

The phone in my hotel room rang the next morning. It was Stella. She was in the lobby to pick me up, and we took a minibus to her village. Both her father and her son were at home. They lived in a small brick house without water, although electricity had been installed. A few nervous chickens were running around the yard in front of the house. There was a well next to a small tool shack. The standard of their home was simple, yet way above the average house in the neighborhood. Still far below what any Norwegian, this side of 1960, would have accepted.

Stella's dad watched football on TV, while John Philip was keen on playing himself.

"If you go and play with him, I will prepare dinner in the meantime. There is a field across the road," Stella suggested.

The eight year old loved playing with a grown up foreigner. We took turns being the goalie. The boy turned out to have some talent, his left foot was made of sledge hammer material.

Dinner was delicious! Beans, tomatoes, beef and lamb was barbequed over open flames in the yard before being served on newspapers where we sat around a white plastic table. An eminent spice mix accompanied the meal. We three adults had iced tea. John Philip drank Fanta. He only ate half his dinner.

"John Philip, you should eat everything if you want to become a big and great footballer," I said for Stella's benefit and big smile.

The rest of the food mysteriously moved from the newspaper into his little tummy in a matter of minutes. I rarely experience being such a source of inspiration for youngsters.

Chad

I probably inspired someone on my way to N'Djamena in Chad too, somewhere in the border area between Nigeria and Cameroon. Or at least I hope that the lucky finder of my wallet could feel some inspiration. I was wearing trousers made of artificial fabric, and therefore very slippery. Especially when combined with a wallet made of polished metal. It slid out inside an old Peugeot taxi. Someone found it and claimed a finder's fee. My account statement showed that someone had paid 10 dollars for a phone card in Cameroon, even though I called on a shaky line to the credit card company back in Norway to block the card immediately after discovering the missing wallet. The worst consequence of it all was that I only had a couple hundred US dollars in cash plus a backup MasterCard. Inside Chad I soon discovered that particular card to be no good. Not even via the internet where I tried to transfer money to myself via Western Union. They were clearly not too keen on transactions initiated from a Chadian IP-address. To make the situation worse, it turned out that my phone company had not bothered sorting out a roaming agreement with their Chadian colleagues.

The result was total phone silence. The solution was the local Novotel hotel located on the bank of the Chari river that runs between Chad and Cameroon. I just about managed to get coverage from the Cameroonian mobile network operator with a base station on the other side of the river, and I finally got through to Øystein.

"Hi! All good?"

"It is indeed, Benedicte and I are up to no good in Oslo, we are soon heading home to Naustdal. How about you?"

"I am creating havoc in N'Djamena in Chad."

"Yes, of course you are!"

Øystein was not always up to date where I was at any given time. But he was soon informed about my situation. And it turned out, against all odds, that he was only 300 meter away from a Western Union branch in Oslo. He transferred a thousand dollars.

"But in order for me to get the money out, you need to give them a password of minimum eight digits."

The instructions I had been given by Chadian Western Union staff had been rather precise.

"57819433," he quipped.

"Hehehe...sorted. Thanks a lot for helping out!"

Our old landline number back home in Naustdal was no longer in use, but we both knew it by heart. It is strange what pieces of useless information from childhood that you will forever be unable to forget.

I was planning to stay in the capital of Chad for another few days. To explore more, but also to secure a visa to Central African Republic. So I roamed the streets of town, a surprisingly pleasant experience given the harsh temperatures there. The center is small, very slow walks came highly recommended.

I eventually found the embassy just outside the town center. A guard stood on the terrace outside the house. He was wearing a way too small and tight T-shirt. Dress code clearly did not apply. It turned out there wasn't even a queue. The guard showed me to the white colonial wooden building and into the office of no other than the embassy's first secretary. He was a very pleasant guy who knew how to carry on a conversation. Not all that strange, really, he must not receive many visitors. Fifteen minutes later he told me that the visa stamp was out of order, but that he would call the airport police in Bangui and instruct them to let me in. He shook my hand and wished me luck. A total waste of time, in other words, had it not been for the industrial strength super fan in his office. I narrowly avoided goose bumps.

The same night I met Robert, the cassette salesman. He ran what he described as a successful business.

"Cassettes? As in audio tapes?"

"Yes, sir! People buy them like crazy. But some people are starting to ask for mp3 files, so I provide that too. On memory sticks. But I personally think the audio quality is better on cassettes. You know, there is just something about that tape. And who the hell will ever create a cover to mp3 files?"

The discussion he had with himself sounded familiar. What people had claimed when switching from LPs to CDs. Very few of the tapes were original. Most of them were "produced" by Robert himself.

"For crispy, sharp sound recording of the Millennium" it said on the labels.

The business man showed me his collection of cassettes. They were stacked on a wooden board surrounded by a frame to prevent the merchandise falling off when being carried. Most of the artists were local. Except for Led Zeppelin and Britney Spears. An interesting selection.

Robert also showed me his so called home. Under a small metal plate on the side of some sort of a restaurant shack. He had a mattress, some clothes in a bag on a wooden shelf on the wall and a double sided cassette recorder. We ordered grilled chicken from the pleasant lady in the restaurant. The salesman explained that she rented out the "residence" for close to nothing. Anything else would have been robbery in bright daylight. It was an outdoor "room" with one wall underneath what someone with imagination might call a roof.

New Zealand

My sister Kjersti stayed in much better conditions when she was an exchange student in New Zealand in 2002-03. Ten years had passed since I had gone through the same in Indiana, and there was never any doubt that I would visit her. We spent our ten days together in a white little rental car that transported us around most of the North Island. Being geography buffs, we saw no other solution but to visit the location in the world with the longest name.

Taumatawhakatangihangakoauauotamateaturipukakapikimaunga-horonukupokaiwhenuakitanatahu.

Kjersti is now a qualified medical doctor, and lives back in Naustdal with her husband Eigil Instebø and their daughter Sunniva. She still remembers the longest name in the world by heart, just ask her. The almost unpronounceable name is of a 305 meter high hill in the south-eastern part of the North island. Where no one lives, barred sheep and owners. The country counts 30 million sheep, 7 times the number of people.

Very few people take the trouble to go to the place with the 85 character long name, despite the world record. When Kjersti and I drove past, we were soon flagged down by the first person we had seen in ages. By a sheep farmer with a sixpence and a tweed coat, with a red pattern.

"How's it going?"

"Good! How are you?" Kjersti answered. With a broad New Zealand accent. And explained that we came from the Norwegian countryside and that this was almost like home.

"So, what are you folks doing here?"

"We just visited the hill with the longest name."

"No, you didn't. That spot with the sign is just for tourists like yourselves. The hill belongs to me and is fenced off."

"Oh."

Her disappointment was hard to hide. At least we had a photo of us and the huge sign. But the farmer noticed our discouraged looks.

"Follow me, and I will take you to the real hill. You've traveled some distance to get here."

We drove slowly behind Brian and the dog, a border collie. Brian walked in front of our car to the farm house a few hundred meters away. I parked, we jumped out.

Three minutes passed before we found ourselves on the back of an all-terrain vehicle, some sort of a mixture of a motorcycle and a car. He drove us between the sheep, across the very green field and up to the top of the hill. It was as spectacular as a hill can be. Not at all. But the view over pastures, forests and sheep was rather grand. Given the surroundings.

And we were, despite everything, on the real hill. The 85 characters mean *"The summit where Tamatea, the man with the big knees, the climber of mountains, the land-swallower who traveled about, played his nose flute to his loved one"*. So there.

Back at the farm we got to meet Brian's wife and three kids. The hospitality in New Zealand is world famous for a reason. The wife spontaneously invited us to a party the same evening. Their oldest daughter, Karen, turned 18, an event that had to be celebrated properly. Guests from the other side of the globe was nothing but a bonus.

The party turned out to be in the sheep cutter barn. And so it smelled. Beautiful! Just like being at home. And the entire neighborhood was of course there too, around forty people altogether. Then again, in these parts of New Zealand you will be defined as a neighbor as long as you can drive to the next house without refueling. People had come from far away. The fields are plenty and they are huge. Let's say there's some space between the houses.

Karen was celebrated until the early hours, by fiddle playing people, a real sheep cutter barn dance routine, potato crisps, dried lamb meat and bottled beer. Kjersti and I were invited to stay in a guestroom of Brian and his wife. The concept of "the nearest hotel" did not exist around here.

We were invited to join their farmer's breakfast in the morning. Or their lunch, rather. They had luckily let us sleep until after the rooster's first call.

I WON'T GO BACK (ANYTIME SOON)

There are some countries I do not feel an immediate urge to return to. Due to bad experiences, a lack of activities or nothing but my failure to meet anyone interesting. I have in either case not really managed to find the pulse or discover the real atmosphere there. Maybe I should have given the country more time.

There are still no countries in the world that I do not want to return to, but the ones in this chapter do not come particularly highly rated for whatever reason.

Kuwait

The desert and oil country of Kuwait is one of the hottest in the world. And conservative as hell. Dry as hell too, with an average of only two rainy days a year. Thanks to a lot of oil it is one of the wealthiest countries in the world, if assessing by GNP per inhabitant. That may also help explain why 40 percent of the population is obese.

Which in turn might make it harder to find a partner. I was surprised to read the classifieds in the English language newspaper Kuwait Times. Next to ads of used cars, discounted swimming pool cleaning and almost-not-at-all-used push wagons, there was an ad section that dwarfed all others. I'd normally call them personals. But these were different. Kuwaiti parents were looking for a spouse for their kids.

"Educated and well-spoken gentleman sought for our 21 year old well-raised daughter."

The phone number was listed below. I presume they prove a higher success rate than what would be the case of joining the hidden private parties where smuggled alcohol is served, but there is still something appealing about being able to decide yourself who to marry.

One of my most vivid memories is from the candy man in Kuwait. He stood in his little stall by the road, proudly displaying a range of known and not so known types of dried fruit and other sweets. The light from a few bare lightbulbs made the contrasts of the shack even sharper. From the dark shadows to the colorful delicacies that have been harvested from Middle Eastern plants unknown to me. It was still not only the various colors that made up the contrasts. So did he, the way he enlightened the hood with his presence. A colorful man. In a country with one of the world's worst cultural combinations.

Extreme Islam mixed with extreme capitalism. I was not particularly tempted to revisit.

The Vatican

Neither was I after in the Vatican, the world's smallest country measuring less than half a square kilometer. And with just above 800 inhabitants. You wouldn't think there was space, but the country allegedly has a secret library with no less than 80 kilometres worth of bookshelves. With letters from British queens, Napoleon and Voltaire. Plus the odd sketches from Michelangelo and a hell of a lot of other stuff from famous, infamous and non-grata persons. And if Dan Brown is to be believed, the library also contains proof that Jesus Christ married Maria Magdalena and lived happily ever after. If that is the case, Ascension Day should not really be celebrated. Not that I am complaining, it provides one day extra off work every year in Norway.

I am in general not a big fan of the Vatican. We are talking about a country that doesn't even actively condemn child abuse. A country which does not support condoms. A country without bars, without women. There isn't a lot more to say, really. The country is not on my list of forthcoming holiday trips.

Bahrain

Temperature is a numerical measurement system for warm and cold. It is measured by detecting heat radiation or particles that emit kinetic energy, or by observing the behavior of thermometric materials. It cannot be colder than minus 273.15 degrees Celsius, also known as absolute zero. The opposite does not exist. There is no absolute hottest.

Except for in Bahrain. Where it is fucking boiling.

The country consists of 33 islands with an accumulated size similar to Lexington, Kentucky. And about as interesting.

In the middle of the day, there are virtually no people outdoors. You either drive with the air conditioner on full power, and then some, or you stay inside. The country uses a fraction of its oil money on keeping the huge shopping malls cooled down. And money they do have. Famous western brands dominate. The more expensive, the better. For those with unlimited amounts of money in their bank account, it seems to be a favorite hobby to brag about how much you paid for an item, not how cheap you managed to get it.

I have never been as close to an overdose as I was in Bahrain. Eight hours in a shopping center was just too much, and I decided to try to venture outside. Despite two attempts, I never got farther than a third of the way across the parking lot before running back into safety. Where I hailed Willis Haviland Carrier. He invented modern air conditioning in 1902.

Qatar

Air conditioning is also essential in Qatar. A country where to be as wealthy as possible is a goal in itself, for no other reason than to show off that you have a lot of dough. Such doesn't really appeal to a simple soul from remote areas of the world. The little country is almost as big as Maryland, but with a third of the population. And awful with regards to gender imbalance. There are five men for every woman in the country. I still decided to visit. On a daytrip. The density of skyscrapers in Doha, the capital, is on par with Dubai or New York. One of the malls downtown comes complete with an ice hockey rink, despite the temperature of over 40 degrees outside. The contrasts were fascinating.

I walked through the sun storm, crossed the Al Corniche road which divides the city and the seafront and entered Sheraton to cool down. The hotel looks like some sort of pyramid. I was drenched in my own sweat after the ten minute walk when I approached the front door. An American stood outside. He was big, if not huge, had an oversized belt buckle and wore baggy Levi's jeans and the mandatory white tennis shoes. His four enormous Samsonite suitcases in metal were stacked on a trolley just behind him. I tried to forget all stereotypes.

"How are you doing? It sure is hot here, man," he said loudly.

It didn't work. I looked forward to a rewarding conversation.

"It certainly is." I decided to keep my answers short.

"So, I am Pete from Texas. Where are you from?"

I was tempted to answer Sogn og Fjordane, the Norwegian county I am from, but I couldn't be bothered to start something I would not enjoy spending a lot of time having to explain.

"I am Gunnar. I am from Norway."

"Wow...Norway! That is awesome, man. Do you guys have global warming over there as well?"

The word global should sort of give it away. I was in the Middle East, not in the Midwest, and I would prefer to spend my time in Qatar on more rewarding experiences than what the stereotypical American could provide me with.

Like counting grains of sand on the beach.

Bangladesh

Bangladesh is also in Asia, on the same latitude as Qatar. There are few other similarities. Can you say anything positive about Bangladesh? Most people have heard few stories from there not detailing flooding, paedophile tourism or child labor. Such focuses don't exactly increase the number of tourists.

There isn't really space for many more either. Over 160 million people live in an area the size of Iowa. But a proactive government has started an offense in the fight against climate change. Then again, they do not have much choice. If the ocean levels increase by much there will be even less space for the people who live there. The government has also initiated several projects to fight poverty, and the results are promising. Bangladesh's economy is booming. The few, but growing number of tourists, can enjoy impressive mosques and archaeologist sites, plus the mandatory beaches and a lot of colorful festivals and markets.

Bangladesh is not my favorite country, but photographers should not think twice before visiting. The country has over 70 ship graveyards that employ 200,000 people. To observe huge decommissioned ships turned into shrapnel is fascinating, but the people who work there do so under inhumane conditions. An average ship contains 7,000 kilo of asbestos and up to 100 tons of lead based paint. Everything goes straight into the Bay of Bengal. The workers walk barefoot, have no protective gear and have to put in between 12 and 15 hours a day. The effort pays them 3-5 dollars a day. Whereas most of the ships come from western countries where owners and people have greatly benefited. Double standards come to mind.

YOU'VE GOT TO GO HERE

Sometimes you just cannot lose, i.e. when visiting certain countries. I have written about some of them here. They have so much to offer that you cannot possibly - not have- an amazing experience when visiting. Several of them are vastly underestimated and rarely even considered as an option by travelers. They should be much more than that by any semi-adventurous holiday planner.

And just to be clear, many more countries could have been mentioned here, but the chapter would soon have grown way too big, so I have selected some candy.

Myanmar (Burma)

Myanmar is one of the world's most undervalued destinations, and it has opened up quite a bit since Nobel Peace Prize winner Aung San Suu Kyi was released from house arrest.

Beware that you will arrive in a country where being overweight is a sign of wealth and therefore a status symbol. You will not see many fatties, though. Myanmar is a very poor country, so there is a chance that you will stand out for more reasons than your skin color and your Louis Vuitton bag.

Buddhist temples, historical towns, extremely pleasant people and a coastline and general scenery that will make people even from the West Coast of Norway gasp. Just do not let creative marketing stunts fool you. Exceptionally beautiful girls walk from pub to pub and from restaurant to restaurant where they will sit down on your lap and give you free cigarettes or shots of vodka. I have never smoked or had a desire to do so, but the marketing girls I encountered were so gorgeous and well drilled that they most definitely have fooled many before and after me. Their point exactly. I managed to avoid the temptations, and rather chose to try local wine. It is plentiful, but not of Australian, Chilean or Moldovan standard. It still tastes surprisingly interesting.

So does Icelandic rotten shark.

Let me not ruin your trip by saying more. Almost no one has been here before you. Just go. But bring good shoes. And hurry! Most sanctions have been lifted, something that is turning the country into a trendy holiday destination. A lot of the big and famous hotel chains are building luxury properties, but most people will still wait a few years before they dare visit from their newly expanded comfort zone, Thailand. You should take advantage of this window of opportunity.

Ethiopia

Selam and I met on the street in Addis Abeba, the capital of Ethiopia. He worked in the flower industry. I naturally stood out from the crowd where I was exploring one of the markets in town.

"You have to visit our national parks. They are world famous," he declared. More impressive terrain than what you can see in the Simien mountains and Rift Valley is hard to come by. Simien must be one of the world's most attractive hiking destinations. The view is unique. Add the silence, the rare animal life, the varied fauna, the sun guarantee and the hospitality, and there really isn't much doubt. Follow Selam's suggestion, the trip is a must.

He also took me to one of the many flower farms in the country, outside Addis. Ethiopia has perfect conditions for roses and tulips, something which has propelled the country into the fourth biggest flower exporter on the planet.

"We love how Valentine's Day has become so much more famous in Europe only the last decade or so! 90 percent of our exports go to your continent."

Selam was one of the main managers on one of the farms and drove a pickup. "I need it to get to rural areas. The roads aren't always great."

I have never seen that many flowers at once. Given flower prices in Europe, I don't blame Ethiopia for exploiting the opportunity of mass production.

The same evening we visited an Ethiopian restaurant not far from the airport. Traditional food was on the menu. That means *wat*, various forms of thick stew. It is being served together with lenses on *injera*, some sort of a pancake. To an untrained palate Ethiopian food tastes pretty much the same as Eritrean. Just don't tell anyone that I have said so. The countries are not best of friends.

It still wasn't the food that impressed me the most. Selam wanted to show me some of the local culture, and he had taken me to a restaurant well known for dance shows. I usually hate such shows, they tend to be touristic as hell, but I turned out to be the only western person in the building. And the show was truly fantastic! Ethiopian dance goes thousands of years back. A handful of women in traditional folk costumes kicked off the performance on stage. Nice, but not spectacular. Oh, was I in for a surprise. Six guys in brightly colored clothes literally ran on stage and danced wilder than I have ever seen before. They kept doing the splits in unthinkable ways, jumped higher than Javier Sotomayor and made Monty Python's "silly walk" look like a piece of cake.

Interspersed Ritalin.

Madagascar

No drugs are needed for a trip to Madagascar. I stepped out of the airport and into one of the countries I had always dreamed about visiting. I anticipated an experience out of the ordinary. And I wasn't disappointed when I walked out of the airport and inhaled the smell of the eighth continent, a two thousand year old history, an avenue of "upside down" baobab trees, a dozen gourmet restaurants, too many stray dogs and beaches, so many beaches.

I had landed just outside Antananarivo, the capital with the longest name of any one word capital out there. No wonder the locals call it Tana instead. The country invites all your senses to work overtime. They may have been slightly triggered or teased by the Madagascar cartoons. As they sort of indicated, Madagascar is an amazing country. Then again, as much as 90 percent of the plants and species there are to be found nowhere else. A range of biologists and zoologists do, therefore, not call it a country but a continent. The eighth continent. What fascinated me the most was the lemur, the monkey-like creature that lives its entire life high up in the trees. It was great humor to see them jump from tree to tree at a hell of a pace together with the rest of the family. They never venture on adventures alone, always together.

To travel around the giant island wasn't always easy though. I was not allowed to rent a car. Not without a driver, at least. The roads are too appalling for the rental companies to allow such. The result was that I traveled with Henry, the driver. He spoke little English, but drove me wherever I pointed to on his detailed map. We were on the road together for several days. At first I wondered how to accommodate the driver, at night. Neither of us were particularly keen on sharing a bed, but it turned out that most hotels I checked out offered free accommodation for the driver, as long as I paid to stay there. Henry still insisted on staying in the car, a huge 4x4 vehicle. Stay at your post.

We drove to Mahambo on the East Coast. The 400 kilometers took us 10 hours. Not even turtles envied our speed along the roads that are in an awful state. Something youngsters know to take advantage of in rural parts of the country. They use shovels to fill a few of the potholes with sand, then they stand next to the road and ask drivers passing by for money. It may seem commendable, but the sand disappears at the first rainfall. Which means soon. At least near the coast, where the seafood is incredible. Coastlines tend to have that effect on cuisine. The food there still didn't compare to what I had back in Tana. Where the selection of gourmet restaurants are unrivalled anywhere else in Africa, with the exception of Cape Town and Johannesburg. And so cheap that I more than once examined the bill to see what they had forgotten. They hadn't forgotten anything.

Except for marketing themselves better.

Cuba

There were four of us visiting Cuba, one of us certainly knew marketing better than the others. Ola, who lost the beer bet. Then again, I am not quite sure if threats to crush my kneecaps unless I visited him in New York count as marketing. Målfrid, who I was seeing at the time, and I nevertheless flew across the pond to visit him and his wife, Hege. He worked, she studied.

Målfrid Hansen and I first met in London. I was speaking at a conference on mobile services, and I instantly noticed Målfrid's long blond hair where she sat among a bunch of men on the ninth row in the audience. She came over to me in the break, she asked loads of questions. They were work related. Sort of. She seemed interested. The feeling was mutual. We ended up in Soho for dinner, drinks and dancing. The result was a big good night hug. And her business card. I was Director of Mobile Services at the time. I should therefore have known better, but I mixed up her own mobile number with that of her company's main line. The text message I later sent her soon went viral on their intranet, and all her colleagues soon knew that some Gunnar dude had invited her out on a date. We started dating a few months later. She coped with me for two years.

When in the US, we decided to take advantage of the proximity to Cuba. Then again, that may not be the most logical thing to do. Cuba is the only country in America without a direct flight from the US. That is of course due to the malicious trade blockade that has been in place since 1960. You should therefore not be surprised by seeing old US cars from back then still roaming the roads in near pristine condition. Maintenance becomes very important if supply is non-existent. Until 2011 only cars made before 1959 could be freely traded to individuals. That isn't all bad, however. Nowhere but Havana can offer plenty of incredible photo opportunities in old streets, surrounded by fascinating and very photogenic cars from another era. We're talking about living museum gems. A trip to Cuba is like traveling in time. Hurry though, not even the Castros will live forever.

We rented rooms from a family in Havana. Ola and Hege shared one, Målfrid and I another. That kind of rental is one of very few ways individuals can access forex, in a country where every employee as a rule should earn the same.

The country is also naturally the origin of Cuba Libre. But it no longer comes with Coca-Cola. The sugar, water and caffeine mix is neither sold in Cuba nor in North Korea. Not officially, at least. In Havana and surrounding areas you have to settle for Tu Kola. Perhaps not the best of names around there since "tu cola" means tail or ass in Spanish.

That didn't prevent us from drinking while there. We found a cocktail bar where the bartenders knew what they were doing. We consumed Cuba Libres, Mojitos, Daiquiris and Cubanitos. The Cubans know their rum. Which is a consolation. Since they have no idea on how to cook. I have rarely eaten as poorly as on the Caribbean island. We ended up booking at the best restaurant in Havana to avoid critical weight loss. The quality there was barely OK, but nothing to write home to your mother about. Unless she works at the Food Safety Authority.

No wonder Cuban restaurants outside Cuba are a novelty.

Brazil

You don't have to fare far southwards from Cuba to find Brazil, the fifth biggest country in the world. It is only half as big as the biggest, Russia, but it contains a far more diverse and impressive fauna and selection of animals. The Amazon alone is home to more than a third of all species known to man. And a lot of species not yet known to man. Given the speed of deforestation, many of these may never even be known to man.

Foreigners typically think of Brazil when it comes to football and the carnival in Rio. I ended up in the latter on my second trip to the country. I watched the parade from the side, and clearly stood out with blond hair and a corpse colored body. Not to mention my lack of body paint and costume. Still I was invited to join by a lot of parade goers. I politely declined until I was dragged into the parade by a hunk of a guy. His girlfriend gave me a canned beer, and I was trapped. Uncomplainingly so. The girlfriend coincidentally had a lot of single female friends. I was taken all over Rio that day, as a participant of a never ending party. Or parties, rather. We eventually ended up at a concert in some big warehouse where a local band played. It was packed, no fire regulations seemed to exist. And no other rules, guidelines, moral codes or commandments either. People drank, sang, vomited or screwed each other. Everywhere. The five man band played as if everything was normal. And it was. It was carnival.

Carnival or not, there are a lot of stunning girls in Brazil. I was back a few years later, and a tall blond girl came over to my table while I was eating at a biff and sushi restaurant in Curitiba, southwest of Sao Paulo.

"You are the crazy traveler, aren't you? It is unreal to meet you! I just told my friend about you a few days ago and I told her that we had to travel more. And then I suddenly see you here!" Suellen said enthusiastically. The physiotherapist produced a wide and wonderful smile.

Small pleasures on the road.

Bhutan

A good road is a novelty in Bhutan. The mountainous country is, contrary to popular belief, not hard to visit, it just demands some planning and patience. I am good at the previous, I struggle with the latter. But it is so worth the hassle. Because it is unlike any other. For several reasons. There are, for starters, two national sports in Bhutan. Archery and darts. You think you can compete on the dart front? Well, it is a hell of a lot more difficult than in a Manchester pub. The dart board is much smaller and the darts are heavy, and lethal. They are thrown from a distance of 20 meters. The archery takes place on 100 meter long fields, and there is a target on each side of it. More shooting, less walking.

Actually, Bhutan is also the only country in the world to ban the sale of tobacco, since 2004. Perhaps a good place to stop smoking? People can still smoke, but the cigarettes must be purchased abroad - and even then a maximum 200 cigarettes per person per month. And needless to say; there is a black market. You would usually expect to find the following only on the black market also; penises. There is actually a long tradition of painting large penises on private houses. These are not acts of perversion, although the taste can be discussed. Penises mean luck, and also work as symbols of fertility. Not everyone stops short of painting them on house walls, though. There is an example of a drinking fountain for water shaped like one, as well.

Bhutan naturally figures on the list of Gross National Product, but the king has decided to also opt for his own variant. They measure happiness through the less famous GNH scale (Gross National Happiness). One reason for the happiness might relate to the environment. Bhutan is carbon neutral, as the world's only country. That means that the country absorbs more CO_2 than it produces. How? Thanks to huge hydropower output and forest that covers over 70 percent of the country.

The nickname is "Druk Yul" which means the Land of the Thunder Dragon. That is due to all the powerful and noisy thunder storms that regularly come in above the country from the Himalayas. And you ought to eat like a dragon to visit too. The locals enjoy spicy food and look upon chili as a vegetable. "Ema datshi" is their national dish. It's made from green chili peppers mixed with a local cheese sauce. Much needed food if you plan to climb one of the many 7,000 meter peaks. The problem is that the country is a little tricky to visit. You need to pay the entire trip in advance as well as having your tourist pass approved. You will, depending on the season, have to pay at least 200 dollars per day you intend to stay in the country. And yes, all in advance. That may sound like a lot, but it includes your hotel accommodation, all meals, the mandatory guide, a driver and a car or a bus.

There is only one international airport there, Paro. It may be your worst nightmare, given that you have a fear of flying. Any pilot that intends to land there needs special training, just a handful have. You will understand why following your first landing. Mountain sides and houses have never been so close to you before, while inside a flying aircraft. No fear of flying? A window seat is mandatory! Sit on the left when flying from Kathmandu and you will see the peak of Mount Everest at a distance. Clouds or no clouds. The highest mountain in the world hovers above them anyway.

I had decided to visit the most spectacular building in Bhutan. Tiger's Nest. Or Taktsang Palphug Monastry as it is officially named. It was built on a cliffside near the airport. The hike from the parking lot demands stamina and shape above average. Lack of such has never been among my problems, and I beat the guide and the driver by half an hour to the top. Not that I was timing them.

All up and inside, we were even invited to join a traditional prayer session. Around ten monks performed their daily routine as if we were not present. I have never felt more spiritual as I did when among the men dressed in their traditional orange garments, high up on the mountain. Magical.

The website Couchsurfing enables you to meet someone who will offer you a free sofa, who is happy to show you around or who is dying for a chat over a cup of tea. I got in touch with Tshering, a girl my age. She lived in the capital Thimpu where I met her in a coffee shop. Without a guide. Bhutan is one of only three countries where a guide is required. The others are North Korea and Turkmenistan. You may however walk around without one in both Ashgabat and Thimpu, and I seized the opportunity without hesitation. I do by far prefer to be guided by friends, rather than by hired randomers that come with governmental instructions and that often also get a cut of whatever the shops they take you to manage to convince you to buy.

Tshering and I hit it off right away. Both of us liked bars, beers and sleazy stories. She showed me a cellar bar with 7 tables and old worn-out sofas for seating. Rather comfortable. I cannot say the same about the walls. Their horror orange virtually raped our eyes. But there was more to the bar. Creative karaoke, for instance. An old 20 inch television set with questionable color settings showed the lyrics, as in any other karaoke joint. But it wasn't connected to any amplifier or speakers. The music was performed live by the house band. Very cool!

We had company later that evening. She introduced me to her friend Pema. It turned out that Denmark is one of a few countries with diplomatic representation in Bhutan, and Pema told me that she had been screwing one of the embassy guys for months. The problem was that she wasn't the only local girl one he had fun with. He had allegedly helped himself to many of the local girls in Thimpu. Other foreigners there had allegedly followed his example, and Western guys in town had started getting a reputation.

Tshering grabbed my shoulder forcefully two rounds of beer later.

"We have to go. I'll explain later."

We were on our way up the stairs in ten seconds. Our unfinished beers remained on the table.

"Did you notice the guys at the table next to ours? I heard what they were discussing. They thought that you were picking up two local girls at the same time, and they were going to lynch you for it."

"Bloody hell. Thanks for telling!" I said in a high pitch.

"Don't flatter yourself! I would have been in major trouble too."

We walked over to another bar 100 meters away. The selection of drinking holes wasn't huge.

"You can pick me up," Pelma whispered to me after yet another drink. She was tipsy, and had started eyeing the possibility of yet another Scandinavian conquest. There wasn't enough beer in town to generate mutual interest.

EUROPE BY TRAIN

My classmate, Tor Egil Hovland and I started planning a train trip around Europe as 16 year olds. The scheme was called Interrail and enabled us to travel to most European countries for one month with the same ticket pass. It would my first trip abroad without parents. The two of us shared interests in computers, graphics, newspaper production and ultra-local radio. We had published our own newspaper a couple of years earlier, and spent countless nights in front of a computer to play games, create simple programs or design the pages of our paper. The last year in secondary school we also made shows and newscasts for Radio Naustloftet, the only station in the village. We had dozens of listeners.

Our first year of high school was spent researching and planning the big trip in detail. We even tried to learn the constructed language Esperanto in order to qualify for free accommodation. Those who spoke it and joined the international Esperanto association were entitled to send letters to other members and ask for a spare bed. It didn't work. Several reasons were to blame. The language was first and foremost boring, and also had no use in the real world. Secondly we never managed to plan the route in enough detail to be able to send off letters weeks in advance to arrange for accommodation. Chances are we would have been revealed as fake linguists, in any circumstance.

Luxembourg

I was too young to remember Radio Luxembourg, but I had often heard about the radio station by those older than me in Radio Naustloftet. They told me it was a real source of inspiration. Not bad for a tiny country in between Belgium, France and Germany. Tor Egil and I had taken the train from Maastricht in the Netherlands via Liege in Belgium. Our goal was the youth hostel in Effelbrück in Luxembourg. The receptionist asked us for our passports, and I experienced my first travel panic attack. My passport was not where it should be, in the safe hidden pocket of the backpack. We sat down for a council of war. Our reconstruction of events took us back to the youth hostel in Maastricht. We had slept in a dorm, hence no key to return and no need to check out. Denmark had actually won the European Championship in football the same night, and everything had been a little hectic. We had to return to Holland before yet again invading Luxembourg. I have ever since watched my passport as a valuable paper. As it is. Teenagers have a lot to learn about the art of traveling.

Yet another challenge awaited back in Effelbrück. We were not allowed to check in. I recently consulted my Interrail diary to find out more. "We lacked Belgian and Luxembourgish Francs, and had to go to the town center to exchange a traveler's cheque before we were given a room (nasty bitch at the front desk)".

This was before the Euro, and we had to exchange money many times during our trip. Something which resulted in a lot of unused change and small bills. The idea of the Euro isn't all that bad, especially not all those small countries taken into account.

I have since returned to Luxembourg, but only briefly. There is a lack of activities in the minor country, the world's only remaining duchy.

Switzerland

My Swiss debut also occurred during our Interrail trip. We didn't quite know where to visit, so we used the world famous point-on-the-map-while-blindfolded method. The finger hit Zug, which meant that we had to go via Zurich to get there. Zug is a town the size of Førde, where we had attended high school for a year. We immediately felt at home. Then again, the point of traveling all over Europe was exactly the opposite, to experience something new. The logic was rock solid, we moved on. There was still a parallel motive, according to the Interrail diary.

"Discovered that the youth hostel in Zug was too expensive. We're off to Vaduz, despite 5 (!!!) football fields AND a swimming pool!"

Our stay was still long enough to experience Swiss yogurt and muesli. That opened my eyes. Was there really more to yogurt than what the monopolistic Norwegian dairy wanted us to know?

I have since visited the country on numerous occasions, most often to Geneva where the European Broadcasting Union has its headquarter. Three colleagues in their late 50's and I had dinner there on Valentine's Day one year. We were approached by a rose salesman.

"It's good to see that they are open minded enough to assume that we are here on a double date," Hans Petter Danielsen said. He is Technical Director of P4 and a former colleague of mine.

"Yes, but do we not look like we are in love?" Jørn Jensen replied. We work together at NRK.

"The question is just who is dating who," Hans Petter replied.

Some people call it broadcaster's humor.

Liechtenstein

There are no railroad tracks in the little principality, the only country to entirely lie in the Alps, so we had to travel by the postal bus from Buchs. Tor Egil and I had planned two days there. That was way too long for people like us, without a dime in the bank. Visiting Liechtenstein without financial backing is outright stupid, and will only cause personal pain. Nothing was open on Sunday, something that seemed to shrink the minor town centre of Vaduz.

Having brought a deck of cards was pure luck. We ended up playing "Idiot", an intellectually unbeatable game. Next to the not so impressive cathedral. Cathedral? Well, that was what we called it. The town is so small that even a small stone church looks cathedralish in comparison. I documented my winner's luck in the diary. "Crushed Tor Egil in Idiot loads of times (hehe)." But we were not left alone to play for long. Someone who seemed to be working with something religious threatened us to leave the yard in front of the church.

"No money games in front of the church!" He shouted. As if we had any money to gamble.

We didn't stay long in the country. Two nights turned into one. The reason could be found in my little red notebook.

"Shared a room with two snoring Finns. Enough is enough!"

Austria

We assumed that Austria would have more to offer. We were sort of right. But what is Austria really known for, except for parts of the Alps, a Ferris wheel and a New Year's Eve concert? Let us not forget the father of the sowing machine Josef Madersperge, Ferninand Porsche who founded a car company and Wolfgang Amadeus Mozart. Characters that the Austrians want to forget include Adolf Hitler and Josef Fritzl.

As a sport geek I just had to visit Innsbruck. The town hosts several skiing competitions every winter. Most of them were broadcast on NRK, with me in front of the box. The town needed closer inspection.

Let me quote from the diary: *"Explored town, most places were closed. Witnessed a drug addict lying half dead on the street by the train station. An ambulance picked him up. Decided that we didn't want to stay after all."*

Easily scared youth. We traveled to Vienna instead, the town with the world's oldest zoo and an enormous graveyard counting a million and a half tombstones. That is more than there are inhabitants.

Getting there wouldn't be easy, though. *"We entered an Intercity train where the super slick (!!!) conductor tried to fool us into paying extra. Thanks to two travel books we showed him, he had to give in. 'Ehe…yes, you do actually have Interrail tickets (blush, blush)' he said before leaving. Idiot!!!"*

Vienna proved to be a popular place. Too popular, in fact. All youth hostels were full, and we could not afford a hotel. The solution was imminent. *"We 'slept' in a tiny park in front of the youth hostel. Had nothing but a sweater, it was super cold. Never again!"*

The trip was not over, despite or thinning funds. We decided to also pay a visit to the eastern neighbor.

Hungary

Tor Egil and I stayed in Budapest, and as in most of the other countries, only for a short while. Although we should probably have extended the stay, we were after all in heaven. A night in a youth hostel set us back less than 6USD. And then we were given a big twin room with a sink and a fridge. Luxury for two broke, tired and semi homesick teenagers. Our food was, for the first time during our trip, stored cold. And the sink was used for a hair wash.

Budapest is a lovely city. We were, as nerds most impressed with the underground. Being the second oldest in the world, after the Tube in London, and virtually free of charge. I was used to underground travel from the British capital and soon adopted a new role as a guide.

We overheard a conversation between a local guy and a Swedish traveler, both in their thirties. They discussed Norwegians, and we were just about to reveal our identities, until the Hungarian concluded.

"Norwegians are very smart, but super aggressive and crazy maniacs."

We looked at each other and instantly agreed to keep quiet. And went to a shop instead. Even though I was on a long trip with only a backpack, I decided to buy something for my brothers and sisters back home. All six of them. Hungary was by far the cheapest country we had visited, and I decided to take advantage of it. I spend 9 USD on chocolate for Åsmund, one of my brothers. That meant several kilos of it, and an increase in luggage weight of 20 percent. Not very smart, but educational as hell.

A three-week trip really tested our friendship. We were luckily good at giving each other time and space by letting one of us look after the way too heavy backpack for a couple of hours while the other one explored wherever we were. Hour after hour with the same person can prove less than inspiring. We luckily never tired from playing cards. Then again, I have never challenged anyone to a game of Idiot ever since.

Our experiences were written down by a blue inked pen in my red diary.

- *Make sure that the car you are in is not about to be disconnected from the rest of the train.*
- *Do not pay the surcharge on Intercity trains. Certain conductors are just trying to make some extra black money. Carry a book in English where your rights are stated.*
- *Never (!) trust an Italian train conductor.*
- *If you enter a new country at night, remember to exchange money the previous day.*
- *Do not show up at a youth hostel at night without a reservation.*
- *Bring a deck of cards, reading materials, etc., for the long train rides.*
- *Only bring what you REALLY need in your backpack. It should not exceed 7 kilos. It's better to wash often than to bring extra clothes.*

- *Buy food in markets and supermarkets, not in kiosks, coffee shops and restaurants.*

- *A lot of public toilets are dirty and uncomfortable to use. Go to McDonald's or Burger King instead. The toilets there are usually clean.*

- *Tor Egil's law: If a poster states that the water is safe to drink, it means that you will get diarrhoea if you drink it.*

- *Gunnar's first law: What you need at any given time is always located at the bottom of your backpack.*

- *Gunnar's second law: Should you forget something, rest assured that you are very far away when you discover it.*

- *Gunnar's third law: If you finally manage to fall asleep in an awkward train seat, it is guaranteed that the conductor will wake you within minutes. Especially if he is Italian.*

I DON'T RELAX LIKE YOU DO

To relax on a beach or to stay on a cruise ship an entire holiday is not my style. I need to see something happen, that is when I'll relax. I am happy to lie on a beach for a few hours to read a book, but not much longer. It is too monotonous, I like to explore when I am on holiday, to get new stimuli. Some people claim that I have ADHD. They usually seem to be suffering from a lack of energy themselves. I enjoy my energy overdose. Everyone around me does not necessarily agree.

"You have to watch out so that you don't wear her out," my mom once told me. She was referring to the girlfriend I had at the time.

I tend to not spend a lot of my energy dwelling on problems, being mad, frustrated or upset. Life is now, there is no use sitting still being annoyed with this and that. My energy is better put to use solving problems. Easy is boring.

Jamaica

Not many other people collect countries, to the extreme. Even fewer Norwegians do it. Malene is the exception. I met her in Jamaica, where I had hired a little flat in a boarding house outside of Montego Bay. The owner showed me to my door and asked me where I was from. My answer made him triumph.

"You have to meet one of my other guests."

I dropped my bags and he took me to the common room. A short haired blond girl sat there reading. Blond refers to her hair color, only.

"Malene, you have to meet Gunnar. He is also from Norway!"

Having completed the introduction, he left for his office. Neither of us had expected meeting anyone else from back home, especially not in the tiny establishment on the "wrong" side of town. I sat down next to Malene and we started talking. About travel. She told fantastic tales from Africa, Latin America and the Pacific Ocean. She had clearly traveled a lot. I commented on several of the countries she mentioned, and she eventually realized that I had been on the odd aircraft too.

"You have traveled a bit yourself. How many countries have you visited?"

"112."

"You are joking!" she shouted. It wasn't a question.

She had just passed 100, and presumed that I was far behind her. She did in fact refuse to believe me. Disbelief turned into anger, anger turned into friendship. We had the same goal, and we have kept in touch ever since. Also due to competitive reasons, we did after all have to keep track of our competitor. We followed each other closely until around 160 countries two or three years later when she halted her hyperactive traveling a bit. In the meantime I finalized my project. Malene was among the first to congratulate me via the internet. We have never actually met since Jamaica.

To be white in certain neighborhoods isn't always pleasant. I was on a 10K run in the area around the boarding house when I had people shouting after me several times. I heard "Be careful, white boy!", "Run, whitey, run! We'll be coming after you!" and "Oh, look at the white nigger!"

Not especially pleasant, but understandable. There is a lot of poverty and social differences in the area, and there is no denying that there has been a lot of racism against blacks. Benefits are far from being evenly distributed, and usually the black population has received the rotten end of the stick. That Montego Bay has a range of resort hotels and wealthy tourists from Europe and elsewhere in North America doesn't exactly help, either. When a white person rarely visits an all-black area, it must be tempting to throw a few insults. When Malene and I went out on the town one of the nights, we decided to take a taxi back.

I also met a girl in her twenties with a Jamaican mother and a Belgian father. She told me that she lived in Europe during the summer, and in a simple shack on the beach with her mom and two half-brothers the rest of the year.

"So, no electricity?" was my first question.

"No, we cook on the fire. And I read from the light of fireflies!"

"Seriously? How?"

"I catch many of them in a glass jar with small holes for air. Then I hold it up over my book so that I can read. The only trouble is that I have to shake it every minute or so to prevent them from dimming their light. The fireflies don't like being shaken, and increase the light intensity."

That's what I call a slightly alternative lifestyle.

Nauru

Living in the world's least visited country sure is too. Nauru only receives 200 tourists a year. Most visitors to the little island nation need a visa. But, as so often before, my trip there was made on impulse, and I hadn't had time to prepare as well as I should have. I trusted that my normal traveling luck and a big innocent smile would do the trick. It had worked before. This time it would be harder. I was set to fly from Brisbane in Australia, and the woman behind the Our Airline check-in counter asked for my visa.

"Do I need a visa? I thought I could get one when landing," I bluffed.

"No, you cannot."

"Really? Are you sure? "

"I am sure. I have worked here for over ten years."

I tried to look sad and lost. I am good at that.

"I will see what I can do, but do not get your hopes up."

She walked over to another counter and called someone from a phone there. It seemed like a very long conversation, given the possible denial of service I was facing in the very near future. She came back over and started typing something on the computer.

"So...is it going to be possible for me to go?"

"Hmm. Yes, it looks like it. You're lucky!"

She meant it. And I was. I even got a window seat.

The old Boeing 737 was almost full. Surprisingly so, until I realized that they were throwing an international fishing conference on Nauru. The plane also landed in Honiara, the Solomon Islands where some people left. Two new passengers entered.

I arrived in Nauru late at night, and it seemed like the entire village (or country) had arrived to greet everyone. Some of those there, it seemed, didn't really have a choice. The runway is also a part of the 19 kilometre long road around the island, and the road is blocked every time a plane arrives (which is not very often). Instead of driving the other way around the island, they would rather check out who is coming from the "mainland" (aka. Australia), before continuing their drive.

I had, as usual, not checked in luggage, so I was the first person to go through customs of one of the smallest airport terminals I have ever seen. Do keep in mind that I have traveled domestically in Norway too.

The serious looking police officer behind a tiny mobile wooden counter looked at me for one second, called me over and asked without hesitation:

"Are you *the* tourist?"

The scene was set. It was only me, the locals and some other foreign people working with fish. No other tourists? I was thrilled.

"Welcome to Nauru!" he said and put on a big, white smile.

Of course my non-existing visa meant that the custom guy had to hold on to my passport until I was gonna leave. I wasn't worried. Crime can't be high on an island with less than 10,000 people, one road and nowhere to hide.

There were no taxis outside the terminal, and I decided to walk through the dark. Which worked out great until a guy in a pickup stopped and asked if I wanted a ride. He and two teenagers had picked up a relative coming by the plane, so the car was full, but not the cargo bed in the back. I jumped in. The driver asked where I was going.

"I'm going to the hotel."

"No problem. Just hold tight!"

It was very friendly of him to pick up a total stranger in complete darkness. But then again, the lack of crime probably had something to do about it. And I was alone. The four of them could have trashed me if I were up to no good.

I was dropped off and they all wished me a happy stay. I walked to the front desk when I realized that I had been taken to the wrong hotel. The "resort" hotel was located in rural Nauru. I wanted to stay centrally, in the main town Yaren. I was saved by the local bus driver who arrived 25 minutes later with the other plane passengers. He drove me to Od'n Aiwo, the only other hotel in the country, free of charge.

"Enjoy your stay!" he shouted after letting me off.

Nauru is in fact only one of two countries in the world without a capital (the other is Switzerland), although Yaren performs most of the functions expected by one. The sunrise was not far off when I finally dove onto my pillow in the little hotel overlooking a run-down factory on the sea side. Some hours of sleep later, and I was all ready to explore. But what to do in the world's smallest Republic?

The road around the island is longer than an old football player like me had ever run. But how often do I have the opportunity of running around a country? What I failed to take into account was Nauru's location. Virtually on the Equator. To run half a marathon at noon was not the best chess move ever performed. I understood this after less than a kilometre. I should have turned around and walked back.

"Pain is temporary, glory is forever!" I shouted to myself. And I repeated myself dozens of times on my mission around Nauru. It took me two hours of intense sweat production. I have never before lost as much salt.

Back at the hotel, I discovered that the water was switched off. Apparently as usual. It would be off until 18:00. There is not much fresh water in the middle of the Pacific. Luckily I dried fast in the heat, and I walked into "town". There was a choice of one food market, a couple of bottle shops, an Internet cafe, a police station, the city hall and two restaurants. I immediately felt at home.

Nepal

The capital is very different from the rest of Nepal, as is the case in most countries. But maybe even more so when it comes to Kathmandu than elsewhere. The city is in many ways a less than pleasant place. Yes, there are many restaurants, bars, clubs and shops, but the mountainous country has so much more to offer than the filthy capital. It pales in comparison.

And no, I am not talking only about Mount Everest. Most visitors will never get close to the mountain, nor should they want to. To climb it requires extreme expertise and an extremely deep wallet. You must first of all have climbed at least one other 8,000 meter peak. Secondly, it will set you back about a hundred thousand dollars. If you do it the cheap way.

There are plenty of other majestic mountains that will impress and make most of us more than happy. I have not been higher than 4,300 meters, my goal is to pass the 6000 meter mark. Just to achieve tourist peak number one, Kilimanjaro in Tanzania with its 5,895 meters. After a mountain hike, or even just a bus trip in the thin air of the Himalayas, Kathmandu isn't all that bad after all. Hot and fresh food, comfortable beds. Beds at all. Dry rooms, nightlife, live bands and English speaking people. Even tourists are welcome. Just don't expect the typical resort tourists up there. There is a lack of all-inclusive establishments.

I was one of two foreigners in a bar. A local band was performing. It was only natural that I soon got talking to Helga. From Hamburg, a tall and very fit girl with long brown hair and browner eyes. She had spent four weeks in Nepal. The conversation flowed along nicely, we had a bunch of travel experiences to share.

Some of them were obviously about Nepal. She had come here to climb a mountain, although she never got that far. Because of a man, a local hunk she had met in a bar. The athletic and tall guy had been extremely fascinating, and they had seen each other several nights in a row. He had eventually shared with her that he was a monk, and that he snuck out of the monastery every night after "having gone to bed". He biked from the "prison" outside town, to his mother's house just outside Kathmandu. She was always asleep by then, so he could change clothes in peace before hitting town, usually to the bar where she had first met him.

He had told Helga that he was one of "the chosen ones", potentially a future spiritual leader.

"Seriously, as in a future Dalai Lama?" I asked a little too loud.

"Well, he never went that much into detail, but some sort of a very senior religious leader."

"And you slept with him?"

"In the end, yes. And we have slept together several times a week since."

I had to laugh.

"You are aware that you are fucking with a religion? Literally, I don't think he is neither allowed nor supposed to have sex with anyone."

"Well, he hides it well. What they don't know won't hurt them."

"And how does he get back in time to their super early morning prayers?"

"Well, he always leaves by four in the morning."

"And what if he is telling you all of this just to get into your bed?"

"He isn't. I have been to the monastery. He was there."

"And you are his only lover?"

"Of course not. He is way too hot for that. He can have anyone he wants."

I didn't know if I could believe what the German girl had told me, the story seemed to be too insane to be true. It was in any case a perfect end to my Nepal stay. I slept a few hours and left early the next morning. Not as early as the monk, of course. I have certain limits.

Cambodia

It was early afternoon when Øystein and I walked across the border from Vietnam to Cambodia, the only country with a building in its national flag. Then again, Angkor Wat is somewhat more impressive than your average skyscraper. A minute after passport control, we had arranged further transport; two guys on motorbikes. The rain started pouring down a couple of kilometres later, and they stopped. We were each given our own raincoat to protect us and our backpacks before the lads continued driving. They had no other protection and were absolutely drenched by the time the rain stopped and we were in a village big enough to accommodate a taxi driver. The couple of dollars we paid the bikers were well deserved.

The taxi driver offered us a ride. Unfortunately he didn't have any competition. His Honda must have been excavated from underneath Angor Wat. It still somehow worked, even on the 4x4 wannabe road the driver insisted on going down.

"Shortcut," he claimed. The word was a large part of his proven vocabulary in English. We also heard the occasional OK and a thanks by the time we reached Kip, a calm little village on the coast.

The driver located a hotel with a swimming pool, and we were happy. Anything would have been good following his less than luxurious ride. Øystein is also restless to the extreme. Luckily. We would otherwise not travel that well together. We dumped our gear, borrowed some bikes in the lobby and ventured into the unknown. To explore.

The first point of interest we came across was a Ford Sierra. Half way into the ditch of a gravel road. The ex-driver, a local man in his 50's with a beer belly and a way too small football shirt stood next to it. He was stereotypically scratching his head in frustration. We stopped and asked if he needed any help, despite the Manchester United logo on his breast. He nodded slowly, but without hope. How could these young kids help? Øystein has a black belt in judo and knows a thing or two about how to beat gravity. I, on the other hand, have nothing but will power, although a fair amount of it. With a little help from our friend, the driver, we managed to get the battered vehicle up onto the road again. I have rarely seen a man go from a state of depression to pure happiness so fast. He shook our hands and hugged us. He hadn't showered that day.

"How can I repay you guys? Do you like beer?"

We are huge fans of rhetorical questions.

The man re-debuted as a Sierra driver and slowly navigated the kilometre or so to one of the bars that hung over one of the beaches in Kep. We followed suit. The dozen or so locals who were drinking there were soon told of our deed of the day. His story had an instant hero effect. Free beers were all of a sudden plentiful.

But a man with a dyed mullet wasn't happy. He refused to acknowledge our inhuman strengths, and challenged us to body lifts from the wooden beams underneath the ceiling. Øystein did 25 and humiliated the local celebrity. That didn't make him less grumpy, and he quietly blamed an old shoulder injury and left the bar.

Indonesia

Indonesia isn't far from there. And it is particularly easy to visit from Singapore, which is only a short boat ride away. Similar to visiting the Statue of Liberty, just add a passport control. The first town on the Indonesian side is however not much to write home about. Batam has a shopping center. And traffic. I traveled there with Veronica from Singapore. We had met each other on the street, she wanted to practice her English, I was looking for tips on what to do.

"Have you been to Indonesia? I asked."

"Never."

"No? But it is only half an hour away."

"So is death if you're bit by a spider."

"That's the most stupid parallel I have ever heard. So are you gonna join me or look around town for leathal spiders?"

Veronica joined. The shopping center in Batam contained an amusement area with all sorts of games and competitions. She kicked my ass in air hockey. A car simulator provided me with a revenge opportunity. I buried her.

The score was 1-1. We needed a decisive third game. A karaoke machine stood half hidden in a corner. The management had presumably put it there due to previous bad experiences. They had even installed some sort of noise screen.

"Let's sing!"

She said enthusiastically.

"Veronica, if I make it as a pop star, Danny DeVito will go pro playing basketball."

I spoke to the deaf. But she would certainly suffer, as my sole audience. She started, and sang like a goddess. She received well deserved, but computer generated appraisal from the machine. And an older couple passed by and wondered which artist that was performing. The karaoke machine did not judge in my favor. "Tone deaf", it claimed. Veronica won 2-1. I couldn't take it too hard. I had mentally admitted defeat the moment I understood singing would be a part of our competition.

Indonesia is a country that deserves so much more. I humbly apologize for my way too short visit to such a big country with limitless travel possibilities. I will return immediately following my next lottery prize.

Suriname

Which might take a while. I have only won a lottery once. When I was two. My mom had bought me a ticket at the local shop in Havøysund, a tiny island in the Arctic. It turned out to be the winner, and I could claim a cake. It must have been big, it is the first memory I have. My next prize came 35 years later, on board an airplane. My seat number won me another flight ticket from Curacao to Paramaribo, the route I flew. I will buy my next lottery ticket on my 72nd birthday.

Suriname used to be a Dutch colony, something the architecture of Paramaribo clearly indicates. There are now as many Surinamians in the Netherlands as in the old country. But Suriname was never totally Dutch. They have always driven on the left side of the road, thanks to influence from neighbor Guyana, formerly known as British Guyana.

To go jogging is an excellent way of getting to know a new city, also in Surinam. The center of Paramaribo is small, yet it contains several distinct districts. I rarely decide on a jogging route in advance and the route was made while running. I passed several proud and old buildings and some run down shacks by the river. All of a sudden, an armed uniformed guard shouted at me and pointed angrily in my general direction just when I was about to pass a particularly nice house. I froze and lifted my arms apologetic above my head.

"What do you want? This is the residence of the prime minister. You cannot come here. Turn around!"

He said, and touched his weapon to show that he wasn't the joking kind. I apologized and started jogging again. My route had gone even more flexible. And that is just the way I like it, when it comes to exploring new areas. Or literally tripping over them. The new route took me to a park of palm trees. Thousands of trees. They were planted on the immediate outskirts of town. No one else was there, the atmosphere was somewhat eerie. I ran through it and came out on the other side where a nightlife scene appeared. It was early afternoon, but the terraces outside the bars were already swarming with men. Dutch men. All, without exception, had glasses of beer in front of them. I returned at night only to see the same guys in the same spots but with new glasses of beer. A number of them had been joined by local women. Some of them were clearly hookers, others seemed to be girlfriends, or applicants for such positions. If they were successful, a safer and more luxurious future awaited on the other side of the Atlantic.

I wasn't in Suriname to find a wife. I discovered an outdoor restaurant in the neighborhood instead. And I consumed a delicious meal before walking home to my hotel. It was midnight and I was determined to go to bed. A lucrative alternative was however introduced to me when I passed the receptionist. She suggested that I visit the hotel's casino instead. It was dark, smoky and with a dubious clientele. I chose bed.

Malta

A large number of the passengers on the plane to Malta came straight from the casino in Paramaribo. Both my girlfriend Mali and I wanted sun. It came with a guarantee of deliverance on Malta. That I had never been in the country before was a bonus.

Målfrid's sister Ingjerd with boyfriend Willy and kids Eira and Nicolai traveled there too. We rented a flat each, a stone's throw apart, not far from the sea. The crystal clear sea with a greenish shade and temperatures that I had yet to experience in Europe. We would stay on Gozo, the little island a ferry ride north of the main island Malta. Not much happens in Gozo. Said the guy from Naustdal.

Xlendi is a sleepy little holiday town. It comes with a handful of restaurants, a bunch of flats and a beach. Two relaxing days by the sea were painfully quiet. I depend on a certain level of activity to be able to "relax". Luckily the others were having a blast. The kids developed fish shell skin and webbed feet, while Målfrid read a couple of books and caught up on much missed conversational time with her sister. Willy kept himself and the kids active in and near the water.

The barista really knows his coffee, and he frowned upon my British coffee habits more than once. Black coffee with milk and sugar. A crime towards coffee. Then again, I do it with a twist. I use honey instead of sugar, for a little bit of an extra taste.

"How can you drink that stuff? You are destroying the coffee," Willy protested. To no avail. He does of course have a couple of points, but since I don't like black coffee it all turned into a war. A cold coffee war. He made better and better coffee from various types of beans just to tempt me using the amazing aroma into admitting defeat and drinking it black. I returned the favor by trying different kinds of milk and honey. Both of us were escalating, but no one won the friendly war.

My dormant hyperactivity was just about to kick in on the third day. I needed something to do in the hot sun. Gozo's coastline constitutes just over a marathon. I decided to take advantage of it and run around the island under a cloudless sky just before lunch. The move of a master. On a positive note I discovered a number of incredibly nice bays and beaches, some of which I later showed to the others. By car. But I also almost caused myself a sun stroke, shin splints and a sprained Achilles. I forced myself around in 6-7 hours, and was finally greeted by Målfrid who came with a big towel and made sure that I finished off with a nice and cooling bath at the end of the day. Madness, at least I lowered my pulse a bit, and we spent the fourth day exploring the island in our two rental cars.

The fifth day was set aside for an excursion to The Blue Lagoon. I assume that the winner of the name competition received the Malta award for creative originality. Excursion.

I could smell group travel from a distance, but I was determined to try to exhibit that I did in fact have social intelligence a little above zero. It turned out that excursion meant a chartered bus. We entered and found our seats in the vehicle that was parked on the square in Xlendi. The more Swedish, Norwegian and British tourists that entered the bus, the worse I felt. I started feeling physically ill. I had been on a group holiday once, in Crete a few years earlier, and I was not able to repeat the hellish ordeal.

"I am actually not capable of taking part in this," I whispered to Målfrid. "I will take the rental car, drive to the local ferry and come after you."

Done deal. I enjoyed my individual trip, taking small detours to the villages I felt like visiting, while the others enjoyed the comfort of the bus and the organized excursion where they didn't have to think about anything else than which way to swim. I got to The Blue Lagoon too, but by the boat the locals used. When it came to holidays in the sun, Målfrid and I weren't entirely compatible.

Easy is boring.

HERE COMES TROUBLE

How come I have never experienced anything that has really frightened me, after 198 countries? There has of course been the odd semi creepy, half scary or at least somewhat educational episode. Luckily corresponding relatively well to my travel experience, the barrier for what I perceive as scary seems to increase proportionally to how much I travel.

It would have been bloody close to a miracle had I traveled to every country in the world without any close encounters with the police. Even though I was never looking to break any laws or rules, I have often stood out enough for the long arm of the law to become sufficiently curious to start talking to me. Or to try to get a little additional income on the side. I still have never been arrested, kidnapped or found myself in major trouble. Then again, it is all in the eye of the beholder.

Central African Republic

I got my visa to Central African Republic in the airport of the capital Bangui two days after my embassy visit in N'Djamena in Chad. Despite a complete lack of phone calls from first, second or third embassy secretaries. A smile usually goes a long way, just not in Niger. The border police stamped the visa in my passport less than half an hour after having landed there. I was free to go. The problem was still a lack of money, following my lost wallet en route to Chad. The cash Øystein had transferred was diminishing too quickly, and I only had a MasterCard I could not remember the PIN code for. A taxi took me to town, where I surprisingly discovered a French bakery. *The* French bakery. Coincidentally just across the road from what looked like quite a modern travel agent. The bakery even had free and well-functioning WiFi. Was I really in Africa?

I was indeed.

My hunt for a bank with a MasterCard logo on its door, window or wall continued. And the search finally seemed to pay off. A familiar logo in yellow and red was painted on the wall of a worn-down cement building. I was about to enter, but discovered that something was happening in the bank next door. The entire building was filled to the rim with mad people. Curiously I entered. People were angrily discussing between them in French. No one was shouting, but there was a rumble of mumbling in the room. There must have been a couple of hundred people inside. No one cared about the sole white person in the crowd. Not until I had taken up my phone and snapped a photo. An old man with a walking stick started shouting and pointed at me. People started screaming loudly, and at least four people grabbed me. One of them had pulled a rusty knife with his other hand.

"Shit!"

The cocktail of smells didn't exactly calm me down. I remember tropical sweat, clothes unwashed for weeks, teeth unbrushed for days – and even old oil from one of the guys holding on to me. He was presumably a mechanic in blue workpants with bright yellow suspenders.

A man in his twenties put his arm around me, in quite a friendly manner. It calmed the crowd down a little. He even spoke English.

"What are you doing?" a furious man practically roared at me. And the entire crowd in the bank turned to watch what was happening. Many of them had murder in their stares.

"I was just taking a photo," my voice trembled when I tried to explain. Admittedly, not very well.

"No photos here! These people have not received their paychecks in months. They are really angry. Show some respect, white man! Or do you want them to kill you?" the young guy asked rhetorically. I showed him and the three men who still held on to me tight that I deleted the photo from my phone. People were pressing towards me from all sides.

"I am really sorry!" I said and bowed my head slightly. For dramatic effect more than anything. But I was most of all annoyed that I hadn't been more discreet. The photo I deleted had looked quite good.

"Come with me. Fast. Before they lynch you."

My savior then said something in French, and the six hands holding on to me finally let go. Seemingly reluctantly. We walked fast down Avenue de Independence, a very fitting name following my near death experience. The crowd had all of a sudden got someone to project their anger towards. Me. Hadn't Emanuel been there, I would most certainly not have left the place alone. Or alive. We passed four armed soldiers and arrived at the river bank.

A few shabby stalls lined a little pathway there. Chickens ran everywhere. It smelled of barbeque, not from gourmet sausages or salmon filets, but from chicken legs and sides of goat. Quite a few grown up lads were bathing in the river. They were all in their nude, and they all came out from in between rusty ship wrecks in the Ubangi River to rub themselves with white soap. The Democratic Republic Congo was on the other side of it. Barges were being pulled by slow moving cargo ships on the important waterway. I noticed that all the naked men were particularly well equipped. Was it a coincidence, or is the well-known myth not a myth after all?

I bought two half chickens and two beers for Emanuel and myself. That was the least I could do following one account of life saving. He knew that he had saved me, and wanted money. I declined firmly but politely. By doing so I valued my own life to one Mocaf beer and half a local chicken, but so be it. I was almost out of money after my wallet mishap in Cameroon.

I said goodbye to Emanuel and walked to Congo's embassy. I could have my visa the same day, but I needed to show them a valid plane ticket. It turned out that the travel agent by the French baker's did not accept credit cards, and I called a travel agent back home. They had no deals with any airlines in this region and could not help me with tickets to Brazzaville. I decided to rather opt for an Air Maroc flight to Douala before continuing with Air Burkina to Benin instead. I hadn't quite clicked with the locals in CAR.

Benin

The narrow little country between equally anorectic Togo and big fat Nigeria is very fascinating. And it felt much safer than Central African Republic. I could feel the outlines of an interesting stay already in the airport. I realized at passport control in Porto-Novo that this was not a country you could just travel to without a visa. I blamed the airline and the check-in personnel who had told me that I would be fine picking up a visa after arrival. The policeman wore a police hat and glasses. He was not particularly impressed. Neither did he seem very keen on the paperwork he would have to engage in should he send me out of the country. He led me through customs and asked me to hang around by the baggage claim belts.

"Wait here. I will be back."

He walked over to a small windowless office nearby to speak to his boss. And there he remained. For half an hour. For two half hours. The strategy was well-known. I should walk over and offer them a few dollars to speed everything up. Too easy. But I finally gave in, and walked over. I was given a penalty of 20 USD, which wasn't too bad. He even gave me a receipt.

I was harassed by a "horse-fly" upon leaving the airport. A horse-fly is an intrusive guy (always a man) whose goal in life is to talk you into something you are not really interested in doing. They are everywhere in some countries. I am usually quite skilled to recognize them and I avoid them like the plague. But this guy was too young, in his early 20's he managed to get under my radar. He asked me if I needed a hotel downtown. I did. He promised to drive me there. Free of charge. The hotel would cost 40 USD per night, not at all bad. He showed me to a green minivan of unmentionable standard, and the driver took off immediately. We drove through the center and across a bridge over the river. Past where I wanted to be. And then we got stuck in traffic. There are not a lot of new cars in Benin, and the exhaust was really bad. Combined with the heat, regular horn outbursts and a horse-fly who was about to take me outside the center made me cross. But I luckily traveled with hand luggage only. I put my backpack on one shoulder, opened the sliding door of the van, patted the guy on the back and jumped out.

"This is not the town center, mate." I said before walking against traffic and back towards town. The horse-fly was furious and shouted after me. I couldn't be bothered to turn around. He probably disliked being patted. Most horse-flies do. I found a hotel next to the sea. It came with a pool, and I would get my own balcony overlooking it all. 50 dollars. Perfect! It all called for a celebratory swim in the pool and a shower before I walked to town. I sat down outside a corner restaurant and ordered chicken and rice. The other option was chicken with French fries. I soon got talking to Carlos, a large friendly-looking man with a bulls' neck. His first question was whether I liked Obama. The American president is popular in Benin, so popular that he has his own beer brand.

"You have to try," Carlos said.

I would indeed. Although I had severe doubts to whether The White House had ever licensed the name to the Benin brewery. I was totally certain about it after one sip. I have never tasted worse beer, and I have tested quite a few strange beers in miscellaneous countries. Carlos didn't complain. He was happy to take over the bottle of Obama.

In between sips, he told me about high unemployment, a lot of corruption and the crime that was largely related to the two first problems. He moved on to his two daughters who lived in the countryside in Northern Benin and that he traveled there every weekend from his Porto-Novo based job as an accountant in an insurance company.

"I hate it, but I need the money. My daughters and the missus need the money. Insurance companies are like mosquitos. They will suck your blood out and give you an itch. And when you need something in return for your blood, the itch will contaminate your body and paralyze it. While the mosquito invites his friends over to suck more of your blood out. You cannot win."

I wanted to call home and cancel my travel insurance, but I had no phone connectivity. My telecom operator clearly didn't see much business opportunity by offering roaming in Benin.

The next day, I was off to Lagos, the biggest city in Nigeria. But I had to cross the border first. That turned out to be hell. Unless I paid the various crooked bureaucrats there a little under the table I would not get my passport back.

"Give me a little extra, sir. Otherwise..."

And the blood suckers were not only employed by the police. Health workers were equally bad. I needed a stamp from them to cross the border, or so they claimed.

"Give me a little extra, sir. Or maybe I cannot help you."

The customs officer wanted his share, as well. His reasoning was the same. As usual, while traveling in Africa, I had quite a few dollar bills of low denominations in one of my pockets. But they all disappeared faster than ever on the Benin-Nigeria border.

Which is where I was met by another horse-fly. Horse-fly v. 2.0. This time I recognized his type the moment I saw him. He was in his early 20's, taller than average and extremely fit.

"I am not interested, my friend," I clearly told him while I walked towards the parking lot on the Nigerian side of the border. He did however not give up, and walked next to me, never more than a meter away. Even when I ordered coffee and chicken for lunch from a stall by the road. The woman who ran it had two gas flames under a plastic cover. The chicken came on a plastic plate, the instant coffee in a much used red plastic mug. She had no milk, but I got something that looked like milk powder. Horse-fly v. 2.0 sat next to me on the plank that functioned as a bench. I couldn't really prevent him from doing so.

But I refused to buy him anything. Despite his claims of being my "buddy", something he repeated frequently to anyone who could be bothered to listen in.

"This is my friend. He is my friend."

The others knew about his routine. I didn't. Yet. All I could do was to ignore him. I thanked the chef for the food, the chicken had tasted great, and I continued by foot to find a taxi. The driver and I agreed on price and I entered a red Toyota which had seen better days.

"Let's go." I told the driver. Horse-fly version 2.0 was starting to be annoyed on the outside.

"You have to pay your friend."

"He is not my friend. Why does he want money?"

"He says that he has protected you."

Of course. This was his business model. Protected me from what? Too hot coffee?

"He has not. Just drive, please.

The con man got the picture and instantly turned absolutely furious. He ripped off his shirt and showed off an upper body with muscles that would have made Jean Claude van Damme blush. Even back in the 1990's.

"I will fight you, I will kill you."

He shouted. Just another fear tactic, the doors were all locked. But the driver seemed scared stiff and refused to start the engine.

"You have to give him something. Or I will be in trouble when I get back. I know who this guy is. He is a psycho."

The driver knew the art of underestimation.

This was turning into a matter of principle. I refused to pay anything to Horse-fly version 2.0. Full stop.

"I am not paying this fucking piece of shit. And that's final. You can pay him if you want, I am not paying. But I am paying you to drive me, so please drive."

The driver was clearly not happy having been made middle-man, but he actually picked up a bill and paid the lunatic through a slit in the window before we finally got going towards Lagos. I paid the driver a few extra dollars for the job. Nothing of this was, after all, his fault. Unless they had set it all up. I will never know for sure.

Niger

The Air Burkina plane landed late at night at the Diori Hamani airport in Niamey. Hamani was the first president of a democratic Niger. Until he made all other political parties illegal. He even achieved international respect as he relentlessly seemed to work for African interests, but domestically, he was fiercely accused of corruption. Things may have improved since then. I had checked online that I could buy my visa on arrival. That turned out to be highly inaccurate, and I was taken to the police office inside the terminal. For interrogation. Although I spent most of the time arguing for why they should let me in.

"You think you can do what you want in Africa just because you are white?"

"Absolutely not, sir. The internet says that I can get a visa on arrival."

"The internet says everything."

"That is very true, sir. But this is Wikivoyage; it is updated by people locally," I said, and showed him a printout from the website. He closely examined the few sheets of papers.

"This is old information."

"I even asked at your embassy in Kano only ten days ago," I complained.

He finally decided to call his boss.

"She will be very mad. I have to wake her up." He sighed. Louder than expected.

"I am sorry about all of this, but I would very much like to visit your country, sir."

Another hour passed, and I was driven downtown by two police officers. I had the pleasure of staying overnight in the main police station in Niamey. The watchman sat outside, under a small roof, and watched a particularly bad soap opera on a tiny television set. I was shown into a small dirty room with light blue walls, a pile of rubbish on the floor and some sort of a mattress less bed.

"You can sleep here, if you want. Or you can watch TV with me."

They even let me have a mosquito net. Luxury!

I watched telly for a couple of hours. Until I became too sleepy and I entered my "cell". I was awoken the next morning by a new "guard" who checked on me. I got up and went back to watch television. Another, yet equally bad soap was on. No wonder, it was six in the morning. Then a young girl came into the police station. She smiled, and started preparing coffee. Apparently the in-house barista. She put coal in an old metal bucket, lit it and got started. Most policemen arriving at work stopped by, had their cup and paid her a coin or two.

The new guard was less rigid than the guy from the night before, and I was allowed out on the street to buy water and have a look around. As long as I was back by nine, I was told. Then the police chief would arrive. And he did, spot on. An elegant and extremely militant looking guy with a thin moustache and the police hat hanging a little to the side. His hobbies did not include smiling. I realized that this guy, clearly trained in the army, would never grant me a visa. At least I observed that he was given my passport and my paperwork. Two hours later a huge policeman came over to me. He seemed to have a high status in the force. Then again, what do I know about Nigerian police?

"Come with me."

I wasn't exactly going to disobey orders. He commanded me into a police van. A 4WD black car. We were back at the airport 30 minutes later, and he walked slightly behind me to the check-in counter of Air Burkina. He gave his orders, and I had my boarding card in hand within a minute. Before leading me to the screening area. There he threw some new orders to the security personnel, in French. And suddenly I saw him smile, for the first time. When he shook my hand.

"We don't want journalists here. Goodbye!"

Someone had googled me. And probably found a connection to NRK. What would Doctor Vodka have done?

I was on board the airplane back to Ouagadougou five minutes later. Deported. At least I didn't have to pay for my return ticket; it turned out to be my first free flight ever! And I had been allowed to explore the area around the central police station, and lived to tell the tale. I was happy.

Burkina Faso

Back in Ouagadougou in Burkina Faso I checked into quite a nice hotel with a pool. I was looking forward to a proper shower following my cell treatment. But I first called my travel agent to cancel my ticket from Niamey to Ouagadougou the next day. I was refunded the full amount, except for a cancellation fee of 25USD. Bargain!

Ouagadougou has been my favorite capital since high school. I was bored in a Norwegian lesson, and took the opportunity to browse an atlas. The Ouagadougou name was so special; I had no choice but to remember it. To my fellow students annoyance. But almost 20 years passed before I actually visited. And discovered little. There is a marked, a few hotels, a river and the odd restaurant. I was slightly disappointed. This was my hero town for so long? At least there were no resorts there.

One night I picked an outdoor restaurant for dinner. Several other people were seated by tables on the pavement, including a fair amount of expats. I ordered barbequed chicken and rice. Within half an hour there were no free seats left. I was approached by a tall and skinny drug dealer in his late twenties. He started nagging me.

"Do you want hasjis?" He whispered.

"No, thanks."

I did not.

"I have very good quality stuff."

"No, I don't smoke."

"It's the best in town"

"I don't care. I am not interested!"

"Man, you really shouldn't turn this down."

I had in fact turned him down three times, but he still didn't seem willing to take a hint anytime soon. I was getting sort of annoyed. I stood up on my chair and shouted.

"This guy here keeps telling me he is selling really good hasjis. I am not interested, but maybe some of you want to buy? He is really persistent."

The dealer started running before I had finished. Some of my fellow diners laughed.

"Nice touch, man!"

Some of them even applauded. I smiled, sat down and finished my meal. A potential little trick for next time I am approached by persistent narcotics salesmen.

Jordan

Jordan is located in a region with its share of conflicts and violence. The last few years have been relatively peaceful within Jordan, but the country has not been spared historically, much due to its strategically located position. At least 8 empires have controlled the area that became Jordan following WWII.

The capital Amman is certainly a stereotypical Middle Eastern town. Most houses are made of cement and painted white. They look pretty identical to an untrained eye. There were few, if any, landmarks to be seen when I entered by road. I had hitchhiked with a local perfume dealer from Damascus in Syria. He was rather talkative, uncomfortable silence was never an option in his car. Uncomfortable talk overdose, on the other hand.

"There is so much money in perfume, my friend! All you need is glass bottles and something smelly to put in it. Why pay for the real Chanel when you can have my Chanel for a tenth of the price?"

"But can't your customers tell the difference?"

"It is all about image, it is all about color, and it's all about marketing. To tell you the truth, it is all about the idea of romance, the idea of beauty. Nobody cares about the smell."

He might have had a point, but I was not convinced. When he let me off in Amman, he gave me a bottle of "Chanel Sport". The original is my favorite cologne. The present looked real, and it didn't smell too bad. But it certainly wasn't "Chanel Sport" as I knew it.

I thanked him before he continued on his journey. I put the bottle in my backpack before I ventured into unknown territory to locate a hotel. My mission was accomplished 40 minutes later, where I showered, tried on the cologne and walked to one of the markets downtown.

The barbequed chicken was world-class! I have never tasted a better bird, and I went to bed smiling shortly thereafter.

The next day called for some major exploration of the capital. Houses with flat roofs, colorful clothes hanging from them to dry, people in small stalls selling everything and a fair amount of donkey transport. It was like walking around in stories from the New Testament. Only Jesus was missing. Some BMWs, a couple of Chevys and the odd motorbike didn't quite fit in, though.

It was by a stall selling spice in the main market that I met Amira, a tall, dark and beautiful girl from the upper middleclass. Her brother was a pilot, her father a diplomat. I asked her about recommendations for restaurants. She spontaneously invited me for a coffee nearby.

"It's better to sit and talk than to stand and bullshit," she said. I did indeed agree.

We ended up in what was both a restaurant and a bar. The fake "Chanel Sport" must have worked. We soon discovered mutual interests and ended up having an amazing time discussing everything from fly fishing to monster trucks. Later that evening we were stopped by the police, while walking on the pavement. The two police officers were under the impression that we had been indecently close to one another. Amira gave them hell, in Arabic, and asked them to go where the pepper grows. It actually grows near Amman, but nevertheless; they took Amiras semi polite hint. Eventually.

We had not done anything illegal. But if we had kissed or held hands, we would have been in major trouble. Couples in Jordan do not kiss. That's the law. Especially not if one person is local, and the other one is foreign. Live with it.

"We were _so_ close to jail," Amira said and illustrated her point by holding two fingers less than an inch apart. She elaborated that the fight had been for real, and that she even had threatened to call her powerful dad. Whoever he was, I was quite contented not knowing.

We hugged each other goodbye outside my hotel. After having double checked for police officers. She allegedly lived nearby and I waved to her when a taxi took her away to her home.

The desert country is the size of Maine. It is best known for Petra, which is Greek for rock or stone. The incredible stone city was carved into the mountains over 2,000 years ago. An Indiana Jones film made the place famous, and the area has had the dubious pleasure of tourist overdoses ever since. To explore Petra takes quite a while when no one is there. It takes forever if you have to queue. And expect having to line up during peak times, the only access point is through a 300 meter high, 1.5 meter wide canyon. The name, Petra, is very much to the point. The city consists of 800 stone monuments plus buildings and memorials that have all been carved out from the many mountains there. At its peak, 20,000 people lived in Petra. Now none do, although tourism has given rise to a thriving industry just outside the historic city. A number of hotels are located in Wadi Mousa, just outside the narrow canyon. They all still claim to be located inside Petra. Then again, Newark Airport claims to be in New York City.

I visited the stone city early in the morning, and avoided the worst tourist traps. I am not particularly interested in donkey safaris or "authentic" souvenirs".

Israel

I got my first Israeli passport stamp in 2001 when I visited my girlfriend Heidi. She was unbelievably skilled in sorting out scholarships and grants to study in various countries. This time, she took a course on Israeli politics in Jerusalem.

We had met each other when I was on holiday back home in Naustdal, just one week before I was to return to my studies in the UK. Rather typical then that I met this stunning and smart girl, Heidi Torkildson Ryste, shortly before leaving. I still tried to make the most of it, and I invited her on a dinner date to the only expensive restaurant in neighboring Førde. Way out of my budget range, but I had no choice. She worked part-time as a waitress in the only affordable restaurant there. It still worked out, although I had to live off beans and toast the first month in England. Following countless phone calls, emails and even old-fashioned letters we agreed to start going out. Via the phone.

In Israel, three years later, we decided to go to a nightclub. A bunch of gorgeous girls lined the dance floor. They knew their fashion, but they were clearly in the army. Each and every one of them sported an IMI Galil strapped over their shoulders. The semiautomatic Israeli weapon is similar to Kalashnikov AK-47 and looks dangerous enough to the untrained eye. Especially when seen on a dance floor. I would never have asked any of them to dance, even if I had been single.

But why such weapons in nightclubs? The explanation is simple, really. They were doing national service. When they start, they are given an IMI Galil each. If they somehow lose the weapon, they are automatically thrown in prison and kept there for seven years. Or so I was told. They would therefore not risk leaving their weapon at home, not even when out on town.

I never had anything stolen on my trips to every country. Except for in Israel. My sunglasses were nicked from my backpack which I had left in our microscopic Old Town hotel. The experience wasn't scary at all, even though I did not have a lot of travel experience back then. To report the theft was worse. The police officer on duty knew no English and was as service minded as an underpaid Russian bureaucrat with a migraine. I still needed a proof of theft certificate to get something back on my travel insurance, and I somehow managed. I didn't have a lot of money, and would like to take advantage of my insurance policy. Even though my sunglasses weren't exactly Prada.

Bolivia

To touch down in the highest capital of the world is cool. You will then just have witnessed the wild and pointy Andes peaks with snow on top. Just as you can do on the Norwegian West Coast. Then again, the Andes are 5,000 meters higher. The airport of La Paz is located 4,000 meters above sea level, whereas the town itself stretches 800 meters down a valley. My goal of what to do in Bolivia wasn't very ambitious, I aimed to eat llama. Gourmet llama.

I walked around La Paz a full day. It never stopped drizzling. The city is truly fascinating with all its colorful small brick houses located next to one another alongside the hillsides, and the density of locals wearing their homemade traditional costumes.

The nicest part of town is at the bottom, where the temperatures are a little more human friendly. And where galleries, good coffee shops and expensive restaurants fight for the best spots. I asked around and finally found a restaurant where llama was on the menu. It tasted really good, like a quality steak with a touch. Chilean red wine accompanied it well. But both eventually ran out. My energy did not. It was only half past eight, and I was not ready for bed. The waiter recommended a bar several hundred meters higher up.

"In the bohemian part of town," he said. Most cities oddly seem to have a bohemian part of town, these days. I guess people think it sounds appealing. A preordered taxi took me there, the price was agreed on by the lovely waiter. I could have flagged one down on the street, but I would have been easy prey for a greedy taxi driver. Any South American one-year-old would put my Spanish to shame.

The bar was as crowded as a bee hive, but I managed to fight my way through the human chaos to the only free seat in the bar. I ordered a beer. A woman in her 40's sat next to me. I remember thinking that she single handedly must have supported a dozen jobs in the cosmetics industry. All of a sudden she turned on her stool and spoke to me.

"I heard you speak English. Where are you from?"

"Norway. And you are local?"

"I am indeed. My name is Carolina," she said. With a big smile. She was blinking at high speed. Her fake eye lashes couldn't quite keep up. We talked for about 20 minutes. And that's what I can remember.

I got back to my senses a few hours later. The clock behind the bar said just after midnight. I had been half lying over one of the tables by one of the windows.

The woman was gone.

My wallet, phone, money and passport were not. But I had a headache. Big time. It would likely have put migraine sufferers to shame. The woman, a jealous "competitor", the bartender or some random person had decided to conduct a chemical experiment on my drink. It had been spiked. Unless the all but well-done llama had had its revenge.

I left La Paz by air two days later. I became bored on the plane as soon as the incredible view was obstructed by clouds, and I went through my wallet. Where I found a note.

"Gunner, I am sorry to have put a little something in your drink. I was going to take advantage of you, but you were too cute and your stories from Bhutan just got to me. Don't judge me. Best of luck with your last countries. 3 paracetamol and a vodka shot will kill your headache. XOXOX Carolina"

The headache had luckily vanished.

Gabon

I would experience different kinds of headaches in Gabon. The atmosphere in capital Libreville is calm and continental. The language and a lot of the inspiration is French. The lively part of town is to the north, between the embassy district and the Atlantic Ocean. On Boulevard Joseph Deemin you might even visit a super trendy restaurant, bar and lounge. Le Bistro could have been located in Paris or London. It doesn't quite fit in there. But it comes highly recommended. I entered and sat down on a stool in the bar. The bartender quickly made me a freshly squeezed orange juice. I was in celebration mode. I had just received my visa to Equatorial Guinea, one of the world's hardest countries to gain access to. Unless you are American, that is. US citizens are the only ones who won't need a visa to visit. I have lived in the US, but I am not from there. So a personal visit to the embassy on the outskirts of Libreville was needed. I guess I had been a little bit of a nuisance, but I was on a mission. I had worn a suit jacket and waited semi patiently on the terrace of the embassy building. They showed Nigerian soap operas on the old Phillips television set that hung on the wall with a tiny tailored roof above it. It was muted, but the intrigues were impossible not to catch. The plot seemed to be from the hit show Dynasty back in the 80's. The actors were not.

Two hours of waiting paid off. I was shown into the office of the ambassador himself. His accent gave no room for confusion. He had studied in the US. "Please have a seat. What can I do for you, sir?"

He sat in a big office chair behind a huge desk made from mahogany. There were some letters scattered on the work surface. A green glass lamp provided the needed lighting. An old-fashioned black phone had probably been there for decades, but was without a single piece of dust. The ambassador himself was tall and he clearly worked out. His initials were woven onto the arms of his shirt. The blue-striped tie was not purchased locally.

"Ambassador. I would very much like to visit you beautiful country. But to do so as a Norwegian citizen I will need a visa."

"What do you know about my country?" he asked. He seemed genuinely interested.

"I have read a lot about it. Your capital is on a small but beautiful island while the majority of the country is just north of us. I also like that you are the only country in Africa where Spanish is the official language.

"You know a lot. I am impressed."

He picked up the phone. It was still in use!

"Kareem. Please come."

One of his employees was in the office less than ten seconds later.

"Give this gentleman a visa."

I stood up and shook his hand.

"Thank you very much, sir!"

"Do enjoy your trip."

I received my passport with the fresh visa in it an hour of soap consumption later. I double checked the validity dates. They were correct.

In Le Bistro I took out my passport from my inner pocket and admired it. Before returning it carefully. Geography nerding. But the difficulties to get that particular visa justified my behavior. I had experienced the difficulties first-hand only two days earlier. By waiting outside the Equatorial Guinea Consulate in Douala in Cameroon for a couple of hours before being let in by a janitor. The Consul, a lady in her 60's with too much time on her hands, had ignored every single attempt at reasoning. She was simply not having it. I finally had had no other option but to leave.

In the bistro, my juice tasted really fresh and delicious. Clearly no added sugar or water. Two men in their 40s walked in and sat down at the neighboring table. They spoke Norwegian, and a very particular dialect of Trøndelag, a region in the middle of nowhere. I nodded to them. The guy with the moustache nodded back. They ordered a beer each and continued talking. The guy with no facial hair told the other about his business in Trondheim and how he had found the perfect way of not paying taxes, thanks to a loophole. It didn't sound legal. At all. He said that he had saved millions. They gradually moved on to another topic; the best hookers in Africa. They agreed that Nigeria and Tanzania offered the best, whereas those in Mozambique were supposedly expensive and useless. The guys had clearly been around a bit. And soon got tired of hooker talk and moved on to their wives and kids back home.

For a while I contemplated walking over to their table and introducing myself as Mr. Nielsen, Norway's chief governmental tax inspector, but I was a little afraid of how they would react. They obviously didn't know I was a fellow countryman, and they had discussed some topics that ought to remain off limits to any other Scandinavian person. I nodded to them when I left. They both nodded back this time. They should have known.

There was time for yet another visa the next day. I passed by the little embassy of São Tomé and Príncipe down by the sea. It was Wednesday and I was planning to fly there on Friday. And not by just any airline. By Ceiba, the only passenger airline from Equatorial Guinea. Or to put it like Wikipedia did:

"…in 2009, the boss of CEIBA, a Senegalese citizen of Gambian origins named Mamadou Jaye, left Equatorial Guinea with 3.5 billion CFA francs and spare ATR aircraft parts in a suitcase to negotiate trade deals and to establish a West African office for CEIBA. Jaye never returned to Equatorial Guinea."

That kind of an airline.

Ceiba is not allowed to fly in Europe. But it is the only airline to fly between Gabon and São Tomé and Príncipe. I didn't know that the flight that particular Friday was cancelled until I spoke to the lovely lady in a Libreville travel agency. Apparently cancelled due to Easter. Good Friday is Good Friday, also in this particular part of Africa. My option was to wait until the next Monday, but that would've been too late as I didn't have unlimited Easter holiday. There was always the possibility of flying via Luanda, Angola, but with no direct flights from Libreville, and at substantial cost.

"But there might be a boat," she said. The travel agent did her job.

"There might? You do not know?"

"Well, there are no scheduled ones, but ask down at the harbor."

I thanked her for her help and walked down to the port with my backpack. There I asked my way to the Sao Tome ticket office, and found some sort of a shack where they sold tickets for local routes. I asked for assistance, and one of the guys behind the counter took me to a friend, a guy called Ricardo on a very small cargo boat named Andrea, carrying loads of colorful mattresses and some oil barrels. I frowned.

This is the boat to Sao Tome? It would sink if a seagull shit on the wrong side of it.

And yes, Ricardo was definitely going to Sao Tome. But not until the following day. If I needed to leave immediately?

"Yes!"

I almost shouted.

"OK, OK. Wait, I will check."

We walked into a run down, badly lit warehouse. It was not exactly designed on carefully monitored customer behavior pattern in Harrods, but rather designed on the mind of Alfred Hitchcock. A metal shop, two sleeping workers, a stairway, a narrow hall and an open door later, there were to my surprise no thugs to be found, but two lovely ladies. I asked how long it would take to go by boat to Sao Tome.

"15 hours," Ricardo translated.

Well, this is Africa and they are trying to sell me something. I'll add 30% to that. 20 hours is still bad, very bad actually, but given the options. Or lack thereof. I nodded. They started writing out my ticket, I paid for it and I felt safe. Kind of. Until they told me, again through Ricardo, that my passport had to go to the police and would be returned before the departure of the vessel.

I hate leaving without my passport, especially in semi-dubious countries. On my way back to the docks, I picked up 1.5 liters of water and 1 liter of apple juice plus 6 bananas and 4 oranges. Enough for 20 hours when they include a night.

After getting my ticket, I had to wait for over 2 hours to board the ferry. M/S Marstal of Sao Tome was docked, being loaded, and seemed pretty ready to leave.

"So, how fast can that ferry go?" I asked Ricardo. He seemed to have finished his duties of the day and was chilling next to me on a bench in the shadow of the harbor.

"Well, you are not taking that ferry. That one is going to Cameroon," he said and smiled at my ignorance.

"So, which boat am I taking?" I asked. More than a little uneasy.

"That one!" he grinned and pointed past the ferry to a pretty run down cargo vessel.

Beautiful! From a shabby ferry of the type that could have been seen roaming the fjords of Norway only 20 years earlier to this, this, this…floating thing. Bloody hell!

I bit my teeth together, again remembering my alternatives. The police brought back my passport shortly after, and we were all set to sail.

São Tomé and Principe

You mean you are impatient, restless or just bad at relaxing? Well, if that is really the case, please skip this chapter. The paragraphs that follow are not for you. What I am about to tell you will make painting the fourth layer of a very white wall seem like Christmas Eve to a six year old, in comparison.

I am impatient, restless and bad at relaxing.

I had found myself rather thrilled after easily obtaining my visa to São Tomé and Príncipe, and even a ticket. The country in the Atlantic does not accept people without a visa. Should anyone still make it to the border, they are sent back by the same mode of transport at their own cost and risk. I would not have such problems.

The only thing between me and São Tomé and Príncipe was M/V Maryvana, the floating object I had finally boarded in Gabon together with five other passengers. Two gentlemen I had seen earlier at the embassy, two women and a baby. I walked onto the vessel at 17:18 and for some reason checked the time. At 18:20, everything was loaded, unloaded and the boat unhooked from the dock. We were off! Sort of. The boat moved exceptionally slow at 7 knots (10-11 km/h), according to my phone's built-in GPS.

I soon befriended the chief engineer.

"I am Fidele, like Fidel Castro," he said in pretty decent English. And told me that he had a sister working in a hotel in Oslo before complaining about African wages and saying that he also wanted to move to Europe.

Not having planned for this boat trip, I had no sleeping bag or blanket in my backpack. Only clothes, toiletries and my laptop. I found a pretty quiet spot on the 58 meter long but narrow boat and laid down on some plastic covers that were tied up. Kind of soft. Softer than the steel plates, at least.

I tried a couple of dozen sleeping positions and eventually fell asleep. After a while I was woken up by one of the women. It had started to rain a little. She spoke no English, but she handed me a blanket. Hers. And she directed me to underneath the roofed part in front of the cockpit area. I was too tired to protest and laid down on the blanket on the steel plate. I somehow kind of managed to sleep again before waking up after feeling big rain drops on my face shortly thereafter. A storm was approaching. The captain ordered us below deck to the galley. It was cramped down there, but no rain. The storm could still be heard and very much felt. One of the São Tomé guys puked a couple of times. I do luckily not get seasick easily. Presumably thanks to trips with my dad on the rough Norwegian coast as a kid.

All of a sudden Fidele appeared in the galley. He asked if I wanted to stay in his cabin while he worked. The tiny room had a narrow and very short mattress. I happily accepted, and managed to get some sleep. I have not been that close to a fetal position since 1975.

I was woken by Fidele at 07:00 in the morning and I went back up on deck while he took over his bed for some well-deserved rest. Still pretty rough, but no rain. We'd been at sea for almost 13 hours. But I could still not see land. Why not? I checked my phone with built-in GPS.

"We're only 40 percent there. Fuck!" I said to myself. I never speak to myself.

We would, with the same speed, need another 18 hours to get to São Tomé, totaling over 30 hours, twice as much as what Ricardo had told me. Where's the voodoo doll when you need it? I considered a variety of self-torture methods in order to rather experience physical than mental pain. None were evaluated as cruel enough, and I somehow managed to convince myself to start looking at this as the perfect opportunity for self-realization and meditation. I have always loved the sea breeze and smell of the sea, so it kind of worked. But slow it was, slow it was. And my self-imposed meditation was made less effective by the occasional Ceiba curse. At 15:10 (14:10 São Tomé time) we started seeing the outline of a mountain. Of São Tomé!

"It cannot take more than six hours from here," I said to myself. Again. I was going insane.

9 hours later we were close. Really close. Maximum 20 minutes away. Then the engine stopped and the anchor was dropped.

"What's the problem?" I asked.

Fidele explained. The customs check had closed for the night, so we couldn't go to shore. I had two options. Exploding, or not exploding. I chose the first, but it didn't work. Another night on deck.

Lovely, really.

This time, I took my backpack and used a t-shirt as a pillow and a shirt as a blanket on the steel. Not too bad. With the gentle sea breeze and a great view of the stars. But two nights in a row on deck of a cargo vessel? And with only a few bananas and an orange to eat?

I was woken by local fishermen in boats with outboard engines at around 6. My fellow passengers were already up, seemingly enthusiastic. For no reason. It took another 2.5 hours until the captain could start the engines and navigate us to the docks. And then we still had to stay aboard 30 minutes for the customs officers to go through the vessel (after all, being called Maryvana, drug smuggling would not be a surprise) and check our passports.

At 09:17, I was on land, yet again. 39 hours and 59 minutes after boarding.

I walked from the port to the center of São Tomé in a matter of minutes, and I found a coffee shop. Complete with amazing coffee, freshly made food and Wi-Fi. I was in heaven. My fellow guests were not. My body odor wasn't exactly award winning following two nights at sea. I found a hostel, checked in and showered. For quite some time.

There was only one problem. I still hadn't booked my onward flight to Equatorial Guinea, and the travel agent in the country only accepted cash. That none of the cash machines in the hood were operational added to the challenge. I luckily had American dollars, British pounds and a few Euros. The travel agent preferred dobra, but they finally accepted my currency cocktail. The transaction left me with 20 USD. And my flight wouldn't leave until three days later.

I harassed the receptionist at the luxury hotel Pestana sufficiently for him to agree on letting me use my Visa card to get cash. As long as I ordered a cocktail in the bar, that was. Cashback! At an exceptionally bad exchange rate. Had he only known his bargaining position he could have done even better. I suddenly found myself with local currency in my pocket. Millions of dobra in my pocket. Less than 70 USD had made me into a millionaire. And the local bills made it far easier to get in touch with people. I could now pay for the eminent street food, meat and corn that were prepared over coal on old car wheels.

"What are you doing here?" a local English speaking man in his 50's asked, and sat down next to me to eat his skewers.

"I am just visiting. As a tourist."

"A tourist? But why are you eating here with us? Why aren't you in one of the posh hotels?"

"I wouldn't have met you there, would I?"

He agreed with my logic. We continued discussing world problems, even solving a few. He purchased two beers from a teenager who pulled a wagon with a homemade ice bag on it. He handed me one of them. I later returned the favor.

And that's how the night continued.

Equatorial Guinea

My flight ticket was accepted. By the rather oversized woman behind the CEIBA check-in counter in São Tomé. And the flight on the propeller plane turned out to be rather uneventful.

Given that this was CEIBA, it called for a celebration. The restaurants in Equatorial Guinea are rather modern, but most people are unlikely to ever experience them. Unless coincidentally invited there on a work trip, anyone but US citizens will struggle to get in. To get hold of the precious visa can be a bureaucratic nightmare, although I had been lucky in Gabon.

The country is unique in other ways too. No other of the 55 African countries has Spanish as the official language. Portugal, France, Belgium, the Netherlands and United Kingdom divided the rest among them. E.G. has a lot of oil, but the revenues from it are divided unevenly. Very unevenly. The mortality rate from lack of clean water and illnesses among children under the age of five is sky high in the police state. Almost 80 percent of the 700,000 inhabitants live in poverty. There are still relatively few people there, something that leads to something positive; no other country in Africa has a higher literacy rate than this country on the equator.

I was surprised by the intense construction work, the moment I arrived. But none of the construction workers were local. They were Chinese. Instead of employing locals, the government hire cheap labor from the Far East. They then have no obligations after completion, and the workers will leave the country.

Then again, the importance of maintenance is underestimated, something you are usually reminded of wherever you are in Africa.

Equatorial Guinea is widely known for being corrupt and having a lot of red tape. All over the place. I was nearly arrested for photographing the presidential palace, but I was let off after deleting the photos and paying a fine of a few dollars.

"You are lucky! Normally we'd thrown you in jail!" the police officer said. Or shouted.

I had given him less than 20 USD from my pocket change pocket. My hundred dollar bills were tucked away in another pocket, due to the likelihood of such incidents. He ran off, down a side street while counting his money. His, not the government's. The people of E.G. would never benefit from the so called fine.

The entire episode pissed me off. Out of spite, I returned to snap some new photos, just a little bit more discrete. Discrete? Well, not consistently. I also photographed an armored tank with a cannon on top. Possibly not my smartest move, ever. The policeman sitting on it shouted at me, and started turning the big gun in my direction. Usain Bolt would have been envious of my sprint. I managed to throw myself around a corner, before continuing at a slower pace. I walked very fast down the street and soon disappeared inside a shop.

Equatorial Guinea is smaller than South Carolina, whereas Bioko, the island where the capital is located, is the size of Delaware.

The country has little tolerance when it comes to freedom of speech and the press. And there is a lot of trafficking originating here, according to international reports. Not much to cheer about, really. It might be just as well that it is a difficult country to visit. There are a few issues to resolve before tourists will come flocking here.

Laos

Tourism is, however, very important and still on the rise in Laos. Although I was actually there for work in Vientiane, the capital. I met with the public service broadcasters there, a BBC in miniature, if you like. The technical equipment could also have been BBC's. In 1956.

The Minister of Culture waited after the meeting with the broadcaster. We would discuss digital radio in a country that never bothered to introduce national radio via FM. Why not go straight to digital? No one was unwilling, but there were a couple of financial issues that needed to be dealt with first. Unless I proposed a solution that included substantial amounts of money, digital radio seemed very unlikely to happen in Laos this side of my retirement.

The prominent meeting concluded my work in the country, and I had set aside a weekend with Haenim from South Korea. She was my girlfriend at the time, although she had been so for just a couple of months.

We decided to explore the outskirts of Vientiane, and I rented a fierce 4WD vehicle. A lot of the roads near the city are fucked. To put it nicely. The mean road machine took us into the jungle where an insect safari awaited. I have never seen as many strange creatures before. They were everywhere, although I would admittedly have spotted none had it not been for our local expert guide. He took us on a three kilometer long hike through the bush to show us what he called "the incredible animals". We saw bugs, stick animals, spiders, butterflies, crickets, bats, worms and who knows what else. He was rewarded a few kip, the local currency, for his troubles.

We returned to the hotel rather late, and decided to take the monster for a drive by the Mekong River, which acts as the border to Thailand. I had never visited the country before then, and I would at least have a peek at the unknown. There was some sort of an industrial area next to the river, the ground was covered by rocks and dirt. Our vehicle didn't disappoint, and easily transported us to the river bank. The moon was almost full, the river flowed past. Slowly. A song by the Beatles was playing on the AM radio. Let it be, Lennon said.

There was no question about it, really. We were alone, in moonlight. We had music, we had a view and it was way past midnight. Haenim climbed over on my side, I put the seat back as far as I could.

We came at the same time.

So did a young man on a motorcycle. We saw his headlight when he was 30 meters away. Haenim got off me and jumped back to her own side. I managed to get my white linen trousers back on. Inside out. That I didn't have a shirt on wasn't too bad. It was still hot enough for that to be perfectly legitimate in Laos.

"Not legal!"

The police officer had left his vehicle and walked over to the side of the car. Someone had probably tipped him off of an illegally parked car, or he had seen us himself when driving on the road 200 meters from us. His English was virtually non-existent.

"What is not legal? We are just admiring the view," I said. The truth, although not the complete truth.

"Not legal!"

"What is not legal? There are no signs saying that we cannot be here."

It soon became obvious there was no point in continuing the discussion.

"Come! He said."

Haenim had managed to fully dress in the passenger seat. I put my T-shirt on and switched the ignition on. We were to follow the motorcycle man. To a little police station in the northern part of town where we were commanded to stop.

"Sit here! Wait here! Please here! Thanks!"

Another young policeman knew at least five words in English.

We were shown into the police station, a brick building. Or some sort of a shack, rather. The linguist showed us to two small wooden stools in front of a metal desk. Before he walked into another room to wake up a senior police officer who was sleeping on a mattress on the concrete floor. Five minutes of waking up, getting dressed and briefed later, and he sat on the other side of the desk. He was still sleepy, his hair pointed in every direction.

"Hello, sir!" I said and smiled. We had probably broken some rules; I did my best to play down the grade of our crimes. My smile was not returned. Surprise. He had been given the much sought after night shift and would rather sleep than talk with two horny foreigners.

"What were you doing by the river?"

"Enjoying the view, sir. It is such a lovely night in Vientiane."

We went through what had happened, and I soon realized that it had been illegal to drive off road. Despite a total lack of road signs or posters informing us of such. I had to write down our names, birth dates and the name of our hotel on a worn notepad.

But the policeman wasn't done yet. He had after all been briefed by the junior officers. He blushed when asking his next question.

"Did you...ehe...have...ehe...sex in the car?"

The officer almost whispered the word "sex" while looking away. He was not feeling comfortable with this particular interrogation. To have sex in a car by the Mekong River could be illegal in Laos, and we weren't even married. My goal was not to talk ourselves into a possible prison sentence.

"Oh, absolutely not, sir. Why are you asking?"

I hoped that this was not some sort of a case that would lead to a rapid career rise and that he wasn't going to order a biological examination of the car.

"So, you were just enjoying the view, without a shirt on and with your trousers the wrong way on?"

I could sense the outline of a triumphant little smile.

"It's the latest fashion in Europe, Sir."

"It is in Korea too," Haenim said. Good job! We were very much aligned. You ought to be when you are in a police station in Vientiane at 2 AM.

Everyone did of course know what had really happened, but no one was hurt and it was way too late for the officer in charge to take the matter any further. That we would receive a fine was given. I still insisted on a receipt. And I got one. Written on the back of a dry cleaning receipt. Very official. At least we avoided prison. Neither of us did however carry cash, so four police officers on motorbikes escorted us to the nearest ATM. They got money; I got the receipt. It all happened a few stone throws from where the eager policeman had picked us up in the first place. What comes around, etc.

Ghana

I will get to police troubles in Ghana too. Let me just provide some much needed background info.

Haenim and I almost married. So did Øystein and Benedicte too. On several occasions. Haenim never became my spouse, but Benedicte finally became Øystein's. On the third attempt. Not because she nagged a lot or because they cancelled any weddings.

But because Øystein is a sadist dick.

He proposed on two occasions, and the very much in love Benedicte answered yes with her huge Bambi like eyes, both times. Before Øystein responded.

"I was joking."

That he still has perfect eye sight and that his face is without visible punch marks is a mystery. Then again, he actually meant it when he asked her the third time. On a mountain in Ecuador. They had narrowly managed to conquer a 5,000 meter high peak, and both were struggling with low oxygen values. Benedicte did of course think that Øystein was calling wolf, yet again. But he managed to convince her that this time he was serious. They descended as an engaged couple, but kept what had happened a secret. Friends and family were to be fooled, when they married at what everyone believed was Benedicte's 30th birthday, in Naustdal. Practical jokes are not uncommon in the Garfors family.

By that time, Øystein and Benedicte had been together for years. Also when she did work placement as a nurse in Ghana - there was no doubt, we would visit. Øystein, my then girlfriend Nicole and our friends Anette and Kenneth booked a Lufthansa flight and headed south. We explored Accra, the capital that hasn't seen a paint brush since the Brits left in the 1950's. The metropolis is huge, hot and dusty. Which meant that we spent most of the time in Kokrobite, a charming little beach west of town.

But even Kokrobite turned hectic on the weekends. We rented a minibus with a driver and had him drive us east. We were stopped by the police just outside Accra. Two uniformed gentlemen were standing next to a police car parked on the shoulder of the road. One of them had a pistol in his belt. He held a red and white stop sign into the road. The other one had a semi-automatic machine gun over his shoulder. Our driver stopped, and was asked to pay a "fine". Not an official one, for sure.

"Corrupt crooks!" he whispered. Not exactly happy. But what could he do? He paid and we were allowed to continue.

For a while. Until we saw another two police officers with another stop sign 30 kilometers further east.

"Bloody bandits," Øystein sighed loudly. The rest of us agreed, and started discussing how this country would never get out of trouble with such behavior. The driver was about to slow down, but suddenly floored it and passed the crooks. They were standing in the middle of the road and had to jump to the side to avoid being hit.

"Are you crazy? Why didn't you stop?"

Nicole wasn't exactly impressed by the maneuver.

"They didn't have a car," the driver said, before he turned around with a big smile on his face. "High five!" he cheered.

We couldn't argue against his logic.

We thanked him for the trip a few hours later. We had reached our destination, a village by the Keta Lagoon. Our accommodation for the night would be a typical Ghanaian hotel, made of concrete and painted green. The standard was simple, and the water temperature inside as high as the sun wanted it to be. It was warm enough for a fast shower, not hot enough for a bath in the rusty old tub.

It came as no surprise that all of us got up early the next day. We were about to explore the islands in the lagoon, and we had to hire a boat. Small villages were scattered around on the islands. It turned out that the villagers produced some sort of rum-like liquor, based on local sugar canes. It didn't taste too bad, so we even purchased a couple of liters. They came in used plastic water bottles. Our purchase would not have made rocket scientists proud. The liquor turned sour, real sour, during storage. It did in fact taste so bad, that it wasn't even drunk in the very late hours of the wedding of Øystein and Benedicte. And at that hour, there was nothing else to consume either. At least it worked well as a tool to threaten the guests to leave. It was, after all, 7 AM. Øystein later used it to open the drain of an old sink.

Georgia

The liquor in Georgia is as strong, if not stronger, but of way too high quality for it to be used to open filthy pipes. The amazing country in the Caucasus comes with a sad history. Not surprisingly, the biggest celebrity is called Josef Stalin. There is still a statue of him in his hometown Gori, and the first toast of every party is traditionally given in his honor. Despite the millions of lives he has on his conscience. Given that he ever had one. A celeb is a celeb for a reason.

Minibus is the most important form of transport in the mountainous country. It won't get you anywhere particularly fast, but it is cheap and used by many. The concept is simple. A bunch of colorful minibuses gather in city bus stations or by a roundabout or a gas station in towns and villages. They are called "marshrutka", and can be found in most of the former Soviet Republics. The Russian word is rather logical, really. It has been put together by "march" and "route". There is only one problem for you, as a passenger. The buses wait for other passengers, and will rarely leave before they are full. And en route they will stop at random places to pick people up or let people off. Or to pick goods up, or to deliver goods. Expect to see anything from car tires via fresh eggs that are to be sold at a market to chickens on their last journey. It's chaos. And in the middle of it are you and your fellow passengers. You will slowly but surely get from A to B, only via C, D, E, F and G. The trip from the capital Tbilisi to the harbor town of Batumi should take six hours, but might take five. Or more normally seven. It was on a marshrutka from Poti to Zugdidi that I had forgotten to to think for a few seconds. Despite all my travel experience, I had managed to leave my laptop in my backpack under my seat.

Braindead at the time of the crime.

You just don't do that. Not in Georgia. Leave any valuables anywhere not in your line of sight at all times, that is. My backpack was underneath my seat, and the inevitable happened. One of the youngsters that sat behind me must have had a field day in my backpack. My laptop, and the power supply disappeared. Nothing else. He knew what he was after. And I had something stolen from me for the first time since the 90's. On my second trip to Georgia. In 2014. 198 countries and 15 theft-free years still isn't too bad, statistically speaking. I had luckily saved the most important computer files in the cloud.

I cannot leave Georgia without having experienced the food. The fantastic food, yet with big regional differences. They do primarily serve meat, vegetables, bread and stews. Don't expect spicy dishes, but very tasty. Garlic, cheese, walnuts, eggplants, spinach and beans are commonplace. All of it harvested from a rich soil that produces taste bombs. The meat *khinkali* or dumplings overflow with delicious juice while barbequed *Badijani* eggplant comes with a highly addictive walnut mixture. Not to mention *khachapuri*, the eminent round and soft bread that often comes with cheese, and occasionally with an egg in the middle.

Somalia

I decided early on during project 198 to visit the divided country in Eastern Africa. Its reputation was not among the best, and I figured that I should start with the most dangerous and dubious countries. At least I wouldn't have wasted a lot of time traveling to a lot of "easy" countries, should the unthinkable happen. Mogadishu was not the preferred destination in 2008, and I decided to go to the less dangerous North. To Saylac, a tiny coastal town, technically in Somaliland which claims to be independent but which has not been acknowledged as such by any country. Somalia is therefore considered a part of Somalia. And it comes with its own tourist office in London. Where they were service-oriented enough to give me a visa on the same day as I applied, but not without some interrogation in the windowless office in one of the less attractive parts of the British capital.

"Why do you want to travel to Somaliland?" the officer in charge asked.

"I am a tourist; I want to see the country for myself."

"Are you not scared?"

"No, not really."

"Have you not heard about the pirates?" the first guy wondered while filling out the relevant boxes on the visa sticker, which he placed in the middle of my passport.

"I am sure I will be fine."

He stamped the sticker and passed the passport to his boss.

"You are a crazy, crazy man."

"Normal is nothing," I said, and smiled. Slightly uneasy.

"Do you want to die?"

"I will be fine, no worries."

The boss signed the visa, shook his head and gave the passport to me.

"Good luck, mister. You will need it!"

"Thank you very much!" I responded, stood up and walked towards the door. There was no use in staying. I would get nothing but negative propaganda anyway.

"We will cross our fingers, they shouted after me."

Tourist office, my ass.

To get to Somalia I first flew into Djibouti, the northern neighbor. A taxi took me to the border; I crossed it by foot and was received by a nice border guard.

"Welcome to Somaliland!"

There was nothing but a few wooden shacks and a gas station in the border town, or village rather. Some of the shacks doubled as houses and shops. Nokia chargers were sold at half price. No surprise, electrical outlets were far apart. I tried to hitchhike to Saylac, 30 kilometers further south. The first guy who stopped demanded 100USD. As if. I walked to the gas station, or should I say barrel with a pump. A 35 year old man had his daily dose of diesel given to the Land Cruiser he sat in. He demanded 10USD for the ride. Still bloody expensive, given where on earth I was, but the transportation options were somewhat limited. I accepted.

The driver commanded his young wife to jump into the backseat. There were already four people there, but they seemed accustomed to sit in crowded places.

Two minutes later, and we were off. And the man turned wild. He drove at 140 km/h through the desert. There were no roads, and the sand made a huge dust cloud behind us. To put on my seatbelt was out of the question. In many countries that shows contempt for the driver as I would signal a lack of trust and respect. The driver is king, and he knows how to drive. Or so the moral goes. I wasn't too keen on offending him and risk being thrown off in the middle of the desert.

Out of the sand another 4WD car came up from behind and tried to pass. The race was on! The other guy managed to overtake us, the sand cloud made it impossible to see anything. Anyone else would have slowed down, but not the wild man. Not even a little bit. Luckily, the other car had a bigger engine and got away. Visibility returned!

We arrived safely in Saylac at dusk. I had done some internet searches and knew that the town should have a couple of hotels. There were also allegedly good diving conditions. I asked the driver where the hotels were.

"There are no hotels here. Goodbye!"

Around 10,000 people lived in shacks; there were no hotels, guest houses or boarding houses. I walked around between the shacks, looking for somewhere to crash. An old man stopped me after a few minutes.

"What are you doing here?"

"I am looking for a hotel."

"There are no hotels here! You are not allowed to walk around here. Come with me," he concluded.

The man showed me the way to one of the shacks. Four old guys sat directly on the ground. The floor was non-existent. The man who had led me there said something in a language I didn't understand. The oldest one there took charge.

"What are you doing here?"

"I am looking for a hotel. Do you know of any hotels here?"

"There are no hotels here! Have you broken the rules?" the man said and raised his eyebrows.

"Ehe…I don't think so. What rules?"

"Do you have a visa?"

I picked up my passport from one of my inner pockets of my suit jacket and gave it to him. He wore some sort of a red cloth that was wrapped around him. They all flocked around the oldest man to study my visa. They almost seemed disappointed when they realized that it was legit. I was brought to two other "houses", where the same thing happened.

"What are you doing here?"

"I am looking for a hotel. Do you know of any hotels here?"

"There are no hotels here!"

Two men sat on the floor of the last place. They turned out to be the mayor and the vice mayor. And in what was as close to a house that could be found in Saylac. There was even a floor, but no windows.

"What are you doing here?" The mayor asked. He was chewing khat and watching TV. Khat is a mild narcotic from the plant Catha edulis. When it is chewed, the user will enjoy a mild amphetamine like stimuli. Rumor has it that the user will be excited and euphoric, as a result. Another side effect is a bonus for many. The lack of appetite. To achieve a strong effect, large amounts must be chewed, something that may cause an extended chin. They appear to have chronic one sided mumps.

"I am looking for a hotel. Do you know of any hotels here?"

"There are no hotels here! So, where are you going to sleep tonight?"
The mayor spat khat in a dustbin on the floor and seemed to be looking forward to my answer.

"I dunno. I guess I'll just go down to the beach and sleep there."
He held his hand towards me, to signal that I should wait. While discussing with the vice mayor. The latter did not seem impressed.

"You can sleep in my house," his boss declared.

"Oh, really? That is very kind of you. Thank you so much!"
I later understood the reaction of the vice mayor. It turned out that I would stay in his room whereas he had to sleep on the floor in the living room. That didn't make me particularly popular. Then again, I wouldn't have voted for him anyway.

I was woken up by a journalist student at seven o'clock the next morning. The rumor of a foreign guest had reached the rest of the town. He was clearly very proud of where he lived, and he showed me the port which he claimed was used primarily for offloading khat that had been smuggled from Yemen. The hospital was next up on my guided sightseeing trip. It came with a maternity ward that might have been modern in the 1950's. Before he took me to school. The hundred or so kids there had probably not seen many westerners before. They went wild, and some of them insisted on touching me. The pupils, they must have been around 10 years old, sat on wooden benches in the classroom. The school, a rectangular one-story green brick building, did not have any windows, and a lovely breeze made the temperature in the classroom just about right. And a lot cooler than in the desert outside.

It was time for breakfast, and we walked to a restaurant. White tablecloths were few and far between. And no sign of a roof. We sat down on shaky plastic chairs in non-matching colors and were served grilled goat meat and vegetables. Not bad.

Suddenly a police car approached and stopped a few meters away from us. Two police officers and a VIP stepped out. The governor of the area, I was told.

First I stayed with the mayor, and then had breakfast with the governor. I couldn't complain much about my reception in Somalia.

The governor was, as everyone else, curious about what I was doing there. I explained that I like to travel and to see new countries and cultures. He wasn't too interested, but that didn't worry me too much. I assumed that he had a few other challenges to think about. We were after all in Somalia. I do not have any idea how much a governor there gets paid, but probably not more than an average Norwegian salary. I wanted to show good faith, and asked for the bill. The response was instant.

"I will pay!"

The governor's look was not to be mistaken. He meant what he had just said, and he was not about to discuss the matter with a young Norwegian. There is just something about certain people with power. Everything about them indicates respect. The governor was such a person. I thanked him and shook his hand.

The journalist student took me to some sort of a tea house. Or shed. The "roof" was made by a stretched tarpaulin. Several men sat on big sacks of coffee beans while two young women served tea. Most of the men chewed khat. A few words were spoken between them here and there. The oldest person was almost 40. He had a wide smile, and introduced himself as Tony. His English was good, despite the slight American accent. I mentioned it to him.

"It must be the movies. But not those with Arnold Schwarzenegger. His English is worse than mine," Tony laughed. And inserted more khat. A couple of hours of small talk passed, and I started becoming a little restless. I would prefer to leave Saylac before dark. The goal was to reach Djibouti on the other side of the border as there were plenty of hotels there. I asked Tony for advice, and he acted swiftly. He was clearly a fixer.

A Land Cruiser arrived a couple of phone calls and twenty minutes later. This was Africa, and no one leaves until the vehicle has been filled up. Since I was first, I got shotgun! Tony even opened the door for me and waved me in. Another twenty minutes passed, and a young fellow appeared. He had a big knife in his belt. He opened the passenger door, grabbed my collar and was about to throw me out. Tony was not having it. No one gave his mate hell!

The two men had some sort of a short fight, but Tony was both older and bigger. There was no doubt about the outcome. I was his guest, and I would sit in the front. No arguing about it! There was only one side effect. The unstable knife man would sit just behind me. I was not too happy, and I leaned forward on the entire trip. There were no seatbelts anyway.

The trip to Djibouti luckily turned out to be very uneventful, except for the odd crossing camel. The border guard from the day before was again on duty.

"Are you leaving already?"

I just smiled. And nodded.

"Such a shame. There is so much to see!"

"I am sure there is! But I have to save something for next time," I said. And blinked.

Iraq

So, I visited one dubious country with a bad reputation. Why not another? Iraq was an obvious candidate. Doctor Vodka and I were ready. Øystein had a few doubts.

"Bloody hell! It's a war torn country," he complained.

We needed to tempt my brother. A plan was made. Over a few beers in a dark pub in a shady area of Oslo.

Expedition Powder. It needed a name, and we intended to pulverize the country. The term is used in Naustdal and neighboring villages for a great party. Asbjørn and I purchased three plane tickets to Athens, and decided on the logistics. If Øystein managed to turn our plan down, he would at least suffer mentally when we were on tour. By just knowing what he would be missing out on. He should be in as much pain as he had been while we were in Afghanistan, without him. The aim was of course not to hurt my brother. Just to hurt him enough so that he would join us in order to hurt no more.

The expedition plan was sent to Øystein as a Power Point presentation. The last slide was of his ticket to Athens, with his name on it. Øystein could, as expected, not resist. He surprised us at Oslo Airport, 60 minutes before departure. The complete expedition team was intact.

We landed in Erbil in the middle of the night. Our visa was stamped into our passports two minutes later.

"Welcome to Kurdistan!"

Kurdistan is a region that includes Northern Iraq. And ancient Irbil, a small trading town that was protected by a fortress on a hill. The ruins are still there, while the town itself has expanded in all directions. We visited the ruins and got talking to an archeologist who was working there. He told us that the oldest houses were over a thousand years old. The newest part of town is in the north and comes with modern shops and restaurants. It is predominantly Christian, which in this part of the world means that they drink alcohol. A lot. Not exactly the stereotypical Christian picture we see in the West. We took advantage of the nightlife options and did not return to our flat until late at night. Everything except for the ceiling was tiled. It made the joint very cold, and the three thick woolen blankets on each bed were put to the test.

It is sad that most of us only know about the Saddam ruled Iraq. And lately that of the so-called Islamic State. Which is anything but Islamic. There is so much more. But even after all my travels, I could feel the uncertainty. The uncertainty that Iraq really was nothing but bombs and grenades. And then tourists would be easy targets. It didn't make things better that Øystein traveled with a suitcase. Small enough to go through as hand luggage on planes, but nevertheless, a suitcase. We already stood out, quite a bit. And having to carry a suitcase when we walk 10K a day for exploration purposes isn't exactly a winning strategy. He received a fair amount of well-deserved hell for his choice of luggage. He has since wisely left it at home.

In the little village of Dokan, there is a market where you can get pretty much anything from one of the little stalls. How about a complete 7 piece pan set, in a flower pattern. Or maybe bed linen in gold fabric, or anything with lace? And let me not forget a wide variety of animals, dead and alive. We were stopped by three black haired young locals next to a shoemaker's store. They explained that they were students and that they would like to practice their English. We were happy to help, and asked them about their studies, the village and the security situation in the area. After some small talk, one of the lads manned himself up. We had just told them where we came from.

"Wow! You are from Norway?"

"Yes."

The one who appeared to be the oldest took a break.

"I know something terrible from Norway."

"Really? What?"

"I can't tell you. It is really bad."

"Don't worry, we are nice people. Pretty nice, at least. You can tell us anything."

"I dunno."

"Really, you can. We won't be mad."

"Well, OK. It's...Mullah Krekar."

We were gob smacked. The man known from UN's terror list, currently residing and causing controversy in Norway, was known in Iraq too! Not bad.

"We thought he was only known in Norway."

"No, everybody in Kurdistan knows who he is. He is a horrible man. Very, very evil. Please do not send him back to us."

Reassuring, really. He was not a hated man only back home. Maybe our Secret Service were doing their research after all. A lot of people want the terrorist expelled from Norway, but he is fighting this, and has been successful for now. We spoke some more to the students, and were invited to give a guest lecture about our country in the local college the following day. With free accommodation in the student dorm thrown in. We learned that the doors of the dorm were locked between 21:30 and 06:00. To be locked up in rural Iraq wasn't extremely appealing. We politely declined the offers, but exchanged email addresses before locating a chauffeured car for hire. Sulaymaniyah next.

I have never eaten such an amazing kebab, perhaps except for in Afghanistan. They know their *bab* around here. And we are not talking about a nasty dry piece of pita bread with a fat meat mixture of unknown origin. We are talking about quality, non-defiled lamb meat, barbequed on a skewer over red-hot coals. There were no doubts between us, six thumbs up for the local specialty. Oslo kebab, never again.

First night in town, and we decided to explore the nightlife. It was however a Tuesday, so we didn't have high expectations. But there is always a bar. In Sulaymaniayah the waterholes are located in the western part. Imams and other people that do not approve of this, rule the town center and the eastern parts of town. The dark bar of our choice had one dimly lit Heineken sign, and the odd candle that sort of contributed to some sort of visibility. There were 6-7 other guests, divided on three tables. Two of them, men in their 40's came over to our table and started chatting. We asked them for more lively venues. They told us that they knew the nightlife king in town, and offered to take us to his top spot. Øystein was sensible, and went back to our hotel. The Doctor and I lack the sensible gene, and we joined them in their 4x4 vehicle. They drove us far. Very far! Out of town, and up a hill. The hill turned into a mountain, and we soon drove onto a snow covered road. We were becoming a little nervous in the backseat. A possible retreat was planned in Norwegian, should they turn out to be up to no good. Then again, we were probably 6-8 kilometers from the nearest house. We finally reached the top of the mountain. And there it was. Timberline Lodge, from Kubrick's The Shining. Or at least, a not very distant hotel cousin. A guard, or a bouncer, stood outside on a patio that was lit by a single lantern. The hotel was dark and seemed eerie. Very much so.

"This is it."

We walked through the snow, and tried to get the snow off our shoes on the patio. The inside revealed a huge ballroom and a bar. But not a living soul.

Our new friends were clearly disappointed, but managed to get hold of the manager. A bartender showed up from nowhere five minutes later. We had drinks in our hands within a minute. Cuba Libre. And suddenly a lady appeared. No one with any brain functions intact would call her anything but a hooker mama. Based on a combination of age, make-up and dress style. Or lack thereof. But she wasn't.

"Welcome! I am Arina, the dance director," she ensured us. "Would you like to see our famous dancers?"

"You mean strippers?"

Asbjørn put it bluntly. The director did not approve of his comment.

"Of course not! This is a reputable establishment. We have quality dancers from all over the world. And *no* strippers, my dear!" she said, and sarcastically stroked Asbjørn over his right chin.

We had traveled far. We couldn't just leave this strange place up in the mountains, and we decided to stay. To see the dance show. Food was even included in the 50USD. So was a bottle of Jim Beam.

"Can we get vodka instead?" Doctor Vodka asked. The bartender made his wish come true.

Less than 20 minutes later, and the dance floor came to life. 12 dancers entered it. There were five of us in the audience, including Arina. And the girls could certainly dance. The show lasted for three quarters of an hour and included a handful of dancing styles. I don't know the names of any of them.

"And they are from all over the world, you say?"

I was curious. All 12 were tall, blond and astonishingly beautiful.

"Yes, they are from Russia, Kazakhstan, Belarus and Ukraine."

All over the world might be a slight exaggeration. But who cared. We were invited to join them on the dance floor. We accepted, although I have a feeling that we didn't add much to the dance. Except for making the girls laugh. I have admittedly never attended any dance classes, and they could tell.

It was 4 AM before we were back at our hotel. Øystein was having a deep sleep. And we soon followed his example. The three of us had a late breakfast. Øystein did naturally not believe a single word about our story from The Shining. Which meant that we got hold of a taxi to show him. There wasn't much evidence there. Except for the guard from the night before. And a dog. We were not allowed to re-enter, although there were tracks in the snow. Supporting our tale.

Øystein still doubts the entire story.

Lithuania

I traveled to Lithuania with Nicole. We hadn't been there, and cheap flights gave us the opportunity to visit a new country. And why not explore Kaunas, the second biggest city after the capital Vilnius. A lot of money has been invested in the latter city, not in the first, and the contrasts between them were huge. Two foreigners walking the streets were met with suspicious looks from many of the locals. Young people were more curious than others.

"Why do you come here?"

Two teenagers on bikes had eventually found enough courage to ask us. They had been biking near us for some time.

"We're here as tourists?"

"As tourists? The only thing to do here is to gamble."

They were pretty much right. And they inspired us to give gambling a go. We entered the first casino upon arrival back in Vilnius. And decided on Black Jack. Ruta, a girl younger than us was our dealer. She was backed up by a gorilla of a man who made sure everything went according to house rules. He tried to stand discretely behind her, although that was an impossibility for a man his shape and size. We exchanged 50USD for nice shiny chips. I have a tradition of collecting fridge magnets from the countries I have visited, what would fit better on my fridge than a chip with a magnet glued on to it? I asked Nicole to sneak one into her handbag. They had hundreds of chips, and surely wouldn't notice. We played for an hour or so, before all the money had left our possession. At least we had a souvenir. Or so we thought. The body builder had full control over the chips too. He whispered something to Ruta.

"There is one chip missing. Would you happen to know where it is?" she asked sarcastically.

There was no one else at the table. Something which narrowed down the number of suspects a bit. I have never seen anyone go scarlet red as fast as Nicole. She produced the chip from her bag in a matter of milliseconds. I apologized, and we left the casino in shame.

"I have never been so embarrassed in my entire life," Nicole said. With emphasis on "never". She has since ditched the career as a chip thief, and is now a teacher. Theft is not on the curriculum.

I later purchased a normal fridge magnet in a souvenir shop. To Nicole's relief.

Tunisia

Tunisia has been a common package holiday destination since the 1960's and tourism is actually important to the country's economy. That people long to go here is understandable. It's a varied country with beaches, deserts, good food and archeological havens. The ruins of Carthage are indeed worth a visit, it was one of the biggest trading towns in the classical age. And you will actually land at Carthage International Airport if you fly into the country.

What is great is that you'll be only five minutes from town, and not much longer from the ruins. What is not so great is that the taxi drivers know that you don't know. Which means that you will pay way too much. That is a secret you may not discover until you return to the airport in a metered taxi, only to discover that you pay one twentieth of what you did when coming to town. Tunis is a big city, but the center feels small and compact. That means that any foreigners are rather visible there. Two nice guys came over to me while I was strolling down a street. They introduced themselves and asked the standard questions. Where I was from, what I did and how long I planned to stay.

"Do you want to have a drink with us?"

They seemed harmless enough, and I let them take me to what they called the best genuine restaurant in town. Genuine, indeed. It was very much a local restaurant. Forty something men sat around the room on wooden chairs. There were no women and no tourists. We were shown to a table, and given menus. But something wasn't right. The two guys, they were in their 20's, ordered beers and 4-5 courses. I suddenly realized that they wouldn't, couldn't and had no intention whatsoever of actually paying for any of it themselves. That would be their reward for showing me the joint. They were not friends, they were sharks.

"Actually, I am not very thirsty. Have a nice day."

I got up in an instant, waved to them and left the restaurant. I realized that they cancelled their orders in panic before they ran after me out on the street.

"Oh, you weren't thirsty either?"

I did nothing to hide my sarcasm.

"Fuck you, man!"

They had been revealed as con men, and they knew it. I smiled at the bogus hospitality. Before I crossed the street and walked towards a guy next to a homemade grill. The chef grilled lamb skewers on it, and I soon had a con free meal on my own. The swindlers were nowhere to be seen. I assumed that they had located another foreign victim around the corner.

My dad had said nothing about such attempted cons in his cassette distributed tales towards the end of the 1970's. To travel really is the best education out there.

Greece

He hadn't said anything about countries threatened by bankruptcy either. Broke Greece was the first country I ever visited. Norway I was born into. Mom and dad took me on a beach holiday when I was one year old. I cannot remember anything from it, although I recall a photograph. My mom was pregnant with my brother Øystein at the time, while she carried me on her back. There was a semi-crowded beach in the background. The caption read "Gunnar on the back, Øystein in the tummy."

I have since visited Athens several times, and long enough to observe that virtually everybody smokes when in bars and restaurants. I was one of 24 people in a pizza restaurant in the capital. The only one not smoking was me. The financial crisis may have knocked out the country, but clearly not the tobacco industry.

The crisis has also lead to spontaneous and untraditional ideas. Something as simple and inexpensive as a cup of coffee has now become a symbol of solidarity. If you have enough money to get by, chances are that you can afford an extra cup of coffee. Cash out for it, get a gift certificate in return and put it on a board in the coffee shop. Those less lucky than you can later pick up one of them and exchange it for the cup of coffee. The initiative was started by the street paper "Shedia" and has been rather successful in the Greek capital.

One of my visits was en route to Iraq. Doctor Vodka, Øystein and I had five hours between flights and we figured time could best be killed over a pint or two downtown. A bus got us there. We walked along the streets when I got a work related phone call. A gorgeous girl outside a bar asked the two others to join her. To say that they were hard to convince would be a lie. I entered a few minutes later and discovered that they had been given a menu and free drinks. It turned out that the beer prices were way higher than in Norway, the most expensive country in the world, and that the girl had gone. Another one that was far less attractive, as in butt ugly, came over to take our orders while a huge local 40 year old with a tiny moustache and a pinstriped suit jacket stood at the door. He was clearly overseeing that business progressed as intended.

"Free ouzo, dubious women and beer prices the wrong side of 30 dollars? You are aware that this is not a normal beer joint?" I said in a high pitch. "Yeah, something wasn't quite right," Asbjørn said. He had been too eager for a drink to notice.

"You'll walk past the grizzly bear at the door first, Vodka! This smells humbug," Øystein said. And we were out. The bouncer said something about us having to pay for the "free" drinks, but we arrogantly ignored him. Giant Doctor Vodka is a priceless friend in such circumstances. We ordered a couple of beers in a less shady joint before returning to the airport. And agreed that bars with female bait would be out of the question in the future. Acropolis and Parthenon were saved for next time.

Kosovo

You will find Kosovo a few gunshot lengths west from Greece. Kosovo is not a member of the UN, although it has been acknowledged as a country by over 100 UN members. Serbia still looks upon Kosovo as its own region, and has managed to get veto power Russia to support that view. I am however not about to let Putin dictate my list of countries too, and I count Kosovo as one of the 198 countries of the world. Crimea is not among them, either.

The newest country in Europe is not known for much but its dispute with Serbia. And for a ten meter high portrait of Bill Clinton on the side of a shabby residential building in Pristina, the capital. What I noticed in particular there were all the cafés, bars and restaurants. It is, after all, a small town with a lot of thirsty people. The atmosphere was so attractive and people so smiling and welcoming that I decided to stay a couple of extra days. Available hotel rooms were plentiful.

After having roamed the streets of Pristina, I decided to spoil myself and burn some money in the best restaurant in town: "Dinner at Tiffany's". It usually hosts quite a few foreigners, locals from the upper class and ladies in high heels not there for the food, but for the male eaters of it. You do not go to such a restaurant wearing shorts; I was reminded by numerous rude stares. And I have rarely, if ever, experienced more arrogant and patronizing service from waiters. Or a lack of interest from those of my fellow guests that wore high heels. Very high heels.

Clear and obvious criticism is rarely bad. Shorts in a restaurant simply means poor service and will do you no favors with regards to whichever sex you are interested in. At least I had an out of country gourmet experience. The chef might not have known who he was cooking for. Or he was a practitioner of non-discriminatory cooking.

Kosovo means "the field of common blackbirds" by the way. None of them were on the menu.

Macedonia

Go southeast from Kosovo, and you will enter Macedonia. Skopje, the capital, doesn't really stand out, and the locals weren't exactly looking for new friends. I don't think they were hostile or rude; it simply seemed to come down to a lack of English. It meant that I got to explore town alone, in a quiet manner.

But it hasn't always been quiet in that particular neighborhood. Alexander the Great, or Alexander III of Macedonia lived there 356-323 BC. He died at age 33, which back then was acceptably old. The warrior never lost a fight, and he is still looked upon as one of the most successful warlords in world history. That is a fact not easily forgotten by the Macedonians, in a country where masculinity is important to many. The heritage of Alexander the Great remains.

The country reminds me of the Mid West in several ways. Hunting is a much loved hobby, by many. Weapons, animal trophies and 4WD vehicles are important symbols. Something I was reminded of in a little café in Skopje. There were only 3 or 4 other people inside. One of them, a man my age was the only one who greeted me when I entered. I smiled, and nodded back at him. He invited me to join him at his table. It turned out that he spoke perfect English, although with an accent.

My coffee with milk and honey was soon brought to the table; we had already started an engaging conversation. I have never hunted, but I know a little about it from back home in Naustdal. And Dejan liked to tell stories. After some hunting related bragging he suddenly showed a softer side of himself. Or so I thought.

"Do you like cats?"

"Cats are cool. My sisters love cats!"

He laughed, and showed off perfectly white teeth. Although they had been thrown into his mouth. Real Macedonian men don't wear braces.

"I once came home after a hunting trip. I was a little bit pissed off, because I hadn't shot anything. I had even missed a couple of rabbits. Back home I was cleaning my shotgun. Then Trooper, the name of my neighbor's cat came along. It wanted to be cuddled. But I was still a little mad. I held up my gun, pointing towards the ground. And I said 'puss, puss, puss, puss.' Trooper was curious and sniffed the barrel. And then I just couldn't resist, and I pulled the trigger. Little Trooper was no more. I could only see some blood and some fur remains left on the ground."

"Bloody hell, that's awful!" I shouted.

"I know. I had to re-clean my gun."

Shocking. Most people I had already met in Macedonia had been reserved and shy. Dejan was not. He would have been, should have been, will hopefully be forcefully diagnosed. And not in a somatic hospital.

"What about the cat?"

"It died."

"Yes, of course! But didn't the neighbors miss it?"

"They probably did, but I washed away the evidence by throwing a bucket of water on the remains. Hey, it wasn't my fault that the cat was so stupid!"

I would never again see a cat without thinking of Dejan.

It didn't take me long to finish my coffee and re-enter the streets. Alone. To get my mind off less violent matters.

THE TOURIST HELLS OF THE WORLD

I have never liked holiday resorts or all inclusive holidays. Not only do westerners travel to some hot country within a given distance to the equator, we rarely even show the locals any respect with regards to their customs and culture, not to mention speak to them. And usually we travel in groups, without feeling any shame. Then again, when hordes of Japanese tourists, Germans with caravans or Eritrean asylum seekers arrive at an area near our homes, we look at them hatefully and tend to freeze them out. But when we do the same, in some hot country far away from home, then it is ok.

I also wonder why so many people switch off their own judgment and sense of adventure, and instead join package group tours. Usually led by a young guide, who'd rather be out on the piss with friends, who shows you the must-see sights and tells you carefully memorized fun facts during a strictly planned and enforced schedule, before yet again hurrying you into a bus for a repeat of the above. Instead of challenging their own curiosity and risk discovering hidden pearls or possible befriending local people.

The way of the sheep flock never appealed to me. I am too curious, too restless. And I don't particularly enjoy being governed by planned schedules that eliminate flexibility and impulsiveness. Schedules that would have made dictators proud. I rarely moralize over those drinking too much, dating too many or ignoring local customs. But I don't understand why such should necessarily be done in a group of people from back home. It eliminates the chance of experiencing something potentially unique, and exchanges it with devaluating the genuine, the real, and the outstanding.

Would you have been yourself or provided especially good service if a bus full of drunken tourists arrived on your doorstep? I become physically ill just by witnessing such behavior, even at a distance.

Then again, it is of course a blessing in disguise. That all these people tend to travel to the same destinations every holiday makes the rest of the world a better place for individual travelers like me. So let them by all means go to the resort villages and towns out there. Or tourist hells of the world, as I call them.

The Maldives

The world's lowest country qualifies. The title belongs to the Maldives, with an average height above the sea of 1.5 meters. Even tiny Tuvalu has an average of double that. The highest peak in the Maldives doesn't really stand out. Leave your climbing gear at home. It is 2.4 meters high and doesn't even have a name. You mean you still care to visit? It's on Vilingili Island in the Addu Atoll. The Maldives is famous for subsea experiences. Don't forget your diving mask.

But enough marketing of a place which doesn't need it. Merely uttering the name of the country will make many women dreaming of their top honeymoon drawl without control. This is the prototype of honeymoon hell. Yes, there are white beaches, crystal clear water and private islands. You will have your food prepared by gourmet chefs and be served the finest wines. Not to forget private jets, private boats, private water scooters and private helicopters. And your own butler. You get what you pay for, and you always pay a lot.

Quite a few do however return home rather disappointed after a week or two in "Paradise", having set them back tens of thousands of dollars.

Because they purchased dreams.

Dreams are easy to sell, hard to deliver.

The glossy marketing magazines show the most amazing things you can think of. But newlyweds tend to hit the wall after a day or three. When they have explored their luxury bungalow, politely chatted with their private butler and had a couple of swims on their private beach. There simply isn't enough to do there to keep you happy. And the other couples there are on honeymoon too, so you don't feel that you can intrude. Which means that you are stuck with one person and one person only. In honeymoon hell.

I skipped the private islands and opted for Male, a capital in miniature. I even met a couple of couples of honeymooners, couples that were tired of the private island prisons. The Muslim town comes with thriving market stalls, small shops and a number of sleepy restaurants. Just do not expect to be served alcohol. Only the private resorts have been given exceptions from the law in order to be able to continue to offer their less than perfect dreams.

I had met Myriam on Couchsurfing and we had agreed to meet up for a coffee. It was noon, and way too hot. The coffee in the shack by the stadium (there is only one) was pitch black, and on the harsh side. Myriam did not belong to the most conservative of Muslims. She sported a hijab that was hanging dangerously low on her long black hair.

"The police cannot say that I do not wear it. They can object to it not covering enough, but you know, accidents happen. 'Officer, it must have fallen down without me noticing', I tell them."

A very pleasant girl with a stunning smile. She was just too nice; she must have been interested in something more than friendship. But I did in any case have a girlfriend at home. And even if I hadn't, I would have thought thrice about hooking up with a girl from a Muslim country thousands of miles from Norway. We were talking cultural differences, Cosmo scale.

Later that day she invited me for a little drive in her knackered old Mazda. It was cooler, cool enough for the "air conditioner" to sort of work, at least.

"How fast have you driven this hunk of shit, I asked."

"Hey, don't insult my friend! He has taken me around the town in up to 90 kilometres per hour. That's as fast as he will go."

"Oh yeah? I bet that I can get him to go faster."

"How?"

"I'll drop him from a plane."

It wasn't a particularly good joke. Myriam still almost suffocated from her laughter overdose. She was luckily not driving at the time.

We said goodbye, but kept in touch. Via the internet. A girl that laughs that much from such a poor joke is in high demand. I would meet her later. She would not be wearing a hijab then.

Thailand

Thailand is often looked at as a place to swim, drink, sunbathe and not much more. It is so much more than that, although way too many package tourists are not really keen on knowing about other options. Depressingly many hail sad places such as Pattaya and Phuket as heaven. They are rather like hell.

The country is the only one in South East Asia to not have been colonized by Europeans. Something which may explain the name of the country. "Prathet Thai" means the land of the free. A proud people. With a lot of admiring tourists. The capital sees a lot fewer tourists. Although its name should be an attraction in its own right. It is the world's longest city name. The real name of Bangkok demands a reasonable amount of your time.

Krungthepmahanakhon Amonrattanakosin Mahintharayutthaya Mahadilokphop Noppharatratchathaniburirom Udomratchaniwetmahasathan Amonphimanawatansathit Sakkathattiyawitsanukamprasit – which is 2514 percent longer.

The meaning? Simply "City of angels, great city of immortals, magnificent city of the nine gems, seat of the king, city of royal palaces, home of gods incarnate, erected by Visvakarman at Indra's behest" according to Wikipedia.

A name such as Boston suddenly seems a little pale.

Bangkok was the first place I was offered a foot massage by fish and intimacy by lady boys. They are men that want to become women, but cannot afford the necessary surgery.

I accepted the first offer, the fish, I declined the second.

Egypt

I have been fooled or almost fooled in a lot of countries. Usually in Africa, unfortunately. The stereotypes seem to occasionally hold up. And in Egypt I was properly busted. Although actually not in Giza. I visited the pyramids at six o'clock. In the morning. No tourists were to be seen, and I had ample time to really admire the ancient buildings in peace. Impressive! Although, the tourists did indeed arrive two hours later. There was like a wave of them. Bus after bus after bus with tourists from all over the world swamped the area in no time just after eight. And more or less suspicious local guides and traders were busy converting tourist cash into guided tours, camel rides and souvenirs. When I rarely visit major tourist attractions, I do it at dawn.

I was conned in Cairo. As usual, when exploring a city, I walked for hours. I covered ten miles by foot on this occasion. A smiling young man invited me into a shop on a side street not far from Tahrir square. I immediately associated him with the sleazy guys trying to lure people into restaurants in France and Spain. He wanted my money, but I had no cash and wasn't worried. He had managed to get me into a souvenir shop with miniature pyramids and sphinxes. But paintings dominated the space. Typical Egyptian motives were painted on what appeared to be old parchment paper. He asked me if I liked the art. I nodded. It wasn't actually too bad. He claimed to be the painter.

"I like you. I will give you a painting."

"No, I don't want anything."

"Don't break my heart. I want you to take this one. It is from me to you. As a gift. You pay nothing," he promised and signed the bottom of it.

"What is the name of your wife or girlfriend?"

He wrote "To Haenim" in big black letters at the bottom. The writing wasn't particularly beautiful. There was no way that he had managed to paint the pictures in the shop. The 30 year old was busy conning, and in a hurry. He swiftly took up another painting and signed that one too.

"What is the name of your mother?"

"Ruth Berit."

And the con artist wrote "To Ruth Berit" underneath the new painting. He kept doing the same until he had signed five of them.

"And you will give me all of these?"

"Only the first one is a gift, sir."

"And how much for the others?"

"That is up to you, sir. I will accept whatever you and God are willing to give."

I knew that this was a scam, rather professionally done, but I felt that I had a moral dilemma. He had written the names of several of my family members on the paintings.

"I don't have any money."

"Not a problem, I take Visa, MasterCard, American Express, and Diner's Club. What do you want?"

I should just have left the building. I didn't want any paintings, but I was squeezed into a corner. He had, after all, ruined several paintings that had a certain value. And he knew that I knew. He knew his psychology. I was definitely not the first he had managed to cheat in his shop. He got 50 dollars, thanks to

MasterCard. And he still put on a show pretending to feel hurt that I offered him so little. I was pissed off with myself the next two days. It was not a matter of money; it was a matter of stupidity. How bloody annoying to fall for the oldest trick in the book.

Mauritius

There is a far smaller country with far fewer swindlers far from anywhere in the Indian Ocean. Mauritius is smaller than Rhode Island. The island nation wasn't discovered until early in the 16th century, there are now over a million people there. Which makes it the densest country in Africa.

I flew in on a scheduled flight from Johannesburg, accompanied with a lot of Bermuda shorts wearing people. I shivered. It almost felt like a package tour. They were looking forward to a week or two on the beach. Tourist bus drivers, private guides and employees of rental car companies were lining the area just outside the passport control. Most of them held signs up high. Signs with the names of individuals, families or tourist groups.

None of the buses were public; I decided to rent a car. From a sleepy man with a moustache and a colorful sun hat. I didn't expect a luxurious car and I wasn't disappointed. The white Hyundai had been around the island before, and managed the feat yet again without too many protests. I passed white beaches and was greeted by quite a few locals who waved to me when I passed them with the windows all open. The car didn't come with AC. In Africa I'll rent from Sixt next time.

The hotel I ended up at was, against all odds, run by a Swedish speaking Finnish woman in Grand Baie. She recommended that I get seafood for dinner. I have rarely tasted fresher or better dishes. In restaurants that were built literally on the beaches, with waves hitting the sand a few meters away. I wasn't in a hurry to leave. Not then.

As several of my friends back home, of unknown reasons, support Arsenal, a football club in London, I felt obliged to visit the Mauritius village that shared its name. Maybe I could find something to use against them. The village has a football stadium, although it can't exactly compete with Emirates stadium back in Europe. I stopped the car and got out next to the field. There were no seats, and only a couple of advertisement boards along one of the sides. A local man in a blue car stopped just behind my white rental, got out and walked towards me. A western tourist in the football field must have been relatively unusual.

"So are you a fan of Gunners?" That is the nickname of the English football club. I laughed.

"Well, my name is Gunnar, so I guess it must be my team," I said.

Something I could never be quoted on. Although Øyvind Vasaasen, my boss at Norwegian Broadcasting Corporation, would have liked it. He is a hard core

Arsenal fan. Which means that he automatically hates my team, Tottenham Hotspurs, intensively. The result is that I work from home every time Tottenham beats Arsenal. To avoid having my pay check slashed in an inevitable moment of rage. I have repeatedly worked from home the last few years.

The man in the Arsenal of the Indian Ocean told me that the odd soccer fan came to the village to take a photo of the signpost. But the locals were not influenced nor impressed by the name of their village. I noticed a teenager outside one of the houses. He was wearing a Manchester United jersey.

Mauritius is paradise for some. It also used to be for the now extinct dodo bird that has never existed anywhere else. The little island is too touristy to me, although a range of small roads do make it possible to find seemingly remote spots. As long as one has their own wheels, at least. Unfortunately, even these spots are never far enough from a resort. I also drove to Mahebourg, a coastal town near the airport. Where I was truly disappointed to hear someone speak Norwegian. And even the Bergen version of my language. A man in his 40's was conversing loudly with a fellow Norwegian woman.

"It is extremely annoying to travel so far away from home for some sun, only to discover that it is bloody raining. Not to mention that our football team lost. Again!"

I could sort of understand the frustration. Bergen is the rain capital of Norway.

She did not seem to share his frustration as she walked with a semi-professional Nikon camera around her neck. She was wearing a Baywatch red, but not Baywatch sexy bikini. Over-dimensioned sunglasses hid most of her face. They were not Ray-Ban, but made to look like they were. I somehow resisted the urge to say hello in Norwegian. And spun off.

Seychelles

Your own wheels are required also in the Seychelles. At least these days. A couple of hundred years back the islands were used as a safe harbor for pirates and their feared ships. One of the most famous and feared pirates was called Oliver Le Vasseur. Some people do still search for a mythical treasure he allegedly left somewhere on one of the islands.

But that wasn't why we traveled there. American Mindy and I studied Chinese together in Taipei, Taiwan. We soon decided that we liked each other. As friends. It might have had something to do with the fact that we were very competitive. In the art of telling very bad jokes. Which reminds me of the Indonesian word "jayus" which is slang for someone who tells a joke so bad and unfunny that you can actually not help laughing. Mindy in a nutshell. In 2012 she called me out of the blue.

"Gunnar, how are you?"

"Yeah, yeah, yeah. Don't ask questions you don't want answers to. It is so typical American, and you guys don't care about the answer anyway. I am great, as usual."

"At least we are polite! That's more than we can say about you rude Norwegians. Listen, I didn't call you to fight."

"Wow, that's a change."

"Shut up! Listen. Hey, do you wanna go traveling together?"

"I am never hard to ask when it comes to such. But, did you ask the only person likely to say yes, or am I the last desperate bid on your list?"

She didn't answer, but we agreed to travel together, although I demanded that it would be to a country I had not yet visited. That narrowed the selection down considerably, and we agreed on the Seychelles. It turned out that there were 500 couples there. Plus Mindy and I.

She had rented a flat. A one bedroom flat. We played stone, scissors, paper. I won, and chose to sleep on the sofa. I figured I had more experience than her in sleeping on troublesome surfaces in far-away places.

Besides, only the living room had direct access to the terrace. And the beach.

The rental car made it possible to easily get away from the worst resort hotels, even on Mahe, the main island of the Seychelles. The smaller islands should be preferred by anyone not particularly keen on being vastly outnumbered by more or less happy western couples. Some of those islands are virtually tourist free, but they still come with guesthouses that don't cost the world.

Mindy and I hadn't met in quite some time. She had decided to become a vegetarian since then. And not only that, she insisted on eating nothing but canned greens.

"I've gotta watch my figure. I am not gonna get fat!"

"You're as fat as an anorectic spider. You'll be a skinny poisoned bitch. Do you know how much metal that gets into your body when you only eat canned food?"

"I'd rather be picked up by a magnet than to be supersized, mister!"

She is an American, which means she sees a lot of propaganda, i.e. fat people, on the streets back home. And the canned food diet certainly kept her figure in shape. But it also made sure that going to restaurants was somewhat less of a social experience. There is obviously a lot of great seafood in the Seychelles. And although she joined me to lunches and dinners, I was left alone to consume the food. She had downed a can of something green in advance, and left it at that. Still great company, but not a partner in gourmet.

Mahe has almost been ruined as a destination by all the tourists. It is always possible to find nice remote beaches, but foreigners are usually looked upon as love tourists that want to be left alone. Or as bags of money on legs.

Spain

That is occasionally also a problem in Spain, especially in the parts where the number of Scandinavians and Brits are the highest. I visit Barcelona every year in February/March to attend the world's biggest mobile conference, in what is the official mobile capital of the world. It is also the unofficial pickpocket capital of the world. A colleague of mine traveled there for the first time a few years ago, and had his wallet stolen early on. While he was in the police station to report it, his hotel room was cleared out as well. So he had to return to the police station, only to meet 20 Japanese. All their suitcases had been stolen from the luggage areas underneath the bus that had taken them from the airport. By the time they had exited the 50-seater bus; half the suitcases were already long gone, stolen by fast moving locals. My colleague pledged never to return to the city.

There are also other places I tend to go back to in the country. I have friends outside Malaga. That means that I usually pop by to see Thomas, aka. Psycho Thomas, and his girlfriend Anne-Lena Løvdahl Hoff. They had enough of cold winters in Norway and moved south. To Southern Spain. Understandable from climate points of view, although I never really got why they wanted to move to the most tourist populated area on the continent. Then again, I assume that it might feel OK to be able to buy newspapers from back home in the shops, to eavesdrop on gossip from Oslo in the bakery and to be able to buy moonshine from the Norwegian countryside in certain bars.

They moved to Fuengirola several years ago. Thomas has demanded that I visit ever since. I sometimes give in. There are dozens of bars, restaurants and coffee shops by the beach there. Amistad is the odd one out, where hardly a tourist can be seen. Only residents go there to relax in the big comfy sofa on the pavement. I do too, when there. This spring was not an exception. But the transport from the airport in Malaga was. Thomas had decided, at the innocent age of 41, to get his driver's license. He met me as I left the terminal building, and we embraced in a big hug. Before we spent 15 minutes looking for the car.

"How the fuck do I know how to find my way around a parking garage? Everywhere looks the same!" he nagged.

We eventually found the bright red Micra. There was not a non-dented square inch on it. The passenger door was properly banged in.

"I've crashed a few times. Most recently when I parked it to pick you up."

"As in just now, half an hour ago?"

"Yes, this is not as easy as it looks."

He said, just as he started backing out. And crushed the side mirror on his side on a giant concrete pillar. A long and loud "fuck" followed. From Thomas' mouth, mind you. I could not not laugh. And I generally laugh a lot around Thomas. The amount of laughs have not decreased since he got his driver's license, although he has eventually acquired some experience and now drives relatively damage free. At least in low gears. Reverse is not one of them.

Portugal

Portugal comes with the same borders it has always had, it claims to be the oldest country in Europe with an unchanged shape. The southern coast has become almost as attractive to sun thirsty people from more northern parts of Europe, as Spain. No surprise, really. The coast comes with beaches but is more rugged and exciting than Spain's. I visited Portugal together with Nicole from Chile. We had driven our rental car to our hotel near the seaside. In the lobby I somehow managed to virtually crash into a former fellow student from Norwegian School of Economics. With husband and kids. And we weren't even on a package tour. But the south coast of Portugal is the south coast of Portugal. Touristy. So was the hotel. It was big and the rooms came with no sign of individuality. Neither did breakfast. Then again, who were we to complain? It was cheap and a fair distance from tourist hot spot Faro. Our solution was to drive away, far away on the hired wheels. Away from the feeling of being cattle.

We ended up driving for hours on the smallest roads that we could find. On dirt roads, roads made for tractors, paths and even a pasture. It can be demanding for car and driver to seek individualism. But also liberating. As long as you don't get stuck in the mud. A local farmer pulled us out of the dirty misery.

We had dinner late that day in a village that was divided in two by a paved road. My girlfriend and I were seated on the terrace, a couple of meters from the little traffic that occasionally passed us. The restaurant was informal, with white tablecloths made of paper and big candles in glasses that kept the wind out.

The sardine paté that comes with the bread in Portugal is usually fantastic, but in this restaurant it was divine. We continued with king prawns as a starter and fresh fish for our mains. Before sound pollution took over. A Japanese motorcycle with a made to impress engine drove past us at speeds usually reserved for sound. We noticed that both the driver and the passenger wore helmets. A giant bang followed a second or two later. A tiny Peugeot had backed out from its parking place in front of a house, less than a hundred meters away.

The bike rider had had no chance to react, and crashed into the back of the car. The bike was split in two, the driver died instantly. The lack of a head on his body gave that away. The passenger laid severely injured quite a distance from the crash site. The driver of the car, a grey haired man in his 60's was panicking. So did Nicole. She started crying. Such should not happen. Not to such young people. Not on holiday. Not during a romantic dinner. Not.

Cyprus

Cyprus was the last "new" country I would visit in Europe, and a celebration was called for. Marmite Sera from London had been invited to join, We had been flirting for some time, and she had previously proved herself as an excellent travel companion. She wasn't hard to ask.

"Will I get shot?"

"Highly unlikely."

"Cool! See you there in three weeks."

Cyprus had never been high on my list of places to visit. Binge drinking, teenage holiday alcoholics and vomiting girls had contributed to my low expectations. I selected to visit in January, with fewer package tourists than normal. And perfect timing also thanks to Sera's birthday, which called for a double celebration. We started off with a five course meal at a rooftop restaurant in one of the highest buildings in town.

"Happy birthday! This is your birthday present."

A fancy dinner is the ideal gift. Not only did I not have to prepare anything, visit loads of shops on search for something I hoped she might like. And besides, I now sort of got half of it myself. If she didn't like it, there was even a waiter to complain to. No need for that in Cyprus!

Our hotel was 20 meters from the Mediterranean. Every night we fell asleep to the sounds of waves that touched land. Sometimes gently, other times fiercely. It was January, and the waves were on the violent side on her birthday. We had finished dinner before midnight, and taken a taxi back to the hotel. But it was too early to go to bed on such an occasion. A terrace had been built partly above the sea, on hotel property. It was not in ship shape, and would probably fall to pieces in not too long thanks to the sand, gravel and rocks underneath that were being dug out by the waves. But safe enough for a bottle of midnight wine. We reckoned. And we should know after five courses with corresponding and well-matched wine. And a drink or two. And why stop there? A bottle of Chablis tastes exceptionally well outside, at midnight. Especially above the Mediterranean. That the waves occasionally licked our feet only made the date all the more special. And contributed to a memorable celebration.

The gift was received well. And I finished off Europe with satisfaction.

Belize

I always liked Belize in North America. There is just something about the name, something about it being a small country that hardly anyone talks about and that fewer have been to. Its interesting mythology only adds to the legend.

I find it somewhat peculiar that parents actively scare their kids to politeness through stories. One of them is about the thumbless midget El Duende. He is only 90 centimeters tall, lives in the forest and punishes all kids that kill or hurt animals.

Or Belize's own "Big Foot" named El Sisimito. To become a mythical figure in Belize, a handicap seems to be required. The El Sisimito creature has no knees, comes with the feet pointing backwards and eats human flesh. "If you don't go to bed, El Sisimito will come get you!" Parenting, Belize style.

But, oh was I to be disappointed when I eventually visited. And that was no one's fault but my own. Research sometimes pays off. A lack of it took me to San Pedro. Fat Americans, over-weight Americans, thick Americans. Traveling in groups. Obnoxious and nasty! I found myself in tourist hell on earth. Flock tourism had taken over the place, and there was nothing to be had except junk food and watered down beer. To make things worse, the nutrition above was ordered loudly by the rude Americans, who asked for, or rather demanded, swift service from underpaid staff. And while in the US they pay between 15 and 20 percent in tip, as a rule, here they rarely tipped at all. They even told the waiters and waitresses that they should be more thankful and smile more in return for their generous business contributions. I decided to cut my stay short. One night was more than enough.

Research would have shown me that I could rather have visited Cockscomb Basin, the world's only jaguar reserve. As in the cat, not the luxury car. Or the tallest building in the country, a Maya temple. Or to the forests to search for El Duende or El Sisimito.

The only good thing about San Pedro, in addition to the frequent boats leaving the place, is in fact the diving. More than 400 fish species live here. And you can easily get to the Great Blue Hole, one of the world's most famous diving destinations. Relatively crowded, but fantastic.

Monaco

I have visited Monaco twice, once for work. I was heading for the world's biggest mobile conference in Barcelona together with NRK colleagues Andreas, who had been stopped for speeding by the same police officer as myself in the US, and Bjarne Andre Myklebust. We had decided to take a detour to the tiny country that only borders France - and the Mediterranean.

Bjarne Andre had hired Ola, Andreas and myself at NRK. He has always been a curious dude, ready to try out everything from how much explosives that are needed to destroy a mailbox to how to make quality Champagne from cheap white wine. The latter can easily be done in a Soda Stream machine.

In Monaco we would check out one of the casinos, dressed according to local expectations, all three wearing black suits, shirts and ties. But "face control" is enforced in Monaco too, although informally and unofficially. My Zara suit did not do the trick. Neither did the small sums of money that we anticipated to gamble away. We ended up in a restaurant instead. Together with a lot of other wannabes who had encountered the same problems as ourselves. Not to mention the locals. They are also banned from gambling in their own country. Monaco is the second smallest airport-less country in the world. And a country where the visual plays an important role. The density of luxurious cars and boats is sky high. And the filthy rich usually have enough room for the first on the deck of the second. In the port of Monte Carlo I saw the wildest variants of Bugatti, Ferrari and Maserati. Parked on board yachts and in the harbor.

Curious middle class people are not all that popular in the harbor society, and I was not surprisingly asked to leave the harbor, after a little swim. By a man two meters tall, with biceps the size of lumber. I smiled, he didn't. I left voluntarily on foot. The yacht owner followed suit. In a brand new Rolls Royce.

Monaco is touristy, although in a different way. The tourists have more money in their pockets than the value of your house. I clearly didn't fit in, but I still very much enjoyed swimming in the center. The water was crystal clear. I assume vast amounts of spilled Champagne had contributed to it.

Antigua and Barbuda

I don't usually get stuck in traffic caused by walking chairs. It is hard to avoid if you walk between the cruise ship port of St. John's in Antigua and Barbuda, the casino literally on the pier and the souvenir shacks just up the street.

The island country in the Caribbean also belongs in the tourist hell on earth category. In my opinion, at least. Barbuda is luckily far less crowded, but prices there are higher and the average age of visitors is far above mine. Although not high enough to include licensed registered walking chair pushers.

I walked around the capital, and discovered that the walking chair zone ended a few streets from the port. Probably due to a slight hill and a fair distance to oxygen. Darwin had a point or two.

I started talking to a few youngsters. They asked me what I was doing there, I clearly didn't quite fit in. Something I perceived as the biggest compliment since I was asked for ID when buying tickets to an ice skating rink a few years ago. Age limit 12.

"I am a tourist, I am just sightseeing."

"But you are so young. Why do you not go anywhere more exciting?"

I displayed my teeth in what must have been a major smile.

"I am working on it. Fancy joining me at Equatorial Guinea next month?"

"Equator where? We are on the Equator, man. Chill!"

Some people are never happy. I walked down to the harbor again, and entered a casino. I should probably have felt guilty for taking all the money from a group of retired holidaymakers in Black Jack. But I didn't. I looked upon my winnings as compensation for time lost in walking chair traffic.

Barbados

"What the hell am I doing here?"

I hadn't spoken to myself since on the cargo ship to São Tomé, but it is both allowed and required in the tourist Mecca of Barbados. Where most women have hair with a shade of blue, where most drinks contain large quantities of sherry and where a lot of visitors die in hotels. Of old age.

I have been to the airport a number of times. It is the hub of LIAT, the Caribbean airline with the small propeller planes. I have however properly entered the country only once, I then soon found myself in one of the two nightclubs in the country. Just out of reach of British hearing aids you will find Sugar Ultra Lounge, in the suburb of St. Lawrence Bay which is a few kilometers from Bridgetown, the capital. The place where the young amongst us gather and ask each other what we are in fact doing. In Barbados. The country comes with eminent tap water; you can and should indeed drink it without hesitation. It is delicious! I can also mention the good bus service and a range of beaches. But there is a critical lack of people my age. At least that means it is easy to get in touch with the few of them that are there. A little bit too easy.

"How was your surf trip?" a French girl with the semi-long brown hair, cute smile wrinkles and shiny blue eyes asked me when I passed her in the bar. She proudly showed off her teeth.

"Ehe…Surf trip?"

"Doh! Yeah I saw you with your board earlier!"

I had landed a few hours earlier, without a surfboard and without any sand between my toes. Several planes had taken me there from a work trip in San Francisco, California via Dallas, Texas and Miami, Florida. Sanja had clearly mistaken me from someone else, presumably another blond foreigner. Should I let her know about her mistake, or readily exploit it?

Bailey from Chicago saved me the decision making. He was a lot better at picking up girls than me, and he had noticed Sanja's flirty tone from the other side of the bar. It took less than three minutes from the time he introduced himself until French-American liquids where exchanged above the bar. I had to smile, while sipping my Banks. It is far between attractive young girls in Barbados. Hesitation is punished by a single room.

GUINEA PIGS, DOGS AND OTHER DELICACIES

Good food is important to me. I am at the same time not afraid to experiment and to try new dishes or ingredients, however awful they sound. Which leaves me prone to the occasional date with the nearest toilet. Then again, if I do not at least taste whatever is on offer I will surely never come across new culinary treasures.

Such an approach has ensured a wide variety of restaurants and "restaurants". From paying a dime or two to the chef that roasts the meat on coal in old metal containers straight from the trash via ordinary establishments that specialize in snake meat, oysters or steak to gourmet restaurants in their own league, with or without Michelin stars.

Worms do for instance taste better than most people think; the same is the case with crocodile meat, insect crisps and dog. I can't stand licorice, though.

Marshall Islands

There is a lack of people who have even heard of the Marshall Islands. Despite it being the fishiest nation on earth, with 1,059 registered salt water fish species swimming around the 29 atolls and the 5 islands. To enter the country, as a Norwegian, you will need a visa. I soon realized that Marshall Island embassies are far apart. Junior Aini is first secretary at the embassy in the US. And I did as I was told on their website; I sent the visa application via email. But I never received an answer.

Until I politely reminded Junior. He then asked me to send my application to the ministry of immigration in Majuro, the capital. I would not have time for that, so I printed out the entire correspondence between Junior and myself, and put it in my backpack. Official looking papers usually satisfy even the nastiest looking border patrols.

It worked in Majuro airport too. Despite the particular policemen on duty. He looked mean and experienced behind his thin grey moustache and round metal framed glasses. I often wonder whether policemen stationed at borders are being trained into looking a particular way in order to scare immigrants away.

I wanted to visit the Bikini atoll, where the US once upon a time tested nuclear bombs. And where the only diveable aircraft carrier, USS Saratoga, lies on the seabed. Those not keen on witnessing that particular side of WWII will find an alternative too. Japanese HIJMS Nagato, the war ship that led the attack on Pearl Harbor, is on the bottom of the same lagoon. The Americans had their revenge.

The only problem is that the dive is so demanding that special equipment has to be flown in and transported to the site by a dive boat. Which means expenses of 15,000USD or more. My wallet would commit suicide. Besides, my basic

PADI Open Water diving license would not suffice. I skipped the entire Bikini dive plan and decided to explore Majuro and surroundings, instead.

If you love pork chops, you don't book a gourmet weekend in a Muslim country. And if you hate fish, dodge Marshall Islands. Fish is cheaper and better than any available meat product.

"And you don't even wanna think about eating in Jasmine. They serve maybe-meat."

Polan put things straight. I met him and Lloyd in Flame Tree, a combined youth hostel, bar, nightclub and pool room. Polan was not asked to elaborate what he meant by "maybe-meat," but I certainly took Jasmine off my list of future dining options.

My top restaurant experience in Majuro was in DAR, which reminded me of an old American diner. I have never had bigger sashimi portions. 20 large pieces set me back a few dollars. You can't get it fresher or cheaper anywhere, and I built up an appetite for fresh tuna while in Marshall Islands. It wasn't exclusively by choice. Most restaurants, street cafés and bars there serve the same. Always sashimi, although you can also ask to have it pan fried. I had tuna sashimi a dozen times during my four days there. Heavenly!

What really fascinates me is that the tuna is fished by helicopter. Not literally, of course, but still. Any fishing vessel of any size comes with a chopper. The pilot finds out where the tuna swims any particular day, and he directs the captain to steer his ship there. Possibly not ethically impressive, but bloody effective.

Estonia

Estonia does as a matter of fact have two independence days. People there celebrate independence from the Soviet Union on February 24, 1918. And believe it or not, the country was freed yet again from the Soviet Union on August 20, 1991. It may come as no surprise that this is one of the countries in the world with the fewest religious people. Only 14 percent claim to be believers.

Maybe they spend their time writing folk songs instead of going to churches, temples or mosques. There are 133,000 folk songs in the country. One for every ten inhabitants. A third of them live in Tallin, a harbor city with a Viking past. I visited with Nicole. We rented a small flat that was used as our base for exploration of the very well preserved old town from Hanseatic times.

There is a special and rather cool bar just outside the ancient city walls. The only music played there is by Depeche Mode, one of my favorite bands. Very cool, indeed! Although non-fans might find the repertoire slightly repetitive. We were satisfied, and hungry, after two beers worth of tunes. To find a restaurant was however not easy. The selection of tempting options in Tallin is great, and we were unable to make a decision on which one to pick. So we didn't. We opted for starters in Baltazar, which has garlic in every dish, our main courses in an Indian restaurant and desserts in a local café. Before finishing off the night in a dark Baltic bar. The experiment was in fact so successful that it kicked off a new dinner tradition. The small walks between the dishes and the variation between the different cuisines make the eating experience last longer and more exciting. The record, so far, is five dishes in as many restaurants. Not in Tallin, but in the gourmet capital of the world. No city beats Tokyo in that respect. At least not if counting Michelin stars.

The Estonian inspired way of eating comes highly recommended.

Belgium

Seriously, who has anything good to say about Belgium, without thinking about it? Except beer and chocolate. The country produces 22 kilo per Belgian per year of the latter. Then again, I guess lovers of precious stones might also have a liking for this particular country. Antwerp is the diamond capital of the world. 90 percent of the world's raw diamonds are cut and polished here. The city also has a lot of surprisingly good restaurants, although it falls way short of Brussels, the powerhouse of Europe when it comes to international politics and shameless lobbying. It is fascinating to go to expensive restaurants and just observe the neighboring tables. I usually guess on who is the lobbyist and who is the politician. The correct answer is revealed in the end. The lobbyist always picks up the bill.

I have visited Brussels quite a few times, through work. This time, I was there for a conference. There were few people I was keen on hanging with the entire evening, it ended up being just Harald and me. Harald is a ladies man from a town outside Oslo. He knows his Kamasutra and is more advanced in the kitchen than Jamie Oliver. We attended the same conference, and had shared a few beers and good company on earlier occasions.

This time, we opted for oysters. We found a restaurant on St. Catherine Square. It is one of Harald's favorite places in town and comes with a range of quality seafood restaurants. Lobster, crab, oysters, cod, salmon and halibut; you name it. Something as unusual as an outdoor oyster shack can even be found there, but it was unfortunately too chilly outside. It would have been quite an experience to go for takeout oysters, the first time I have seen such. The only thing missing was a drive-through. But our pick of the evening came with a ceiling. And temperature fit for two Norwegians on tour. Well inside, and Harald started telling me about oysters.

"You are aware that oysters are among the sexiest things you can serve a woman?"

The topic came as a surprise. We had never discussed much but work, beer and football before; although I had picked up that he had been around the block when it came to girls. It turned out that I had signed up for story night. He started on a long tale. Over a bottle of bubbles and two slim glasses. He told me about Kari, a girl he had been flirting with for months, and whom he finally had been invited home to.

"I had picked up 36 oysters, herbs, white wine, butter and onions and I was certainly in an upbeat mood when I pressed the doorbell outside her flat. I was about to give her something she had never had before. But bloody hell, I almost collapsed when she opened the door. High heels, black stockings, an indecently short skirt and a see through blouse," Harald smiled. He could still picture the moment, while he told me the story. Presumably one of his favorites.

"I enjoy bossing around the kitchen, and she had to accept that I immediately owned it. The looks she sent me were so flirty, I could barely stand still. Now, I will explain how I prepare oysters, I heard myself say. An oyster is so good, so beautiful, and so feminine that I refer to it as a she. I was at it. There was no turning back, and I kept going. You know that I have taken my time to pick only the best. That is why I am here with you, I said. Let me explain how this is best done. I held firmly around her. As in the oyster."

He just had to specify.

"I look at her, study the uniqueness. Every oyster is different, unique and beautiful. I get ready to make my move, and then she has lost. While I hold her tight, I place my tool, a blunt oyster knife, towards the place where I know she is the weakest and where she will open for me."

Harald gesticulated while talking.

"When I have decided that I want inside her, I press the knife through the opening and I twist. A little bit of a tip, and she can be opened. Her juices flow out, and she lays naked in front of me in my hand. I enjoy the sight of the most intimate details, and she has lost. She is mine forever."

I couldn't help interrupting.

"Seriously, Harald! That's just totally sleazy!"

He just laughed. And continued. He was virtually inside his own story, and he talked as if in a trance.

"Don't interrupt! When she has been opened, the next operation awaits. She will be placed on her tummy, with her back towards me so that most of the liquid will drip off her. I turn her around after a bit and put her on her back. That is when she blots her little mussel for me, and I can touch it with my finger. It is very sensitive and immediately withdraws when I touch it. I then put her on a bed of beautiful silver foil and pour the delicious liquid inside. Made by white wine, cream and herbs. I fill her up to the edge so that she cannot take anymore. Finally she will be properly heated and baked in the glowing hot stove until she is done and again ready to be united with me. In my mouth. I swallow her in one piece. Kari had just been standing with a smile on her face next to me. 'Lovely', she said. 'Do that to me too!' The kitchen alarm clock was the only thing that prevented the oysters from becoming severely over-baked. The oysters tasted delicious, and they disappeared very fast. So did we. To the bedroom."

Harald finished with a grin. The Champagne bottle was half empty, and the waitress was ready to take our order. Oysters, naturally. I ordered mine as they were picked up from the sea. Harald wanted his prepared in a special way and started explaining just how to the pretty waitress.

I went to the restroom.

India

Bad oysters can cause serious food poisoning. But India is the mother of unruly tummies. The gigantic country deserves collective punishment for uncountable food poison victims. Øystein worked as a marketing manager in Chennai for six months. He claimed that between 70 and 80 percent of all foreign tourists in the country experienced runny asses. With various amounts of pressure and coverage. This liquid side effect is one of the few reasons not to visit India.

I was invited to a wedding there in 2001. A friend from university was marrying her carefully selected man and we would celebrate for four days. I took the opportunity to first go there on holiday together with Heidi. We traveled to Mumbai and explored the metropolis by foot, taxi and cockroach. The small yellow and black motorcycle taxies with a roofed three-seater on the back are named after the hated creature, as they totally look the part when observed from above. They zig zag through traffic just like hyperactive cockroaches.

A few days full of impressions later, we headed for Goa. We were aiming for walks on the beach in fresh air. We were told it would take us eight hours, by train, to get there. Food was therefore needed. Toilet paper is unfortunately not among the items found in a modern India; most people use their left hand as a substitute. This seems to also apply to waiters and chefs. A meal in what seemed an acceptable restaurant turned out to make our train ride unforgettable. Both of us threw up before entering the train car. Before our tummies exploded. The toilets in third class on Indian trains are holes in the metal floor. I was standing in a jockey position while disposing of, what had recently been a curry, through both exits. I have never ever felt closer to dying. That the train was eight hours delayed due to a train accident ahead of us didn't exactly help, either. We were not up for swimming or any kind of beach activities in Goa. Had I possessed the contact details of the guy who did not wash his left hand that particular day in Mumbai, he would have been no more. We flew Jet Airways back to Mumbai. The train ride there had somehow scarred our minds forever, and we were willing to pay top rupee to forget.

My tummy wasn't back to normal until five weeks later. And it would take several years until I stepped on Indian soil again. Then together with my brother

Håkon, my sister Kjersti and my girlfriend Nicole. We were going to visit my other brother Øystein in Chennai.

What he did not know was that his wife Benedicte had also joined. She could not officially afford it or even manage to get time off from work, but had in secret purchased a ticket. Lufthansa had an offer she could not resist. Our homesickness present to Øystein, famous Norwegian brown cheese and a cheese cutter had been taken from us by useless security personnel in Germany. They feared that the cheese was a chemical weapon and that I would slowly cut one thin slice at a time from the pilot's head while forcing him to crash into the nearest skyscraper.

En route to Chennai, Benedicte planned on what to tell Øystein when she would surprise him. They had not seen each other in three months. We came up with more or less creative suggestions.

"How about 'I have traveled farther than far. Would you like to come back to my hotel room?'"

"Well, a little too long," Benedicte said.

"Or, 'Around the world just for you'?"

"Better, but no cigar."

Håkon, Kjersti, Nicole and I were sparring partners. There were no clear winners, despite a variety of suggestions. Benedicte would have to say whatever she decided on saying on impulse.

We tested sending a text message between our phones while waiting for the luggage. None of us had been to the airport before, so the layout was new to us, and we could not possibly know where Øystein would be waiting. The text message came through in ten seconds. Perfect! We agreed that I would send Benedicte a message as soon as we had found Øystein and made sure that he would not look towards the airport exit.

As said, as done. We hugged our long lost brother in a careful manner. We could not risk that he would accidentally see his girlfriend. She got her electronic message while Øystein was hugging Kjersti.

"Come!"

Benedicte had spent uncountable hours on what she could tell Øystein when he suddenly saw her far and away, but it all ended up with a long "Heeeeeeyyyy!" before Øystein's response, an extremely surprised and equally long "Noooooooooooooo!" before it transferred into a kiss. It was all even captured on film, showing a man totally taken by surprise. Before a mutual state of happiness.

We explored large parts of southern India together, including beautiful Kerala. Øystein had been advised by his local colleagues and made an eminent itinerary. He just had to improvise a little when it came to arranging an extra double room in a hotel. There was no room for her in the tiny apartment he shared with some colleagues.

We also rented a boat with crew and our own chef in the backwaters of Kerala. The food was amazing and we really managed to find peace on the long narrow wooden boat. Håkon introduced crime to the area when he showed them how to steal coconuts from palm trees. The computer-wiz has a talent for climbing logs. It was his first trip abroad without our parents, and he really got the taste for travel to untraditional destinations. He later passed on the favor to his girlfriend Rebecca. She is from Albany, New York.

Guatemala

I hardly knew anything about Guatemala before I visited. Except that it is a little bit bigger than Iceland, but has 50 times the number of people. Iceland can however brag about more volcanoes, the country has six times more than Guatemala. And infinitely many times more rotten shark. There is however more to Guatemala than that.

The flag has a blue stripe on each side and a white with the country's coat of arms in the middle. The blue stripes represents that the country is between two bodies of water. And Guatemala means "The country with many trees" in one of the Mayan languages. There are also a range of forest reserves there.

It is less known that chocolate was discovered by the Mayas in Guatemala. They should have patented it. As well as the jeans that they also claim to have invented. The Mayas were a clever bunch. Mathematics was important to them, and they are alleged to have been the first to start using the concept of zero. It is unknown how football matches were played prior to that.

More than half the people in the country are descendants to the Mayas. They are proud of the fact, and can often be seen in traditional national costumes at important parties. Such celebrations have a tendency to go a little off the rails, and every Christmas several people are killed by returning bullets that have been fired into the air as a part of the celebration. The risk is low, but you may want to wear a helmet.

I didn't need one when I drove into Guatemala from Honduras in a huge pickup truck I had rented in El Salvador. The village of Esquipulas was my first stop. It is the home to only 50,000 people, but it is known as the second most visited town, after the capital. That is primarily due to pilgrims coming to see Black Christ, El Cristo Negro. It is not a person, actually just a metal statue of Jesus on the cross. The metal turned black, unknown to man why, following the production of the statue by a local artist in the 1500's. Hence the name.

My visit was less noble. I was hungry for lunch. There were a range of food stalls in the local market. I scouted for something tempting. An old lady sitting in one of the stalls commanded me to come over to her. There was no question about obeying or not. She did not even speak English, it was just something about the way she spoke, I would eat there. Full stop.

Mexican food is getting the fame in the region, but Guatemala does certainly also deliver. It is based on the cuisine of the Mayas, and the diet contains a lot of corn, beans and chili. *Tamales* is a favorite, some sort of a burrito with tomatoes, vegetables, chili, herbs and meat. I can't be much more specific, there are hundreds of kinds of tamales. Red, black, with corn, with potatoes and with rice. Plus mini tamales. To name a few. I am not sure which one I was served in the market, I just know that it tasted heavenly. The old lady, the chef, was carefully monitoring my eating. I gave her thumbs up with an accompanying smile several times, she responded by nodding and a big toothless smile. She also served me what I thought was chicken stew, but she just shook her head at my "pollo?" question. It was rooster. *Gallo en chichi* also tasted great!

I thanked her so much for the food and tried to pay. By quetzal, the local currency. It is also the name of a little bird, the national bird of Guatemala. The Mayas did supposedly use the feathers of it as their currency back in the days. The old lady was not accepting my quetzals, she was in fact not having any of my currencies. And she was as stubborn about it as when commanding me to eat her food. Being a tight guy from the Norwegian West Coast I didn't protest for too long.

South Africa

I had dreamt about visiting South Africa for years. A lot of it thanks to René Smith who I studied with in Falmouth. We were two of the three foreigners in our year, and we got along great. Despite me not being a huge fan of theoretical studies, while René and Adrian were among the very best. I compensated in practical work. Unfortunately the theoretical aspects of the course counted for 75 percent of the grade. I have no idea how I passed.

René had brought her friend Donna Claire Arend, a sporty girl who I immediately got on well with. She was going through a divorce and had her hands full selling the house and splitting up everything. Working in an international bank, she traveled a lot to Europe on business. We were to eat in Sophiatown, a combined restaurant, bar and lounge, in Johannesburg. The unusual venue was charming but simple and came with both indoor and outdoor seating. Sophia provided an untraditional menu and a live band too.

Semi normal dishes like ostrich, crocodile and squid were among the menu selections. Norwegian cuisines had a hard time topping any of those, but both René and Donna Claire were rather impressed by the sheep head dinner tradition from the Norwegian West Coast.

"Have you tried worms?"

I asked. "Worms in chili sauce" was listed on the menu.

"Yikes! Hell, no! Is that another Norwegian 'delicacy'?"

René occasionally shows an interest in sarcasm.

"It's on the menu here. In this restaurant. In your country. And you haven't tried it? That's an absolute disgrace. Isn't it painful to be South African, yet not have eaten worms?"

They laughed.

"I will take you out of your agony. I'll order worms, and you can have your worm debut right here," I said and delivered on my promise.

Worms. Should they be fried? Boiled? Baked, even?

The special dish soon arrived. Worms marinated in white wine, onions and garlic. With a chili sauce on the side. The worms were a lot thicker than the worms I have seen, played with as a kid and used as bait when a little older. And they were black. Mopani worms, allegedly. What a texture. And a relatively neutral taste. Not particularly delicious, but far better with the chili sauce.

René and Donna Claire also tried half a worm each.

"Congratulations, girls! It's just a little worrying that it takes a Norwegian to introduce you to this gourmet dish."

"Shut up!"

None of us have ordered worms again. Despite the extreme percentage of protein.

China

Only France, the US and Spain have more foreign tourists per year than China. That should not come as any surprise, really. No country has a longer border to watch than China. Or to quantify, tourists can cross 22,117 kilometers of borders from 14 countries. Only Russia borders as many.

I got talking to one of the cabin crew on a half empty flight to Shanghai.

"We call China flights cup noodles and hot water flights. That is all they ever want."

It may beat the alternatives. Plane food certainly has its limitations.

I have visited China repeatedly, and I am very fond of the food and the culture. But the food must be eaten at restaurants in China; Chinese restaurants outside the country's borders do not deliver the real deal.

There is one part of the Chinese culture that is non-existent. Queue culture. Of course, if you are one of 1.3 billion people to only think of yourself and your immediate family might be a good excuse. There are, after all, 160 cities with over a million people in China. There are only ten in the US.

In some cases different rules apply to westerners. On a study trip to Shanghai I managed to sprain my ankle. Or so I thought. I woke up in the middle of the night, after a dance move gone wrong. The pain was unbearable and my ankle had doubled in size. I then figured it must actually be broken, and I managed to hop to the bathroom and put cold water in the dustbin to cool it down. Early in the morning I hopped to the elevator and managed to get to the lobby. A young man from the hotel staff took me to the hospital in a taxi. I was first waved into an office, allegedly because I was a foreigner. There were no doctors there, only a cashier. I had to pay 15USD. For a VIP card. Which turned out to be an eminent investment. With the piece of plastic in hand, I was lead through a range of hallways through several buildings. We were going for an X-ray, the helpful hotel guy told me. He was patiently following me around. My mood had a downward turn when we came around the last corner. There were approximately 30 people in the queue. All of them were local, two of them had brought goats, and several of the others had arms and legs tied up in scarfs or home-made bandages. This would take forever! But my newly acquired VIP card did the trick. I was waved past everyone by the doctor who was walking with us. I tried to protest, a lot of the people in the queue were surely much worse off than me, but to no avail. I was pushed into a new room. A middle aged Chinese man was sitting on the prehistoric X-ray machine. He was literally pushed off the machine, and I was told to get on it. The X-ray showed no signs of a fracture, but I was given some strong painkillers. They certainly worked. I still don't want to know what was in them.

I always try whatever strange I came across on the menus when I am in China. With that amount of people it may not be so strange that some of them eat the unthinkable. How else could they feed everyone? The most peculiar thing I tasted still wasn't worse than dog meat. A little Chi-chi, apparently. Dog meat is tasty and healthy, but not very exciting. The head turner being that we in the west usually think about dogs as friends, with names. The story about my dog eating has at least made a lot of people very angry. I have, although, not eaten cat meat. If I had, I have some sisters that would have denounced our family links. The cat, not the cow, was holy back home.

My first visit to China took place in the late 90's. Heidi and I were to take a bus to the biggest city in the country from Tsingtao. They called it a small coastal town. In China, that means the population of Los Angeles and Phoenix. Combined. The bus was supposed to take 8 hours, it took 20. And we were then accompanied by live pigs, huge bags of rice and a sleazy old man who only knew three words in English.

"I love you!"

Heidi wasn't the only one who experienced the pleasure. He repeated himself at least 20 times throughout the journey, and as often to me as to her. I had a hard time producing any jealousy.

With three hours to go, we had to change modes of transport, and we decided to have breakfast while we were at it. Boiled rice and eggs. In no time, half a circle of almost 20 people stood around us, just watching us eat. They could hardly ever have seen white people before, at least not breakfast eating ones. We felt like celebrities. A Kodak moment, but with no one to do the shoot. To travel in the Chinese countryside certainly is different. No one speaks English, and people feel no shame. Then again, the same applies to certain parts of rural Norway. Heidi told me about a friend from university who had invited her boyfriend, his parents and two of his siblings on a bus trip to certain outskirts in China. They encountered particularly bad food poisoning, and all had to go to the loo at once. At the bus station they were at, there were only unisex facilities. That meant a long bench with eight holes in it. Next to each other. Without walls in between. Five adults and two teenagers sitting next to each other in a synchronous blowout session.

"My friend and her boyfriend broke up after that particular holiday. She felt that the exposure to her family-in-law had turned too intimate, intense and smelly," Heidi said.

We laughed together.

Argentina

A cousin of my dad had a prominent position in a Norwegian owned company in Buenos Aires, Argentina and he had promised to show Nicole and me around. He had told us that we would be picked up at the airport. We were. By a private chauffeur with a Sr. Gunnar Garfors sign. Awesome!

Dad's lovely cousin met us in the lobby of the hotel before taking us to a restaurant nearby. It was large and simple. The temperature indicated that we would be eating outside, sitting on plastic chairs and eating from a plastic table underneath a Coca-Cola parasol.

"It might not look like it, but this is the best steakhouse in town. And that says a lot, we are in steak country - number one in the world. This place isn't pretentious, the food is always top class, the staff is very friendly and they definitely know their food," he said.

And he knew his way around the gourmet scene of Buenos Aires. His company was owned by one of Norway's richest men, who he had dined with several times. At those occasions the price level of both steak and wine had been many times higher. Then again, to choose a fancier restaurant over this might not be a smart move. I have eaten amazing dinners since then in Michelin star restaurants boasting one, two and three stars, but the brick sized ultra-tender steak still is the best I ever tasted. Heavenly, and then some!

But why is Argentinian steak so good? I asked the head waiter via translator Nicole.

"It takes a lot longer to prepare the steak here than in Europe and the US, and we cook it on a wood fired barbeque, not a gas fired one. The top must also be made of ceramic, not metal. Otherwise the heat will not be sufficient," he explained.

But that was only the end of the story. The meat also needs a good start.

"The cattle need exercise! While you gringos let the cows stand inside to chew dried grass and artificially produced "cow feed", we let them roam around on the Pampas to eat fresh grass, good grass. They are happy. And please, with a hug thrown in, ditch the awful antibiotics!"

I didn't get what he said, but he was certainly really into his story. Nicole's translation lacked quite a bit when it came to articulation.

Lebanon

Beirut in Lebanon is a Mecca of nightlife, but do not let me forget about the food. They for sure know their way around the kitchen in this Mediterranean country, and they know it. You can feel the pride in many of the best restaurants, and the chefs often come into the dining room for a chat with the guests and to check that the waiters have done justice to their dishes.

The tastes of fresh vegetables and newly slaughtered poultry, lamb and goat. The olive oil, the herbs, the garlic and the lime juice. All the small dishes. My waiter asked me what I wanted. The menu was huge. I browsed through it and decided in a flash.

"Whatever you recommend, sir! And as many courses as you think I can eat."

Not a ground breaking order, but the waiter lit up in a big smile. It was just a little tip I had gotten from Thomas in Spain, the ex-waiter.

"If you really want the best, let the kitchen decide. They know what is fresh and what is good, and you give them a challenge. A la carte is boring, it's routine."

He explained with passion. As usual. The Thomas trick resulted in hummus, home-made yogurt, pepper steak, pickled vegetables, and okra stew with lamb, chicken *shawarma* and peppers filled with goat cheese. Before *baklava*. And I have probably forgotten something. I got at least ten different mezze.

Following my memorable meal, I tried to walk out on town. But where is the carrier chair when you need it? I needed a long stroll to walk off some of the food. The nightlife just had to wait. It is primarily in the northern part of town. The bars, pubs and night clubs are impossible not to see, almost to walk straight into. And then chances are that you will remain there. The hospitality is legendary and local bar patrons are always curious about foreign visitors. However, the best experiences are always found in narrow side streets or back alleys, in the underground bars and clubs. Where you can really chill. If chill is drinking, dancing, talking and taking part in havoc until four o'clock the next morning.

Jonathan was a member of the Hells Angels, I was sure of it. With a long braided beard, fully tattooed arms, cowboy boots and a leather jacket. But he didn't quite fit the stereotype. I cannot remember having seen a single non-white

Hells Angels' member ever before. He sat at the bar; I sat on a stool by a round table a few meters away. I had sipped my beer, and was reading The Economist. "Fancy a toast, educated guy?"

I must have looked a little lost when I looked up from the magazine. Or the newspaper as the weekly publication likes calling itself.

"Sorry?"

"You are sitting alone. I am sitting alone. That's fucking stupid, isn't it? Would you mind drinking with me?"

"Sounds like a fabulous idea. Who are you?"

"My name is Jonathan. And I am not a member of the Hells Angels. Before you ask."

"Really? You totally look the part."

"I know. That's the idea. I like challenging stereotypes."

Jonathan lived in Beirut, but had studied a few years in Ireland. It was easier to get accepted there, he claimed. The Lebanese now lectured at a university in Beirut.

Our conversation covered various subjects. About Norway's role in the Israel-Palestine conflict. About The Economist compared to Newsweek compared to Time Magazine. About people reading such magazines in public and whether they did so because they were interested in the content or whether they just wanted to look interesting enough for other people to reach out to them. About how well it had worked if the latter had been the case. About why old men like dressing up. About how that might just be a method to get closer to people. About Kilkenney, Guinness and Heineken. He hadn't heard about Hansa, the Norwegian beer.

Romania

Romania has the biggest parliament in the world; the palace that much hated Nicolae Ceaușescu had built during his reign. It is 86 meters high, but comes with 92 meters below ground too. Ceaușescu was killed on December 25, 1989 during the Romanian revolution that started in the town of Timisoara eight days earlier. That's where I met Flory years later. The revolution marked the end of communism in the country, and made a strong impression on her, even though she was a little girl back then. She lived in Sibiu, a medium sized town not far from Transylvania, the roaming grounds of Dracula. Bram Stoker's novel from 1897 is about Duke Dracula's attempt to move from Transylvania to England. But there was actually a real Vlad III Dracula who lived in the area in the 1400's. Legend has it that he killed up to 100,000 people. Flory wasn't too keen on the focus on Dracula, but appreciated the much needed tourism that it brought to the area.

"People should come to Transylvania for the beauty, not for the beast," she said.

I agree. The castles on the mountain and hill tops are impressive and surrounded by mystique. Although the latter is primarily thanks to Stoker.

Flory and I traveled to Sibiu where I got to meet her Polish boyfriend. We all had dinner together in a nice restaurant by the square in center of town.

"You have to try *cărnați*, our famous sausages. And *ciorbă*, our famous sour meat and vegetable soup. And *jumări*, the famous dried pork."

"You sure eat some famous food here. There is no way that I can eat all of this!" I replied, and smiled.

Flory was over the top enthusiastic when it came to introducing a foreigner to local cuisine. She had given up on her boyfriend's eating habits a long time ago.

"You should come to Poland, we have no famous food. But it is good," he uttered quietly.

Flory's revenge came when he was in the bathroom. I got the truth about his language.

"Polish is like a broken radio."

She clearly hadn't heard about DAB radio, the new digital standard being rolled out on four continents.

They later showed me the nightlife in the town famous for its culture and festivals. Quite a few of the basements from the Middle Ages had now been converted to discotheques. And the acoustics there did no one but ear doctors and manufacturers of hearing aids any favors. I have never heard louder music anywhere, and I have been out on the town in a few places.

Romania is like most Eastern European countries when it comes to nightlife. The girls dress very sexy. The goal is to be noticed. Flory accomplished that with style, and her boyfriend proudly held her on the dance floor. I decided to leave them to it. The volume was just unbearable.

Dominica

There is a lot of noise on board the propeller planes of LIAT too. I landed on the short runway in Dominica relatively early at night, but it is dark in the Caribbean as soon as the sun has set. My hotel was only two kilometers away from the airport, and I decided to walk. It was as dark as the inside of a coffin six feet under, and I eventually regretted not having taken a taxi. Only the sound of waves to the left and the firm feeling of the hard top on the road helped me manage it all the way to Father's Place. The guesthouse has been named after the late dad of the two sons now running the place. A German friend of the family and me were asked to join them for dinner, in Pagua Bay Bar & Grill a few kilometers away. We were there in a matter of minutes in a huge 4WD.

"Brad Pitt eats here." One of the brothers proudly proclaimed.

He didn't say anything about how often. Rumor has it that Dominica has turned into an island for rich and famous people that want some peace and quiet

among unspoiled nature. I don't blame them. The paradise fe
almost touched. That the airport is big enough to take down
small for big commercial jets, is a plus.
"How about Angelina Jolie?"
Pitt's wife was more interesting, I thought.
"We never saw her. But once he ordered two take-away r
They sure like their conspiracy theories in Dominica.

Ecuador

My mom has traveled to Ecuador yearly for quite some time. She teaches aid and traveling courses at a folk college in Norway, and takes her students to visit prisons, schools, orphanages and other institutions. These always have a much lower standard than at home, and helps the youngsters open their eyes a little. They are required to stay with host families, and get to see how things work or how they don't work at all. In Ecuador. The first country in the world to have included the rights of nature and the ecosystem as part of their constitution.

My mom's students always have to eat guinea pig, or at least taste it. Grilled guinea pig or hamster looks bloody awful. The teeth are bare, and the head looks like it comes straight from Alien with Sigourney Weaver. The body itself looks a little like a barbequed chicken. Mouth-watering! I had already heard quite a few stories about guinea pig consumption performed by Norwegian folk college students. The tales involved vomiting, crying and threats of lawsuits.

I had to try! Quito was well suited. There is a great selection of restaurants, youth hostels and various kinds of joints in Mariscal, the fun part of town. People had already started drinking when I arrived just after lunch on a Friday. And they were pretty much hammered by the time I got back, after walking around for a few hours. I wasn't there to drink, though.

I entered one of the better guinea pig restaurants in town. I had, for once, done a little research. The full bodied guinea pig came with a healthy looking salad on the side. It didn't taste too bad. There wasn't much meat inside, and the texture was somewhere between that of fish and chicken. Form over content. As with Ola's sheep heads. It is more the mere thought of eating what looks awful that scares them than the actual meat. Which many may not even try. It doesn't taste fantastic, but OK enough for everyone to try a little. Sheep heads on the other side actually taste very good. Ola's at least. I haven't tried anyone else's.

Mauritania

My trip to Mauritania started in the idyllic coastal town of Saint-Louis in Senegal. I was on the bus that was all set for departure to the border, and it had finally filled up. 30 big sacks of various food produce had been loaded and secured on the roof, and everyone was ready to get going. Except for the engine. It did not

n the first, second or 90th attempt. To push start it was also a waste
and the local mechanic could pull no rabbits out of his tool box. We
d a new bus, and all the sacks were thrown from one roof to another. The
re bus shook every time a new sack hit it. I was waiting for it to collapse
altogether, but somehow it didn't.

We finally arrived at the border river late at night in bus number two, too late
for the ferries to still be crossing the Senegal anymore. That meant an overnight
stay on the border check point, a little police station near the river bank. I
managed to occasionally power nap sitting on the concrete outside, only to
abruptly wake up every time a mosquito came dangerously close to one of my
ears. That particular sound is incredibly discouraging, especially in malaria prone
areas.

The police officers finally woke up, opened the station and stamped me out of
their country. They did the same with Emmanuelle King, or Issa as the pleasant
guy from Sierra Leone called himself. The self-declared businessman was on his
way to visit his brother in Morocco. But first, some business awaited in
Nouakchott, the capital in Mauritania. We got talking.

"What? Have you been to my country? Why?" he almost shouted. Issa soon
managed to get over the shock, as we took the ferry together. A few travel stories
later, and he had a nickname for me.

"Hey, Mr. Move-around. Let's have breakfast together on the other side."

Crossing the river on the long narrow wooden boats was fast, and I had no
problem crossing the border there either, my visa had been sorted out in Dhakar.
Emmanuelle on the other hand had big problems and I told him that I would
wait outside so that we could dine together. Half an hour passed, and no
Emmanuelle. I called him, told him that I couldn't wait any longer and that he
would have to call me back when he finally got through.

I stopped at the first and best restaurant in the border town of Rosso. A thin
local man grilled goat skewers over coal in half an old oil barrel. I asked for three
skewers, and was instantly served white bread on my table under a blue parasol
ten meters away. The goat meat arrived a minute later, dazzling hot. White lumps
of fat where placed in between the pieces of meat. I am not a big fan of pure fat,
so I left them on my plate and walked over to pay. The pieces of fat had
disappeared before I reached the man by the barrel. Three street boys 10 years of
age had jumped to the table and swallowed the fat as fast as they could manage.
Their thin bodies were clearly in need of nutrition, and they had just had it served
on a plastic plate.

It soon became hot in Rosso. Very hot. Luckily, the market place there was
covered by big sails. The shade was much appreciated, and I spent quite some
time there. The selection wasn't great, the break from the sun was.

I didn't hear from nor see Emmanuelle again that day. But I did weeks later. Via email. I had given him my business card. It was pretty much straight forward. He was trying to swindle me outright, Nigeria style. A guy I had actually met in person. He sure had some nerve. Surprisingly enough, given his smiling and polite manners.

"Hello my dear friend,

I has some amount of money befor my coming to Morocco that i send thrue diplomatical channel, now i have some problem to resiv this money, i wanted if you can help me i will give you some parsentag, this is a money my father took in the time of war in my country.

My father can not leave the country for any international investment, There is 15 million US dollar, that my father kept in a conservetions box, in West Africa securarite company.

This conservations box has been in the company for long time, now my father is sick, he cant able to even work, so he told me about everything about this money. this money is not yet in my hand, i have some tax to pay to the company and i will offer you ten pasent. It is not easy for me."

We have not agreed on any new breakfast meetings.

DRINKING AND PARTYING

A party without alcohol is a meeting. Or so the saying goes in Mid Norway. Although all drinking stories do not include alcohol. People in different parts of the world drink this and that given the time of year, the situation, their faith and other contexts.

Sharing a bottle of wine or having a couple of beers may be a great way to help some people socialize. And Norwegians clearly need it more than anyone. We aren't rude, really. Only shy. Alcohol is the social glue that helps people get in touch with each other easier, establish friendships and maybe do stuff or go to events together.

I am not going to reach speedy conclusions, but I have also seen that alcohol can reduce tension. In for instance Swakopmund in Namibia. There is still a big difference in where people go out. The whites have their own pub, the blacks have another one. At least until around midnight. Alcohol has intruded into people's blood streams, and segregation suddenly seems like less of an issue. There were all of a sudden white people in the "black" nightclub" and black people in the "white" bar.

The social aspect related to alcohol may be the easiest to notice, especially while traveling. I have often been approached by people who've had a few glasses. Many of them would otherwise never have built up the courage to talk. Although it of course also happens way too often that people drink too much, approach me for the wrong reasons or become violent.

Everything in moderation. And especially while abroad. You do then not know the culture and may not wish to insult the locals or be easy prey for people with less noble purposes. Western people on group holiday already have a bad reputation. There is no reason to add to it.

South Sudan

The world's newest country became a UN member in July, 2011. And it all kicked off with a huge party all over the country. I was planning to attend, but the Sudanese embassy in Oslo wasn't having it. They refused to issue me a visa.

"We don't do that, they claimed."

Working hard for the service of the year award, clearly.

They rather passed me over to a travel agent in Oslo. No one picked up the phone on my first, second or third attempt. So I skipped Sudan and South Sudan. For the time being. I would in any case have had to get a Sudanese visa and enter Sudan, then go to what would become South Sudan and wait for it to become its own country. When that happened, and the celebration would be over, I would have had to leave South Sudan, a country I had never officially entered. There would of course have been a transitional period to cater to such cases, but it shows the difficulty of traveling somewhere which turns into a country while you're there.

I traveled there the following year, instead. To Juba. The selection of hotels wasn't among the greatest I have experienced, and I decided to screw my travel budget for the time being. Donna Claire, René's friend from South Africa, had also decided to join on short notice. She had never been to any other country in Africa than her own. To ease the culture shock a first time traveler to the real Africa, I opted for what was supposed to be the best hotel in the country, with a swimming pool and all. It was unfortunately not very central, but unparalleled use of motorcycle taxis to and from the center of town solved that particular problem. The establishment was run by James, an eccentric Brit who could brag about a fair amount of rather original guests. There were ambassadors and their wives, embassy workers, owners of security companies, salesmen and some employees of NGOs.

"So what do you do in South Sudan?" James asked while checking us in.

"I am a traveler. We're here as tourists."

He went totally quiet.

"No, really."

"I am. I love traveling," I reassured him.

James started laughing. At the volume of jet engines. One of the guests who ran a Blackwater inspired security company came over to see what was up.

"Alan, this fella says he is a tourist. Hahaha…hahaha…hahaha."

Another laughing spree started, now in stereo.

"You're not fucking kidding me, are you? I have been here for five years. I have never seen a bloody tourist. Are you out of your fucking mind?"

James swore a lot. It is more or less a necessity unless you want to lose your mind in South Sudan.

I'd still say this way to greet a new guest was slightly unorthodox.

"Well, it's better to be mad and happy than safe and bored."

I tried to defend my choice of destination. James giggled again.

"I'm gonna treat you to a god-damn drink. It might be your last."

It was not.

We stayed in the bar for quite some time. And were joined by Alan and one of the ambassador couples. As in any place where there are a limited amount of foreigners, the few that are around produce a lot of gossip. About each other. You would think that people would become almost like supportive family members in such an outpost by the Nile, the reality is the opposite. Small groups backstab each other whenever everyone is not together. When they are, there is little but superficial small talk.

It fell natural that I spoke to the guys, while Donna Claire chatted with the ladies. She soon picked up that the elegant and seemingly successful ambassador couple were sleeping around with numerous people, each on their sides. And I was told about one of the salesmen who drank heavily and who was not afraid of needles in his arm either.

James took the opportunity to introduce me to several of the guests.

"That guy over there works for Alan. He has shot dozens of people."

"The guy in the blue shirt?" I asked.

"No, he's an idiot. The man with the hat."

The hotel manager always put it straight. And he enjoyed telling stories. "The idiot" had an extremely animated face. I could have bet a lot he was a puppet from Wallace and Grommit, had I not been able to shake his hand and talk to him.

The stories soon evolved, and I heard about shoot-outs, cowboy flick style. The man with the hat, Alan, and his people often took part in such. Owning a security company, you can demand pretty much what you want in order to protect businessmen, embassies and NGOs. And Alan did. He was minted. And every Friday he invited everyone staying in the hotel to a major barbeque with pork chops and drinks for everyone. Everything was paid for.

"This business is risky. There is no point in saving up for a pretty tombstone. A toast to you, my friends!" he said. And lifted his cup of whiskey. The foreigners in Juba drink a lot.

There are surprisingly many good restaurants in Juba. As in three. Notos is the best. It's owned by a nice Greek who has lived in Juba for years. Donna Claire and I decided to test it out. It's been built around a big stone grill. We had a delicious fish kebab, tandoori style, and a perfectly cooked *makhani* chicken as starters. The tender steak also disappeared quickly where we sat under the stars with candles on the table. There was no wine list, but the waiter assured us that they did indeed have wine.

"Could we have a Cabernet Sauvignon, please?" I asked.

"Sure, sir! Would you like that to be red or white wine, sir?"

We ended up with a South African Pinotage from 2009.

I would fly out of Juba to Khartoum a few days later. Donna Claire had just returned to Jozi via Nairobi. She had been declared both an idiot and a genius for her choice of travel destination when back home. South Africans should stay in South Africa. Allegedly.

I met Giuseppe in the airport. The Italian and I had spoken a fair bit back in the hotel. He sold generators, a lucrative business in a country with a very unstable electricity supply. He was returning to his wife in Nairobi, and asked me where I was heading.

"With what airline."

"Tarco Air," I responded.

"Oh, my god! You are kidding, right? I flew them from Khartoum a week ago. I have never been so scared in my entire life. Shit, I made the sign of the cross on my chest ten times after we landed safely. And I am not even Christian!"

"Thanks, mate!" I said sarcastically.

I would not be disappointed. The Soviet Yak-42 hardly managed to take off. I have never experienced a plane take that long to reach cruising altitude. The turbo fan engines struggled. The cabin crew had scared looks on their faces. The sounds were different than what I had experienced on any of my several thousand flights before. I promised myself to add Tarco to my blacklist as the first airline. As long as I made it down again alive.

Rwanda

Rwanda is unfortunately best known for the genocide in the 90's. And still, most westerners didn't hear much about it until they watched the film Hotel Rwanda ten years later. It made the hotel used in the film world famous. It is called Hôtel des Mille Collines, and is as luxurious as they get. In Kigali. Donna Claire had come with me; she had not been scared away from Africa by our trip to South Sudan. We landed at 5 am. And we had five hours to kill in Kigali before continuing to Brazzaville.

"Champagne breakfast and sunrise at Mille Collines?"

I made the suggestion just before landing.

"Hahahaha....are you serious?"

"Am I ever not?"

She giggled and shook her head.

"That is a question I will not answer. But I am in."

The taxi from the airport took us past quite a few early risers, going to work. But we also saw people on their way home from town. And a few still sat drinking outside typical African pubs, with loud music blasting out the windows and vents. A little something to hate about Africa, the music volume is always on full from the smallest and the dirtiest of places. The less people, the higher volume. Sound pollution. There might be a correlation, but I personally think they are wrong when thinking that loud music will attract business. I have at least yet to see evidence of the contrary.

We entered the hotel. The restaurant by the lawn and the pool doesn't serve breakfast, so we had to go upstairs to the top floor. We got a table and ordered the breakfast buffet and a bottle of champagne.

"I am sorry sir; we do not serve alcohol this early in the morning."

Shocking. But I had been in Kigali twice before and knew of a solution. I asked Donna to wait, and ran 300 meters to the best supermarket in town. It is open 24/7 and has a great selection for Africa. But no bubbles. I opted for a bottle of Chablis, paid and walked back to the hotel. The sunrise could start. And it did.

A minister from South Sudan was also there, enjoying the fantastic breakfast buffet. He was in town for a conference, and came over to us asking where we were from. And whether we had heard about the newest country in the world. "Of course! Juba is an unpolished gem!" Donna exclaimed. "You have been there? When?" The man was almost in shock. Not only had we heard about his country, we had actually bloody been there too. "But, why?" The conversation had not developed as he had foreseen. "Would you like some wine, sir? It looks like you need it." He declined. He was about to attend an international forum for ministers from large parts of southern Africa. We still managed to finish the bottle before taking a taxi back to the airport.

We were en route to Brazzaville.

Congo Brazzaville

French Italian Pierre Savorgnan de Brazza explored Africa. He was in active opposition to slavery, and he got along well with local Africans. He founded the capital of Congo in 1880 and called it Brazzaville. Not among the most modest of men. The city is still there, very close to Kinshasa in Congo. They are technically the closest capital cities in the world, although the honor is shared with Rome and the Vatican.

To take part in religious ceremonies in various countries is underestimated. I don't chase them, but I often pop by if I happen to walk past. It was Sunday and there was a sermon in the large church with the green roof, Basilique Sainte Anne. We got there towards the end, and asked a lady with bleached curly hair if we could come inside. She nodded and showed us two free seats. Patricia came up to us again after it had all finished ten minutes later and invited us to the church party.

"It must be a 'party'," Donna Claire said. "With cake and coffee."

I agreed and nodded. We were wrong. Big time.

The party took place on a little square just below the church. There was a new priest in town, and he would be celebrated. We were the only westerners there, and had to line up for photographs with old and young alike. Plus with the priest himself. An honor. The party started with a gospel choir and a couple of hundred people dancing, before hot food was served. And Primus beers. The priest was the guest of honor and didn't only have beer, but also whiskey and two bottles of wine. The bottles were all opened, lined up on his table. It was clearly expected that he drank it all, too, and he gave it a good try. Poor man! He wasn't the only one drinking, of course. Everyone, except for the kids, was hastily drinking from 0.6 liter big brown glass bottles. Everything was free! People became more and more drunk, and brought the big bottles to the middle of the little square. A cemented area was used as a dance floor.

We stayed for a couple of hours, before we tried to say goodbye. They were not having any of it, and we did have to invent an appointment in the end, to be allowed to leave. Long live Congolese hospitality!

I wonder what would have happened to membership numbers at western churches that did the same, instead of church coffee and cookies. My guess is that it would give churches some leverage and make them more accessible to most people. Most churches should at least do something. Membership numbers are declining rapidly.

The border to neighboring Congo is in the middle of the Congo. We decided to calm down following the religious party at restaurant Mami Wata by the river. We had a great view over the waterway and Kinshasa. The heat called for a few bottles of Ngok beer. The logo consists of a crocodile. There are many of them in the river, where both Nile and dwarf crocodiles dwell.

Nicaragua

There are no crocodiles in Nicaragua. I parked the rental car on the Costa Rican side of the border and walked in. The wheels where not insured outside the borders, and I was not planning on challenging Murphy or his law. I took a taxi to San Juan del Sur, a little coastal town with a beach and colorful houses. It is supposed to be one of the most touristy towns in the country, although that doesn't say much. It luckily still hasn't got much of a touristy feel to it.

I checked into a little but cozy and modern hotel. A unique combo. The pool just outside the lobby is the smallest I have ever seen, with space for two relatively skinny people. Most people would have called it a Jacuzzi, but it was too deep, and clearly meant to be considered a pool for marketing purposes.

I walked around the few streets in town, before deciding to eat in a little local restaurant with orange walls and blue window frames. We experienced great service in the lush garden. I had been joined by a polite young man who spoke English well enough to instantly get the job as my translator. That move secured a delicious dinner. My level of Spanish would not have secured the same complexity of dishes.

The night was ageing, and we agreed on walking to a place with some more action. Three bars lined the beach; we picked the one with the roof terrace and the best music. They played AC/DC when we arrived. The bartender nodded at me and smiled. I took the opportunity to place an order.

"Could I have two Cuba Libres, please?"

"I am sorry."

The bar was well equipped, and I could see a number of different types of rum. His answer didn't make any sense.

"Do you have rum?"

"Yes."

"Do you have Coke?"

"Yes?"

"Do you have lime?"

"Yes, sir."

"Ice cubes?"

"Oh, yeah."

"Glasses?"

He was in on the game.

"Certainly!"

"But you cannot make two Cuba Libres?"

"Afraid not. But I can make you a couple of Nica Libres," he said and giggled at his own joke. You can't beat the pride of Nicaraguans. Not many of them will provide you with Cuban rum.

Moldova

You think that your countrymen drink a lot? Everything is relative. 73 countries drink more per capita than Norway. The heaviest drinkers can be found in Moldova. Where every adult person drinks 17.4 liters of pure alcohol a year. Let me translate. That means 1,320 drinks a year, or over a case of beer every week. The average US citizen drinks 9 liters of pure alcohol a year, my fellow Norwegians only drink 7 liters.

One reason for the high consumption is the wine industry. A lot of good wine is made in Moldova, although most is exported.

It is also interesting then to know that Moldova is in the very last place for the happiest people in the world. World Happiness Index does however only measure 60 or so countries. Among Moldovans, only 44 percent answered that they are lucky. The Icelandic are happier than anyone else. 97 percent are happy.

Are you?

I certainly became happy when I met Irina. She is a model and speaks Moldovan, Russian, English, Italian, Spanish and Dutch. We almost crashed into each other in a supermarket. I must have looked totally lost trying to figure out which toothpaste brand would taste sort of normal. She saw an opportunity to practice one of her many languages, and assumed that I could help. I rarely say no to models that coincidentally say hi and even ask me out for coffee.

Coffee was pleasant enough for me to be invited to join Irina and some friends in town later in the evening. We chatted and had a few drinks. Suddenly, what to me seemed like an ordinary bar, totally changed character. The volume was boosted and several strippers appeared between the tables. Both male and female.

I was clearly surprised, whereas the others around the table didn't even notice and just kept on talking.

"This happens all the time! Why, you didn't like the sexy girls? Or are you more into the guys?" they teased and laughed. Irina came back to my room that night. She wasn't good only with languages.

I invited her to come to the breakout Republic of Transnistria the next day. I would travel through it, then to Ukraine and fly home from there. We got on a bus. To get through the border police could put anyone's patience to the test, that she spoke the language seemed to help quite a bit. We had dinner and went for a walk by the river Dniester in Transnistria. Before she hailed a taxi that drove us to Odessa.

"If I wasn't traveling with you, it would have cost you ten times as much." She told me upon arrival. A fact I was very well aware of. And usually the way it is when you do not speak the language. I happily paid her taxi back to Chisinau.

Serbia

Serbia is a country for blood suckers. Which isn't necessarily a bad thing. The word "vampyr" is apparently the only Serbian word that has made it to world fame. They believe in vampires there, and Serbia made world news in less serious parts of newspapers in 2012.

The city council of Zarozje officially warned its inhabitants that the local vampire Sava Savanovic most likely had escaped. The old mill that he was rumored to have lived in for years had fallen down, and the council assumed that he was roaming the streets looking for a new place to live. The result? Massive media attention and a sharp increase in the sale of garlic. "Better safe than sorry," the locals must have thought. While stocking up on deterrents.

Øystein studied with Helge Fauskanger from Bergen back in the 90's. Helge worked for years in Oslo, and we occasionally met for long talks and coffees. Before he moved back to Bergen. He is a good, sly and well-spoken man who works in finance. We traveled to Belgrade together with Doctor Vodka and Øystein. He had repeatedly been asked to join before, but he is creative when it comes to poor excuses and had only joined once before, to Prague in 1995.

Doctor Vodka, Øystein and I didn't have high hopes for a re-debut on the traveling front, but we sent him a message. And he actually responded positively. The trio had become four. A boy's trip to Belgrade ought to be a memorable experience. The Strahinjića Bana Street in the Dorćól has for instance been nicknamed Silicone Street. Not for the same reason as Silicone Valley in California, but because of the prevalence of female gold diggers with silicone implants in various places. We were told that they are often referred to as trophies by men in Belgrade. The view was rather nice, but there was a clear tendency. The bigger the assets, the more arrogant they were. The signal they sent was clear;

expect high maintenance costs. We couldn't and wouldn't compete with the wealthy suits that were trophy hunting. Hopefully both hunter and huntee match well together. The question is just who really hunts who.

That both Helge and I were food poisoned didn't make matters better, and our Saturday night partying was way below par. It was reassuring to have Doctor Vodka there. He drinks for three. At least.

Czech Republic

I have been in Prague both when it was the capital of Czechoslovakia and after it became the capital of the Czech Republic. Helge, Øystein and I traveled there together when it was no longer Czechoslovakia. They flew in from Bergen while I came from Falmouth, via London. We all engaged in some hectic study times and we needed a long weekend off.

Of course we went to a few bars in the city. We are after all talking about *the* country with higher beer consumption than any other. 132 liters per capita per year, 2 liters above country number two, Germany.

In a traditional dark bar, we met the leaders of a Norwegian youth orchestra. It was Saturday and they had given the kids time off after having played two concerts in a school on the outskirts of town. They told us that "almost everyone is over 18" and had therefore been allowed to explore the city on their own, given that everyone was up and ready for counting at 9 o'clock the next morning.

The conversation with the two guys, Roger and Joar, opened up a totally new world for us. We had no idea about the culture of such orchestras. The trip usually turned absolutely wild, we learnt. With a lot of alcohol consumption, dirty stories and crazy behavior. Men on a group trip aren't particularly charming. Especially not in Prague where the locals have grown accustomed to such following the arrival of a lot of stag parties the last few years.

"To us, this is a tradition. We have been here three times, and two Czech orchestras have visited us at home in Norway," Joar said.

The previous year, it had really taken off, and eventually they had decided that no one would be allowed to go out on the town.

"It ended in a catastrophe, especially for Roger."

"Screw you. Not that story!" Roger responded indignantly, and without hope in his voice. The story had clearly been told before.

"Roger had been drinking beers all night long, before starting on some cognac. Good shit, even, it was Gabrielsen XO. He still didn't feel that he was getting drunk, so he decided to try a different method of consumption."

Roger went to the bar to get another round of beers. He was clearly not interested in hearing the autobiographical drinking story yet again. Joar eagerly kept on telling it.

"The one liter bottle of XO was almost full. He took the cap off and stuck the bottle up his ass. Before somehow managing to get up to a handstand towards a wall. His theory was that his mucosal would absorb more alcohol than he could drink, so that he could finally become drunk."

"Did it work?"

I was curious.

"Hell no! He stood like that for half a minute before we managed to get him down again. He then took the bottle out of his ass and put it on the table."

We laughed. Joar the loudest. Roger had demonstratively turned his back towards us where he stood by the bar.

"And the rest of you lot must have been eager to finish the bottle?" Helge asked ironically.

We were assured that the bottle had been left untouched. Helge just shook his head in shock over the wasted liquor. Roger returned to the table with a tray of beers. And a little revenge.

"Do not forget to tell about how you used to get your chewing tobacco fix. Putting it under his foreskin. Until it itched so badly that you had to take it away. And then he didn't throw it away, he put the tobacco where it belonged, in his mouth."

We left Norway's finest young men following Roger's round. The stories had sort of ruined the nice atmosphere around the table, and we took the hint. Maybe they should anonymize themselves next time around.

Øystein, Helge and I walked back towards our hotel.

"I do not understand how these brass band people have such a good reputation, while sportsmen do not," Helge complained. None of us had ever been in any youth orchestras.

"They belong to a much more dubious environment than what we have been led to believe. Drunk wife beaters, all of them," Øystein quipped.

Andorra

I cannot lay claim to fame that I have drunk many countries empty for liquor. But we were not far away in Andorra. The little mountainous country between Spain and France has been independent since 1278. People there now primarily live off tourists.

Bjarne Andre, Andreas and I still decided to visit over the weekend en route to the yearly Mobile World Congress in Barcelona. My colleagues are rarely hard to convince when asked about travel plans. I am less uncertain about how their better halves react to all my travel suggestions.

We drove a rental car from the capital in Catelonia to the capital of Andorra, Andorra La Vella. The hotel even upgraded us, and the receptionist recommended one of the better restaurants in town. And in the country. Both Andreas and Bjarne are big fans of steak; I usually prefer food that lives in water. "Do you recommend any of the seafood?" I smiled to the older waiter. He did not return it. His reply was as dry as sandpaper in the Sahara.

"Do you see any sea around here, sir?"

Being relatively stubborn, I still ordered cod. It wasn't the best chess move ever performed in the landlocked country in the Pyrenees. The cod, if it really was a cod, was dry and tasted harshly. Not even the thick creamy sauce could save the dish. The waiter is always right. Or at least so I was reminded throughout the night by my so called friends.

A night that was spent in a bar. Our goal progressed as we drank. The bar would be emptied of rum. Three guys on tour managed in style. Then we had to redefine our tactics and drink bubbles instead. Andreas ended the night in a shopping cart. Bjarne Andre pushed it and I acted as the map reader. The receptionist was not impressed by our mode of transport, since he had to dispose of the cart. This luckily happened before phones came with built-in cameras.

San Marino

We were going to the same conference in Barcelona the following year. And yet again, there was time for a detour with the usual suspects. Andreas, Bjarne Andre and I opted for San Marino, one of the two tiny landlocked countries inside Italy.

Andreas was for once determined to avoid any traveling mishaps. He had even ordered a 12 cylindered Jaguar from a rental company way in advance. Andreas prepared for anything? It couldn't last. Following a delayed meeting he missed his flight to Milano. Seat 5B was empty, between Bjarne Andre and me. We heard from him on the phone just after our arrival. He had been rebooked via Copenhagen and would arrive three hours late.

We felt that we had an obligation not to leave the Jaguar alone. We explained to Avis that Mr. Munkelien had become ill and that he would not need the Jag, but that we were a part of his entourage and that we would do him a favor and take the booking.

"Be careful, that cat is a hell of a car. And it's the last one we've got," the rental car clerk said.

Perfect. It meant that Andreas would have to drive a class A or a class B vehicle. 4 cylinders. At most. And with less horsepower than a motorbike.

We checked into one of the few hotels in the country that claims to be the world's first and still independent and constitutional Republic. The amount of activities in San Marino are rather limited, so we arranged a little test of tax-free liquer in our accommodation, 700 meters above sea level, next to the monastery on characteristic Mount Titano. We had an amazing view. All of a sudden Bjarne Andre's phone rang.

"It is Andreas!" he said, before answering with the call on the loudspeaker.

"What the hell have you done to my Jaguar?"

We laughed so uncontrollably that we could hardly speak.

"All they had left was an old ugly brownish Ford Fiesta. Fuckers!"

I have never before heard the gentleman use such language. He was clearly mad as hell.

"No worries, we will guide you! We can see Switzerland from here."

He just hung up. We called him again three hours later. He was freezing; the heater in the Fiesta could hardly manage to keep the frost off the windows.

"We can see you!" Bjarne Andre shouted. The amount of duty free bottles had diminished drastically.

"Turn to the right now."

Andreas was several kilometers away, and there was no chance that we could recognize his particular car on the motorway. He still did as he was told. Chance had it that Bjarne Andre had been right, and Andreas soon had his San Marino debut too.

Italian gourmet food was our choice for dinner the next day. There is a little village at the foot of the mountain. The restaurant is fantastic, and there is even, as close to a nightclub that you will get in the country, in the basement. And we took full advantage of it. Andreas drank with both hands, while Bjarne Andre acquired several alcohol related syndromes. I wasn't far behind either of them, and we refused to stop the party. The owner had to lead us out into his car in the end with a promise to drive us back to the hotel. He told us he could see no other solution to get us out of there. The turnover that particular night must have been way above average. He even gave us one T-shirt each. With the restaurant logo all over.

Iceland

Ola and I have hardly traveled together, despite our bet. At least not with the exception of a few work trips around 2002. Eleven years later I invited friends and family to a party into the last country, number 198. Ola was obviously on the list of invitees. He did after all have a bet to lose. But no. Ola called out of the blue to tell me that he couldn't join. His wife Hege was pregnant, and the trip collided with the due date of his child number two. An acceptable excuse.

We still had to compensate for his non-participation in May, and we decided to visit Iceland together. The famous Blue Lagoon is a tourist hole, but it is still rather charming to go bathing there with freezing temperatures above water and 40 degrees Centigrade in it.

Iceland was discovered by Norwegian Vikings around 800. No one lived there before that time; which means that it is sort of legitimate to claim that Norway has discovered, or even invented the country. It just isn't very popular to utter that out loud. In Reykjavik, at least. Ola and I got talking to two fishermen in a bar in the capital, and we somehow got started on the world famous subject of trolls. The locals claim that trolls are Icelandic.

"How can that be? Norway invented Iceland," Ola replied and lifted his glass for a toast. They did not return the gesture, the conversation had abruptly ended.

The mandatory geyser hunt took place the next day, driving through the strange but fantastic landscape on the island.

"It is extremely depressing that I can't join your celebration in the last country! I have a good excuse, if nothing else."

"You do indeed! We will report from there in great detail."

"No, please do not. I do not want to know what I am missing."

Ola and I drank a few local beers in one of the cozy pubs on the main street in Reykjavik. Before indulging in puffin, horse and whale. Iceland is a winner when it comes to gourmet experiences.

Something I had discovered several times before. With two exes and a Doctor Vodka. On separate occasions. I had also met Erlich, a Filipino mate of mine on a trip there. He now lives in the US, and he has never spoken loudly about the delicious whale steak there.

"People would have murdered me, man!"

Sweden

I have visited our nearest neighbor to the east a lot of times. I do in particular remember the summer trips as a kid. We drove a minibus, towing a large caravan. I still don't quite get how we fit seven children and two adults in it every night, though.

I returned many years later. Without a caravan. It was New Year's Eve 1999 and time for the biggest new years' celebration ever. The switch to 2000. It was all about being at the best, coolest and wildest party. The right one. Some multi-millionaires even rented a private jet to take advantage of the time zones and celebrate more than once. Others allegedly used a Concorde to manage four celebrations. We did not.

Arve had a 25 year old Datsun 120Y. The station wagon was dark green. So green, in fact, that it just got the name "The green car" and ended up as a tattoo on Arve's right shoulder. Arve is a unique guy. Arve Grønnevik, remember the name. He is, was and will always be mad. Mad as in creative genius and brilliant.

He had been pretty tired of university back in his student days. A friend and him took the bus to the airport and walked over to the ticket office. *The* impulsive trip of all times was about to happen.

"We would like two tickets abroad, please."

The message was clear, but the ticket sales person just didn't quite grasp the concept. Several minutes of explanation later, and they finally got their tickets. To Berlin. Where the first flight abroad from the airport was destined.

He was later one of the initiative takers to a pensioner's trip to Sweden. No one signed up, so to camouflage failure he was among 30 students who traveled instead. They purchased the right kind of clothes in a used clothes shop and shaved each other bald on the top. Before taking the bus across the border, checking into a hotel less modern and going to the bar to drink sherry and port wine. They all ended up drunk out of their minds and were thrown out of the hotel after they started hitting each other and random people passing by with their canes.

This man was the brains behind the New Year's Eve of 1999 also, together with fellow student Pål David Blakely. And for once, I joined in. We filled up the Datsun, were joined by a few others in a different car in Trondheim and drove towards Haparanda in North Eastern Sweden.

The temperatures in the Swedish forests were 25 below zero. The Datsun was not happy. The heater was a joke, at best, and we were freezing despite thermal underwear and jackets as thick as mattresses. A piece of cardboard in front of the radiator helped to a certain degree, and The Green Car finally got us to our target. The youth hostel in Haparanda where six of us would sleep in the same room. There was a reason why we weren't on a Concorde.

Swedes, Robert Karlsson and Jesper Hedner, arrived from Stockholm on New Year's Eve. We knew each other well through work in Copenhagen, and they wanted to join the celebration. Karlsson's nickname was Rese-Robban, or Traveling Robban. He had traveled for over 13 years of his 40 year life, and ran his own online travel site. A true inspiration to me. Jesper was the wealthiest among us and walked with a cane. That gave him the nickname Osama bin Laden, thanks to FBI's most wanted website. Under special characteristics for bin Laden, it said "He walks with a cane."

It was New Year's Eve. We fully explored Haparanda. In ten minutes. There is a reason why you haven't heard about the place. We purchased beer, pretzels and potato crisps. We were ready. For *the* millennium party.

Finland

At 23:33 we walked across the border to Tornio in Finland. Where the time was 00:33. It was already January 1, 2000 and we had avoided the transition to 2000. By walking into the only country in the world where they drink more coffee than in Norway. 10 vs 12 kilos per person. Iceland and Denmark are number three and four, Sweden number six. Only the Netherlands splits up the five Nordic countries when it comes to the black beverage.

We continued the celebration "East of Sweden" with loads of stupidly drunk Finns. There is something about these Finnish jokes. There is some reality in them, something I had confirmed by Jørn Jensen. My colleague has a Bachelor's Degree in jokes.

"The jokes about Finns are different than other types of jokes as there is an element of truth in them. We find a familiarity in the jokes about drunken Pirka, based on stereotypes. The point is that the stereotype about Finns matches the joke. We do on the other hand not seriously believe that Swedes are stupid, but we believe that Finns are fast to pull their knife out. It doesn't say anything about real life, but the stereotype is aligned to the joke," Jørn explained.

You would think that he knew a few good ones, having a degree in jokes. He tells the odd great story, but also some awfully bad ones. He was President of WorldDMB, the organization that maintains the digital radio standard of DAB, for four years, and we have attended a fair amount of dinners together. That means that I have heard some of his jokes way too many times. Jørn is over 20 years older than me, but still young at heart. We have traveled a lot together the last few years, and we have indulged in amazing food and drinks here and there. Jørn has the memory of an elephant when it comes to good European restaurants, something I have often benefited from.

Back in Finland our celebration was not like that of the locals. We had met quite a few people on the bridge, walking the other direction. They did the economy version of the Concorde party in order to celebrate the transit to 2000 twice.

It didn't look like they would remember either of them.

Bulgaria

Deadly drunk people were commonplace in Sofia too. We visited the country, as normal, before Barcelona. Andreas and Bjarne Andre were true to tradition and joined me to yet another new country. But also Thomas Weigård, who had been to Ukraine with us, came along this time. Thomas is a large fellow, almost two meters tall. And he has a nose for a good party. We checked out several shady joints and tried a number of beer types. It was late when we were back in the hotel. Bjarne Andre's room was decorated in a proper 1970's style, had mirrors on all walls and a heart shaped bed. It is more likely than not that the room has been location for more than one video taped and more or less well-choreographed orgy.

Around three o'clock the next night we heard music from an office building just across the road from our hotel. It had to be investigated. We walked into an elevator which started running automatically. Downwards. We came out in a very suspicious looking bar, complete with two dance cages in metal, hanging from the walls. Five huge guys sat in the bar with a drink each. They all wore dark grey suits, and could have been on the set of a mafia film. They all turned towards us when the elevator door opened.

We had clearly no business there, whatsoever. They said something in Bulgarian. It was loud and short.

"Sorry, we only speak English," I uttered.

"Where are you from?"

The man closest to us was clearly the boss. He spoke English well. In a no-bullshit tone.

"We're from Norway."

"You are from Norway? Why didn't you say so? Please enter. Enter, please!"

The atmosphere went from tense to strange. The chief Mafioso said something to the DJ who sat in a tiny box on the other side of the room. The bartender also received his instructions.

We had GTs in our hands two minutes later. Just about the same time as Sissel Kyrkjebø, a Norwegian semi-famous soprano started singing. The DJ had put on the first and foremost of Norwegian music that he could find.

The suits told us they worked in construction. Doesn't all Mafiosos? They said that they'd had a few jobs in our home country and that every Norwegian was their friend. We didn't want to offend these guys, and stayed until dawn. We still almost managed to piss them off.

By asking for the bill. For unknown amounts of gin and tonic.

"Friends don't let friends pay!"

We could vaguely detect the voice of an insulted man.

Uruguay

Uruguay had the politician in the world that just got it. Jose Mujica, who stepped down after two terms in 2015, came across as the world's best president. He drove a VW Beetle to work, and lived in the same old farmhouse as he always had done. Mujica also gave 90% of his earnings to those in much greater need than himself. But it wasn't only about image either. He made things happen too. Uruguay recently legalized and regulated cannabis. I will not enter a polarized fight for or against drugs, but by making it legal he immediately undermined large parts of organized crime too, as well as generating tax revenues to most people. The country has also opened up for homosexual marriages, something which is revolutionary in a country where half the population is Catholic. The country still has no state church, and everyone religion is guaranteed equal rights. The little regulatory twist of allowing gay marriages is entirely free, and increases joy and the feeling of justice for those affected.

Or to put it like The Economist did. "Gay marriage [...] has increased the global sum of human happiness at no financial cost." Politicians can now use their time to make the country better. For everyone.

And poor Uruguay does indeed have a few challenges. Garbage is still fetched by horse and carriage in Montevideo, the capital. Charming and sort of cool, but not very hygienic. I was taken around town by Fredrico, a local chap. He told me it is on the beach and the road that goes alongside it, Rambla, where stuff happens.

You will never fit into this country unless you drink mate, or maté. Although the latter works best in English speaking countries. It means "I killed" in Spanish.

The traditional tea is based on the herb yerba. It is ideally drunk from special rounded wooden cups with a metal straw, called bombilla. The straw works as some sort of a filter so that you only consume the tea, not the yerba leaves. The right amount of leaves have very hot, but not boiling, water poured over them. The cup of an average Uruguayan is rarely empty between dawn and dusk, People drink the tea everywhere, but it is no longer legal to drink it while driving. A lot of people got serious burns from the tea following accidents. I also had a few cups, but not enough to Fredrico's liking.

"You will never be a true Uruguayan at this rate!"

And he was right. I had to return to Oslo despite a great and relaxing ambience in Montevideo. Work was waiting. So was the coffee machine.

Trinidad and Tobago

Most of the action in Robinson Crusoe took place in Trinidad, the biggest island by far of Trinidad and Tobago. The smallest, Tobago, only accounts for five percent of the land mass of the well developed country. The island nation gets surprisingly few tourists.

Those few that actually go are well looked after, and I was greeted by juice seller Rocco. He looked like one of those marijuana smoking stereotypical Rasta guys from Jamaica with his baggy trousers and huge earphones plugged into a Discman. He wasn't. He was from Trinidad and Tobago. Music is the soul of the island state, something that is particularly noticeable during the carnival. It isn't as well known as the one in Rio, but it is equally wild. If not wilder. You hear calypso music and steel drums everywhere, and people party more or less continuously for a week, only interrupted by a few hours of sleep here and there.

Rocco told me about the party, with real felt enthusiasm.

"Everybody dresses up big time. Most people save all year to be able to afford the best of parties at carnival. And the girls are just damn hot and horny!"

"So, you don't have a girlfriend then?"

The question called a big white smile that morphed into a loud and long laugh.

"I've had the same girlfriend for five years, man. But we break up for the duration of carnival each year. We rather do that than be unfaithful."

One way of doing it. And not particularly unusual, according to what I heard from others too.

"Seriously?"

"Absolutely! This year I fucked five girls, man. You know, you just can't do that when you're hitched."

"And your girlfriend?"

"I don't wanna know. I never asked."

"Did she ask how many you slept with?" I inquired.

"Well, sort of. But she thinks I only slept with one girl. She'd kill me if she knew there were five."

"You mean you have this sort of an arrangement, but you still lie about it? That's priceless, man!" I laughed and we toasted in the orange juice he sold from a stall in the middle of Port of Spain.

SUITS AND LOBBYING

I've been on a lot of work trips abroad, both alone and with various colleagues. Meetings, negotiations and conferences have given me a lot of possibilities to travel, although I have still been on holiday in the 25 or so countries I have had work missions in. Such trips have helped me to be able to afford my quest. Let's say that I am at a conference in Johannesburg. I will then go there the weekend before to visit Namibia, come to the conference in Jozi and work throughout the week before going to, say, Mauritius the weekend after the conference. The big trip, to Johannesburg, is naturally paid by my employer or the organizer of the conference, while both weekend trips and extra accommodation are at my own expense.

My work trips usually take me to a few standard destinations such as Barcelona, London, The Hague and Seoul. I luckily enjoy returning to places, as I find it fascinating to see and feel changes from my last visit.

The Netherlands

Ronald Haanstra and I first met in a sterile meeting room in the Netherlands. The walls were green, without anything on them. The coffee was instant and the coffee milk had expires three months ago. Ronald is CEO of MTVNL, a company that deals with digital radio and mobile TV, and we had met on neutral ground to discuss how to work together. We decided to establish an international organization and International DMB Advancement Group (IDAG) was born. It would give us more power and legitimacy. The head quarter would be in Oslo, with a local office in The Hague.

Ronald became vice president, I would be president. A rather pretentious title, maybe, but very important and effective in meetings, especially in Asia where titles are Alpha and Omega.

Through a range of visits I discovered that I enjoy The Hague better than much more famous Amsterdam. It is more Dutch, less busy and with a lot less tourism. The cities are of similar size, so the restaurants and nightlife on offer is similar. And The Hague comes with a beach close by.

I have been to countless meetings in the Netherlands. And got to know Ronald very well. He is 15 years my senior, but we get along great. Both of us enjoy partying, conversations with new people and to travel. And food. We have had dinners with budgets way above what I am used to. I used to collect countries, Ronald collects Michelin stars. He owns several companies, has sold others and is rather well off. He knows "everyone" in the Netherlands, including the royals. Our stories are plentiful, and are usually exchanged over a nice meal. Sometimes in one of his restaurants.

We once decided to go to Ron Gastrobar, one of the two star Michelin restaurants in Amsterdam. Ronald had brought his colleague Ron, so I was with Ron and Ron in Ron. Molecular gastronomy delivers. It means that science is utilized in order to create dishes in new ways, and to better understand what happens throughout the cooking process. The result is new tools and new ways of preparing dishes, and often incredible dishes. Including at this particular Dutch restaurant. The combination of scallop tartar, duck liver, neck of lamb and lobster works perfectly well.

A very well dressed older couple sat at a neighboring table together with the equally suited up son in his mid 30's. None of them seemed to mind showing off their wealth. The son politely sat conversing with his parents, although it looked as he would rather be somewhere else.

"He is politely sitting there waiting for his inheritance," Ron said. Eloquently.

Ron also dresses well and has enough money to do what he wants. He used to be CEO at the European office of one of the world's tele giants, something which has resulted in a massive network and a lot of respect. He is now above 60 and has decided to do exactly as he pleases. I was there when Ronald introduced Ron to Derek, a very elegant and influential British business contact, gone friend, who always wears a nice suit and delivers contagious laughs. A shame about his jokes.

"It's nice to meet you," Derek said and reached out his hand. Ron did not take it.

"Well, that remains to be seen."

The answer was priceless and unexpected. Things usually are with Ron. A liberating man.

Germany

Berlin is one of my favorite cities. It just has everything. Except salt water. The bars, the restaurants, the canals, the people, the quirky little shops. I visit at least once a year.

Sometimes for work. To be at a conference abroad with other Norwegians is always a little odd. The organizers in most countries plan for socializing or networking as it usually is presented as in the agenda. What it really means is coffee or cocktails, with the possibility of meeting and talking to people you don't know in order to create new business possibilities, to prepare new deals or contracts. Everyone understands the value of this and will move from person to person in order to find interesting and potentially good contacts.

Except for Norwegians.

We are shy, almost scared of meeting new people. What we usually do is to locate the nearest corner, preferably near the coffee, and hang out with other Norwegians. And the occasional Swede or Dane. It is fascinating and strange, but rather entertaining to watch. I didn't think much of it the first times I participated in conferences abroad, but I now sometimes take a little break and observe this phenomenon. The positive bit is that we get to know each other rather well. We just have to realize that we won't be perceived as less strange by foreigners when acting in this way.

I took part at an event in the German capital when I myself ended up talking to another Norwegian. Frank was almost 50. And unmarried for the third time, as he put it. Two ex-wives, there. And three kids semi evenly divided between the exes.

We stayed in the same hotel, and decided to skip the formal networking dinner.

"I hate the organized mingling," Frank said.

"Fair enough, but do you not miss out on a lot of contracts with such an attitude?"

He worked for a company selling technical equipment. I thought he would be dependent on networking, even as a Norwegian, in order to achieve the desired results.

"I manage my goals with a very good margin, and I make enough money as it is," he said, and smiled.

"Good! I assume that means you will pay for dinner?"

Catch 22. But Frank could afford it. Then again, he had a budget for wining and dining. A big budget, judging by his choice of restaurant.

"You are aware that I am not a potential customer?" I asked, or stated, rather.

"Hell, yeah! But my boss back home doesn't."

We eventually came to the topic of women. Inevitable. Frank told me that he had a girlfriend, that he was very much in love and that she might very well become his third wife.

"OK, but have you told you that you love her?"

"No, no, no. But she knows that. Of course she does!"

"And therefore you won't tell her? It may not come as a surprise that you have been divorced twice."

He just laughed. But there was something there. I barely knew him, but continued with rather personal questions.

"Of course you told your ex-wives that you loved them?"

"No, never."

"Never? But did you not love them? And if not, why did you then marry them in the first place?"

"Of course I loved them."

"But you never told them?"

"No, but they knew. I showed them in different ways."

"Have you ever told any girl that you love her?"

He hesitated. Not too pleased with the rapid line of questions.

"No, I have not."

"What's the name of your girlfriend?" I asked.

"Monica."

"Come on, Frank! You are almost 50. And you have never told anyone that you love them. Are you aware of what you are missing out on? And are you aware of what feelings you deprive them of? Or yourself?"

I offered him my hand.

"Here is an offer. If you tell Monica that you love her, I will then take you out to a restaurant of your choice in Oslo. It'll all be on me. I just want a full report on her reaction."

It would be bragging to say that Frank particularly liked my suggestion. And he did not shake my hand. Not until after another bottle of wine. The bet was on.

He called me a couple of months later.

"You owe me a dinner!"

His voice was triumphant. And I took him out for dinner. Not in Oslo but coincidentally in Germany. In Munich. We opted for the ten course menu and had a lot of time to talk.

"I have never had so much and so great sex as after your genius move."

"Mine? What the hell, it is just you that lack manners! If you love a woman, she deserves to hear it. It is a tradition. Even the Vikings did it, a thousand years ago. You must have missed the memo."

He ignored my speech.

"You know what? Now I get oral sex too! I have never had that from a girlfriend before."

"Oh, no? From whom, then?"

Frank blushed, but not for long. And it only became more and more evident that the "I love you" trick had worked way beyond expectation since he had used it for the first time a couple of weeks earlier. We had good wine too, in the south of Germany. But there were no new bets. And Frank insisted on paying for dinner.

"Forget about paying! You have done me a favor with your idiotic bet. And Monica comes over to mine tomorrow. I will just enjoy."

The conference we were attending was coincidentally organized at the same time as Oktoberfest. I wanted to take advantage of that, and had booked my hotel over the weekend. I had assumed that other colleagues would have done the same, but I was wrong. Neither Frank nor any of the other people I knew prioritized plentiful beer toast in Munich.

I ended up going to the Oktoberfest area alone. It was Friday night, and the 13 giant tents there were extremely crowded. There were over 8,000 people in each tent, and I entered one of them. People were already shouting and dancing on the tables. I stopped one of the waitresses and asked her for a beer.

"You have to have a table to order."

"Oh," I blurt out. Clearly disappointed.

"You mean you are here alone?" she took the time to ask despite being super busy.

"Yes."

"Let me find you somewhere," the beer maid said, grabbed my arm and took me to a table full of girls in their late 20's. She asked if they could look after me. They were friendly and not at all hard to ask. I sat in the midst of 8 girls, all very curious of why I was in Munich alone. We too danced on the table a couple of hours later. It was a memorable night in Munich.

Despite a few black spots.

Russia

Norwegian Broadcasting Corporation was a world leader in its use of mobile services when I was Director of Mobile Services. I will not take much credit for that, except for being curious and rather restless in trying out new stuff. The position was mainly due to Norway being very advanced when it comes to technology overall, and mobile usage in particular. Not to mention highly skilled and enthusiastic developers. Ola and Andreas were among them, Bjarne Andre was our boss. I pretty much had it all served. In any case, it meant that I was often invited to speak at conferences at home and abroad.

I had the agenda to the two day conference in Moscow sent to me in advance. The organizers had even set up a special agenda for me, as a foreign speaker, and I would be taken to a museum and the opera. Not quite my cup of tea, I asked to test drive a Lada Niva, the legendary 4WD, instead. They were a little puzzled, but took care of the necessary arrangements. I was driven to a dealer on the outskirts of Moscow and got to steer a blue Niva around an off-road track. There were no seatbelts in that particular car, and my guide Natasha was almost thrown from one side to another. She was luckily strong enough to manage to hold on pretty well, although she cursed me for choosing this over going to the opera. At least I was happy.

So were the organizers with my contribution, and i was invited to come back to another conference a couple of months later. A bigger event, albeit a one day happening only, on a Friday. To get me to accept they even offered to fly my girlfriend in too and to pay for a five star hotel the entire weekend. Målfrid took a direct flight from Oslo and was picked up by a private driver. I flew in from Kiev in Ukraine a few hours later. The same driver was there too fetch me too. The organizer had yet again asked me if there was anything I wanted to do while in Moscow. Having enjoyed my Niva trip, I asked to test drive a Ferrari. Before immediately letting them know that was just a joke. Målfrid and I would manage just fine alone.

But you shouldn't joke with Russians. Oliana was our guide this time around. She and the private driver took Målfrid and me to the posh part of Moscow. The Russian capital competes with Istanbul of the biggest city in Europe throne, but Moscow has no competition from anyone in the world when it comes to the city with the most dollar billionaires. The houses, villas, mansions, even palaces are lined up in the luxury villages of Barvikha and Skolkovo.

Our target was neither of those, but the Maserati shop. The brand is less known than Ferrari, but certainly delivers very high RPM figures and a hell of a lot of horsepower. And Maserati comes with a Ferrari engine. A nicely dressed salesman in a full suit and tie took me to the white car. There was no way that he could be older than 25, he would join me on the test drive. Målfrid got to sit in the back, virtually on top of the engine that is placed in the rear.

We first drove on some curved roads on the outskirts of Moscow, so that I would get to know how the car handled. It didn't feel too bad. I have had six cars throughout my time; the most expensive one cost 800 dollars. This one was 400 times dearer. In Russia. I wouldn't even think of what it would set me back to buy it in Norway, with a range of creative road and car taxes. It wasn't until we hit the ten lane motorway that I got to really test the Maserati. A car that doesn't need much of a hint from the right foot before the engine reacts. Fiercely. I'd claim that Målfrid never ever had a better back rub. By the engine. We soon hit 250 kilometers per hour while driving zigzag between slow Mercedes's, BMWs and Porsches. I wasn't allowed to go any faster. By Målfrid. The salesman didn't frown even a little during the entire test drive, but the back seat driver wasn't at all pleased when I turned too quickly or drove faster than 200. Then again, I'd probably not be entirely happy if we had switched roles.

I think I managed to compensate by the dinners later on the same trip, but I would never be allowed to buy such a car. As if I would ever have enough cash, or wit, to drive one.

Malaysia

It wasn't extreme speeds, but extreme spice that was on the program in Malaysia. Being fond of hot food, I often see it as a little challenge to try the spiciest item on the menu. That happened in Kuala Lumpur too. I was there for a conference on digital radio with Jørn and Ronald.

Dinner was as usual one of the day's highlights and the waiter of a local restaurant came to get our orders. I did not surprise anyone but him when I asked for the strongest dish on the menu. A chicken course, I was told. We were served our food less than twenty minutes later, and the waiter checked up on us.

"How is your food, gentlemen?"

"It is good, but your strongest dish isn't exactly spicy," I complained.

"Oh, I will see what I can do."

He was back in a flash, with a chili sauce on a glass bottle. The mixture looked homemade.

"How about now, sir?"

I tasted, he stood by politely waiting.

"It is very good, but it still isn't very spicy."

"Really? One minute, sir."

Before he was back yet again with a small glass bowl with some sort of a spice paste. I took a full tea spoon of it and ate it all in one gulp. The waiter gasped. I tasted.

"No, still not hot."

"I surrender! Please accept my apologies, sir. You have the taste buds of a dragon."

Poland

Norway is the 8th biggest country in Europe, area wise. Poland is number nine. Both countries are replacing FM radio with DAB digital radio, and Jørn, Ronald and I were in Wroclaw in Southern Poland for a conference related to this. The town is well known for a good nightlife and plentiful parties. That has made the place a renowned destination for stag night participants. It should therefore not come as a surprise that our taxi driver assumed that we were looking for non-committing relationships.

"There are a lot of good whorehouses in town, but many of them will con you and make you pay way too much. You should never pay more than 70 Euro for the full package, and I know exactly where you should go for beautiful and affordable ladies," the driver lectured.

Overly blunt and absolutely not expected. We had just entered the cab, and not asked the driver for anything else than driving us downtown.

"Ehe...thank you. I suppose," Jørn said. It was May, and we ignored the taxi driver's well-meaning advice. We had coffee on a café on the pavement instead.

"It must look like we are looking for prostitutes," I said.

"Yes, I almost felt bad disappointing the taxi driver," Jørn responded.

"Are you insinuating something?" Ronald asked.

"No, no, no, I have a girlfriend at home," Jørn answered.

"No worries, I don't think the taxi driver will tell," Ronald smiled.

There are always some bad jokes on work trips. But this time Jørn was actually not to blame.

We had dinner later in the evening. Ronald had a phone call just after finishing the first course, and he excused himself. He was back after 15 minutes.

"I do apologize. But I have just sold one of my companies."

"How much did you get?" Jørn asked.

"Let's just say that dinner is on me," Ronald said smiling.

Before upgrading the three course menu to a seven course one. And ordering a magnum bottle of champagne.

Italy

Lake Garda is the biggest in Italy. Surrounded by wild and very steep mountains. It's beautiful there, and I can easily understand that many conferences are organized around the lake. I was there to speech on digital radio to Italian colleagues. All the seats in the conference hall in Riva del Garda were sold out.

Jørn and I had flown in, and then picked up a rental car to avoid having to ride in the cramped minibus. That also made it possible to take a little detour and explore some villages. We enjoyed dinner in a cozy little restaurant in the charming village of Costermano.

We met a German we knew while checking into our hotel in Riva del Garda. He is well known in the industry as an obnoxious guy, and we politely declined his dinner invitation.

"We might join you for a coffee later."

Jørn and I rather had dinner at a small and informal cellar restaurant. Walking around town on a detour back to our hotel we saw the German again. He sat outside a bar, together with two women, clearly hookers. One of them was rather large and black; the other one was small, skinny and white. He spotted us and enthusiastically waved us over to their table, with his gold ring covered right hand.

"Guys, you have to join me for a drink. And I will not take no for an answer!"

His two ladies soon went together to the restroom.

"But, don't you have a wife at home?" Jørn asked.

"Come on, I have problems in my marriage like everyone else! Let's drink to Garda!"

We toasted. Once. Before the Norwegian delegation left the party and headed for the hotel. I was awoken by the hotel phone ringing loudly at 2 in the morning. I was startled. I was in the middle of a dream about pirates.

It was the German.

"Gunnar, you have to help me out! I do not have enough money to pay for the hookers, and they have started destroying the room. Can i borrow some money?"

I had to say no. I didn't have a single Euro. Even in Italy credit cards are accepted almost everywhere.

"Please, can you come and take my credit card and go to get some cash at an ATM? The bloody hookers are refusing me to leave. They think I will run away."

I got dressed, walked to his room and knocked. The German pushed his credit card underneath the door.

"They won't even let me open the door."

He sounded desperate. He also pushed a note with the pin number on it. I took it and ran off. The nearest ATM was luckily not far away, I was back with a big bunch of Euros in less than 15 minutes. He had either hooked up with very expensive girls, or he had used me to get money for the entire weekend.

"I hope the sex was good!" I said and put the money through the little gap between the door and the frame. The security chain was on. The German was clearly not at all trusted by the two girls.

WHY IMPULSIVITY BEATS PLANNING

Not everything can be planned. Or should be planned. Sometimes things just happen. You meet the right, or the wrong, person. You are invited for dinner or a party. Or you just have a kick and you do something that wasn't particularly thought through but that in hindsight contributed to eminent holiday experiences. Too much planning is overvalued. Impulsivity is not.

Australia

Australia is the sixth biggest country in the world, but also one of the most urban ones. Over 80 percent live less than 100 kilometers from the coast. Australia can also claim to have the biggest cattle farm in the world. Anna Creek Station in the south is 24,000 square kilometers big. Similar to the size of New Hampshire. Or Vermont.

That the capital is relatively unknown Canberra is due to a huge compromise. Neither Sydney nor Melbourne would give in on becoming the main city, so Canberra was chosen back in 1908. It just had to be built first.

I had been pondering to friends and family about the least possibly productive, but still rather impressive trip that I could think of.

A day trip to Australia.

Impossible, of course, given the long flights, but 24 hours there sort of qualifies. It should ideally have commenced on impulse on a Thursday night, but that might have been pushing it. I was invited to speak at a conference that could fit the bill and that I could take advantage of. Ericsson organized an event in Sydney and asked if I could come there to speak about an agreement with NRK on personalized ads on mobile TV. The seminar was on a Friday afternoon. Perfect! I left Oslo after work on Wednesday and arrived Friday morning after transit stops in London and Singapore. A visit to the fish market, the mandatory visit to the opera house, two speeches, an incredible work dinner and an overnight stay later saw me back on the plane towards Europe. I was there for lunch on Sunday. You are depending on one thing to get full effect from such a manic trip; that someone on the Monday asks you what you did over the weekend. The ultimate answer is "I popped down to Sydney". But what were the odds that no one would ask me about my weekend on that particular Monday? No colleagues even took the hint when I tried to switch coffee break conversations to weekend activities.

At least I enjoy plane food, can sleep in airplanes and do not suffer from jetlag.

Armenia

It was Christmas again six months later, and I had to come up with a Christmas present to Målfrid, my girlfriend at the time. People in the Western World have everything anyway, and I prefer to give experiences, rather than objects. I still gave her three darts. And a map.

I had marked 12 places in Europe and Asia on it. She also got a sheet with some simple rules.

1. Put the map on the wall.
2. Stand five meters away from the map.
3. Throw the three darts.
4. Find the dart hat is closest to one of the 12 marked destinations. If two or three darts are equally close to a destination, you pick the one you want.
5. That's where we'll go on holiday for your Christmas present.

Before a little greeting:

"Have an amazing Christmas. I love you! Gunnar."

Selfishly enough, I had of course only marked places in 12 countries that I hadn't been to yet. Both of us celebrated Christmas with each our own family, and I was not told about the result of her dart throwing until a phone call late at night. One arrow had hit Turkey, another had penetrated Portugal. But in the spring we traveled to Armenia. Målfrid had thrown the darts pretty spread out.

Armenia is the oldest Christian country in the world, but that doesn't stop people there from drinking. A lot. Cognac is big here too! That only French brandy can legally be called "cognac" doesn't really bother them. The most famous cognac is called Ararat, and is named after the mountain where Noah supposedly grounded with his arc. The mountain is actually in Turkey, but the view of it from Armenia is breathtaking.

We flew via Warsaw, and had to spend a night in Poland. I had never been to the country, and Målfrid launched a conspiracy theory about us going via there for that reason alone. I refused to comment. And we soon had other things on our mind. Armenia's capital Yerevan fascinates with all its old Soviet style propaganda statues. We soon discovered that the place to be was the main square. The plentiful coffee shops there never seem to run out of guests. Coffee is served during the day, wine, beer and cognac at night. Having explored the city for a couple of days, we wanted to see more, and we rented an old Toyota to go to Lake Sevan, the holiday destination for a lot of Armenians We even came across a huge Ferris wheel in a small village by the lake. Some kids played in the old rusty wagons that still somehow hung at the bottom. There was nothing but sad, grey apartment blocks, Soviet style, in front of a rather anonymous looking mountain. A Ferris wheel has never been built in an odder location. But what a motif!

The roads there weren't exactly great, and we ended up with a flat tire en route back to Yerevan. I had to change the wheel, and my hands were covered in black oil. Resolving agent was unfortunately not in our luggage. There was luckily a tiny kiosk nearby. Half a bottle of vodka cost a dollar or so. Vodka dissolves oil, and my hands were tip top super clean in no time. The three youngsters wearing jacket made by jeans fabric who just hung out by the kiosk watched in dismay. Imagine wasting so much good vodka!

Latvia

There is a lot of vodka in Latvia too. But it was still not the reason for going there. Øystein and Øystein Djupvik, the guy from the world record trip, and mates Jon Christian Vie and Einar Solberg had tried to get me to join on a boy's weekend to Riga. I would normally jump at the possibility, but I had meetings in London and had to decline.

John Christian has a name too long to our liking. We rarely call him anything but Jonna. As a music and football interested guy from our home village, we got to know him well back in the 80's. He taught himself to play the guitar and bass, and eventually became good enough to tour large parts of Europe with Tåke and Gorgoroth, two of the best known black metal bands in Norway.

Einar is one of the world's most hardcore Depeche Mode fans, although he might not quite fit the stereotype of one, being a sheep farmer, dog owner and avid fan of mountain hikes. He occasionally DJs at clubs and bars on the Norwegian West Coast.

I managed to move around a couple of meetings in London, and I headed to Riga after all on a last minute ticket. Unannounced. I knew what kind of music they were into, and raided every little darkish rock bar and rock joint in search for them. With no luck. I could of course have called them, but that would have ruined the surprise.

So, I checked into a youth hostel instead, and was shown a bed in a dorm. I woke up next morning only to find out that I was sleeping next to Auri from Sweden. We immediately hit it on. She was cool, bubbly and with a good sense of humor. I told her about the failed surprise attempt, and asked if she could call Jonna and pretend that she was Laura from the night before. They would, without a doubt, have been drunk enough to not fully exclude the possibility that they had indeed met a Laura.

She called from her own phone, but he didn't pick up. We assumed it was due to a day after nerves or a heavy hangover. I borrowed her phone and wrote a text message instead:

"Hey J! Such an amazing night with you guys yesterday. Still meeting by the tourist info on Rätslaukums at 14:00, right? Julia and Alice coming too. Kisses Laura"

I was confident that they would swallow the bait. If for no other reason, to find out who this was. There was no immediate response, and Auri and I split up for exploration purposes. I got a message from her at 13:30. They were on their way. I found a dark corner and could observe the four guys strolling uneasy to the arranged meeting place. Three of them wore sunglasses, one had a sun hat.

Classic! All ready to meet three girls they couldn't even remember having talked to last night. They sat on a little wall by a statue. I snuck around the square to attack from the back.

"Hello, I am Laura from yesterday!"

I shouted with as close to a girl's voice I am capable of producing. They were visibly startled, and turned around in perfect synchronization.

"Fuck you, you bloody wooden cock! I knew we hadn't met a fucking Laura yesterday! Fucking bastard!"

I always appreciate a warm welcome. John Christian wasn't all that impressed though. I still hugged them all, and received less nice names in return. Einar and Øystein were almost killing themselves laughing. Jonna had clearly been picking his brains for hours trying to remember who Laura was. We spent the rest of the weekend together. And they got to meet "Laura". Starring Auri. She too was quite chuffed with the stunt.

Lesotho

The unknown mountain country is fully surrounded by South Africa. And it has to be discovered. It is the size of Belgium, but much more hilly. The lowest point of Lesotho is at 1,400 meters above sea level, making it the country in the world with the highest low point. There is always a claim to fame.

My visit to the kingdom started as part of a wild plan. Kjersti, who studied medicine in Botswana, met me at the airport in Jozi. We picked up one of those miniature Fiats from a rental company and drove off. The red little thing would be our mode of transport through eight countries. The first one after South Africa was little Lesotho. We drove to Katse, a village with a guesthouse and a shop. The shop is called Lucky Seven and includes the only gas station for miles and miles. If gas station is the right word. It is first of all 200 meters from the main road, up a muddy path. Small Fiats do not come recommended. And unless you drive the kind of a car that Arnold Schwarzenegger usually does in the movies, don't even think about trying going there during rain. Should you still manage to get past the goats and up the hills, you will discover that there isn't a gas pump. You have to ask Nelson to fill up the car with as many liters as you need. He will then find the right gas barrels and a funnel before he fills up your car. It takes quite some time, but the price is half of what it is in Europe. And feel free to explore the 10 square meter big shop while Nelson is at it. The view is also fantastic. Then again, that's the least they can offer after that elevation.

Katse is better known for the biggest dam in the country. The impressive engineering efforts can be seen up close, if you take a guided trip inside it. And behind the dam, a couple of companies are farming trout. There is actually also a botanical garden in Katse. And we had a guided tour. By Rele, who normally works on the biggest trout farm. She has even been to Norway. Not a bad idea, given the possibility to learn about fish farming.

Kjersti and I drove through the villages of Thaba-Tseka and Mohlanapeng before crossing some sort of a bridge, made up by two parallel concrete constructions. The Fiat wasn't too happy, neither was Kjersti, but we got across on the narrow lines of concrete. We were stopped in the mountains, a few kilometers later. A mother and her two adult daughters were hitchhiking. We drove them to Linakeng, almost an hour away. They told us about farming and tough conditions in the cold mountains. We were however also told that the mother's husband was the chief of the village. They were grateful for the ride. I got a big hug from the mom, who used the occasion to propose to me on behalf of one of her daughters. The prettiest one, even. A future as chief son in law in the middle of Lesotho was tempting. I would presumably take over the chief title when my potential father in law would call it a night. The average life expectancy is only 48 years there, so a transition of power could happen relatively soon. I showed some interest for the offer. My sister wasn't equally impressed. She may not be high maintenance when it comes to luxury, but the dirt huts in Linakeng came without running water and electricity, and she hinted that I might be tired of such a life relatively soon. And besides, she added, it would be a little far to come visit. I politely turned down the marriage proposal, but they weren't having it.

"Please come back, Mr. Gunnar."

I might have reconsidered if they had thrown in a fancy title. Or a crown.

Our Fiat took us further afield, on roads with the odd patches of pavement, to the town of Mokhotlong. They even had a video store there. And a hotel. But no daughters of chiefs wanting to marry. Disappointing. We walked to the combined restaurant, shop and gas station. Where they even had real pumps. But we still had half a tank following Nelson's efforts in Lucky Seven and ignored the gasoline possibility. That may be a grave mistake when driving around Africa.

We had "papp" for dinner. In the gas station, of course. Papp is a mixture of corn, and it is often used across Africa instead of potatoes, pasta or rice. It may remind you of mashed potatoes, but it is lighter. Barbequed trout from Katse came on top of it. Yummy!

We were getting ready for a return to South Africa when the sun rose. We had figured that Sani Pass, a famous mountain pass from Lesotho down towards Durban, would be the perfect route. We had checked the map, and the road was drawn in. Did I say road? The gravel road soon became a mud path. A little bit of rain, and we would be stuck. We passed a lot of goat herds on our way up to the pass, sometimes there was a herdsman there too, and we frequently had to stop for goats. It certainly took its time, and the gas was diminishing rather fast.

We finally got all the way to the top, and were stamped out of Lesotho in the border police shack on the edge of the pass. They giggled when they saw our car, although we didn't quite understand why. The road hadn't been all that bad, despite a lack of pavement and an overdose of goats. It was when we started driving down from the top that we realized what the giggling had been about. As we would have known had we read about Sani Pass on Wikipedia.

"It is a notoriously dangerous road, which requires the use of a 4x4 vehicle. This pass lies between the border controls of both countries and is approximately 9 km in length and requires above average driving experience. It has occasional remains of vehicles that did not succeed in navigating its steep gradients and poor traction surfaces, and has a catalogue of frightening stories of failed attempts at ascending the path over the Northern Lesotho Mountains."

Such small wheels have rarely climbed bigger ditches. The pass has on many an occasion been used for car adverts. To show the properties of 4WD vehicles such as Nissan and Ford Ranger. Never Fiats. We had our first instance of oncoming traffic a couple kilometres down the road. The driver of the Range Rover laughed heartedly when he saw us, but then waved encouraging. Unless it was mockingly.

Kjersti got out quite a few times. Officially to see how the chassis was bearing, unofficially because she was slightly nervous and would rather take a break from the abseiling Italian car. The chassis was severely beaten, judging by the sounds, but we had no leakages. And she eventually came back into the car. The "road" had become slightly better, but the fuel gauge was not a positive sight. The lamp had come on ages ago, and I switched the engine off to roll down. The South African border guards luckily didn't say much about our chosen transport. They smiled and shook their heads, but stamped us in and wished us a good onward journey.

We finally found a gas station in Underberg. The tank was supposed to fit 40 liters. I filled 44. This particular Fiats had the ability to run on fumes.

Mozambique

Kjersti and I continued on our African roundtrip in the little car. Next up was Mozambique, the only country with a gun in its flag. A fully automatic AK-47 machine gun, even.

It might be better known as a Kalashnikov, after it was launched in 1949. It is by far the most popular machine gun in world history, thanks to its low cost, its high quality and its relentless stability in use. More AK-47s have been produced than all other machine guns, combined. It has therefore allegedly also killed more people than any other gun. But why is it in Mozambique's flag? The explanation is simple, even logical. The current leaders fought their way to power thanks the machine gun. Although it does officially symbolize resistance, alertness and the struggle for independence. The flag was meant to be replaced in 2005, but the parliament later voted against a new flag. It does, after all, also contain an open book and a dirt pick.

We had earlier on our tour fortunately been warned about fake police officers in Mozambique. That we might actually encounter one was not on our minds. A policeman stepped out in the road and waved us to the side of the road not far from capital Maputo. I did as we were told.

His English was poor, but he still uttered something about "license and registration." I gave him the documents.

"Problem. Problem. No insurance!"

I knew that we had insurance, and I showed the insurance paper to him.

"Not valid."

That was when I remembered what we had been told about fake police officers. It had only been a day or two since we had been warned, it just didn't occur to me. I noticed that he did not have a police car, and I could not see a police belt. The blue shirt wasn't exactly newly ironed, either.

"This is a fake police officer," I told Kjersti. In Norwegian.

"How do you know?"

"Where is his police car? And why is he alone? And where is his radio? His police badge also looks homemade. There is no way he will get any money from us."

I leaned out the side window. The con man stood next to the car with my license in his hand.

"Sir, there is nothing wrong. The insurance has been paid. May I have my license back, please?"

I snapped the documents away from him, and drove off at acceleration previously unknown to Fiat. We clearly had the wrong car for a car chase and he shouted something, but I decided to ignore him. He only had a normal old white Renault. Which would hopefully stand no chance against the Italian car, already at decent speed. He did not pursue us in the end. We finally felt safe after spotting a real police car without anything happening.

Finally in Maputo, we found a fantastic fish restaurant that served catch of today, picked up at the local fish market. Which has to be experienced due to the atmosphere, the people, the variety of fish you don't know the names of, and the other sea animals on offer. To forget to taste the fresh giant lobsters is a crime in its own right. But it may be a challenge to find the right stall. There are plenty of salesmen that won't think twice for selling you today's catch at quadruple the price. Or who won't sell you today's catch at all, but that of Tuesday.

Mozambique is also a country with virtually empty beaches as good as they get anywhere. I am surprised that there aren't more foreign tourists here. Just don't tell anyone.

The Bahamas

There are no countries where I have stayed shorter than in The Bahamas. I am not really into those kinds of typical beach holiday countries anyway, but it is a country, and I wanted to visit. I have a good reputation for finding plane tickets, and I was given the task when Målfrid and I would travel together with Ola "The Sheep Nazi" and his wife Hege to Cuba. They lived in New York at the time, where Ola took the opportunity to visit the original soup Nazi from Seinfeld.

We first stayed a few nights in the biggest city in the US before going to JFK airport. There are no direct flights between the US and Cuba, we would have to transit somewhere. None of them objected to my tickets conveniently being booked via The Bahamas. But we were short on possibilities of what to do there, with only three hours to spare.

"How about a trip to the beach?"

Ola's suggestion was ground breaking, and Målfrid did not object. She loves the beach.

"Seriously! There are beaches all over the world. We can go swimming in Cuba."

I was not impressed.

"OK; but you have to do something to count The Bahamas," Ola responded. He was thinking about the bet even back then.

"Didn't just Anna Nicole die there?" I asked.

"Anna Nicole Smith?"

"Yeah. So there might be a tombstone to visit."

They all actually liked the unusual idea. We found a taxi upon departure, and gave clear instructions.

"To the tombstone of Anna Nicole Smith, please."

The grave clearly stood out from others on the little graveyard, a couple of stone throws from the sea. It was much bigger, and covered in flowers and silk ribbons. The visit had to be documented, and we snapped a few shots. Suddenly another taxi stopped on the parking lot. A fat American got out. He walked with his head lowered towards Smith's tombstone. He was crying and spent a quiet minute by her final resting place before asking if we could photograph him with his heroine. Målfrid is a photographer, and volunteered. He handed her his compact camera.

"Please wait. Please wait," he said, dried his tears, buttoned his shirt up properly, straightened his suit jacket and combed his hear. Before trying to smile bravely. He didn't quite succeed. Not quite Elvis tendencies, but the once so barmy Smith clearly still had some hardcore fans. None of us where among them, despite our visit to The Bahamas exclusively to visit her final resting place.

Senegal

I happened to experience a couple of fans in Senegal. Two guys in their 20's all of a sudden became very good friends with me on the street of Dakar. They grabbed me, one from each side, clearly looking for valuables. I shook myself loose from the sharks and ran as fast as I could along the street, while checking that they hadn't managed to steal my passport, mobile phone, money or wallet. They chased me for a few meters, but soon gave up. Luckily so. They most probably knew the neighborhood much better than me.

There are a lot of poor people in the center of Dakar; to carry expensive looking things does not come recommended. Then again, I'd rather have the essentials on my body, as opposed to leaving them back in the sleazy hotel I stayed in. I also visited Gorée, an island with beautiful old houses and limited population. The boat trip takes less than 30 minutes. Upon my return, I decided that I'd had enough of Dakar, and I took a taxi to the minibus stand. Where I ended up sitting next to Angelina Jolie. Or at least her black double.

Paulina was much younger, but could easily have stepped in for Jolie in the Tomb Raider films. She was heading to Saint-Louise, I would travel via there an onwards to Mauritania before returning to the town. We agreed to meet when I would be back.

Following a bumpy and dirty minibus ride from the Mauritanian border, she greeted me at the university where she studied and lived. She shared a 30 square meter little flat with three other girls. They had no air conditioning, but one fan each, aiming at their beds. I was showed the campus on the outskirts of town, and I was impressed by the standards. Relatively speaking, given which country this was.

Paulina's roommates seemed very keen on us getting together, but neither practicalities, distance nor the difference in age made that seem like a good match. That had not been the reason for us meeting up again either. To see how people live in other countries is always fascinating. And who knows, I might find contacts in Northern Senegal useful in the future. Friends living locally usually beat any other way of information gathering.

I invited all four for dinner.

"I'll buy. Do you know a good restaurant where we can eat?"

We ended up in gas station a kilometer away, the only restaurant they knew. Student life in Senegal is not quite the same as in Boston. They ordered spaghetti Bolognese, hamburger and lasagna.

A typical student menu.

I opted for barbequed chicken. Fried fish also sounded quite nice, but perhaps not in a gas station. My experiences from roadside stops along US motorways are bad enough, and I didn't really have a lot of faith in the Senegalese alternative to Exxon.

I walked the girls back to the university campus, received four hugs and took a taxi to my hotel in town. I would leave early next morning, they had lectures. "We'll be studying even harder now to be able to travel like you," Paulina said. I am not sure if she realized how many hundred thousands of kilometers in the air and on the road that would actually mean.

Western Sahara

Western Sahara is not a UN member. The partially recognized state is called Sahrawi Arabic Democratic Republic, and is slightly bigger than the UK. Still, only half a million people live in the desert country of North West Africa.

There aren't many serious country collectors around. But I meet Mike from Britain who was into much of the same as me. The 40 year old had visited over 90 countries; his goal was to reach 120.

"There is no way I will do all of them like you are planning to. I am not that crazy!"

Nicely put. He had worked as an engineer in England for years, until an offered he could not refuse had landed in his mailbox. He had just been employed by an international oil company in Angola. He would just travel a little bit before starting his new life.

We flew Air Maroc from Casablanca, and got talking in the passport queue. An Icelandic guy was just behind us. He imported and exported fish, and had been to El Aaiún, the capital, a lot of times before. The blonde giant recommended us his hotel, and we shared a taxi there. Before he excused himself and headed for a business dinner with local contacts.

That left Mike and me. We wanted a beer, but couldn't find anyone who would sell us. Western Sahara is a Muslim country, and alcohol is not sold openly. We settled for orange juice. Which was not a bad idea in the desert heat. Skewers and rice made up the remains of my dinner. Mike stuck to rice, hummus and vegetables. He is a vegetarian.

We decided to rent a car together the next day. With a driver. To rent one without is a challenge in Western Sahara. Our destination was a pelican colony further north, towards the border of Morocco. We were out of luck. The pelicans were too far out for us to even get a glimpse of them. But we were happy. We saw a lot of sand. Sand dunes are actually much more impressive than what most people thinks. And I tried camel meat for dinner. The camel's head had been chopped off by the bottom of its neck, and three heads hung next to each other outside a butchers shop in a small village.

It tasted really good. Like a mixture of lamb and steak, just a little rougher. And much more macabre looking. Or as Mike put it:

"I am even more determined to not give up on my vegetarianism now than ever before. Not even, or should I say especially *not*, ten wild camels, would be able to change my mind."

Albania

Not many airports in the world have been named after women. The international airport in Tirana, the capital of Albania, was named after Mother Theresa, probably the most famous Albanian of all times. The country has a reputation for being a less developed one, and its peoples as warriors.

King Zog who ruled in 1928-1939 is also known to be the only leader in modern times that had fired back during a coup attempt. He lived through it, in other words. I like less developed countries with a bad reputation. They pretty much guarantee positive surprises and a lack of mass tourism. There are actually quite a few tourists in Albania, but most of them come from neighboring countries, and go beneath the radar of most westerners. A mate that I met in Jokkmokk in Sweden and I decided to visit the country in two days' notice.

We stayed in Shengjin for two days, a town with big contrasts. The old part is rather run down, whereas new apartment complexes are being built everywhere to cater for tourists that want an uncomplicated beach holiday. We weren't in for such, and soon headed southwards on the motorway, then westwards on anything but to the Patoku lagoon. In the middle of nowhere, you can see a range of restaurants, made up by little dining islands standing on stilts in the Adriatic Sea. Like oil platforms in miniature. They are all connected by bridges, and there is one table on each island. The restaurants do not surprisingly specialize in seafood, and they do indeed prepare it properly too. Just do not expect non-Albanians at the next table. Nor any English speaking staff. You are, after all, in rural Albania.

I later returned to the country with Asbjørn and Øystein. My brother was sensible, as usual, and went back to our rented flat relatively early. At three o'clock. The doctor and I could not possibly leave at such an early hour, and we ended up in a private underground club in what looked like an office building in central Tirana. Vodka performed his usual beer drinking shows, and attracted an audience from all over the club. I would have walked among them and taken bets on his drinking abilities had only more of them spoken English. He downed half a liter of beer in 2.4 seconds, according to a guy who timed my friend. They did not believe their own eyes.

"What is your trick? This is not humanly possible!" a tall and skinny girl with platinum blond hair exclaimed. And we agreed.

"That's what we think too. How can drinks be so cheap?"

Colombia

You should know which taxi companies to take in Colombia. It is the ninth worst countries if measured by murders in absolute numbers. The country fares slightly better per capita, then it is number 12. If the lists are "combined", only four countries are worse: Honduras, Venezuela, South Africa and Ivory Coast. A lot more pleasant, but presumably not related, is the fact that capital Bogota has one of the best networks of bike paths in the world. And on Sundays and bank holidays several of the main roads are closed too to open up for even more biking. A nice scheme that enhances health.

Øystein and Benedicte had decided to adopt. They early on knew that they would do so from Colombia. I had not been to the country, and promised them to visit while they were there to pick up their child. But five years went by without much progress, and I was getting close to finishing my visits to all 198 countries. My promise to visit them was maintained, but I decided to first pop by to complete my country collection.

I therefore opted for a day trip. I landed and neglected the warnings of not taking a taxi. The country has a bad reputation for a fair amount of taxi crooks. They will drive you, and then suddenly stop to pick up a mate. He will be armed, you will be driven to the nearest ATM and threatened to deposit whatever it is that you have of cash. There are also stories of people being kidnapped and held in captivity while a credit check is being performed for themselves and their entire family. A demand is then sent to family members back home. The size of the demand always correlates well to income and accumulated wealth.

A car from the official taxi queue at the airport is however supposed to be safe. I took one to the center of Bogota to visit the free entry gold museum. Before I explored the old town and took a minibus to Parque De La 93. It is in one of the nicer areas of town, and has a good selection of restaurants.

I have always had an above average sense of direction, and I soon realized that the minibus had taken off towards west, and what wasn't hard to understand was among the less attractive neighborhoods. Judging by houses, cars and clothing styles of the people there. I left the bus and eventually managed to stop an available cab. Cars of such low standard are not common even in the poorest countries in Africa. It would have been forcefully scrapped back home. But that was exactly what made it safe in Bogota. Not a potential kidnapping victim in the world would ever voluntarily get into such a car. I was safe. Unless the driver crashed.

It did not, and I found a local restaurant that delivered. But Parque De La 93 is clearly an upper class area, and not even lose to how the common Columbian lives.

Six year old Miguel eventually became a part of the Garfors family three months after I had visited all 198 countries, and I did as promised come to see all three in Colombia. Despite some linguistic challenges, we soon hit it off. I even got a bright yellow and blue Colombian football jersey as a present from him. Øystein and Benedicte had prepared him well, and he called me "tio loco Gunnar" from day one. Crazy Uncle Gunnar. In addition to occasionally, on random, say "Ashgabad". It goes without saying that we got along well from the start.

LOVE AND MARRIAGE

On all these trips to all these countries, the odd romantic adventure has been inevitable. Despite what we were taught in Christianity class, formerly a mandatory subject in elementary school, sex is actually a natural thing. And totally amazing. Usually, at least.

I have flirted, dated and been serious. Most guys are reputed to have their wild period late in their teens. Mine came after four long and serious relationships. And bizarrely being an avid traveler helped me finally make some girls turn their heads. It may sound strange, but it isn't really.

Because deciding to travel will have consequences for your social life. You will not be able to afford all that tempting stuff. Neither those gadgets from California, Taipei or Seoul, nor the smallest of cars from India, Russia or Italy. Your flat will not be the flashiest or biggest one around. If you even can afford one. Your wardrobe will more likely than not consist of a wide range of strange garments. They may all be very fashionable where they were purchased, but mix them or wear them in the wrong country and you will be the cause of widespread whiplash around you. Not ever being at home when the party in town takes place will lower your social standing to a depth not yet explored by man. You will of course never be able to afford the "right" presents to your potential better half, as any month's salary will be spent on impulse on that bargain flight to Dushanbe. You even purchased it before contemplating why there would be bargain flights to the Tajik capital. And cutting that romantic date short because your plane to a new territory leaves very early in the morning just kills your score rate. Your date will be here when you get back, you think. Or hope. Before you are consequently proved wrong.

But when eventually settling down for someone, only a traveler will do.

Just think about it.

Would you like to hang out with someone who has the right handbag, shoes or pair of jeans? Or rather with someone who can share incredible memories, that money cannot buy. That sudden wedding invitation on two hours' notice in Afghanistan, the bow and arrow competition in Bhutan or the boat ride down the river in the sunset on the Congo.

Would you like to be with someone who needs to plan everything even when going on the smallest trip, only to freak out when nothing goes according to plan? Such is the curse of traveling plans, they change.

Or would you rather be with someone who is calm and laid back about the trip, who knows how to behave when on unknown territory and who realizes that everything will work out just fine when you get there? There is no need to stress, you won't get killed. If the train doesn't go today, a bus, taxi or donkey will. And when something breaks, it can be mended. Even in the 21st century.

And let's speak about that long needed holiday. Would you like to travel with slaves of guidebooks or be led by tour guides with little red flags held high? The same beach, the same hotel and the same pizzeria aren't all that fun the umpteenth time. Or would you rather like some stimulation, some excitement, and some adventure? Travel guides promise to deliver it to you, but most do rather the contrary. The travel guide writer passed through a town or an area in a few days or maybe a week. In 2010. To do what? To explore for you. To ruin the pleasure of exploring, to stop you from enjoying the satisfaction of discovering for yourself. Like you did when you were a kid, when you couldn't even read but had to let curiosity help you find out the hard way. Will you really allow them to do so? Has curiosity left the building? Towns change, people change, cultures change, and you change. Dare explore. How else will you find the hidden gems, the small secluded restaurants and the new bar in town?

Will you share your life with someone who lacks curiosity? Or rather with that certain individual who wants to find out why, who dares talk to locals and who are not afraid of tasting snakes, worms and fried bush crickets? They have Heineken in 172 countries. That still shouldn't stop you from trying Polar, Tusker, Primus or Kubuli.

Travelers have learned that arrogance is their worst enemy and that being humble goes a long way. Only by acknowledging that people you meet are your equals can you understand and appreciate the world genuinely and truthfully.

Travelers know how to appreciate home, however unimpressive it may be. They have been in dusty towns, on rocky roads and in salty waters. They know why and how to smile because of the little things in life. They know how lucky you are for even being able to travel. And they have seen the world from a different perspective, from an unusual angle.

Travelers are a strange breed. They may not immediately come across as Aphrodite or Adonis with their hiking boots and the worn backpack. But I'd say they are worth searching for. People with stories to tell, images to share and problem solving skills usually are. They even kiss better too. Chances are they haven't only kissed in French.

My extensive traveling made sure that the number of girls that found me interesting increased.

A hell of a lot.

Slovakia

Bratislava, The Slovak capital is a nice little city. Doctor Vodka and I once somehow ended up there following some sort of a party bet. The apartment we had found online turned out to be more of a tiny flat, without the advertised sleeping sofa, the brand new bathroom or the state of the art sound system. The

Doctor was still happy with the Ikea mattress in the living room while I planned to sleep on a semi soft carpet on the kitchen floor. We were in any case not planning on staying there much.

We met two girls outside a bakery in the old town. Asbjørn liked one, I preferred the other. And what do you know, the interest seemed to correspond. Highly unusual. Both of them were bakers and had worked since 5am. Their eye lids became heavier and heavier, their drinks were emptied slower and slower. It was only a question of time before they would have to go home to sleep. But not until we had exchanged phone numbers and secured a double date the next day, a Saturday. They promised to return with more energy, and we got big hugs before they went home to their apartments.

But the night was still young. Asbjørn and I started discussing our next trip. Perhaps we should go to Africa next, I had been to all the "Stans", but I was still missing 8-10 African countries. Then a gorgeous girl with shoulder long light brown hair came over without notice. That pretty much thwarted our ongoing discussions. I am shy when it comes to girls. Friends call me incapable of even starting a conversation with a random unknown girl as long as my only intention is to pick her up. It was therefore very convenient that Martina did the job. She is a professional photographer. Her photos are amazing. Then again, she would not have done a worse job on the other side of the lens. As a model. She might be a little bit too short for the catwalk, but perfect for 173 centimeter tall Garfors.

"I noticed you speak Scandinavian," she said. As in a really bad pickup line. Not that we complained.

"Sort of. Scandinavian isn't really a language. We speak Norwegian," I replied. She ignored being corrected.

"I knew you had to be from up north. I am Martina."

We politely said hello and offered her one of the empty chairs.

"I have traveled a lot in the Nordics, and I so love it there. The midnight sun, your mountains, your fjords."

"When are you coming back?"

"Is that an invitation?"

"It sure is."

Everyone laughed. We taught her "skål", Norwegian for "cheers". Highly original. On an Android tablet she showed us some of her photographs. She explained that she used between 30 and 60 minutes in postproduction on each and every one of them. I was not surprised. She really knew how to shoot. And how to "Photoshop".

"And that is after taking 50-200 photos of each object," she said.

And thanked God for the digital camera.

Martina's friend Katia showed up an hour later. She had long red hair, and wore a pretty liberal skirt and high black heels. She worked as a designer. By the end of the night Asbjørn and I had yet again successfully invited two girls for a double date. The only problem was that we had to return to Oslo on Sunday. We either had to cancel one of the double dates or find a very short program for advanced speed cloning.

We agreed to try the impossible. Two dinner dates in one night with a little bit of an overlap. The first date with the bakers was agreed for 18:00 whereas we managed to delay the date with Martina and Katia until 21:00.

Dinner number one started very well, although both Asbjørn and I ordered salads for main course. That has never happened before. It will never happen again. But we needed some space for main course number two a little later. The conversation flowed well and the atmosphere seemed great. But the two Norwegians could somehow not concentrate. The dessert still had not been served by 20:30, and our stress levels rose a bit. They were, as bakers, no strangers to a little something with their coffee either. Asbjørn and I took a whispering time out and agreed that I would come up with an excuse, that my brother had some computer problems at home, that he needed help and that I had to call him. Not the best of excuses, but still all we could think of under self-initiated pressure.

I left and walked to restaurant number two. We had, if nothing else, been clever enough to order tables at two restaurants not far from each other. I was there five to nine. Martina and Katia were there fifteen minutes later. I told them that my friend was a little delayed, but that he would be joining shortly. I suggested a drink together in the meantime. At 9:30, I "had to" make a phone call, and I walked outside and returned to restaurant number one where I apologized for the long absence. Just when I got there, it was Doctor Vodka's turn to perform some world-class acting. He claimed to have been food poisoned, excused himself and got ready to "go home".

"It must have been the salad. I will never eat salad again, he whispered with a dramatic voice." And left.

I was left to get rid of the bakers. Asbjørn went to restaurant number two to cure his food poisoning.

The problem was only that the bakers were both thirsty and keen on continued company. I needed another plan. Fast. International etiquette states that a phone call during a dinner date should not last much more than a couple of minutes. At most. Mine had lasted for 25. I sent Asbjørn a text message. "Call me in 5."

He did.

"Shit, it's my brother. Sorry, I have to take this," I said, and left the restaurant yet again, with my phone to my ear. I was back two minutes later.

"My brother has been arrested for fraud. The fucker is a little bit of a crook, but I have to help him get out of this one. I am really sorry about this, but I am gonna have to beat it. Let me at least pay for dinner."

The message was not met with standing ovation, but the story was insane enough for them to actually believe it. I paid, hugged them, promised to keep in touch and walked out while "on the phone".

The Doctor was in the middle of some wild stories from various stan countries. His audience of two listened enthusiastically. They did not seem to miss me much, despite of my unacceptably long absence.

The Doctor ordered steak, I ordered chicken this time around. The girls went for our previous arrangement and ordered salads. Their bodies implied that they ate a lot of that. We had a fantastic evening. Until we had finished wine bottle number two. When Martina and Katia announced that they were getting married. With each other.

Jaws have rarely dropped deeper.

Our flat was anyhow not suited for a perfect end to the double date. A champagne bottle later, to "celebrate" their forthcoming wedding, and we were gone. The girls were left snogging. They had been too shy to do so earlier, but some bubbly usually helps.

The doctor and I walked along the cobbled streets in the old town. The odd street light showed us as giant shadows.

"Should we call the bakers?" Asbjørn asked.

Zambia

Back in Africa, this time in Zambia, and the huge blue car behaved like a sledge on the dirt roads. Thanks to Øystein's Toyota Condor, a model unknown outside Africa. He was at the wheel and usually had a steady hand on it too. But this particular car had 12 years on Malawian roads, something that made it feel both loose and sloppy. It was just before dusk, and we hoped to beat darkness in reaching Chipata, a godforsaken intersection with 100,000 people around 130 kilometers from Malawi, where we had started our little drive. We almost succeeded. The thousand meter lights on the car proved crucial the last few kilometers, and we managed to find a hotel. Or was it a school? It smelled like the latter, and totally looked like it too. The dining hall was the size of a gym. But any pupil having had cooking classes in school would have made a better breakfast.

Øystein and I were shown to our room, the size of a small class room. It was sparsely decorated and only came with a little sofa, a wooden table in front of it and a 20 inch television set. There was a hand woven wooden basket on the table. Full of condoms. Flat screen TVs had not yet found their way to Chipata. Neither had Durex, Trojan or Rough Rider. We opened one of the anonymous looking, locally made condom packets. It smelled of cheap rubber. Probably not the best bet in the fight against HIV, but still way better than nothing. If you are single and open to sexual encounters, do not travel to developing countries without rubber from home. I had early on discovered that there were no condom vending machines in any bathroom in any pubs in Africa. And I could never expect to find a pharmacy on any corners, either. Not that it would have mattered, of course.

This was Africa, so the local condoms were in any case way too big for me.

We continued to Lusaka the next day. The Zambian capital feels typically African. A crowded main street with a few shops, small markets and the odd bank. We walked down the street on one side, took a U-turn and returned on the other. To see more and to meet others. There are usually a lot of people who are keen on a chat when someone obviously a foreigner roams the streets in Zambia.

We eventually found a youth hostel. The manager there, Preeti, showed us to our room. It came with four bunk beds. There were no other available rooms; we might as well save some money on our accommodation budget. We were anyhow the only guests in it, so if we were lucky we'd still get some sort of a twin room. We dumped our backpacks on two of the beds and Preeti showed us the way to the backyard where there was a bar. A blackboard told us about the option of tonight. Common dinner at 20:00, a couple of hours away. We ordered a couple of Mosi. The local beer, named after Victoria Falls. The mighty waterfall is called Mosi Oa Tunya there. Preeti served us. She was in her late 20's and was typical boss material. She knew what she wanted, and how she wanted it.

A Brit sat down at our table. He worked as a teacher, and told us that he had arrived a couple of weeks ago and that he still hadn't found a permanent residence.

Preeti came along after a while, serving some sort of a stew. Before pouring herself a GT and taking the fourth seat at our table. I joined her in a taxi three hours later. Øystein had been notified that he would get the eight man room alone. The car, an old banger, drove to a posh villa neighborhood. The standard of the houses was high, the roads leading there was not. I don't know if it is typical for Zambian girls, but Preeti sure knew exactly what she wanted. We went straight to the bedroom. Which is when I noticed the huge framed poster, two meters across. A team photograph of Liverpool Football Club. Rather fishy.

"So, you like football?"

"No, that's my husband's."

The answer came without hesitation. As if it was the most natural thing in the world to bring a guy into the master bedroom. Under your husband's football poster.

How on Earth she could afford a villa on a youth hostel salary was suddenly evident. But what the hell did I do there, in the home of a married woman?

I all of a sudden had very cold feet, and asked her to order a taxi. It arrived an hour and 20 minutes later.

TIA. This is Africa.

I didn't exactly feel very brave while waiting for transport back to safety. Every little gust of wind made the gate to the villa move while squeaked loudly. The hinges were desperate for oil. And at every little sound I pictured a very mad husband looking like Chuck Norris enter with a machete in one hand and a sawed-off shotgun in the other. I was relieved when someone finally knocked on the wooden gate. I knew that it had to be the taxi driver. Chuck Norris doesn't knock on doors.

Iran

That I would ever end up kissing an Iranian girl, in Iran, wasn't even a thinkable option when I decided to travel to one of the world's oldest civilizations together with Øystein, Doctor Vodka and Marius who I had just been to Afghanistan with. It was all in all extremely strange to go straight from Turkmenistan to Iran. From Oleg's vodka kingdom to a highly conservative police state, complete with its own religious police. The acclimation is such instances usually take some time. Marius had in the meantime left us; he was meeting up with a Norwegian mate. As you do, in Iran.

We had taken a taxi from the border to Turkmenistan up north to the easterly located Mashad, one of the most religious cities in Komeini country. Øystein and I volunteered to go get tickets to Esfahan, an ancient trading town 10 hours away, on railroad tracks. There was luckily an own hole in the wall for foreigners in the train station. Anything else would not have been very efficient. Virtually no one speaks English in Iran. I noticed two attractive girls, when we were queueing. Their headscarves were sitting worryingly far back on their heads, and hardly covered any hair at all. A common trick used by more and more girls in the country. And beyond. Myrian in the Maldives had done the same. The religion police can't really give them hell, let alone tell them they will go there. The girls would just argue that the scarf had slid a little, and instantly move it back up. They risk a warning, at worst. In reality, they won't get much more than a few frowns.

The nicest girl was 27 years old, it turned out. I was 34. Her name was Neda, and she spoke English too. Sort of. Ten minutes were enough before she gave me her name and number on a note. I wouldn't want to be impolite, and I gave her my contact details back. She seemed cool.

Two days later, just after narrowly avoiding being conned by a Swedish speaking souvenir salesman in Esfahan, my phone rang. It was a local number, and I answered in English.

"Hello, it is Neda. Where are you?" she asked.

We saw each other again the next day. In a hotel lobby in Teheran. Neda had brought her bodyguard. He introduced himself as Alexander and said that he was not only a strong man, but only her professor.

"She has her own professor? You are her bodyguard and professor?"

"I have two doctor's degrees from Oxford University and Harvard Business School. As you have noticed, her English is not perfect. So I am helping her father to prepare her for the world."

"What does her father do?"

"He owns real estate. A lot of real estate."

He said, and blinked with the left eye so that Neda couldn't see it. There was no doubt that she was backed up with money and that she usually had it her way. I assumed that Alexander was paid well too.

Doctor Vodka was going through the mother of all tummy troubles and was momentarily out of play. We got him into the three man room in our hotel. Before Øystein and I joined Alexander and Neda. To an Iranian gourmet restaurant.

Three musicians played muted music in a corner as we came down the stairway and into the basement restaurant. There were long red Persian rugs on the floors, and we were shown to our table by a highly professional waiter of the quiet type. Øystein and I sat down next to each other. Big mistake. My brother was politely ordered by Alexander out of the seat and over to the other side of the table, opposite me. We didn't quite get why, but assumed that it was some sort of Iranian etiquette that brothers or family members should sit across the table from one another. Neda sat next to me, Alexander next to Øystein. The wooden chairs had figures carefully carved into the backs and underneath the broad armrests.

The conversation was relaxed and flowed freely. Neda didn't talk too much, but her bodyguard slash professor told us a lot about her background and about himself. Primarily about himself.

Ten minutes passed and Neda suddenly stroke her right hand over my left hand that was laying on my armrest. Neither Alexander nor Øystein could avoid seeing what she had done. The armrests were at table's height.

"Gunnar, you will be Neda's husband. You are very lucky!" Alexander proclaimed.

Neda produced a shy smile. Øystein and I had to engage every bit of self-control we had ever possessed to not laugh out loud. We avoided all eye contact with each other the rest of the night. One error in that respect would have caused spontaneous and inevitable laughter cramps.

"Really?"

"Oh yes, she knew it the first time she saw you in Mashad. And Gunnar, her family will provide generously for you. She has a *very* fortunate background."

Neda just smiled. She was beautiful, with dark brown eyes. And she hardly stopped smiling at all throughout dinner. Ten minutes with me was clearly all she needed to fall majorly in love. She couldn't be particularly smart or reflected.

I can actually not remember what we were served for dinner, the situation was too bizarre, but it was delicious and expensive. Neda had discreetly picked up a silk wallet at the end of our meal and taken out brand new, seemingly ironed bills of high denomination. She insisted on paying and totally ignored our objections. They walked us back to our hotel, and we agreed to meet the next day.

It turned out we would then be given a guided tour. With Alexander as our local fixer and the network of Neda's family we had no problems getting access anywhere. We were, among other things, taken to one of the Shah's eight palaces i Teheran. The last shah ruled for 38 years. He lived in constant fear of being toppled by his enemies; hence he needed a lot of palaces so that no one would know where he was at any given time. Not a bad strategy for someone with unlimited money in his pocket and enemies behind every bush.

We would return to Norway the same night, and Neda became more and more sad the closer to departure we got. Her feelings certainly developed fast. She wanted to marry after the first night and was in urgent need of Prozac due to my departure 36 hours later.

Øystein has rarely smiled as much as he did in Teheran. No wonder, to be able to freely observe the very much in love girl with his own brother playing along out of curiosity. Maybe I had been a little too open to other cultures and impulses. We had ended up both holding hands and making out in the dark corner of a coffee shop. The religion police would have had a field day, and Alexander clearly disapproved too. He had demonstrated by turning away from his own employer, Øystein later told me.

United Arab Emirates

It had slipped my tongue, while in Teheran, that I would go to Dubai in United Arab Emirates for a conference only four weeks later. Neda had taken notice, and later demanded exact dates and details.

I was met in Dubai Airport by Stig Sunde, a mate from home, who worked as a financial controller for an Abu Dhabi based company building nuclear power plants. His Lexus was still gas driven.

"Cheaper than a Ford Fiesta back home," Stig said with satisfaction.

Norwegian car and road taxes must be annoyingly high. For those that engage in such self-transportation. I live in the middle of Oslo and don't need a car.

"Do you mind if we wait another 40 minutes? A girl from Iran will come too," I said to Stig shortly after having arrived.

"Is she beautiful?"

A classical Stig question.

"Would I otherwise have asked you to wait around?"

He giggled. Neda arrived on time. We drove downtown and had a really nice lunch. But it was obvious that Neda wasn't too keen on Stig's presence. She hadn't traveled to Dubai for a meal. Something which was made quite clear while my Norwegian friend was in the bathroom.

"When do we go to the hotel?"

"But we've just met Stig. He's my friend from back home."

"I want you. Now!"

Well, what should I say? Stig was asked, in relatively polite manners, to explore Dubai for a couple of hours. Neda knew what she wanted, and she was not concerned about waiting for the wedding night to accomplish her dreams.

Stig had in the meantime thoroughly enjoyed the two hours in an air conditioned mall. Before he met up with us again for dinner and later headed back south to Abu Dhabi, a much more conservative city than Dubai.

Neda and I later ended up in a lounge. Where we soon snogged by the bar. Not the cleverest of moves in Dubai, people have been arrested for much more minor offenses than that. The bartender was with us, probably faster than he had ever attended a customer before, practically begging us to find a room.

"Otherwise you will be given one room each. For free. By the authorities."

The Iranian background has made sure that Neda has other values than any girl I had ever encountered before. Iran is, for instance, very patriarchal. I was in Dubai to speak at a conference on mobile TV, and I would be in the conference venue all Sunday. Our last day of the week is the first day of an Arabic week, a normal weekday in other words. I asked Neda to relax, order room service if she wanted anything and just explore town and have fun. The conference was about to finish at 17:00 and I was in a meeting with a guy that looked more like Steve Buscemi than he ever did himself. Then Neda called.

"Where are you? I am hungry."

"You are hungry? But haven't you had lunch somewhere?"

"No, I am still in the room".

The hotel rooms in Dubai are far larger than what Paris Hilton has ever dreamt about, but still. A full day in such a room must be overly boring for anyone.

"You are still in the room? But didn't you order room service?"

"No. And I am hungry."

"I'll be there soon."

Such a lack of initiative. It annoyed me, but what to do with such a patriarchal society? Women in Iran have a few rules they should stick to. Regardless of who her father is or whatever he owns.

I took a taxi to the hotel to pick up Neda so that we could find a place where they served an early dinner. It turned out that she wasn't all that hungry, after all. Not for food, at least. I changed outfits before we actually got down to dinner. I had done some research and found a good and romantic Italian restaurant by an artificial canal in Dubai. We were given a huge menu each.

"What would you like, Neda?"

"I will have what you have."

Clearly a very normal procedure when Iranian women visit restaurants.

"Neda, I want you to eat what you really want to have. What you enjoy the most, independently from me. What would *you* like to have?"

We had a little session of ping pong. And eventually, after 15 minutes or so, she gave in and decided for a main course. Chicken breast with fresh spinach and mushrooms in a white wine sauce. That was typically exactly what I wanted too, but I had to choose something different should my attempt to get her to think for herself not be totally wasted. I opted for grilled fish instead.

"And what would you like to drink?"

"I will drink what you drink."

Here we go again. Easy is boring.

This time it only took three or four minutes to get her to make a decision.

"I want whiskey."

"Whiskey?"

"Yes!" she said with determination.

"For chicken?"

"Yes."

"OK, let's get you some good whiskey."

Neda was given a mild 20 year old Highland Park. I ordered a glass of Italian red wine. I have rarely seen anyone make faces as obviously as she did every time she forced down a zip.

"Do you not like the whiskey?"

"Yes, it is good."

"It is good?"

"Yes. Very good!"

Liar. But she could of course not admit that she didn't like the whiskey after I had practically forced her to freely choose something.

I later told about Neda to some mates back home.

"And you didn't marry her! Are you a complete idiot?" one of them asked. "She is wealthy, beautiful, good in bed, does exactly what you ask her to do and has no free will. She is the woman of totally unrealistic dreams!"

His words. I would have died. From boredom.

I didn't return to Dubai until years later. To visit Agata. We had met when she visited Oslo on holiday with her boyfriend. They had found me on Couchsurfing and had stayed several nights in my guestroom. She was later employed as cabin crew and moved to Dubai, where Emirates is headquartered. It is one of the airlines that flies to most countries and has thousands of cabin staff, all based in Dubai. Most of them aren't local, and they need a place to live. The airline has therefore built several building complexes of very nice flats, where you as cabin crew will share one with two others, as part of your wage package. Everyone has an own big room, but they share living room, bathroom and a modern kitchen. The least attractive of these complexes is located in the desert, half an hour drive from the middle of the city. Between three and four thousand employees live there, and shuttle buses go between the complex and the airport 24/7. There is also a shuttle to Dubai once every hour. The complex contains several swimming pools, a dry cleaners and a Costa Coffee café. And nothing else. Except for large amounts of sand. Everyone being employed as cabin crew will start out living here, in the middle of nowhere. To be able to move to the more luxurious and far more centrally located complexes, one of several skyscrapers in Dubai will later be an incentive in order to get people to work longer in the company.

I'd say 97 percent of the cabin crew are females, judging by those living in the desert complex. And there are allegedly virtually no straight guys among the males. It may therefore be tempting for the girls to invite external men to the flats. But Emirates is not keen on tarnishing its image by accepting such behavior. So, to visit Agata, and actually stay there, we had to be related. That wasn't too hard to organize. We are both blond, and Agata said that I am her cousin. That was enough to secure a paper permit that I had to show to the receptionist every time I wanted to enter or leave the complex. They want full control of who is there at any given time, and for how long.

Employees of Emirates are typically given a 30-70 percent discount on pretty much anything in Dubai. Which includes the bills in restaurants, bars, coffee shops and nightclubs. And of course they get in for free to all the best nightclubs. Emirates do not employ visually challenged girls. And world history proves that pretty women attract paying men.

The discount is also valid when it comes to rental cars. So, instead of picking up the usual class A Fiat I ended up with a Ford Mustang with 8 cylinders. At the same price. Agata didn't want to drive, which meant that I had to. Doomed. I haven't driven such a fast car since I test drove a Maserati in Moscow. The response was swift and the 325 millimeter wide tires got accustomed to high temperatures caused by friction. We cruised down to the yacht club in Dubai where I was introduced to three Greek colleagues and friends of hers.

Iriela Kasemi was previously a football agent, but had to go out of business when the financial crisis hit Greece at full strength. I believe that she must have owned the title "the world's most beautiful football agent". Of course, competition is not too fierce. Dimi Koutraki was a teacher, and were hit by the same crisis as the youngest teachers were the first to be fired. To be a professional ballerina was likewise no longer an option for Maria Mittakou. Such high culture was not on top of Greek minds anymore, either. And it didn't help that she drove motorbikes as an expensive hobby. The solution for all three was Emirates in Dubai.

I hadn't had the car full of girls since I volunteered as a weekend driver with my parents' Subaru as a 19 year old. And none of them back then got into the car for any other reason than to be driven to and from the local pub. There was only one.

In Dubai I had a stunning car with four stunning girls inside. And a slightly better selection of entertainment options.

We drove Agata to the airport the next day. She was heading to Milano. The rest of us would remain in Dubai. The Mustang delivered and took us to the beach. Eventually. Map reader Iriela was not paying as much attention as expected and we were suddenly half way to Abu Dhabi. There aren't many exits once you get onto the 10-16 lane wide motorway. But what a detour! Long stretches of straight road. Neither football agents, teachers nor ballerinas turned out to be particularly negative at high speed. I was all of a sudden doing 240 kilometes per hour.

"Come on, faster, faster!" Maria cheered. She sat just behind me. The motorcycle driver enjoyed the smell of rubber.

"OK, since you're twisting my arm."

The engine put up no fight, and we were doing 260 before a curve that approached fast. Very fast. The breaks of the Mustang are luckily custom made, and we safely made our way to the beach. It turned out that you don't rent a sun chair on the beaches there. You rent a double bed. Which comes with a waiter wearing white gloves. Being the designated driver, I skipped the bubbles, but still had a great time with Maria, Iriela and Dimi who flanked me in bed.

"Bloody bohemian life lover!" A friend shouted at me. He was not at all envious when I told him the story over a coffee back in Oslo a few weeks later. He changes diapers in his spare time.

South Korea

I have been over 15 times to South Korea. Or Korea as they insist on calling their country. North Korea is their only neighbor, but that particular country is hardly even mentioned in daily chitchat. There has just been too much scaremongering, too many threats, too much propaganda and too many broken promises. Too much bollocks from the Kim dynasty up north, in other words.

Haenim is also named Kim. They are not related. We were set to marry in Seoul, the Korean capital, in 2012, but we never got that far in the end.

We had been going out for no more than 18 months when I proposed. I was very much in love, and scared to lose her. And I had tried every other way. She had been invited to live with me in Oslo, but that was an invitation she did not accept. Not without being married. So I proposed. A classical mistake. A desperate measure to try save a relationship that wasn't 100 percent. Better than making her pregnant, at least. But idiotic, nevertheless. We had, after all, never been physically together longer than three weeks in one go.

Not the best of backdrops. Which also made me less serious about the forthcoming marriage. The opposite was the case with Haenim, and certainly her family. Kids live with their families until they marry. Full stop. In Korea, at least. There are virtually no exceptions, and living together as a couple is unheard of.

And surprise, surprise. Traditions in Korea are totally different than in the West. We had certainly discussed the challenge, but not reflected particularly much over it. Love makes blind.

In Korea it is for instance common to take wedding photos many weeks before the wedding takes place. The reasoning behind it is that the wedding guests should be able to see the photos during the celebration. And the photo shoot is a big thing too. It takes all day, and the bride to be will be photographed in at least three wedding dresses, her future husband will have two or three suits or tuxedos. The photographs are naturally taken in several locations to which friends and family join in as well. A great excuse for an evening party. Haenim had planned everything carefully. We had pictures taken in a photo studio, on a bridge, in a forest and outside a luxurious villa that had been rented for the occasion. The day had started early, at an eminent hairdresser. It was one of those few times I have been styled and had makeup applied. I was 35. I looked like a teenager in the photos. Not necessarily a bad thing, Haenim is 11 years younger than me. And we finished the day with some sort of a stag night party with all her best friends present in the villa we had been photographed outside, on the outskirts of Seoul.

I had slowly realized around the time of the photographs that we were in fact not a perfect combination. We fought about everything and nothing. About details and the big questions in life. About dishwashers and how to pronounce words in English. About life philosophies and traveling. It didn't do us any favors that both are stubborn as a donkey in its terrible threes. We discussed how to escape the vicious circle, but without much success. We agreed to be nicer to each other. We failed. We broke up two months after the photo shoot, having finally realized that we were incompatible. The wedding was cancelled, the wedding venue as well. I still have the wedding photos, though. On a memory stick somewhere.

The wedding invitations had luckily not gone out, but I had still talked enough about it all for Øystein, Benedicte, Andreas and Bjarne to know about the planned wedding date. When they found return tickets to Seoul costing less than 600USD, they instantly took advantage of the offer. Which meant that four of my closest had tickets to Korea. To a non-happening wedding. I felt partly guilty and joined them as a guide. It ended up as a party weekend.

In Electric Shoes.

Seoul is coincidentally the city with the world's best music bar. Electric Shoes is in Apgujeong in Gangnam, the district that was made world famous by Psy through the song "Oppa Gangnam Style". Gangnam means south of the river. The bar is run by Alex Moon, a woman my age with the world's coolest whiskey voice. And she has any music you can imagine, stacked up towards the walls. She has over ten thousand pieces of vinyl, cassettes, video discs and CDs. Plus a laptop for streaming and music files. We have never been able to successfully challenge her to play something she doesn't have. Except for a Korean tune.

"Come on, I don't do local stuff," she answered a little huffy. But she wasn't for long. She always accepts music wishes from her guests down in the dark basement. Which is hard to find. The bar is down an anonymous marble stairway in an anonymous side street. Only the sign will guide you to it. A round sign with a cannabis plant. Even though she doesn't serve drugs. There are harsh penalties for such in Korea.

I visit every time I am in town, for the ambience and to chat with Alex. If I come without Ronald, Andreas or Jørn she checks up on them. Not strange, really. We have emptied Electric Shoes for bubbles more than once. On real boys' trips.

And again so, during my "wedding weekend". This was Bjarne's first trip to Korea. He has not yet seen Seoul in daylight. At least he didn't have to deal with jetlag.

Guinea

Europeans won't get jetlag going to Guinea either. The country is straight south. The capital Conakry is a chaotic town located on a long and narrow peninsula that goes straight out into the Atlantic.

There are loads of stalls around town, shabby stalls where people sell lottery tickets, fruit and fish. And I noticed rubbish everywhere. Surprisingly much, even for an African city. What used to be the city beach is now covered with layers of rubbish. At least the pigs around there approve.

The beaches on the outskirt of town but still on the peninsula are much cleaner. I was advised to go there by Kai. The German has converted large parts of a giant villa to a hotel, while still living in one part of it. I rented one of his rooms, and could enjoy German hospitality, cable TV and wireless internet.

"You should go to the beach a couple of Ks from here. That's where the locals go. It will be fun!"

I listened to the German gone local and walked through a middle class residential neighborhood, strangely with a few nightclubs and restaurants, to get there. Some sort of a bouncer demanded a dollar for beach access. I couldn't be bothered to protest, even though the locals did not pay. A white person will in certain parts of Africa be ripped off in one way or another for no particular reason. I decided to look upon it as a contribution to the local economy.

I got there just in time for a classical West African sunset. They never fail to impress me. And a party was actually taking place on the beach. People in their 20's and 30's stood scattered around, drinking bottled Guilux beers which are nice and light. Some people were barbequing meat and fish over old empty oil barrels. I only saw two or three other westerners on the beach. A woman came over to me after a while. She was tipsy.

"How are you doing?"

Inspired by Joey in Friends, perhaps? The tone was almost exactly the same, but she seemed to be genuinely interested. I was not, but it is regardless nice with a chat. And as soon as the other people around noticed that I didn't bite, others dared approach me too.

Madeleine was among them. She came over together with her friend Monica.

"Can I get you a beer?" Madeleine asked.

Wow, I hadn't heard that one before.

"Sure, why not."

She clearly had money. The pretty girl asked me the usual questions. I told her about Norway, Kai's hotel and that I enjoyed traveling. And asked if she had any recommendations of what to do in Guinea.

"Soumba is an amazing waterfall. You have to see it!"

"Hehehe...we have a couple of waterfalls where I'm from too," I said. As in thousands.

"None of them are like Soumba. I guarantee it!" she assured me.

"So, how do I get there?

"My driver will take you. Tomorrow?"

"How far is it?"

"A couple of hours."

"Deal!"

Madeleine, Monica and the driver picked me up outside Kai's the next morning. I insisted to pay for gas, they didn't object. But I had to meet Madeleine's family on our way to the waterfall. She lived with her mother, a sister with husband and two kids. No one knew where her father was. They ran a medium sized shop and could afford an apartment of decent quality in an old residential building outside town. There were tiles on the floor, the living room partially furnished. But only one wall had a window, and the room was dark and not very cozy.

I was invited to sit on the couch. They didn't have a table, but I was served a glass of Pepsi on a white plastic chair. The sister's oldest boy had clearly also been givem some sugar water. He had totally overdosed on sugar. The kid was insanely hyper and moved all over the place. What happened to nutritional education in underdeveloped countries?

Madeleine was in her mid 20's and very fit. Her mother was black, while she had substantially lighter skin. I guessed that her father was European. Monica had taken the passenger seat, so Madeleine and I were in the back. She was not shy, and it didn't take long before we somehow ended up kissing wildly while the villages flew past on both sides.

We drove the last few kilometers on a dirt road. There were no one else at the waterfall, but I don't think she would have been particularly embarrassed in any case. The water temperature was high, and we jumped in wearing nothing but underwear. I had seen plenty of waterfalls before, but never kissed underneath one. As taken from a rubbish movie from the 80's with blue and lagoon in the title.

Costa Rica

There are plenty of lagoons, beaches, waterfalls and rainforests in Costa Rica. It is one of the most diverse countries on the world, and has become one of the most popular destinations for ecotourism. It probably doesn't do any harm that the country boasts 1,000 butterfly species, 20,000 sorts of spider and 34,000 kinds of insects. The peaceful country is also one of few in the world without an army. Should they run into trouble, the United States is there to defend them thanks to a defense treaty.

I hadn't planned to visit Costa Rica when I did, but I received an email out of the blue from the doppelganger of actress Penelope Cruz, just younger, with a nicer smile and an even fitter body. The correspondence that followed should probably have made all Nigeria scam instincts kick in, except for the fact that she wasn't looking for money. She just wanted me to visit. I don't know where she found me on the internet, but I didn't really burn many calories wondering either.

I might have seemed a little naive and easily conned, but I hadn't been to Costa Rica and I decided to also visit some other Central American countries while I was at it. The hot and intense dialogue with "Penelope Cruz", or Mercedes as she was called, made buying the plane tickets a no brainer.

Easy is boring.

Mercedes was the sole member of the welcome committee at the airport in San Jose. And it turned out that she was even prettier in real life than in photos. Given that was possible. I had ordered a rental car and we drove towards the West Coast. And checked into a resort hotel in Playa Herradura. It was my first time in such a hotel. And the last. For several reasons. Buffet breakfast where the goal seems to be to eat the most dishes in the shortest possible time, artists with no talent whatsoever that sing while a colleague "plays" a synth, buffet dinner where the goal seems to be to eat the most dishes in the shortest possible time and a price that includes all of the above plus as much as you can drink of the cheapest drinks that can be purchased legally in a so called nightclub where mullets are still considered high fashion.

But she liked it. And as long as Mercedes was happy, she did whatever she could to make me happy. She was addicted to sex, wherever we were. In the pool, in the Pacific, in the shower, in the car.

"Do you want a blow job, darling?"

"Mercedes, I am driving!"

"I love it when you say yes in mysterious ways!"

I was fined, but she was not the reason. The police officers luckily didn't witness the result of her indecent proposal at high speed. And the fine was immediately reduced from 200 to 50USD the moment Mercedes demanded a receipt.

We hung out for almost a week. Before I became restless. There were other undiscovered countries in Central America, and I had tickets to all of them. Mercedes was also a little bit too ready for marriage, I was not at all. I assume that was her reason to get in touch in the first place, but I still wondered why she picked me. Chances are she has used the same trick since.

Paraguay

When you order a bottle of champagne, it will usually be served in a bucket of ice. Beers are served the same way in Paraguay, thanks to the extreme humidity and the heat during the summers. The beers will otherwise not be drinkable after a minute or two.

I arrived, assuming that I was in a Spanish speaking country. But I was wrong. Most people actually speak Guarani. There is no point speaking Spanish on the country side, let alone English. And to get into the country wasn't easy either, but not due to language problems. Maybe I look suspicious when traveling with nothing but a relatively small backpack. I was in any case invited in to the customs office. And their very sterile "office".

I was not so politely asked to strip down to my boxers. To ask for judicial assistance was not an option. Individual rights in such situations are all in all very limited. They were looking for narcotics.

I have a lot of other vices, but I couldn't help them with this one.

They ended up giving me advice on a good and traditional restaurant instead. Which is where I met Lili. She stood outside speaking on the phone holding a yellow helmet in her hand.

"What's up with the helmet?" I asked just after that she hung up and our glances met.

"Why are you asking? Haven't you seen a girl with a helmet before?"

And we were talking. She told me that she worked as an architect and that her work involved a lot more than what took place inside an office. She often visited the building sites to check that everything went according to plan and drawings. She had come straight from a site. We were both starving, and ended up inside the restaurant where we had local beef of top quality. Before it was dessert time. In Paraguay, that involves tea. Tereré is similar to the Mate tea I overdosed on in Uruguay. But there is a big difference, in Paraguay it is cold. The Paraguayans claim that to drink it cold gave them an upper hand in former wars with the other countries. Not having to make a fire to boil the water made sure that their camp sites were not easily discovered. I anyhow had coffee instead. Before Lili ordered stronger stuff. We had beers, not in ice buckets, but in some sort of an insulating foam cup that is placed outside the can.

We somehow got talking about travel. She had been here and there in South America and southern parts of Europe. My extreme traveling came up too. But she claimed that I hadn't really been around much.

"You can't count a country until you've had a baby in it."

"Really? And how many countries did you say you had been to again?"

She pushed me, in a friendly way. We looked at each other and laughed. 1-0 to me. In flirting.

"Why are you so thin, by the way?" she inquired.

"I am not thin; my weight has been the same for almost 20 years."

"Lucky boy! And don't say that I am fat as a revenge. I would kill you!"

I didn't doubt her for a second. Her body indicated that she worked out. I guessed that men and women alike turned their heads after her on the street. Her smile is contagious too. And her brilliant sense of humor didn't hurt either. But she had a typical South America temper. I discovered the moment I looked at other girls passing by. Not to mention the distance between Paraguay and Norway.

But the days we had together in Asuncion were amazing.

Mongolia

I had been invited to the huge country between Russia and by Sharad Sadhu. It was ABUs annual General Assembly again, several years after Kazakhstan. Sharad is a lovely guy, and always up to date on technical issues. NRK was still ahead on mobile services, and I had been invited yet again, despite a few glitches in Almaty.

But ABUs General Assembly didn't really matter. It was much more of a milestone that Mongolia would be my 100th country to visit. One hundred, two zeros, three figures, over half way there. Less than half the countries to go to that distant goal. I had, after all, primarily been to "easy" countries. Still, reaching a 100 was a massive vitamin injection. I had proved to myself that I could and would forsake whatever it took to get there. I don't know if I really ever had my doubts, but I surely shook off any of them in Mongolia and promised to myself there and then that I would indeed finish my quest.

It was celebration time, but my Asian colleagues and I was in for a surprise. The last Friday every month is "white" - restaurants and bars are not allowed to serve alcohol. Until I finally discovered a loophole. The rule doesn't apply to room service in hotels. I was later told about the other loophole. To get to know the restaurant owners well enough to be served drinks in a big coffee mug. It is not transparent and could contain whatever, also beer, wine or hard liquor. But there was one rule. You would have to perform a Tajikistan inspired fifty-fifty operation should the police come to control that the alcohol ban was being enforced. Bottoms up, in other words.

I had as usual traveled earlier than I had to for work. Which meant I had a few days of vacation before the conference. There were only two Mongols and me in the Irish bar. Until Canadian Fiona Smith, let me call her that, walked in. We didn't have much of a choice, really, we started talking. She was teacher at an international school and taught English. She had worked there for almost a year.

"So, who do you know here after such a long time?" I asked. I was actually curious.

"Loads of people, of course!"

"No, i mean who do you know who is also local?"

"Dozens of people!"

"Yeah? Name four."

"Ehe...Boldbayar, Anar...ehe..."

"I knew it! You live here, but you only hang with other westerners. You're such a typical expat."

"I am so not!"

"OK, prove that you know someone. Get them here."

Boldbayar came through the door half an hour later. With his girlfriend.

"I think you owe me a beer." Fiona said and put on a big smile. I got a round of drinks. Before Boldbayar insisted on taking us to a strip joint where there were not many other guests. The Mongol ordered a lap dance to himself. And for me.

"Boldbayar, that is very nice of you, but..."

Fiona touched my shoulder and stopped me mid-sentence. And leant over towards me.

"His father is a big shot around here. You have to accept. It will be very disrespectful, otherwise," she whispered.

So, I had my lap dance debut in Mongolia. Very reluctantly. Unusually after being talked into it by a woman. And the stripper wasn't even attractive.

But Fiona was. And I was invited home to hers. She had a flat next door to the international school, and her alarm clock went off 07:30 the next morning.

"I have to teach. Do you mind speaking to my kids about Norway in a couple of hours?"

"Sure, not a problem!"

"I'll come get you. Just get some more sleep in the meantime. You look really tired!"

"Thanks, Mrs. Teacher!"

The fifth graders loved the Norwegian visit in the class room. Fiona had told them that I would show up, and they had spent one lesson to prepare. It turned out they really were curious and asked a lot of questions. What types of houses we have in Europe, whether I had been to Japan, what kind of food I preferred and what was my mom's name.

"Are you in love with Ms. Smith?"

The last question came from a little girl with glasses all the way in the back of the classroom. Fiona answered suspiciously fast on my behalf.

"No, he is not."

Before cancelling the remaining questions. She told them to get ready for their mountain trip. The class would hike a tiny peak in Ulaanbaatar.

"Can Gunnar join?"

A boy sitting by one of the frontline desks dared to ask the question.

"We have to ask him politely, then, won't we?"

"Would you like to join us, Gunnar? Please!" they all said, as if in a choir.

"You don't have to," Fiona whispered.

"I don't mind. It's my day off," I answered. I was all of a sudden the mountain guide for a bunch of kids. They all wanted to hold my hand. It also turned out that picking up the boy who fell over and hurt himself and letting him ride on my shoulders was a big mistake. Suddenly everyone wanted to ride Norwegian shoulders.

"No, no, no. That is only for injured people."

A boy fell flat on the path, clearly on purpose.

"I am injured!" he screamed.

"Nice try, but no cig...ehe...but no price for you, my friend."

My presentation was scheduled for the next day. It went much, much better than in Almaty several years earlier. Of course, I had gained some experience in the meantime.

Zimbabwe

There were girls in Zimbabwe too, but no conferences to speak at. The Fiat would take Kjersti and me through the country. The economy was down the drains with hyperinflation and a total lack of goods and gasoline. We filled the tank to the rim on the South African side of the border, and brought ten extra liters of gas as well. The container was leaking a little, so the entire car smelled of gasoline. I had calculated that we would just about make it to Victoria Falls and across the border to Botswana where we would be able to refill. Given that I drove very carefully. Then again, all others did not, especially after dark. Quite a few people then drive without the lights on in order to save valuable gas. That causes accidents. We decided to drop driving all the way to Bulawayo, the second biggest city in the country, and to rather check into the first hotel we could find after a few near crash experiences. We ended up in Gwanda, a little town with a virtually empty shopping center, a pub, a church, a bank and Gwanda Hotel.

The receptionist smiled when we arrived, Of course they had a twin room, and they even served us dinner in the restaurant before Kjersti's bed time. We are related for sure, but our day rhythms are quite different. I decided to walk over to the bar, which was in fact inside the shopping center. The receptionist was still at work. Her sign said Belinda.

"Do you wanna join for a beer, Belinda?"

"I would love to! I am off work in five."

I waited for her to change out of her uniform, and we walked together the few hundred meters in the dark. I treated her and we discussed Mugabe and the situation in the country. With caution. Mugabe was never a big fan of oppositional voices and he has supporters across the country. It was a pleasant evening, but I was in bed shortly after midnight. But to invite Zimbabwean girls on a drink does not go by unpunished. I must have made an impression, or a hope of possible love and wealth far, far away. To give her that impression was not at all intended, she still kept contacting me for three years. After two beers and a nice conversation. She even sent me a T-shirt from Hotel Gwanda. I haven't used it much.

Kjersti and I was up early the next day. She is annoyingly incapable of sleeping late. There was a basket with dry bread and a butter container waiting for us on our table.

"Well, we are in Zimbabwe, we could probably not expect anything but a very ordinary or even awful breakfast," I complained.

Kjersti hardly moved an eyebrow and nodded towards the chef. She lived in the region, and new a thing or two about local food traditions. He came towards us.

"How would you like your steaks, madam, sir?"

Kjersti put on a slightly arrogant what was it I said kind of smile. I have never had steak for breakfast since.

We stopped in Bulawayo and walked around town. The selection of vegetables, meat and fish seemed to be OK. But there was no bread anywhere. And in a sports store there was actually no selection at all. There was one pair of football shoes in the shelves. Size 38.

It turned out that my gasoline calculation had worked, and we both experienced having our hair wet by Victoria Falls. Before we narrowly made it to Kasane in

Botswana and a gas station that actually had gas. I have rarely if ever driven as economically sensible as in Zimbabwe.

Guyana

That I managed to get to Guyana alive was not for sure, either. I would travel to the former British colony in South America from neighboring Suriname, and the bus took between 6 and 10 hours. Sometimes even longer. I was not in the mood for spending that much time in an overloaded vehicle, complete with crying kids, frustrated dads and worn out business women. Gum Air came to the rescue. One of the world's smallest airlines only operate tiny propeller airplanes. With no room for cabin crew. That means that the security demonstration happens in the terminal building before departure. The pilot then walked with us to the plane. I ended up sitting next to him, all the way up front. Eight others were in the back. I have never been scared on any flights, but my pulse was higher than usual this time.

The plane left dead early in the morning, and the pilot didn't utter a word the entire flight. I hope he was just morning moody, not hung over. At least the view was unbeatable. Not only did I sit in front, such aircraft also fly a lot lower than normal scheduled flights. Gum Air also operates between the small airports Zorg en Hoop and Ogle that are located virtually in the middle of the capitals Paramaribo in Suriname and Georgetown in Guyana.

The latter comes across as a shabby city, but it has actually developed rapidly the last few years and now has a range of modern buildings in some parts of town. Other parts are just the way the British left them. The locals are particularly proud of their cathedral, which is allegedly the highest wooden church in the world.

I was in need of a coffee after the early flight, and I walked to Oasis Kafé, the best coffee shop in town. That's where I met Rousanna Baird.

"Rousanna is supposed to be French but I can't seem to figure out the accent. Neither can anybody else. Plus it's bloody long! So, please call me Rose."

"Does it usually take that long for you to introduce yourself?"

We ended up talking over several cups of coffee. And the best brownies in the country. Then again, the competition is limited. I asked Rose what happened in Georgetown during weekends.

"We like to impress and we go way out for some good Guyanese fun. We're natural party people, give us any shack, beach or nightclub and we're there with drinks."

She wasn't even 30, but had already run her own shop for several years. A hard working woman. With dark brown eyes, a contagious smile and the most perfect teeth I have ever seen.

We had dinner together before she took me clubbing. That's when I discovered the strangest clubbing custom ever. After midnight, just when people are getting tipsy, the DJs start challenging the females to some sexy dancing. Via the speakers while playing music. Then again, challenge is the wrong word. The girls are almost harassed unless they do as they are told. The girls move their asses to the music and eventually rub them against the nearest men. It seemed like the goal was to provoke erections all over the dance floor. At least so it seemed. But Rose explained.

"We love to dance. And dance we do, in all fashions. But the most common form of dancing is dirty dancing. As you just experienced," she explained enthusiastically and smiled. "It seems extremely sexual, I guess, if looking at it from a foreigner's point of view. But it's no big deal! It's normal and it means nothing sexual. If the DJ says to grind harder into a guy, then you listen to the DJ. It's fun. Provocative and fun."

"And how was I supposed to understand that?" I pondered.

"Well, that's a legit question. Just remember that a real man can handle a nice behind grinding into his crotch. I swear it! It's just dancing. A little Guyana tradition for you," she said and blinked.

Before we split. She walked home, I returned to my hotel.

And she could say whatever she wanted to, but a lot of the nightclub guests seemed to leave together with newly acquired company. The question is whether the DJs receive mainly thank you cards or demands to contribute towards child support.

Singapore

Singapore is both a country and a city. The 64 islands are the size of United States Virgin Islands. 100 percent of the people live in a city, and is together with Monaco the world's most urban country. You are virtually guaranteed to see the Merlion, Singapore's beats of a mascot. There are several statues of the half fish, half lion across the city. The lion symbolizes an animal a historical prince claims to have seen, while the fish points to the history as an important harbor city in ancient times.

A lot of the people here are Chinese and speak poor English. Few of them can for instance not pronounce the letter R; it is often uttered as L instead. At least they have self-irony about it. The name of one of the rooftop bars in town is named Loof.

I had spoken about MiniTV at a conference in Singapore, before dinner with several colleagues. Four of us continued to Marina Bay for a pint on the waterfront. At one point I noticed someone staring at me. I could see a girl with dark blond hair in my side vision. She was wearing red high heels, a short skirt and a white top. I turned around and saw Vera. Beautiful Vera. We knew each other from back home, and had been on a few dates in Oslo together.

"Hi, Vera! What on Earth are you doing here?"

"What on Earth are *you* doing here?"

She was as surprised as me. But we ended up in a big hug.

"I am at work. And you, don't you work in Beijing?" I wondered.

"I do, I am just on a weekend trip here."

The world isn't always all that big. We sat down at a separate table for a chat. She had time for one glass of wine before she had to run to meet a few friends.

"Who the hell was that stunner?" a colleague asked.

Vera has a body and a character that charms and impressed most. My colleagues, included.

"She is just a fan," I shrugged. I couldn't resist pulling a white lie.

"And I presume she will be waiting in your room?"

I smiled, but didn't say anything. They jealously shook their heads and sipped their beers.

Grenada

There are no reasons not to drink beer in Grenada in the Caribbean either. The tiny state consists of only seven islands, and the hundred thousand or so people have 344 square kilometers of roaming space. Or the size of Philadelphia. The country has a typically British look and feel, even though the capital St. George's was built by France. I had visited a local bar, and I was the only white person there. A woman walked over to me with a large bottle of Carib beer in her hand and asked me where I was from. My response put a big smile on her face.

"That is great, that means that I can speak Swedish," she said. In Swedish. It turned out that Claudia was Caribbean, but that she had been married to a Swede until two years earlier. She was 4-5 years older than me, and looked great. Still not quite my type, but superb and knowledgeable company. She sure knew Grenada and we explored the tiny country together the next two days. We tested various restaurants and I discovered that St. George's is quite a nice town, as long as we stayed away from the cruise ship port and the immediate areas. I particularly liked the fruit and spice market in the center. The smells and colors are truly magical.

We had a lot of long and deep conversations on all sorts of topics, including relationships and sex. She was very open and told me about ex-boyfriends, her ex-husband and previous bed mates. It was only natural that I did the same, but we never practiced together.

A few weeks later I started receiving regular text messages from Claudia.

"Your mom's best present to the world was you. I will be surprised if there exists any other guy like you, only single and at least 4 years older than you. I hope you are not dead, kidnapped

or injured on your dangerous journeys. You laugh beautifully, you are kind, fun, intelligent, brave and happy."

I thanked for the nice message, despite not being totally comfortable with her tone. But it would only become even more intense the following days, weeks and months.

"There are few people like you. Make children!!! Make many Gunnar Garfors."

That must have been the biggest confidence boost of a message I have ever received. I have photographed, enlarged and framed it.

"Gunnar! Thinking of you! I admit to God Almighty, myself and you that I am hopelessly in love with you. I would like to be the woman you search, who is always at your side. But I want you to have the one you want and the one who is best for you, my friend! But I would always fuck you to pieces so that you could not manage another girl."

She wasn't exactly shy. But a Thursday I received a message that topped all previous ones.

"Hi Gunnar! I know you. Curious, Norwegian and a citizen of the world. I don't want to know more about you. What I don't know about you are probably only problems. I'll cut to the chase, I want babies with you. Babies that will be loved by me and everyone that loves me. They will grow up without you or with you. Not important to me to marry you or to have a relationship with you. I manage everything regarding kids myself. You don't have to do anything but what you want to. I appreciate if you answer me in earnest."

I refused to enter a thorough correspondence on something I was not ready for. My answer was short.

"Seriously? I am not ready for children. I have to grow up myself first, and that might take a while :) But thanks a lot for the trust!"

Claudia seemed to have thought things through the next day. Or she had started drinking.

"Would you like to marry me? I would like to marry you. I usually know what I want."

I didn't know whether I should laugh or cry?

"Claudia, I do not want to marry anyone. But thanks for the compliment!"

And she went quiet. For almost a year. Before I received the last message.

"Hi! Shall we approach each other just as friends, or shall we for example give us a chance to try out whether we enjoy each other's company, do fun stuff together, comfort each other with great sex? If there will ever be sex between us I guarantee that I will fuck you to pieces! But not to worry, I live nearby the hospital, and they have good orthopedists. What does your impulse say? Big hug."

My impulse this time around was not to answer. Quite a few people would probably have been tempted to return to Grenada. I was scared and have never returned. The orthopedists probably have enough to do without me.

Vietnam

Øystein and I traveled to Vietnam to visit John Christian, the mate from back home who was among those I had surprised in Latvia. He worked as an executive project manager at a shipyard in the coastal town of Vung Tau. His main task was to train local workers, other foreigners were there to do the same. The shipyards in Norway didn't manage to fill up their order books, and a lot of workers had been fired. The solution for quite a few of them was to move to developing countries were shipyards were booming due to lower prices. Foreigners still made almost the same money as at home, as they had better skills which were in high demand in order to pass on knowledge. Jonna had been headhunted to Vung Tau. Not only was he highly skilled, he also spoke excellent English and knew how to teach and communicate with others.

He showed us around on the shipyard where we also met some British colleagues of his. To an untrained eye the near completed supply boats looked great, but he told us that it was rather hard to get Vietnamese workers without a boat building tradition up to the same level as back home.

Our evenings were typically spent in various bars and nightclubs. They clearly catered to foreign ship workers, sporting names as Offshore 1, Offshore 2, Offshore 3, Ocean Rig and Sea Warrior. The interior included a lot of young and beautiful girls. There were obviously prostitutes among them, most of them were however allegedly "normal" girls that hoped to find a man with far more money than what they could dream about locally. We ran into three of the Brits we had met at the ship yard in a music bar, the only joint in town without a suspiciously high girl percentage. Their British wives from back home were there too. Jonna had of course told a few stories, and we had a pretty clear understanding of the life of foreign shipyard workers in Vietnam. A lot of the foreigners picked up girlfriends temporarily while they were abroad, despite of having wives waiting back home. The guilt was painted on their foreheads as they desperately tried to maintain their position as stable and trustworthy family men with happy wives and children at home.

We knew that they knew that we knew.

We said hello and got all six a drink each, but soon realized that they were scared stiff that we would rat on them to their wives, so talk was slow. Turtle league slow. We soon escaped to Offshore 2 where there were no other foreigners. Which meant that the girls immediately flocked around us. We politely turned them down, although it was admittedly not all wrong to be surrounded by attractive girls from the moment we walked into the bar.

What was most disappointing was that they took our refusals nicely.

We felt rather shabby the next day. We had turned the girls down, but not the cheap drinks. Jonna managed to get up in time for work while Øystein and I had a desperate need for relaxing massage. Jonna had recommended what he called *serious* massage parlors. We knew that many were brothels in disguise.

"How do we know which ones are serious?" Øystein demanded.

"Places with those reflexology maps of the feet are usually serious. Go to one of those."

His advice was as clear as it was poor. We followed it. Øystein and I were shown to our own little room, by one girl each, on separate sides of a small hallway. We exchanged stories afterwards. What had happened was pretty much identical. Both of us had been asked to shower in a cubicle, tie a little towel around our waists and lay down on with our faces down on a massage bench. Before the girls started the most pitiful massage plagiarism attempts I have ever experienced. They signaled that we should turn around after three minutes of shoulder "massage". None of them spoke English.

"Bom bom?"

They said. In Vietnam it means "fuck".

"No, no, no."

Neither of us were interested in such. They decided to change strategy, and started to gently massage our erogenous zone to make us change our minds.

"Bom bom?"

They asked again. It had probably tempted many customers before us, but no. Change of tactics followed.

"Bom bom?"

This time around the question came with related gesticulation. They clearly referred to oral bom bom, but the answer was yet again negative, and they finally gave up. The next half hour passed with massage so poor it would have anyone not severely hung over commit suicide. We did in the end get an offer of "happy ending". Not surprisingly. I have never had a worse massage, but that was of course not what they were employed to perform either.

None of them received a tip. Jonna was slaughtered for his massage recommendation.

I was back in the country a few years later. Not at the bom bom ladies, but at work in Hanoi together with Jørn, the joker. We opted for a mandatory visit to a village north of the capital, where they specialize in snakes. As in food. We picked out a king cobra, and it had its teeth cut off before it was killed just in front of us. By a chap who clearly had done the deed before. He wrote a text message while he held the then still alive snake up for us to take photos. The huge venomous animal was made into ten dishes, included snake spring rolls, snake soup and fried snake skin. And this was for lunch. The heart usually goes to the oldest person around the table. I did not protest. The oldest person did. Jørn made faces while eating the heart.

And we got snake blood too, of course. Mixed with vodka. I might pass on that next time.

Our last night in Hanoi ended at a Halloween party in Westlake, the so called posh area of town. We came straight from a work dinner with the public service broadcaster VTV, and were wearing suits. The bouncer wasn't exactly impressed, and stopped us.

"Gentlemen, this is a Halloween party, we require you to wear costumes."

"Of course. We are dressed up as businessmen. The most evil there is," I improvised.

The broad shouldered bouncer started laughing so much that his bow tie started shaking.

"I will let you in. For creativity!"

Peru

Peru has a long and beautiful coastline, high and wild mountains as well as glaciers and of course world famous Machu Picchu. It is a versatile country, just like the potato. Which was coincidentally discovered here.

Cat is always an issue when it comes to food, as it is not unusual to see it on the menu. There used to be an annual cat meat festival in the town of La Quebrada south of Lima, but this was outlawed as late as in 2013. Cat eating was at its most prolific during this, and animal rights activists were fuming world-wide.

My sisters also love cats so much, that attending the festival was never an option. Or they would have denounced our blood line.

I had decided to visit Machu Picchu. It's a very impressive sight, but also touristic as hell. The place had still received enough acclaim by several friends that I decided to give it a shot. The Inca town is 600 years old, and was most likely home of the Inca chief Pachcuti. The town has deteriorated a lot throughout history, but is now gradually rebuilt by archeologists. It provides a good picture of the life of the Incas.

I arrived straight from a work trip in Taiwan, and had crossed the Pacific for a few days off in South America. A little round the world trip, in other words. The town of Cusco is only a few hours away from the famous ruins by train, and has its own airport. I took a small propeller plane from Lima. It landed heavily in the thin air. The runway is practically in the middle of town, but a taxi ride in this parts of the world costs nada, so I jumped into a car and was in my hotel within minutes.

She sat on a stairway by the hotel. The beautiful girl with pitch black hair who delivered a smile to kill for. She wore bright blue jeans and a green woolen sweater that hinted of an incredible figure. I smiled back.

"Do you know any nice restaurants around here?"

That was the cleverest thing I managed to think of. I wasn't prepared for such. Girls in Peru are renowned to be pretty, but this came all too sudden. "It depends," she said. And smiled again, widely. A natural smile.

"It depends?"

"Yes. It depends on whether you will invite me to come along or not."

"It depends."

She did not know what she had started.

"It depends?"

"Yes, I only invite stockbrokers, lawyers and car mechanics for dinner."

"Sure, I might fix your car!"

"You might?"

"It depends."

"Hahaha...it depends?"

"Yes, it depends on how many cylinders it's got."

We laughed together. Before I checked in, and came back out for a guided tour around town. Perfect! The old trick, to have locals show you around. That she was both smart and pretty was not a drawback. The conversation flew smoothly over dinner. We sat by a simple wooden table on small wooden stools and ate alpaca, a llama relative. She had taken me to a charming restaurant in the old town, not far from the square and Sagrada Familia, a little red stone church. The cobbled street outside just added to the lovely setting.

We had a great time together in Peru. Julia worked as a teacher, but had time off the week that I visited. A nice coincidence. And she wasn't hesitant to ask to join my Machu Picchu trip either. It would be her first time, as well. Locals rarely go there.

"Too many Americans," she explained.

The train ride to the little town of Aguas Calientes near Machu Picchu was magic. The old train slowly ascended the mountain from Cusco, before going down a valley at full speed. A truly amazing view of the mountains and the busy Urubamba River. Do sit by the window on the left hand side, and the two hours or so will pass by very quickly. There are a lot of small farms alongside the railroad. The farmers there struggle to get by without tractors or any modern machinery. Some of their produce is sold in Aguas Calientes, where most of the economy revolves around tourists. Buses go from there, delivering tourists to the ruins. Machu Picchu is a unique place, just be there very early in the morning to avoid the cramped feeling. We were on a day trip as Julia had to meet her mother in Cusco the following day. The train from Aguas Calientes took us back in time. Just about.

Canada

The gigantic northern country is the biggest in the world, after Russia. Canada has only two borders, both to the US. The one not bordering Alaska is the longest in the world. And that's not all. They can also brag about the world's longest street. Find the right street sign and you may still be 1,896 kilometers away from the particular street number you want. And let me not forget the longest coastline of any country. 202,000 kilometers makes it exactly twice as long as Norway's, the runner-up.

But what exactly is the difference between Canada and the US, anyway? A lot of people who have never been to either country see none. And they have no idea that celebrities such as Michael J. Fox, Keanu Reeves, Bryan Adams, Pamela Anderson, Justin Bieber, James Cameron, Leonard Cohen, Celine Dion, Dan Aykroyd and comedian Leslie Nielsen are in fact Canadian. Not to forget that the brother of the latter, Erik Nielsen, was vice prime minister in Canada for two years.

Canada is easy to visit from Europe, so I had prioritized other countries in North America on my holidays. Then, in 2009, I had a phone call out of the blue, from an office in Toronto. It was no one else than Myriam from the Maldives. We had got to know each other rather well following our short meeting in Male through phone calls, emails and chatting sessions. She had in the meantime been offered a high profile job in Canada's biggest cities. Following a year long rocket career in the UN in Africa. I was impressed.

The story that follows was never to be shared with anyone. But Myriam and I had talked a lot about what had happened, and she surprisingly wanted me to.

"That is because I, beyond my personal experience, am trying to think of how this can help other similar girls. I mean, to tell you the truth, I like the idea of this being shared so that someone in my situation can see that they're not alone, that this happened to other people. I went through all of this on my own. I knew of no other examples and I didn't get any advice. Please share."

It had all started with a minor problem. Myriam had been 29 and a half. And still a virgin. The beauty with the thick, black, silky hair was taller than me and with an amazing body. I was also appealed by her eminent self-ironic sense of humor. That she liked my outrageous jokes didn't hurt either. Her loud but likeable laughter proved that beyond doubt. Often. And she was smart too. Smart enough to be headhunted to the UN.

And Myriam had decided to not turn 30, still a virgin.

"Of course, I would ideally want to do it first with a man I love and to whom I was married, but to meet someone, fall in love and get married seem unlikely to happen before I hit 30."

She'd had her share of intimacy offers from guys from many countries. From colleagues and random guys on the street or on town. But she wouldn't let just about anyone take her virginity away. Somehow, the Norwegian she had met in her home country had made an impression. Maybe not so much the first while, but during the reoccurring conversations.

She asked if I was willing to come to Canada to "make her a woman", as she put it. In case it would still be desired. Myriam was crystal clear about nothing being clear. She had narrowed it down to three guys. One was her German ex. He had been her first choice, but a holiday in his country had not made her feel ready for such. The second one was a Canadian colleague, but she felt that he was a little bit too easy. As if she could expect anything else when looking for this kind of assistance.

I told her that I would be happy to come to Toronto, regardless. After all, I hadn't been to Canada, and it would be great to see her again. Whether we were to solve her "problem" or not.

"You will have to find out whether it will turn into a friend favor or not. I like you and find you attractive, and I am sure that I will feel up for it, should you decide to let the occasion arise."

"Literally speaking," she replied. Her imagination matched mine. We spoke again on the phone a month later.

"I have decided I want you to be the first I do it with."

"You are sure about this? We are friends, this will probably jeopardize our friendship, you know. If feelings and shit get in the way."

"Yeah, sure! I want to do it. But I reserve the right to re-decide when I see you!"

"Hahaha...you mean a disclaimer in case I have gained 30 kilos?"

"Gunnar, if you have gained 30 kilos, I will bloody kill you. Fat boy!"

"Myriam, I'll come to visit you. We'll have fun either way. And you know me. I would never do anything you wouldn't be totally comfortable with."

We spoke about everything and anything. It was all in the open. That she was from a Muslim country was beyond grasp.

I landed a Thursday afternoon and took the bus downtown. I met Myriam in a Starbucks, and we hugged. For a long time. Before the hug turned into a kiss and the kiss turned into a synchronised walk. The two of us were holding hands. She must have looked slightly more gracious than me carrying my worn backpack.

I didn't think an employer like hers would pay particularly well, but she lived in a very fancy flat. Not big, but super modern and beautiful.

Nothing happened there that evening.

"Thanks for not putting any pressure at all on me, you are sweet," she said. And fell asleep on my arm.

I woke up for brunch. Myriam had already got up, showered and prepared an excellent late breakfast. There were bagels, spread cheese, smoked salmon from Norway, croissants, fresh kiwi, oranges and apples plus Greek yogurt and muesli.

And coffee from Colombia. With milk and honey. She knew me well after all the electronic conversations.

She suddenly took my hand, looked me in the eyes and led me to her bedroom. "I am ready."

She undressed in front of a man for the first time. She was almost 30 years old. She was still a virgin.

And then, all of a sudden, the title was gone.

"I demand that we do it again! I need to practise!" she said. With a smile.

It must have been the strangest friend favor ever. We are still friends, and have never repeated the Toronto nights. She is now happily married with three kids. None of them are named after me.

There are, after all, some limits.

Oman

The only country in the world that starts with "O" can actually with some goodwill be said to look like Norway. In the northern part of the country, you will even find "Norway of the Middle East." The Oman fjords certainly do exist, but the surrounding scenery is somewhat drier than back home. Where a day without rain is a day without meaning. They can however boast about dolphins. And nice swimming temperatures. And a severe lack of people (admittedly also true in large parts of Norway).

Further south, in the capital Muscat, there is a lot more going on, albeit in a more traditional desert landscape. That is where I had my debut as a market haggler, in the central souk, or indoor market. A cruise ship coincidentally came to port when I was there. Suddenly prices doubled. The western tourists were in for a surprise. To fool the odd traveler among locals is more difficult than having a ship of fools in one spot.

Robert from Canada got in touch, and we soon decided to go get a drink. He worked as an importer and exporter of various food products, and knew Muscat rather well. That resulted in the recommendation of a juice bar by the harbor. I had never tasted such a delicious mango juice. Or pineapple juice. Or kiwi juice. The selection was impressive, the prices were barely above zero.

Our next stop was a local restaurant where we were served a big grilled fish. Roger turned out to be of the talkative type, and he easily got in touch with other people. In the evening he managed to lure Esther, a local girl, over to our table. Alcohol was not served in the restaurant, and she eventually asked if we would come back to hers for a proper drink.

"I'm having a party," Esther proclaimed.

She was 30 years old and worked as a nurse. It sounded very unusual for a local woman to have a party in Oman, but we were not hard to convince. That she had lived in Meatpacking District in New York City for a couple of years could explain a thing or two.

"Really? You're quite liberal," Robert said.

"Well, it's my brother's party, really. But he's cool!"

Robert's hotel was en route her flat, and we dropped by to pick up a bottle of rum. An unopened 7 year old Havana Club. We would not arrive empty handed. She took us to the fifth floor, the penthouse, of an old building. There are not many high-rises in Muscat. There were two three-seater sofas positioned in a 90 degree angle in the living room. It could have been a random flat in the US. In the 70's. A painted brown wooden table stood on the floor between the sofas. A fake flower in a green vase on the middle of it made out the main decoration in the flat. I also noticed a half full bookshelf. The black television set, branded Konka (which coincidentally means "stopped working" in Norwegian), was the last item in the room, on a wooden box in a corner. A carpet hung on the wall.

The living room also came with people, her brother and a female friend of hers. Not much of a party, but hey, it was in Oman. They each held a glass bottle of beer. We were greeted and given beers. It didn't take Robert long to try to hit on the friend of Esther. She was in her late 20's and not exactly a bowl of fruit. Unless potato qualifies as a fruit. Then again, the selection of willing women in Muscat isn't particularly huge. Esther was the pretty one in the room and immediately sat down on Robert's other side. Tall and dark Robert. The girls had clearly started a competition. Who could get the Canadian?

Ahmed was Esther's so called brother, in his mid-30's. We took a hike into the kitchen from where we could hear that the party of three opened the rum bottle. We were happy with the beers and got talking. As in a polite conversation. Then, all of a sudden Esther's friend left the flat, we could see the hallway from where we were sat. I assumed that she had lost the competition, and didn't think more of it. Not until the two remaining citizens of the living room clearly had succeeded what they were there for. It was hard to say who was the loudest, but they both shouted for god. I am not sure if they called for the same one, but it was all over a minute or two later. Silence. Maybe their prayers had been heard.

There was, needless to say, sort of an uncomfortable silence in the kitchen. Ahmed had also lived in New York and didn't seem to care much that his sister had come in the neighboring room. If it really was his sister. He seemed to not give a toss about what had just happened, I would certainly have reacted differently if I had been the brother in the same situation.

The uncomfortable silence never got time to become really uncomfortable. The show wasn't over. The friend reappeared out of the blue and entered the living room. Hell in Arabic followed. The girls were loudly shouting at each other.

"She too wanted your friend," Ahmed explained.

We laughed and toasted with a fresh set of beers from the fridge. Robert was desperately trying to calm the situation down. Before he entered the kitchen. Only one button of his shirt was done, and the shirt was not tucked into his trousers.

"You got any rubber, mate? I need two more."

I had to concentrate not to laugh out loud. I gave him two condoms from a pocket and wished him luck. He returned to the battle field, I said good bye to Ahmed. I felt no urge for yet another erotic radio drama.

I met Roger in the juice bar the next day. He was rather big-headed.

"My first threesome, man! Farida was really upset that I fucked Esther. So I had to do them both afterwards."

He had my full sympathy.

"I presume that they will be much prettier when you tell the story to your mates."

Croatia

The looks of Marija, on the other hand, can be described by a range of adjectives. She is cool. She is pretty. She is sexy. And she has long dark blond hair. She also smokes 40 cigarettes a day, drinks two figures of mugs of very black coffee and has a voice to match the habits.

That she doesn't sing jazz is a loss to the genre. I saw here in Zagreb. She is stunning, and I looked at her one second too long.

"Who the fuck are you looking at?" she snapped.

"I have no fucking idea. Some bitchy girl, apparently. What's your name?"

"Why the fuck do you care?"

"I like to know the names of people who insult me. You will then be listed in my black book which I'll pass on to my personal contract killer. Or you will be sued. Whichever I feel like at the time."

"Ha! I'll seduce him anyway."

"Who said it's a he?"

"Fuck off!"

"And your name?"

"Marija."

"I'm Gunnar".

Marija actually doesn't live far from Mars. Our solar system can be found in miniature in Zagreb. In 1971 artist Ivan Kožarić made versions of the sun and the then nine planets in the scale 1:680 million. That means that the earth sculpture is only 1.9 centimeter in diameter and that it is located 225 meters from the sun. To find Pluto I had to walk almost 8 kilometers. Her flat was luckily only 500 meters away. A stone throw from the red planet.

"Welcome! I live here with my mom."

"What?" I said, sounding somewhat surprised.

"No worries, she is at work until late."

I have rarely had wilder, more amazing sex. Rarely as in never. "I have never been thrown around like that in bed before. It is always I who has to dominate. I love it! Do me again," she asked. Or commanded, rather. I decided not to play hard to get.

I received a text message a few weeks later. I was at work in Oslo. "*I've been wanting you all day...*" Or so it started. The continuation is unmentionable. The result was that she came to visit. Although not only because of me. She works at a coffee bar in Zagreb, and wanted to try out the world famous Tim Wendelboe coffee bar at Grünerløkka in Oslo and Java on St. Hanshaugen. She is one of the people who love coffee with such intensity that she knows exactly what kind of beans she wants at any given time, and how they need to be ground. She does, overall, know exactly what she wants. And how.

UNREAL COUNTRIES

Some of the world's countries are crazy, eccentric or pretty untraditional. They may offer experiences found no other place, but there are often tragedies or stories of people being suppressed too. That a country gets a bad reputation is usually well deserved. Some travelers and tourists may see that as a curiosity, something that must be documented and shared. To the locals it is a forced reality, a prison, a life sentence. The rest of us just pass by.

I am often asked how I can support such regimes by visiting them. I do not agree with the question. A visit can help open eyes, to meet those who live in them and possibly give them a voice. If I do not travel to for instance North Korea or Central African Republic there will be one witness less to give the local people a little hope that there is something better on the outside. And a little bit less money inserted into local economies.

I know that I, as a traveler, am likely to be used as a prop in their propaganda, but I refuse to let that stop me. The hope is that my, relatively modest amount of traveling, may help a tiny bit to internationalization and possibly a small hike in increased understanding between country and cultures.

Eritrea

There is a lack of positive news from Eritrea; I traveled there to try find some. You should too. As one of a very few visitors, an attraction in its own right.

Because Eritrea as a tourist destination is virtually unheard of. Except for some adventurous Italian tourist groups, thanks to the countries' shared colonial past. But travelers who rule out a trip to Eritrea are missing out. The architecture of Asmara, the capital, is art deco to the extreme. And well preserved too. Take away the modern vehicles, and it is like traveling back to the 1930's. Add the bright colors, the old styled shop signs and the thousands of trees that make most central streets into alleys, and you are in motif heaven. Architects and photographers who never visit should reconsider their careers.

The markets of the town are also worth a visit, so are the plentiful jewelry shops. They sell gold and silver at prices unheard of in Europe. Plane buffs and fans of odd building shapes should check out the Fiat Tagliero building, designed by Italian architect Giuseppe Pettazzi and completed in 1937. It may be the building in the world that most resemblances an airplane, having 15 meter wide "wings." It used to be a gas station, but is now only used for storage.

Friends of mine were invited to join my trip, but politely declined. Some of them cited security issues. I have however rarely felt safer anywhere and I repeatedly walked throughout town alone in the middle of the night.

Getting in may not be straightforward, though. Two of my mates slash colleagues of mine and I had sent our visa applications to the embassy in

Stockholm. Our visas were rejected, I still do not know why. It may have been a deciding factor that all three worked for Norwegian Broadcasting Corporation. Because you may have heard about "Reporters Without Borders"? Neither have Eritreans. The country was placed as number 179 out of 179 at the last count in 2012. And yes, North Korea is also on that list (number 178). There are no privately owned media in Eritrea and a lot of journalists are imprisoned.

Our passports were finally returned after six weeks. There was a Post-It note attached to mine.

"Hellow! Visa denied."

I have never before, nor after, seen "hello" written with a "w". I doubt it was done on purpose. I nevertheless tried again half a year later. My colleagues could not come along then. I sent the application to Stockholm over two months before my planned date of travel, together with a letter stating how much I had read about the country and how much I craved visiting it. It worked, although they spent seven weeks to process the application.

I landed just outside Asmara. Only to discover that arrival at Asmara's airport isn't for the restless. To get the stamp in your passport isn't anything out of the extraordinary, but add a second checkpoint, declaration of all your money (regardless of currency) and having your luggage searched make time add up. I had my laptop with me too. Which meant that I had to register it before being able to leave the airport. And that wasn't too easy either. The town center is 6 kilometers away, but I flew in late at night, and there were no buses. The taxi drivers took full advantage of their monopoly. I refused to be ripped off, and ended up walking to town. Through the darkness. I was occasionally greeted by armed, but smiling guards. I should add that one third of working adults in Eritrea work in the army or the police. That should make matters safe. For foreigners. The locals are routinely suppressed by the army.

The nightlife is not to be frowned upon either. Eritreans love their beer which is named after their capital. The only problem is that the bars usually run out around midnight. The brewery just cannot cope with the demand. Not surprisingly so. The consumers of it certainly know how to party. Do expect to stay out until 4 or 5 on weekends if you want to keep up with the locals.

I visited a restaurant in Asmara on November 30. Or so I thought. Late at night someone opened up a set of doors to a room next door, and the restaurant had gone nightclub.

Virtually everyone danced within 30 minutes. That I did not didn't go unnoticed. A woman called Asmara, the same as the capital city, reacted.

"Why aren't you dancing?"

"I am not from around here."

"You don't say!"

"Hahaha...so I do not know how to dance Eritrean style."

Asmara is from Eritrea, but she now lives in Sweden. She visits her dad and siblings in Eritrea as often as she can. She was now in the nightclub together with friends and her brother's maid. They looked upon it as their mission that night to give me a short crash course in Eritrean dance.

"Bend your knees; straighten them out again, step two steps to the side. Repeat. You're now a pro. Come dance with us!"

The dance floor was packed; everyone was dancing the same simple dance. To men in wheelchairs danced too. Or were danced. A handful of guys lifted the wheelchairs into the air and made sure that those that couldn't dance themselves still were able to take actively part in the fun. I have rarely, if ever, seen wider smiles than those of the lads hovering near the ceiling.

Neither Asmara nor the maid had a good sense of direction. The brother didn't live far from my hotel, and I volunteered to walk them home. We were approached by a 30 year old who left a nightclub, before we were half way there. He spoke to Asmara in Tigrinja. I didn't understand anything, but the girls started giggling.

"He says that you are a very cheap guy who picks up to girls and then don't take them home in a taxi."

"Hahaha...thanks!"

We said goodbye on the corner by the brother's house.

"What are you doing tomorrow; it's New Year's Eve?"

"No plans."

"Would you like to join us for dinner?"

New Year's dinner was simple, but delicious. The maid served grilled chicken, steak, lenses and traditional Eritrean injera bread. It still looks and feels more like a pancake. But it tastes anything but. Water and flour are fermented for a few days before it can be baked. We used our hands to pick up pieces of injera and fill it with the dishes. I had eaten much of the same before, in Ethiopia. We were finally treated to coffee that the maid made over glowing hot coal. On the living room floor.

There was not much hope of getting a drink. The brother was a high ranking diplomat, and not a drinking man. That the clock got closer and closer to midnight did not seem to matter. They were all getting ready for bed. I thanked them so much for the hospitality, and started getting ready to leave.

"Skal ni på bar?" Asmara asked. She had switched to Swedish, asking if I would hit a bar.

"Yes, of course. It is New Year's Eve. Would you like to join?"

"Definitely!"

We were in a crowded nightclub only 15 minutes before midnight. I was together with Asmara, drinking Asmara, in Asmara.

"Do they have fireworks here?" I asked.

"No, it is not legal."

But the DJ was of the creative sort. At midnight he put on a recording of fireworks. Almost like the real deal, but cheaper and without the fire risk. Everyone in the nightclub were thrilled and they cheered, whistled and shouted. The DJ had found some sort of a loophole.

I decided to travel to Massawa, the day thereafter. The 1,500 year old town is on the coast, only 110 kilometers from Asmara, but 2,400 meters lower. It took almost 4 hours by bus, on very curved roads. A guy my age in Massawa claimed to do the journey in an hour and 45 minutes, but he was sporting a Michael Schumacher key ring.

To walk around the old town of Massawa is impressive and sad at the same time. A lot of the old houses were still being used; a lot of them were seemingly not. Quite a few of them were heavily damaged, gun holes were everywhere. The civil war was to blame, but not even bombs and grenades had managed to take away old greatness. There was still a charm to the old town, just a little faded, as if someone had try to eliminate it with a poor eraser. It looked like a ghost town during the day. But then something happened every night. The damaged buildings, also the worst affected ones, seemed to suddenly get a second wind, they woke up. There were bars and nightclubs in the least likely spots. Happy tunes from various music genres, aggregated discussions and loud laughter sifted out through the half open doors and windows.

To have a pint in a bombed out town that is on the very slow road to an uncertain recovery can get even the toughest among us to ponder a little extra over our short lives or the meaning of them. Although not everyone would want to visit and possibly go through a rollercoaster of emotions.

"The current state of the town makes me cry. I refuse to destroy my memory of old Massawa. I will never go back," an old man told me, back in Asmara. He sold spice in one of the markets. He might still have been willing to travel to the beaches near Massawa. Gurgusum is the most famous one, and comes with few signs of an ex-war. The amount of water sports, boat trips, dancing and partying shows signs of hope for a better future, at least.

Nothing can still beat the Dahlak Islands just outside the coast. They are unfortunately very expensive to visit, thanks to a lack of transport and outrageously priced tourist permits. The azure water, the distance to civilization and the absolute peace for a long way. An American group of investors so fell in love with the islands that they attempted to buy them for billions of dollars. The plan was to establish luxury hotels, casinos and poker joints to compete with Macau. Their intention sounded noble, they wanted to offer the paradise to everyone. Everyone with money, at least.

They had really missed the point. Entirely so. The Eritrean government luckily said no.

Eritrea is a one of a kind sort of country. Although some people will encounter a moral dilemma by visiting. There is just one legal political party there. It is quite typically called exactly what it isn't.

"The People's Front for Democracy and Justice (PFDJ)."

President Isaias Afewerki was presumably inspired by the well-known democracies "Democratic People's Republic of Korea" and "Democratic Republic of the Congo". New ideas might be overdue. The president has been in power since 1993.

No websites seemed to be blocked, though, but the internet access was extremely slow. Something I might have mentioned once or twice on social media. The response was swift.

"If the country is so great, why do you need internet?"

There is a reason for everything. Even friends.

North Korea

There is no internet in North Korea, but a gigantic intranet. That comes complete with "news", sports and dating services. A lot of people introduce me to others as the guy who has been to every country. The follow-up question is almost always, "OK, but have you been to North Korea?" North Korea was a country last time I checked. Despite the many reasons why it shouldn't be. I still recommend adventure seeking people to visit. Due to a lot of reasons. It is easy to visit; you will have your visa in hand around a week after applying for it and it's totally safe to visit as you are always looked after by two guides. Slash guards. You will also have a unique experience that can be had nowhere else. Even Turkmenistan is far, far away in terms of craziness. Miles away. As in light years of them.

There is no crime, either. Unless you consider oppositional thoughts crime. The government does, but foreigners will have to really push the limits if they are to ever be considered even remotely close to belonging in that category. There are good reasons why North Korea is considered as mad as it gets. Yet, it is still a problem that the reputation is so bad that we pretty much believe anything, rumored, said or reported, that comes out of the hermit kingdom – regardless how insane it sounds. We do no longer look upon it as unlikely that absurd matters may have taken place, and we have therefore virtually seized questioning what we hear. Such a development is dangerous, although quite understandable.

I visited over Easter in 2009. I had prior to leaving put out a status update on the internet that I would go there. I had, just for fun, asked if anyone wanted to come. Seven people did. And I would debut as a group traveler. There wasn't even anyone to blame but myself.

My fellow travelers included Stig who had met Neda in UAE. He had brought Frode Nordeide who I had seen in Førde, but never said hello to. Frode had worked on the printing press of Firda, when I worked there in the summer of

1997. It was clearly far too easy to miss out on each other in such a huge paper, with 14,000 in circulation.

Frode's mate Eirik Ødelien joined too, another guy I had never met before. He worked in a home for vulnerable youngsters on the West Coast of Norway. Virtually all "normal" people in North Korea can be considered vulnerable, and we feared that he would not be allowed to leave, given his essential competence.

Camilla Krog was yet another outsider. We had coincidentally ended up next to each other on a plane from London to Oslo, and just kept in touch ever since. When the offer of a visit surfaced she immediately accepted for a glimpse inside the theater of absurdity.

Not to forget my ex-girlfriend Målfrid. We had remained good friends following the break-up, and had agreed that we were way too fond of each other to screw it all up through a relationship. She also brought a friend, her childhood neighbor Kristine Sevik from Arendal.

And last, but not least, my ex-colleague Vegard Skjefstad. He was contemplating a move from web development into management.

"I might get some fresh impulses from Kim Jong-Il and friends," he had pondered. Vegard obviously purchased "The Leadership Philosophy of Kim Jong Il". Presumably a must-read in any management training program in North Korea.

There were three I had never met before, and one I had only met once, in an airplane. Maybe I should have considered being a little bit more critical to who I traveled with. But it might be a good thing to be several people in the extremely eccentric country. At least we'd have people who could verify that what we had seen was in fact real.

The madness started in Beijing. We were to fly in with Air Koryo, the only airline in North Korea. We're talking about Soviet era airplanes. We are talking propaganda. We are talking hardcore nationalistic brass-band music in the cabin before departure. The cabin crew consisted of beautiful but very strict looking girls. They had clearly been trained not to smile. Contrary to any other airline in the world.

Our luggage was scanned upon arrival. We had been informed that all mobile phones had to be delivered to security personnel who would look after them until we would leave again. Pretty meaningless, really. No foreign mobile network operator had roaming agreements with Koryolink, the monopolist in the country, anyway. Most businesses are monopolized. Not surprisingly.

After letting go of our phones, we were taken to our guides. Mister She and Miss Lee. Mister Che was 63 years old. He looked older. Miss Lee was in her late 20's. They spoke propaganda English, and had been carefully handpicked following an intense indoctrination program. The government was sure that they would not be affected but any "untrue" stories about how nice it is in other countries.

Let me just quote from "The Leadership Philosophy of Kim Jong Il" for a moment.

"North Korea is the highlight of the world as the 'Kingdom of independence', and has become the world's model in state-building and the management of affairs of state."

Just so that you know.

We didn't strictly need two guides, but they came in plural primarily to look after one another. So that temptation wouldn't be too great to ask about or to discuss what really happens outside the borders. Outside the only perfect country in the world. All other countries make hell wane in comparison. They have been told. Repeatedly.

We were given a brief tour of Pyongyang en route to our hotel, and got some sort of a first impression. There were a lot of nice and wide roads, although hardly a car in sight. To walk in the middle of the road or to cross it on impulse was not a problem. To look left, right and left again in this country is a waste of time and will only increase the chance of whiplash.

It took a couple of hours to get to our hotel, and it was dark by the time we had dinner served. This was the first time all of us could properly meet, and we had thorough introductions over a range of Korean dishes. Very similar to those served south of the border, of course. The two countries share both a history and traditions. Until the Korean War.

All of a sudden we heard sharp bangs outside. The staff didn't seem to care, and there were no other guests. Camilla asked Mr. Che what was happening.

"It's fireworks for The Great Leader."

We walked out to get a better view. I have never ever seen as much and as impressive fireworks. It just kept going on and on and on. When we thought that what we had just seen could not possibly be topped, it was. By even more impressive missiles exploding across the night sky. It all lasted for almost an hour, with the intensity only increasing throughout. A great way to use limited resources. Or maybe just some surplus rockets from the army. It's been quite some time since the country was in active war with South Korea, but they are still officially at war. A peace agreement was never signed following the Korean War.

The next day was spent seeing a range of oversized stalinistic statues and other touristic sights. Our guides were there at all times. So were our driver and a film team. They made a documentary of our stay. For us to buy on a DVD upon departure.

I have never been a big fan of guides, and I decided to do what I could to lose them. I told Mr. She over lunch that I always went jogging when abroad and that I would very much like to do follow up my routine the next morning.

"Not a problem. I will go jogging with you. Let's meet at 07:30 in the lobby."

"Well, let's see about that", I thought. Frode had brought a bottle of aquavit, Norwegian liquor. I let him in on the evil plan, and he liked it. The bottle was to be emptied for dinner. And not by us.

We invited the guides to the hotel bar where we had local beers at a dollar a piece. Foreigners are not allowed to use the local currency. "Mister Che. Would you like to try some traditional aquavit? It's like whiskey, just Norwegian," Frode offered. It turned out that Mr. Che liked drinking, and he happily accepted the offer. Bingo! The bottle was emptied in a couple of hours. I only had a few beers. I was going jogging the next morning, I was not so sure about Mr. Che. Who only got more and more drunk. He was helped to his room by Miss Lee around midnight. Frode and I toasted. A goal can indeed justify the means of getting there. Or so I have been told.

At 07:40, Mr. Che had still not woken, and both Vegard and I wore shorts, eagerly waiting for him in the lobby. I was finally allowed by the hotel lobby staff to call him via the hotel phone. He stumbled down the stairs a few minutes later. A cigarette was hanging from his lips. And his clothes were awfully creased. He must have slept in his suit, and there had been no time for a shower.

"Mister Che! Are you ready to go jogging?"

He didn't even ask my rhetorical question, just pointed to the driver who was standing next to us. The driver was absolutely not ready for such, but the pecking order was clear. Mister Che was the boss, and the driver reluctantly removed his suit jacket and joined us to go jogging. The driver started fast, but it soon became evident that he hadn't run in many years. We only ran a short route of 2-3 kilometers before we were back at the hotel. Mister Che stood by the entrance, smoking. Chain smoking, according to Eirik who had also managed to get up.

"Are you happy now?" Mister Che spoke his first words of the day. In English.

"But Mister Che! That was only a couple of kilometers. That is not far enough. We need a proper run."

The elderly guide looked at the driver who was totally out of breath. He was leaning forward, holding his hands on his knees. He frenetically shook his head. He was not capable of another round.

"OK, you can go jogging alone. I will wait here," Mister Che said, lighting a new cigarette. Vegard and I didn't give him any time to reconsider. We ran off immediately. I asked the main guide whether he wanted to go jogging with us the next morning. He still seemed unaware of having been tricked.

"It's OK. You have been jogging alone already. You can go running where you want tomorrow morning. But be back by 08:15."

I did as I was told. And jogged a different, much longer route. It was liberating to be able to move alone in Pyongyang. Despite the odd looks from locals I passed by. They were few and far apart. Some played table tennis by the Taedong, there was the odd person taking a stroll and a few people in buses.

Pyongyang supposedly has three million people, according to official figures, but it certainly didn't look like a metropolis. I could see one military parade at a distance. And the intersections do not come with traffic lights, but with beautiful young women. They stand in the middle of the streets with skirts at knee length (trousers in the winter), big military hats, white socks and black shoes with two inch heels. Their job is to control traffic. The little there is of it. And they have been trained well. I have never seen more robot and army like moves. It is all very fascinating the way they command drivers to stop or to go using nothing more than a black and white stick. And they need stamina too. The shifts last several hours.

Pyongyang is simply unique. You will never see a capital just like it. Or anything even remotely similar.

Belarus

Belarus is also eccentricity on steroids. The agricultural country is called the last dictatorship in Europe and is being ruled by a hardliner. There is a street called Lenin in every city and most statues are of the late dictator. There is one privately owned bank, 30 state-owned. And until a few years ago, every household had cable radio. Due to propaganda purposes. But still not as bad as in North Korea, where every household has a government controlled speaker without a volume knob. People in Minsk were in other words marginally freer than those in Pyongyang. That's always something.

I still remember the first time I read anything about the city, in the guide book series "In Your Pocket". It is free and is written by people who live in the city in question.

"Minsk is as mad as a sack of bent hammers. And so are you for wanting to go there."

That was all I had to show Øystein and Asbjørn. They were in for a visit. We knew we would like it. I arrived a little later than the other two. I came from Moldova, they from back home. I found them sitting by a lake, sipping each their cola. They had already checked into the Soviet style hotel. Asbjørn had based on experiences in various stan countries been forcefully moved to his own room. He snores like a sawmill connected to an amplifier. And the volume only goes up after a few drinks.

Minsk lacks men, something that is quite noticeable when going out on town. We have rarely received more looks from women. Beautiful ones with short skirts and high heels. Something that didn't exactly make us popular among the male population. They already have a hard time attracting the local girls. Despite 24/7 nightclubs and sky high alcohol consumption by both genders. If expensive umbrella drinks do not work when it comes to luring the women home, they can always resort to the night open jewelry shops. They are strategically located, by the entrances of nightclubs and casinos. The women are clearly in good bargaining positions in Mink.

But getting access to the country isn't only easy. A spelling mistake in our visa applications saw them returned. There is a loophole given that you have business contacts on the inside. A letter from one of them secures you a visa on arrival. I took advantage of this on my second visit.

The company has offices in the middle of the city. Not far from where KGB operates from, in a huge yellow concrete building.

"It is many times bigger underground," a random passer-by told us. He went on to tell us about surveillance halls, interrogation rooms and torture chambers. That didn't stop naive Norwegians. Øystein decided that the main stairway to the KGB building was perfect for a handstand. I agreed. The synchronous double hand stand that had been perfected in most of the other former Soviet Republics was yet again performed. Doctor Vodka took a picture of it all. Before we in angry Russian were shoved by a KGB guard. Or agent as Øystein described him as in a text message to Benedicte who was back home.

"We were arrested by a police agent for standing on our hands outside the KGB office. They will take my phone. Vodka was let go. Contact him if you don't hear from us. Love you! Ø."

Øystein knows the art of worrying people at home. There may be a reason why he was not allowed to join us on our trip to Afghanistan.

There is a huge Ferris wheel in a park in Minsk. The cars do not have ceilings and are not secured, but we still decided to give it a go to get a good overview of the city. Before we were one third of the way to the top, a collective fright of height kicked in. And there was nothing we could do about it. All three reacted by uncontrollable laughter. And it lasted all the way to the top, even though we'd prefer to rather cry. London Eye might be bigger, but you are then secured in what appears to be a safe bubble. Not much beats an open Ferris wheel.

Azerbaijan

They don't deal with such in Azerbaijan. And you soon understand you have arrived in a country off the beaten track when one of the best known "tourist attractions" is the most polluted city on Earth. That was at least how Sumgait was referred to by international organizations in both 2006 and 2007. It is located just north of Baku, and it was the hub for the country's industries, primarily chemical ones. The pollution from there sifted into soil and water, and caused a lot of children to be born dead, often with deformed bodies. Or at least damaged enough for them to live very short lives. Maybe three months, perhaps two years. It didn't take long until the need for an own graveyard for fosters, babies and small children became evident. Everyone buried there had strange, often unexplainable deformations.

Øystein and I were curious and decided to visit. We flagged down a taxi driver in a Volga, a type of car that in the Soviet Union was considered much more luxurious than Lada, but also much less exciting. The Volga looked and felt Soviet. You would as a foreign passenger even assume that you were being spied on and that the driver was in direct contact with the KGB. Not even speaking Norwegian felt entirely safe. The KGB does for sure have fast translators, that can work simultaneous as you speak, on their payroll. To openly criticize the Omnipowerful president in the country was not an option inside the Volga.

The death rate of kids in Sumgait was 82 per 1,000 births at its worst. The government has luckily managed to limit the pollution somewhat now. The death rate of kids in Norway is less than a tenth of that. Sumgait is by The Caspian Sea, and the water in it was rumored to be fluorescent at night thanks to the chemical waste that went into it.

In this part of the world it is normal to have a picture of the buried itched into the tombstones by laser or made by a stone mason. The deformations have not been toned down; I would guess rather the contrary, despite never having seen the kids alive. The matter of detail was very impressive, something that made the graveyard even more gruesome. But all the more important too. The world cannot forget this. We could see misplaced eyes, destroyed mouths and empty stares. Some of the children actually smiled, most of them just apathetically glared into the air. Their expressions were as taken from poor horror films in black and white, films where the kids were scared senseless by mean monsters.

We returned to the town center and had a cup of tea in a park. To calm ourselves down. Some pensioners sat by huge chess boards made by concrete to play the ancient game. We were invited to join in, but politely declined. The motivation was still not quite there following an overdose of dead children's bodies.

To further calm down, we decided to stroll down to The Caspian Sea. A couple very much in love walked along the beach. A rusty old ship wreck had ended its last journey on the edge of a tiny peninsula. It was symptomatic for the entire city. Azerbaijan is a rich country. There is a lot of oil, but no one has given a toss about the environment and the people have been ignored for a long time.

A Lada taxi took us back to the capital. They somehow felt safer than the Volgas. Cars do not come simpler and with less options than a Lada. They can therefore not be tapped. The logic was good enough for us. The Lada was not. Its radiator boiled half way back to Baku and the driver had to open the hood.

Kiribati

There were no Ladas in Kiribati. But the laughter heard in Kiribati is very frequent and very warm. The latter is not because of the equatorial temperatures. People are just incredibly friendly, open minded and easy going. We might have been too had we lived in a country with only 2-3 plane departures a week. And sunny beaches in all directions.

They usually have good stories they are more than willing to share too. If you don't find them funny, their laughter bombs will more than compensate for your lack of humor.

But hang on. Had you heard about Kiribati before? Yes? How do you pronounce its name? I bet you a beer that you do it wrong. "Kiribati" is not correct. Neither is "Keereebatee" or anything similarly creative you might come up with through any over creative brainstorming session.

The letter "s" does not exist in Kiribati, but the sound "s" does. So, to pronounce "s" you write "ti" or "tu". "Kiribati" is therefore pronounced "Kiribass". "T" followed by any other letter than "I" or "u" is pronounced "t" as normal. Piece of cake.

"Of course, there is no 'h' either," Kaure told me. He is the only registered taxi driver in Kiribati. He sometimes carries individual passengers, but usually operates as a shared taxi. In that case, a trip will set you back between a few Australian cents and a couple of dollars, depending on the distance.

"No 'h?' What do you do about hotels?"

"We don't have any. We have a lodge, an inn, a couple of motels, a boarding house, a guesthouse and some flats."

Of course there is an "h" in guesthouse, but why let a little detail ruin a good story.

I had great expectations to Kiribati. I even received a heart-warming Twitter message several weeks before my trip there:

"Welcome to Tarawa. We don't have much, but enjoy our warmth and hospitality."

David Lambourne, a local lawyer had picked up that I would soon visit. I never met him, but his fellow countrymen did not put my expectations to shame in any way, form or manner. If you do not like to get in touch with new people, do stay away from this country.

The capital is called South Tarawa and is located on Tarawa Island. This is where most of what might appear like civilization can be found. If you prefer to travel back in time, one of the smaller islands is for you. There, you will find no electricity or running water. Nor official accommodation, but you will usually find yourself staying with friendly locals in their own homes. And if worst comes to worst, the temperatures are never really bad; sleep on the beach.

The Captains Bar has been built on the beach in Betio, the closest you will ever get to a city on Tarawa. That is where I met a group of friends who emptied a few beers at the midday heat. They invited me over and asked me where I was from and what the hell I did in Kiribati.

We got along well in no time at all, and I asked them what they felt about their country being the second in the world to disappear, should ocean levels rise.

"That is bullshit! We aren't sinking. Far from it. Nothing has changed here the last 100 years; it is not going to either."

They were certain of their opinions and did not hesitate at all. Before continuing. They told about politicians who used, what they referred to as a myth, to get world-wide publicity and hence money. Money they would spend on themselves and their families. And, admittedly, to some much needed infrastructure. If the lads were right, politicians in Kiribati should thread carefully. Many people have cried wolf before. Although they have for once been joined by scientists and researchers that cry equally loud.

The first project that has received funding is for a new road between the airport and Betio. Most locals are very much looking forward to this, judging by the amount of time they spend on discussing it. Not surprisingly, perhaps. They have been promised a new road for years.

The work on it "was just about to start" when I visited. They had heard that phrase many times before.

Employees of the UN and Red Cross didn't agree. I met some of them in my hotel. They felt that a new and better road would only remove focus from the main problem; erosion caused by the sea. A new road would also cause more accidents and cause more pollution, they claimed.

There are always at least two sides to any story. Even in Pacific paradises.

East Timor

East Timor is also sort of near the Pacific Ocean, but it is rarely described as a paradise. You sense the feeling that something is strange about the country the moment you land at the airport. It isn't particularly big, but still full of planes and helicopters. All of them are white with two letters on the sides. "UN".

You can smell problem area from far afield.

It is still easy to enter. They are presumably interested in the few tourist dollars that they can get. The facilities are still not quite up to speed. I stayed in a guesthouse. Although I am not sure if inside is the right term. I was taken to some sort of a four square meter large shed. In the back yard. Without any windows. But with a mattress on a homemade bed with what appeared to be clean sheets. Not too bad, really. Totally dark, at least, so I wouldn't wake up super early. At least I wouldn't have done had it not been for the damn rooster that had the impression that dawn was duet time. Together with the rooster who was in charge of music at the farm next door.

The center of Dili is small, but they have still found space for a football stadium. And an international match was on the program. A junior team from Darwin played the local heroes. Just as the referee blew the whistle for the break, it started raining cats, dogs, giraffes and jaguars. I had witnessed four goals and was happy nevertheless. So was the home crowd, their boys had scored three of the goals. It turned out that the locker rooms have windows towards the street. I heard a less than happy Australian manager when I passed by on the outside.

"What the fuck is this, lads? You play like women. No, not women. You play like girls! Like tiny kindergarten girls. Do you want to travel back home in shame?"

I was almost tempted to return to the stadium to see if the attempt of a moral boost helped, but it just rained too much and I had no umbrella. I opted for lunch instead. In Aru the bakery. Where being served took 45 minutes. Still not too bad for East Timor.

Castaway Bar is a restaurant on top of a diving shop, and the view over the Banda Sea is certainly not a reason for any complaints. I was not surprised that this was the location for the weekly expat meetings. The foreigners in town were primarily from Australia and New Zealand, and I must have come across as somewhat exotic. Just not by everyone.

"We can't afford to befriend random passer-by's. In East Timor, you spend your energy on other expats," a guy from Sydney said.

To his defense, let me add that he was very far from sober. And at it trying to pick up a girl from New Zealand. Most of the others were luckily far more positive, also the females. They might have been interested in some new blood in town. But I wasn't really putting too much effort into it. For obvious reasons. I don't think "Would you like to come back to my windowless shed?" would have been the preferred pick up line of the evening. The plane connections to Dili aren't ideal either. Then again, such a challenge has never stopped me before.

Libya

Gaddafi was still alive when I visited Libya, but the so called rebels had made Benghazi a stronghold and the hatred towards Gaddafi could almost be felt. It was in the air. Libya had for a long time been a visa challenge, but several borders were opened by the dictator's opposition as the revolution gained speed. I took a taxi from Cairo to the Libya border, and walked across with my press card in hand. The armed border guards almost pushed me across the border. Journalists were very welcome in order to better balance the coverage than what the regime would prefer.

"Where are you going? Do you want a ride?"

The hospitality wasn't warm. It was glowing hot.

The situation in Benghazi was very tense at the time, and I decided to visit the coastal town of Tobruk instead. My voluntary driver was happy to take me there; he didn't even ask what the angle of my reporting would be. They seemed to assume that anyone who entered the country and experienced the situation and the atmosphere would cover it all favorable to their side. I was driven by a 25 year old in a Ford Sierra with an added spoiler. An older friend sat in the passenger seat. He drank Coca-Cola from a bottle with a screw top and ate banana crisps from a see through plastic bag. The driver consistently drove fast and reached 180 kilometer per hour several times. Get the journalist there ASAP, seemed to be his mantra. He let me off outside Hotel al-Masira, the only so called luxury hotel in town. That's allegedly where journalists usually stayed. I thanked them so much for the ride, and tried to pay. They were not having it.

"You make the truth about Libya come to the world. That is the only payment we want."

I waved them off. A little shameful. There would be no immediate newspaper articles on Libya signed Garfors.

Hotel al-Masira was too impersonal to my taste and also located outside town. I wanted to live close to people, and I strolled alongside the road in the dry landscape. To find a room was effortless. There were no foreigners in town with the exception of a few Egyptian business men.

There were demonstrations on the square in Tobruk too. Gaddafi clearly had the people against him. He would not, could not last long. A dead dictator was celebrated across most of Libya four months later. Some places openly, other places in hiding.

I had no intention of staying long. But I wanted to see something more. The question was only what. Tobruk is a relatively quiet and calm town. Nothing much happens except for in the port, and there are few sights for visitors. The tourist attraction turned out to be a war memorial. A must see spot, I was told. Local advice is rarely to be ignored, and I hired a driver. He stopped at the cemetery. 2,282 allied soldiers from WWII are buried there, in a dirt dry desert landscape a few kilometers outside the town center. A gardener did his best to keep a few trees and bushes alive, but not many enough to keep the depressive and hopeless feeling of tragic mass deaths and lost fates at bay. The driver and I were on our way back to the Egypt border less than an hour later. He told me about his daughters. The oldest was called Sahara.

Whether I was interested? She was 14. I politely declined the offer. And pondered over which other 35 year old man the poor girl might be forcefully married to in the near future. Cultural differences are some times less charming and understandable than others.

Ukraine

A boys' trip to Ukraine. It sounds ace. With a trip to Chernobyl included, where you can only go with a guide. I can't remember whose idea it was to go there, but I was nevertheless given the responsibility of finding accommodation since I had been there before. Needless to say, we ended up in the most Soviet styled hotel that I could find. With one person on duty on every floor, around the clock, to have full control over the guests and to make sure that nothing too unsuitable would occur. The rooms were totally sterile, and every room had a tiny bathroom with some sort of a 90 centimeter long bathtub.

My colleagues Andreas, Bjarne Andre and Hallvard Lid made up the NRK team. Hallvard is a developer, and is usually not hard to ask when it comes to travels. Even though his position as a dad of two makes it harder to combine with crazy boys' trips. We were also accompanied by Vegard "Pyongyang" Skjefstad and his mate Hans Olav Nome whom none of us had met before. He works with computers and is a promising photographer. It turned out that he was less promising when it came to radioactive radiation.

Bjarne Andre brought his fellow villager Thomas who had joined us to Bulgaria, while I had vouched for a friend from back home. Let's just call him Karl. A full delegation, in other words. Almost like a group holiday. I brought valium.

Delegations need a base. The always open restaurant slash coffee bar Double Coffee next to the hotel was selected as ours. Not many hours of the weekend passed by without any of us being in it. Some of us tested out the liquid on the menu of Double Coffee a few hours after arrival in Kiev, and were still there when the others came for breakfast. Karl managed to drop his phone during the night, a hyper modern Nokia that supported various types of document types.

"Fuck, I lost my black book as well! It's on my phone."

"You have names of everyone?" Thomas asked. He was clearly impressed.

"Well, not really, that would have been bragging. One is listed as 'Laila behind the kiosk', another one is called 'blond babe on the plane to Spain'. And so on."

We got the point.

And partied the night away in a nightclub. Before making a pit-stop at Double Coffee. It appeared as if Karl could be in a position to add to his list. Two local girls had joined from the club. Our friends who had actually slept all night showed up for breakfast around nine. They came without beer goggles, and discretely passed on the message that the girls weren't even close to be girlfriend material. They were in a relatively polite way asked to go home. We were asked to get some sleep.

We woke up late afternoon, just in time for dinner. The agreement was to meet in the hotel lobby. Hotel security was performed by a Ukrainian big man, clearly inspired by military operations. He was not happy about our little congregation. Of course, it may have seemed as we were planning a terrorist attack. As westeners do in lobbies of Soviet styled hotels in Kiev. We moved our planning outside.

But one of us was missing. Karl. He had done his homework and had looked up some girls in a Ukrainian dating website. It turned out that he had met one of them, and that he had somehow ended up in her place, on the top of a classical 14 floor communist apartment block.

"That was an anything but cozy experience, so we had to do whatever we could to compensate," he told us the next day. We just got a short text message from him, saying he was late, while waiting in the lobby. "It all depends on how long this blowjob will take" was all we got to know. We ruled him out for the night. And ended up with borscht, potatoes, potato pancakes, cabbage and meat balls. When in Ukraine, eat as the Ukrainians.

To travel with Andreas is always exciting. Our theory is that some evil wizard once upon a time cast a spell on him. A spell that means he can never travel without any bullshit happening. He either misses his flight, has his laptop, luggage or Visa card stolen, has his credit cards skimmed, gets jetlag from Hell, arrives at a fully booked hotel, oversleeps to important dinners or finds that the Jaguar he has rented is gone. Unless he is just majorly hung over. To mention a few examples.

The latter was the problem in Ukraine. Officially, at least. Unless he had sudden radiation nerves. Whatever the reason, he dropped out from the Chernobyl excursion.

We had told local people in Kiev that we were planning to visit the former nuclear power plant. As tourists. We soon discovered that was the same as swearing in church, synagogue and mosque. Simultaneously. It is understandable, if you think about it. We come to see and photograph an area that is still ruined after the worst nuclear disaster in the history of the world. Cursing us didn't help, we just spoke a little bit less about our planned trip. At least in English.

The bus that took us from Kiev let us off by a control post. Before being allowed to enter the area around the ill-fated reactor, we had to go through some sort of a machine that measured radioactivity in us. There were no indication, no alarms, no nothing. Unsurprisingly. We were, after all, going in. The question was only which sound the machine would make when leaving again.

Dimitiriv waited for us on the inside. He proudly worked in the army. Guiding tourists in Chernobyl is among the tasks delegated to the Ukrainian military.

"We are only allowed to work here three weeks in a row before we are sent elsewhere. I think it is a good thing. Then we usually have a pretty bad headache," he explained.

That didn't exactly calm Hans Olav down much. He was by far the most sceptical person among us.

"Let me go through the rules before we drive any closer. Never. Let me repeat. Never go further than I do. Not even a foot. Understood?"

We all nodded. Obedient as second graders visiting a fire station on a school trip.

"This is a Geiger counter. It will make sounds according to the amount of radiation. The more intense the sound, the more radiation. Do not panic unless I do."

Hans Olav was already whiter than Caspar the ghost's albino cousin. The rest of us just nodded.

"And finally, no drinking in Chernobyl. Now, let's go."

The driver took us from one area to the next while Dimitriv told stories and showed differences in radiation. Moss has a long degradation time, and the Geiger counter started screaming as soon as our guide put it close to any moss. Radiation was actually not too bad by the reactor, but relatively high some other places, especially nearby vehicles and other metal constructions that had been in the vicinity of the explosion and the fire on April 26, 1986.

Two hours of our radioactivity tour passed, and it was time for lunch.

"We will eat in the army cafeteria. It is actually quite nice. But first we will stop by the shop where you can buy Coke, beer or vodka for your meal."

"But didn't you say that there is no drinking?" I protested.

"Come on, this is Chernobyl. Rules are flexible!"

Of course.

The lunch was acceptable, but not memorable due to food technical reasons. Neither Hallvard, Vegard nor Hans Olav ate much. We had been informed that some of the raw materials were grown locally, and an eight year old having fish gone bad for dinner would eat more than they did.

The lack of appetite was not commented upon by Dimitriv. He had presumably seen worse. It was time to continue to Pripyat, the city where the workers at the nuclear power plant and their families had lived. It is now a plundered ghost town with a rather big and rusty Ferris wheel as the main attraction on a playground in the middle of it. The town had been evacuated by all the 50,000 inhabitants, but not until a day and a half after the explosion. They had not even been told that anything had gone wrong, although rumors had of course started circulating immediately. Our guide claimed that evacuation had started after a few hours, of course he was telling the official and politically correct version. Other sources claim it took up to 48 hours before the area was cleared. The building blocks we entered had clear signs of having been left in a hurry. Old furniture, stoves, clothing and toys were scattered around. Trees grew on roofs and some places even inside the buildings. There was nothing of any value left. It had presumably been stolen.

Dimitriv suddenly held the Geiger counter up in the air. We were in the minibus on our way out of Pripyat.

"We will now drive through a pretty bad area. It is because of the special vegetation that grows in this spot."

The driver had slowed down, and the car moved slowly. The sounds from the Geiger counter did not. The beeps ran amok. Before the driver stepped on the breaks and the bus came to a complete stop. The Geiger counter did no longer sound like an alarm. The output was a continuous beep. Until it snapped, stopped producing any sounds and the numbers on the display were replaced by incomprehensible lines and shapes.

"Oopps!" Dimitriv shouted.

He knew his Hitchcock.

I have never seen anyone as pale as Hans Olav. The photograph of him in the minibus could later have been used in ads for skin bleaching creams aimed at Indian housewives.

"This particular area, a line only 50 meters wide, is worse than any other around here. It is because of the certain kind of trees that grow here, but even the scientists don't understand it. Should we continue driving?"

That Hans Olav at this stage could even utter anything was impressive beyond belief, but a high pitched "yes, please"-ish sort of sound did in any case come from his lips.

Dimitriv and the driver thanked us for the ride back to the station where we would be measured for radiation. We all held our breaths in fear of having been dramatically exposed, but there were no sounds, no nothing. A person needs to be in the area for quite some time before any harm occurs. What we had been exposed to during the day could apparently be compared to one photograph in an X-ray machine.

T.I.A. THIS IS AFRICA

There is a lot that doesn't work in Africa. We know that. But we don't do anything about it except for donating money when we see offensive footage on our TV screens. And it seems like the images must be more and more spectacular to shock us sufficiently to actually contribute. What usually triggers our generosity is drought catastrophes with extreme hunger, which does warrant our immediate assistance. But traditional aid is one of the main problems that the continent struggles with, or so my brother Øystein claims, who has seen the misery up close when he lived in Malawi for 18 months. Dambisa Moyo claims the same. She is the author of *Dead Aid*, a book that deals with the problems that are caused by aid. She claims that aid leads to corruption, undermines local businesses, maintains toll barriers and destroys impressive local initiatives - big and small.

Generally speaking, traditional aid largely benefits Western employees. It is therefore hard to cut nation's aid budgets since so called *charitable* organizations and NGOs perform a lot of lobbying to maintain their own jobs. Any suggestion of budget cuts leads to mayhem in the media, using the "poor Africans" as an alibi. Whoever hints that a change in the traditional aid system should be tried, is usually portrayed as Satan himself.

Both Øystein and Dambisa Moyo suggest that stimulating local businesses and removing unfair taxes and toll barriers are much better and more effective alternatives to traditional aid. After having seen a lot of nasty shit in Africa, I must say that I agree. "Read *Dead Aid*," I insisted to a friend, who had studied humanitarian aid. This person was strongly disagreeing with my point of view, but changed their opinion after reading the book and has since challenged me to read *Aid and Other Dirty Business: How Good Intentions Have Failed the World's Poor* by Giles Bolton. He touches on a lot of the same points.

TIA is an acronym for "This Is Africa" and is a sarcastic expression that most Africans understand - except in South Africa. Too much work too well for TIA to be a generally known term there. It has an autotherapeutical function and is absolutely necessary on a trip around the continent. As I traveled in Africa, I observed that most of the infrastructure and services can and should be improved. Poor transport conditions frequently lead to delays or to things simply not happening. The indirect consequences may be just annoying, horrible or devastating.

It is rather the rule, not the exception that you have to wait for five hours before the bus finally leaves. Or that you are told that there is no fresh fish available in the restaurant, two hours after you ordered - two hours at the table without even getting anything to drink. Or when you discover a man's hand far down inside your backpack when standing in line. Expect to lose a gadget, a passport, money, or a water bottle.

Sometimes pretty much everything goes to hell. In those instances, it actually helps to say TIA out loud, preferably followed by several exclamation marks. It is a little bit like being exempt from guilt. It even reduces stress. To say "TIA" is a little like taking Valium, but totally free.

Kenya

Kenya was the first African country I visited, together with Heidi in the late 90's. She had received a scholarship to study in Nairobi, and it wasn't hard for me to ask for a visit. I traveled from London by British Airways, and my luggage naturally disappeared. This was before I had realized that checking in luggage was a waste of time, and also something that takes away a lot of freedom. The upside was that I was given 200 dollars in compensation and that the suitcase was delivered to the door of our shabby hotel just 24 hours later. The Kenyan capital had a rough reputation, and I wasn't particularly at ease going there. Still I hadn't gone all the way to Africa to study the cockroaches in our hotel room. So, we explored the metropolis and soon discovered that it wasn't as bad as it had been portrayed through the media, guidebooks and so called *experienced* travelers. However, a few days in Nairobi was more than enough, and we headed to Mombasa by train. The coastal city has its own airport and several hotels with swimming pools. The ambience was certainly more relaxed than in Nairobi, although the slums were just on the outskirts of town there as well.

Heidi and I stayed in Mombasa for a couple of days, exploring it on foot. Colonial architecture and Port Jesus, an old Portuguese fortress, dominated the landscape. But we also found a pub where they showed English football. A few Brits had lined up in front of the screen, each with a pint. Pub owners in Kenya, or anywhere in Africa, didn't pay anything for sports rights back then.

Neither Heidi nor I were particularly interested in watching football, staying in wannabe resort hotels, or hanging with large tourist groups. We soon decided to head south via minibus. To a village boasting a few bungalows scattered around a restaurant building only meters from a snow white beach – simply pristine. The road left something to be desired, best suited for tractors – or pedestrians. We had waited for our contact John by the road leading to the village for 15 minutes or so, when we approached a local couple that also seemed to be waiting for something or someone. We told them we had agreed to meet John, and asked if he was normally on time. They just smiled.

"Hakuna matata." They spoke as they nodded.

It is Swahili and means "no problem". It was the first time that I heard the expression, and for me, it turned out to be the predecessor of TIA. John showed up an hour later, and the 30 year old welcomed us with a wide white smile.

"Welcome! You must be Miss Heidi and Mister Gun!" He said enthusiastically.

We had not yet learned anything about the autotherapeutical term TIA and asked how far it was to the hotel, after spending only a few minutes in the old car on the shabby road like infrastructure.

"Hakuna matata!"

We started suspecting a pattern. Another 15 minutes passed before we arrived in paradise.

The bungalow on the isolated beach became our home for a few days. We could get used to living like this with first class fishing, eminent snorkeling, adventurous boat rides with local fishermen and nothing but total relaxation.

This was also the first time I understood how annoying one tiny little mosquito can be. We had a mosquito net, but what if there was a hole in it? In areas with malaria it is essential to manage to keep them out. The trick is to trust the mosquito net and your own talent in fitting the net without a mosquito on the same side as yourself. Otherwise you will not get any sleep at all, in fear of being bitten by the potentially lethal flying insect.

Tanzania

We headed south yet again, from the paradise beach in Kenya to Tanzania. Even the border crossing was pain free, despite this being so early in my travel career that I hadn't even checked whether we needed a visa. We did indeed, but they were stamped straight into our passports by the police officers on the border.

Heidi and I were the only white people on the bus. A rather large lady with big gold earrings and clothes that indicated upper middle class carried a big bag of sweets - caramels wrapped in golden paper. The road standard had diminished dramatically since we crossed the border from pavement to gravel, from highway-wide to mountain-road-narrow. We twisted between small villages with straw huts that reminded us of those stereotypical cartoons and children's books about Africa. In every village, the gold earring lady took a handful of caramels and threw them out the open window. The bus was cruising at normal speed, and screaming kids ran like crazy after it and managed to pick up a sweet or two each. It even seemed like they shared their prizes willingly. It didn't take long, only 5 or 6 villages, until the generous lady started getting bored. All of a sudden she started counting the caramels before throwing them out. If four kids ran next to the bus, she would throw out three caramels. When there were only three kids, she would throw out two. Then she laughed her head off when seeing the kids diving to get a caramel, and one always ending up crying without a sweet.

Sadistic, TIA style. We still didn't feel that we were in a position to do much about it. And she didn't stop her practice until the bag of goodies was empty and the large lady fell asleep, snoring loudly. Evil bitch.

We stayed overnight in Tanga, I am unsure whether the city is guilty as charged for having inspired to the name of a new kind of underwear. It was the first time

I stayed in a hotel with lizards sitting and walking on both walls and ceiling. The little animals are very fascinating to observe where they slowly and carefully move towards various insects before they suddenly gobble them up with a carefully acquired tongue technique.

Our Tanga stay was short-lived. We wanted to continue to Dar-es-Salaam, and walked to the bus station we had reached the day before. We were headhunted by a ticket shark and payed the equivalent 8 dollars for the two tickets. When we entered the bus only ten minutes later, the conductor asked how much we had paid. He exploded and became mad as hell when we told him.

"Who the hell sold you those tickets?" He demanded.

We pointed to the man who had ambushed us, and the conductor immediately ran over to him. Hell broke loose but not for long. He was back two minutes later. We got 7 dollars back.

"Nobody fools Pete's passengers," he said and smiled.

He got a tip.

In Zanzibar, we picked up a new expression: "Cool as a cucumber". We had been invited for dinner by Jake, who lived with a friend in the charming, but somewhat touristy Stone Town. He had approached us, asking to guide us around town. We were not super enthusiastic.

"No worries, it won't cost you anything. I am just your friend. I am Jake and I am cool as a cucumber."

He sure was too.

Malawi

Malawi is supposedly the poorest country, not at war, in the world. Øystein very occasionally gets a kick to do something charitable, and he once decided to apply for a job there as a business developer in Nkhotakota District Assembly, through Fredskorpset, the Norwegian Peace Corps. 300,000 people live in Nkhotakota District. Øystein would be the only business developer, or advisor.

Benedicte joined too, and worked as a nurse in the local hospital. It wasn't the pay that tempted her. She was only paid 5 dollars a day to see, smell and feel more hellish conditions in a few months than most Western nurses get to see throughout their careers. Øystein was paid a Norwegian salary, and got free accommodations in one of the best houses in Nkhotakota. To effectively be able to do his job, he needed wheels as well. He purchased a blue Toyota Condor.

A business developer in Malawi isn't just a business developer. If your hope is to make any changes permanent, the locals need to feel responsibility and have ownership in the project. No anchoring, no long-term success. A lot of the job is about securing 100% local participation, although this is, in many cases, virtually impossible.

Nkhotakota is on the shore of Lake Malawi, the world's ninth largest lake with more species of fish than any other freshwater lake on the planet. Øystein teamed up with some local enthusiasts that wanted to take advantage of this natural resource. They had built wooden boats, but needed engines to operate them effectively. How could they get a hold of engines in such a poor country without a well-developed or recognized banking system? Someone had to contribute with forex. Kwacha alone would simply not do the trick.

Øystein contributed a fistful of dollars, and the snowball started rolling. Engines were ordered from the United Kingdom, and they arrived quite a few months later, after fights with the government, banks and customs officers. Øystein Garfors had made it as a shipping magnate. And more importantly; Benedicte was the wife of one!

There still wasn't time or occasion to exploit such titles in the social circuit in Malawi, a lot of work still had to be done. My brother had refused to enter the project without local backing, and two hardworking lads had enthusiastically joined. They didn't have any money, but they had strong arms, a network of contacts and motivation made from steel. They made their business plan and budget, researched various fish types, tools and ways of storing their catch. The plans were presented to various local investors, and a local bank finally agreed to join in. In the end, the fishing company turned out to be a reality with 26 employees. Nkhotakota got access to fresh fish, and jobs were created for those who also sold to the market. Smaller fishing boats have long roamed the lake, but they cannot go far from shore without engines, and never been able to reach the best fishing spots.

I visited Øystein and Benedicte when the engines were still stuck in customs, but the optimism could be felt through the hot air. That the fishermen signed their contracts and the company would soon be operational, had to be celebrated by shipping tycoon Garfors with wife, and older brother.

"It is about time for a culture-historical pub crawl in what is alleged to be the biggest village in Africa," Øystein said.

No one knows exactly how many live in the center of Nkhotakota, but most people put the figure somewhere between 20,000 and 50,000 residents. And there is no shortage of bars. After visiting two relatively civilized ones by the lake and the dirtiest bar shed I have ever seen, in a little canyon by a small stream, we decided to head to the joints by the market where the beers are never far away, regardless of which day of week it is.

Although I am not sure if "beer" is the appropriate word. Most westerners would not place the liquid in that category. First, it is served in one liter cardboard boxes; Second, it is extremely cheap; and last, it tastes awful. The "beer" is called Chibuku and must, as an absolute minimum requirement, be shaken before consumed in order to water down the yeast taste a little. Its slogan does in fact reflect the drinking instruction:

"Chibuku shake shake."

Luckily, there are real beers to be had in Nkhotakota too. Usually, at least. Chibuku is drunk by those that would otherwise not be able to afford beer, and is only sold in the most dubious of joints, the real shabby bars. There are many of those in Malawi. In several, you can also buy the services of prostitutes for as little as the equivalent of one dollar. Money is exchanged for performed service in small stalls near the bar.

Do not despair should you not be convinced by the *"Chibuku Shake Shake"* slogan. Their second work of advertising genius might. *"Drink Chibuku, It's Good For You!"* There are a lot of sleazy marketing people out there, but this slogan probably takes the prize. And can be proven wrong by the drunkards that have passed out on the streets with at least one empty carton of Chibuku next to their bodies.

Unemployment in Malawi is high, and often leads to alcohol abuse. Those without money cannot even afford Chibuku. But there is, of course, an alternative, the homebrew Kochasu.

"Rumors are that it is brewed on fertilizer and corn waste," Øystein shared.

He decided that we'd had enough of dubious joints for one night, and led the way to the Nkhotakota Special Entertainment Center in the middle of the village. That is where those "well off" go to drink, they are usually employed by the government, nationally or locally.

The establishment was full on this particular Saturday night. Young and old, the well-dressed and those not so well-dressed, the sober, the drunk and the pissed. Everyone was there. And they were all black, except for the three of us. We stood out. But I still felt at home. Old football jerseys and sport jackets from Førde IL, my team back home had been shipped to Nkhotakota, and several of the locals wore jerseys that were used back in the days when I played football. A bonus is that neither Chibuku nor Kochasu are served in Nkhotakota's most popular drinking establishment.

Øystein told us that both the government and various NGOs arranged courses aimed at public officials on the dangers of unprotected sex, and that these courses are highly popular. Not because people are particularly interested in the issue, but because the participants usually get paid an "allowance" to cover extra costs. The allowance is the equivalent of three days' pay, and comes in addition to their normal wage. Øystein was considered a part of the administration and had to go to some such courses and workshops where spoke to many of the participants.

"I have been told that people usually are very eager and active in the classes. This enthusiasm continues into the night, when they spend most of their allowance on drinking and whores. They might use a condom the first time, until they get too drunk and don't care anymore. A sad story. But far too often true. And at home, their wives are of course also infected. Which means that the virus is also passed on to the tax collector, the shop owner and the guy selling goat meat. Because when there is no money available to pay living expenses, which is normally the case, the payment is sex." Øystein explained in detail on the sad practice which has made large parts of Africa ravaged by HIV and AIDS.

That's when Kingori showed up. The 55 year old doctor and goat farmer is a good friend of Øystein and Benedicte. She had advised me to stay off certain topics.

"Whatever you do, do not start speaking of sheep. He is a goat farmer and absolutely hates sheep. Kingori finds them stupid and worthless compared to goats," Benedicte explained.

We were introduced. The older man had a full beard and nice clean hands. After some polite chitchat, I could naturally not resist. I said that I heard he was a proud sheep farmer. I have rarely, if ever, seen a smiling jolly old man change character so fast.

"Eistein!"

Most Malawians cannot pronounce the name of my brother.

"Are you telling lies to your brother? Sheep are inferior creatures. Sheep are dirty. Sheep are dirty!" He declared. "All sheep should be massacred and replaced by goats," he argued, and lit up when it came to his beloved goats.

"Goats are intelligent. They make the world a better place."

Benedicte was right. This was indeed a true sheep hater. I changed subject to medicine, and Kingori calmed down. A little. My sister-in-law gave me a nasty look for my sheep stunt as she focused on keeping the conversation far away from the woolly creatures. The cooperation worked, and the goat lover's pulse was soon down to normal levels.

Kingori turned out to be quite a character for other reasons too.

"I like dirty places. I like dirty people. They are more interesting and more fun than clean ones."

We agreed, even though our definitions of what qualified as dirty places and dirty people probably differed a bit from his. His mood also improved when I got him a beer. It obviously wasn't his first this evening, and a policeman came over to us a little after midnight.

"Eistein! How are you, my brother?" He greeted us and gave Øystein a big hug. I was introduced and realized that this wasn't a normal copper. This was one of the police bosses in Nkhotakota. Øystein knew him well from getting the permits for various businesses.

But this was not the time for business talk. The police boss was drunk and he wanted to go home.

"Eistein, I need you to drive me home." He instructed.

"My car is at home," Øystein apologized "but maybe Kingori can help. Kingori, can you drive the chief back home?"

"But I am drunk, too!" Kingori wailed, "I was going to take a bike taxi back home. Why don't you take one with me, Sir?"

Bike taxies have both license plates and special permits, even though they are not much more than a normal push bike. Youngsters charge a few kwacha to transport people here and there. It is just like being an 18 year old driver with your own banger of a car in rural Norway.

"Kingori, I need to get home," He demanded. "Would you like to see your Chief on a bike taxi? Really?"

"But Sir, I am drunk. I have had too many beers." Kingori lamented.

"Kingori. I am Chief of Police. I command you to drive me home. I guarantee that you will not be stopped for drunk driving," he promised, while laughing out loud, patting Øystein's back.

"Besides, we have no instruments to measure drunk driving. I would have to take you to Lilongwe or Blantyre to find out whether or not you are drunk, and by that time you'd be sober anyway," the police officer said and laughed heartily yet again.

"But don't tell anyone I said this. Come on, let's go!"

Malawian police logic trumps most others. Kingori drove both us and the police officer home two minutes later. Fortunately without any mishaps. We all got home safely.

Togo

Togo is not a country that is high up on lists over anything. The narrow strip of land between Ghana and Benin has a 50 kilometer long coastline and can be crossed in about an hour, if traffic allows. The country does, however, stretch far enough to the north to be almost as big as West Virginia with four times the population.

I don't know why, but I have traveled quite a bit in Africa with girlfriends. The continent is legendary and full of myths. If you are offered the trip with an experienced travel companion, it would be tempting to say "yes" - or hard to say "no". Nicole accompanied me to Togo. We entered the country from Ghana where we had been with Øystein, Benedicte and their friends Kenneth and Anette. They had had enough of scarce hotels, shady transport options and poor food options, and returned to the safe haven of Kokrobote in Ghana, where the hotel had a certain standard. It was run by a German lady. They were also on a traditional holiday. I wasn't. I never am.

Nicole was almost as tired of African standards as the others, but she still joined. She had a certain understanding for my fascination with new countries. She got infected by the same bug at the mask market in Lomé, but not badly enough to agree to come along to neighboring Benin. We had gone amuck in Togo, buying enough masks for several African exhibitions back home. Some ended up as gifts; others are still routinely watching me in my flat in Oslo.

Tiny Togo was a dry affair, except for the mask mania. It was my first trip to a French speaking country in Africa, and we were met with zero tolerance for our severe lack of French. Our taxi driver from the border didn't understand a thing, and drove us to the wrong hotel - which is exactly when he understood where we were really going. A classic taxi trick. We demanded to be driven to the right hotel before he received any payment. It usually helps, and it did this time too. We got a few nasty French expressions thrown after us when he realized that he wouldn't be paid extra for his detour.

We walked down to the beachfront in the capital, and I ended up playing football with local heroes while Nicole decided to let the sun do its magic on her pigments.

"What is the point of traveling to Africa if no one back home can see that you have actually been there?" she pondered.

I have always played football, and I impressed the lads on the Lomé beach. My career highlight had been several years earlier when I scored all seven goals in a 7-2 league victory back home in 1995. Manager Svein Olav Myklebust and the entire bench had just laughed and shook their heads in disbelief when I scored the final one. It was one of the first matches I started, and the expectations weren't exactly sky high. Old tricks still worked in Africa, and my football opponents were not happy about my skills.

"You're cheating, man!" They complained.

"Hakuna matata," I answered.

But I took the hint, let them alone and walked over to Nicole. She was already noticeably tanner. I was not, thanks to sunscreen 50. She laughed when she saw me.

"I look like a local compared to you," she giggled.

"Absolutely, you will probably never leave this place on your own passport."

Mali

Mali is almost twice as big as Texas, and the fifth biggest landlocked country in the world. I visited Bamako's main market, where you can buy pretty much anything, including the dried heads of several exotic animals. They don't appear or smell particularly appealing. And I find it highly unlikely that they are legal to export from Mali or to import to Western countries. Which means that there isn't much foreign money in it for the salesmen at the market. They needed to adjust their business model. I suddenly found myself in a situation where I had to haggle over how much to pay them in order to be allowed to merely photograph them and their wagon with my own camera. They started at 20 American dollars, we ended up on one dollar. The main salesman still seemed rather satisfied.

What is annoying with this market is the overly eager fixers that actively harass foreigners under the pretext to help with anything imaginable. They will not take "no" for an answer, and end up annoying even the most patient traveler. Of course that is part of their strategy. It makes it all the easier to nick valuables from them. If their nagging didn't annoy you, their ability to cunningly steal from you will. I managed to lose three or four of the fixers by creative and abrupt maneuvers.

A more fascinating market can be found on a steep muddy hill north of town. Anything from television sets to sunbeds; plastic containers to CDs are sold from underneath tarpaulins in colors you didn't know existed. Planks have been put here and there on the muddy surface to make it possible for customers to get between the stalls and stay relatively dry. A similar market is on the same hill, just slightly to the west. Like a giant mall, but with somewhat lower comfort and luxury than those in American suburbs.

Mali is not a country renowned for gourmet food and nightlife, but thanks to French colonialism I found both impressive restaurants and cool and lively nightclubs in the capital, particularly in the street with the nonchalant name "Bla Bla". It is as close as you will ever get to Bourbon Street in Mali. A fair amount of the visitors there are expats in Bamako, foreign friends and some rich or well-off locals. The country is among the poorest in Africa and the world, and more than half of its topography is desert. Despite the high percentage of poor or very poor people in Mali, and in many other African countries, smiles are rarely hard to find. The joy of life witnessed in Africa is simply unique. People come across as happy, even without or with very few belongings. This fact alone makes it even worse to tolerate pitiful, nagging and demanding people. Most of these seem to come from the Western world. WAINS - Why Am I Not Surprised?

The country's only super attraction is located in the desert. The town of Timbuktu is well known from Donald Duck comics and other literary works of questionable quality. Mali is also famous for its music, and many people may have heard about the music festival "Festival au Désert" held in Timbuktu until 2009. Pending better times, it is now organized in exile. In 2014, it took place in Berlin. Naturally.

Sudan

Sudan was dramatically reduced in size when South Sudan became independent in 2011. What used to be the biggest country in Africa is now number three. Its name derives from Arabic "bilad al-sudan" which means "the black's country". Sudan has actually more pyramids than Egypt, then again, it was also a part of that country in earlier times.

The taxi driver who would drive me to my hotel in Khartoum didn't know where it was and called several friends to try to figure it out. This, of course, meant a substantial detour, something he demanded extra money for. I refused, something which made him mighty angry. The large man came out of the car with an intention of showing me who was boss. The receptionist of the hotel luckily came to the rescue and managed to calm the driver down. Taxi drivers in almost every country in the world are full of dirty tricks, and I prefer other modes of transport when possible.

The desert climate in Khartoum doesn't invite too much activity, but I decided to at least see where the Nile starts. The Blue Nile and the White Nile meet in Sudan's capital, and make up the Nile which flows into the Mediterranean Sea. Just be careful when documenting your visit via a compact camera. The police do not approve of photography.

I got talking to a guy calling himself Spider, one night in Khartoum. He wasn't exactly shy.

"So, have you found any girls yet?" he bated.

I smiled.

"No, I am good. How about yourself, have you got a girlfriend?" I asked.

"Oh yeah, but she is at home up north. Tonight I am gonna take that beautiful girl over there home with me," he boasted.

"What about your girlfriend?"

"Not a problem, I will be using a condom!" he assured me.

He gave me a big smile and showed me some condoms he kept in his back pocket. Planned unfaithfulness coming up in a Muslim country.

Risky.

At least he used contraception, even a barrier device. Not something overly usual in Africa.

The taxi driver taking me back to the airport was very different than the first. He even invited me for tea in some sort of a café with plastic chairs under parasols on the side of the road. He insisted on treating me. He was either a lovely chap, or he just felt bad over having demanded too much money for the ride.

It isn't legally possible to get hold of any stronger drinks than tea in Sudan. It is a dry country in more ways than one. Alcohol is available only if you know the right people or end up at an embassy party, according to the driver. He was a practicing Muslim and used the tea stop for one of his four daily prayers, facing Mecca. He seemed open to discuss pretty much anything, and I seized the occasion for a little discussion on religion.

"You have a lot of rules in your religion." I stated, more of a question.

"Tell me about it! I think there are too many. But I am raised a Muslim, so I try to follow them. Most of them at least," he smirked.

"Most of them?" I repeated.

"I will let you in on a secret. I actually eat a lot of pork every time I travel abroad to my relatives," he confessed.

"Wow, isn't that a big sin?"

"I refuse to believe that God will not accept me because I eat a certain animal. What's the difference between a cow and a pig, anyway? It makes no logical sense. Besides, Spanish Pata Negra is to kill for."

A reflective and good man. I don't agree much with the abundance of religious rules either. What made me most curious was how on Earth he had got hold of Pata Negra, one of the most exclusive hams available. Clearly not in Sudan.

Liberia

Liberia is a unique country. It was primarily founded by freed American slaves, and the capital Monrovia is named after James Monroe. The fifth president of the USA worked hard to help establish the new African country.

It may not come as much of a surprise that there is a ban on any form of slavery in the constitution:

"There shall be no slavery within this Republic. Nor shall any citizen of this Republic, or any person resident therein, deal in slaves, either within or without this Republic, directly or indirectly."

I finally managed to get a ride to town from the airport. Three taxi drivers had, reasons unknown, turned me down. I did not carry a single coin or bill - no cash at all. So I bet everything on well-functioning ATMs. The poor driver had to stop at eight cash machines, without any luck, and he was becoming visibly frustrated. So was I. It is not on anyone's bucket list to be penniless in Liberia.

I succeeded on my ninth attempt. The ATM actually accepted my Visa card from my little local Norwegian bank. I am probably their customer that travels the most, they have yet never complained about my withdrawals in one suspicious country after another. They blocked my card once, though, when the credit card number appeared on a list that circulated in dubious circles in Nigeria. Unfortunately, I was at Oslo International Airport when they called to inform me about it en route to South America. My MasterCard performed well as backup.

I paid the driver and started exploring the capital. An alley between two office blocks was full of office workers. They sat typing on their typewriter - future proof. But they seemed to have plenty to do, even with several competing internet cafés within walking distance.

I got talking to Victor over lunch in a downtown restaurant. He told me he worked as a driver.

"And not for just anybody. I drive the head of the prison service and the head of the police."

I didn't doubt him. He wore a suit and showed me a Mercedes key.

"Would you like to join me for a beer?" he asked.

His offer sounded very tempting in the extreme heat except for a small detail.

"Sure! But aren't you working?"

"Of course! I am always working. If they call me, I am there in ten minutes."

"You drive the police and prison bosses, but you still drink beer on duty?" I asked.

"Of course! You know, for every six beers I drink one cold Coke. It neutralizes the beers and I am totally sober again."

"Really?"

"Yes, I always do this. And then I can drive them. Or I have another six beers and then another Coke. And then drive them."

There wasn't much to say about his logic - except for the fact that it was totally, utterly wrong. But who was I to object, he would probably never be arrested anyway. I assumed that it was highly unlikely that the chief of police would arrest his own driver. Unless he crashed, of course.

Another driver took me back to the airport. We were stuck behind a motorcycle for quite some time. A man was sitting behind the driver. He held a lawnmower that nicely rolled behind the bike at 60 kilometers an hour.

Whoever said watching traffic is boring – never visited Liberia.

Gambia

I met Øystein and Benedicte a little further north, in Gambia. I was in the middle of a tour to six African countries; they were on a relaxing holiday and had decided to stop at two; Gambia and Senegal. Little Gambia only borders to Senegal and is a well-known tourist destination, especially for Brits - as in female ones. Gambia is to older women what Thailand, the Philippines, Malaysia, Indonesia, Madagascar, Kenya, Cuba and many, many other countries are to older men. A place where they go on holiday to get laid. This is not, as in the dictionary definition, prostitution - albeit not far from it. People with money from Western countries travel to countries where most people can only dream about cash. By offering a luxurious hotel room, delicious food and often plenty of gifts for a week or two, they receive sex and companionship in return.

A lot of Gambian men have specialized in attracting and pleasing the women that arrive on holiday. It is clearly important to have a well-toned body, and to preferably know enough about history, geography, literature and culture to keep a conversation going for a brief period of time – say the usual two weeks.

We visited Atle, a friend of Øystein's, south of the capital, Banjul. He has had his own retirement home built here, not far from one of the beaches. We had gone down to go running on the white sand. We ran past three local hunks. One of them was called Will and didn't wear anything but a small Speedo. And I will leave the jokes. Will had a body fit; fit enough to wear pretty much anything he wanted to. Except for nice buttoned shirts because his biceps were way too big to fit any mass produced shirt. Not to mention his breasts. They were bigger than those of most competitors in any Miss World or Miss Universe competition. In Venezuela.

Will tried to appeal to British women by doing a lot of pushups and nothing else.

"I am the push up king! I push, I don't pull," he said. And that was pretty much all of what he said that made any sense. The 27 year old did not use conversational skills to successfully be picked up as a two-week partner. He focused on his upper body and did over a thousand push ups every day. He claimed that his record was 160 in one go.

"What do you think, Benedicte? Does he stand a chance?" I teased.

I was curious what a girl would say about such a body. Øystein seemed curious about her answer too.

"Hell, no! I can't go out with a man who has breasts the same size as me," she frowned.

Of course he is aiming at a slightly older clientele.

Congo

There are other things that matter in Congo, in the middle of Africa. I ended up in a visa queue on the border between Rwanda and Congo just in front of a local man. He spontaneously shouted at me the moment he saw my passport.

"Where are you from? I live in Drammen," he said in fluent Norwegian. He had been given asylum in Norway several years ago and now worked with youngsters to persuade them to pick up sensible hobbies, not drugs usage. He was on his way to visit relatives and friends back in Congo.

The town of Goma is located on Lake Kivu just across the border from Gisenyi in Rwanda. Less bureaucracy is needed to visit this part of the country than the capital, Kinshasa. The two G towns are in walking distance of each other, but the atmosphere is very different. Goma has been controlled by both rebels and government forces. It has also been in the center of one of the world's worst refugee catastrophes when two million people escaped from Rwanda due to the genocide there in 1994. Goma had no chance to manage the unbelievable increase in population, and sanitary conditions were inhuman. Outbreaks of cholera could not be avoided.

To make matters worse, the lake contains large amounts of gas that is stored on the bottom of it. This gas could suddenly be released, something that would kill anyone and anything inhaling it. The gas is secure, for now, but an earthquake or any other eruption from the Nyiragongo volcano, which is only 20 kilometers to the north, has the potential to release it all in no time. The volcano last erupted in 2002, and huge amounts of lava flowed through town and into the lake. A lot of it was still there when I visited in 2008. We are talking about a volatile region, but the conflict between government forces and rebels is what gets most of the attention.

The UN has a lot of soldiers in the area, where numerous NGOs are present too. A country can often be noted for the souvenirs they offer since souvenir manufacturers are inspired by local traditions, happenings or events. It may come as no surprise that most of the souvenirs in Goma consist of white plastic play cars with "UN" painted on the doors in big black letters. The vast amount of armored personnel vehicles certainly contributes to the atmosphere, or lack thereof, even though the locals come across as friendly and smiling.

With one exception.

I went jogging along the lake, where a lot of people were walking. A skinny, tall and well-muscled teenage boy ran towards me and pretended that he would punch me.

"White man, go home or I kill you!" he yelled.

I can't blame him, really. These conditions could make anyone in the neighborhood unstable. I turned around, raised my open hands, kept them high and spoke to the angry kid.

"Calm down, boy!"

I turned around again and continued jogging - a little faster than before.

Algeria

The biggest country in Africa is the tenth biggest in the world. I have unfortunately only visited the capital Alger, which almost seems French, maybe not strange given the country's colonial past. Then again, I might not have missed too much since 80 per cent of the country's area is covered by sand.

I found a butcher in the Casbah district of the capital. He sold sheep heads. Ola, the Sheep Nazi, seems to have competition in Northern Africa. Parts of the city come with a range of alleys and buildings very close to each other. They seem to have been built without too much of a plan, it is almost like a labyrinth, and not even my well-developed sense of direction prevented me from taking a few mistaken turns in the crowded hill that ends up in the harbor.

My hotel was just east of town. Frankenstein's brother sat at the front desk. Just as silent, just as dark, just as tall, just as scary. He had a mark in his forehead, probably inspired by Gorbachev. The door to the room had two locks and a security chain. I used all three before finding an alternative escape route from the balcony. A gutter would work as a plan B, should I need to escape from the second floor.

"TIA," I whispered to myself.

What would Doctor Vodka have done?

Probably drunk Frankenstein under the table.

The night passed peacefully, and Frankenstein was off duty the next morning. He only worked nights. Of course.

Ivory Coast

To travel alone is liberating. It is only then that I can truly do, see and eat exactly what I want. A lot of people are reluctant to travel alone; to me it is actually a bonus. But of course, not always. At least not when it's my birthday. I celebrated my 37th birthday in the Ivory Coast with British Sera. I asked if she would like to join me, since she had never been to Africa.

"Will I be killed?" she asked.

"Absolutely not!" I said.

"I'm in," she said hesitantly.

I didn't tell her that the State Department had just warned against visits there. She arrived in the country a few hours before me. We had taken different airlines, and she was picked up by the wife of the hotel owner. She was back in the airport a few hours later to greet me upon my arrival in Abidjan, the biggest city in the country. It was a warm welcome.

"This is amazing! It is so different than anywhere else I have been. The sky is so blue, the smells are different and I just saw my first cockroach!" she said enthusiastically with big eyes. A typical reaction from a first timer in Africa. Although cockroaches rarely bring out any form, kind or shape of enthusiasm. A great girl! I laughed.

"And you have only been here 4-5 hours. Look forward to more cockroaches and other things you have never seen before or even imagined could happen or exist."

We stayed outside Abidjan in a privately run German Ivorian hotel, practically on the beach. With a swimming pool. Not a bad place to celebrate your 37th birthday. But we still had to explore the local area first. Sera agreed to go for a little walk in the sun around lunch on the second day on the beach to the next town, Grand-Bassam, which is on the border to Ghana. 15 kilometers away, it turned out, as we discovered the hard way. Luckily, the luxury hotel La Cote du Repos was located halfway there. Its restaurant is on a terrace next to the beach. Their Tuna Carpaccio is to kill tuna for.

I soon experienced overexposure to the sun and had to use an umbrella as protection. It looked anything but cool, but beat the alternative of third degree burns.

Sera didn't directly complain, but she was anything but impressed by what our little walk had developed into. A GT at sunset before dinner in the best fish restaurant she had ever been to, saved some of her impression. We still took a taxi back to Abidjan. The driver was called George, and he drove an over-styled

Nissan. We saw him repeatedly the next few days as he stopped by our hotel to check up on us. Service - or just a desire for more chauffeur missions.

My birthday two days later was celebrated in the hotel room with take-out pizza. Food poisoning sort of put a break on the celebrations. Maybe we should have skipped the cold chili sauce that was served together with the barbequed chicken the day before. Has it not been barbequed, fried, boiled or peeled, it should neither be eaten. I should have known better, but I was back in shape after only 24 hours. I have encountered much worse in that area.

The contrasts are huge in Abidjan. We saw beggars who were missing several body parts, and who hardly had any clothes on the remaining body parts. They seemed to be located at random. Some were totally out of it; others begged using small paper cups. And quite a few were too weak to even carry their own cups. One beggar was lying down on the sandy surface next to a market place. He wouldn't stay alive much longer. We had ordered chicken and sat waiting for it on plastic chairs a few meters away. The meal cost next to nothing, yet much more than he could dream of collecting during one day of begging.

Hell is widespread in Africa. Traditional aid doesn't do much good.

Namibia

There aren't many NGOs to see in civilized and relatively wealthy Namibia. The country is twice the size of California, but with only two million people. That makes it the third least densely populated country in the world - after Mongolia and Western Sahara. Also, this is not a country for wimps. We are talking deserts, giant cars and huge steaks. So, if you are a girl, leave your high heels at home.

Kjersti and I drove into Namibia from Botswana in the North. We had just been to Zimbabwe, and the contrasts were enormous between the very empty shop shelves there and the US inspired hypermarkets in Namibia. The selection in Namibia is much better than in Norway, the prices obviously much, much lower.

We would stay overnight in the middle of the bush, by the Okavango River. There are actually quite a few hidden camping sites not too far from the road. They offer accommodation in traditional huts or cabins of various standards. Toilets and showers are usually shared, built up in the jungle without anything but bamboo walls that divide the facilities from the path, a meter apart. We also swam in the river in floating swimming pools made of an upside down cage floating in the river. To prevent us from being tomorrow's crocodile or hippo shit. We felt safe, and had an amazingly refreshing dive after a long day's driving.

We walked back to our straw hut after the unusual swim. We hadn't seen crocodiles or hippos, but the animals are skilled at advanced camouflage and might have been close by without us knowing.

"Watch the snake!" Kjersti suddenly shouted.

She walked behind me, but had noticed something I had not. A long and thick snake of unknown origin was relaxing across the path. I was just about to step on it with my right foot, but I miraculously managed to actually leap backwards, practically in my step. The snake was probably not poisonous, but why gamble? We returned to the cabin on a different path.

I was back in Namibia years later. This time with new travel companions. My brother Øystein and Torgeir Halvorsen who I had met for the first time in Cape Verde. There wasn't much vegetation to see this time. Namibia's entire coastline consists of sand, rocks and dunes. Desert as far as the eye can see. Swakopmund, is a "German" town, a divided one too. Those with a German background live in the modern town center, while the local blacks live in one of several "townships" on the outskirts - as in some sort of high standard slums. We rented a flat in town.

One fine day we drove an hour or so north. We stopped for lunch by a coffee shop. The owner, a big German man with a mustache, sat outside. We had read about a seal colony on Cape Cross, yet another hour's drive north. We were not too keen on making the journey unless the seals were there. The local German should know.

"Sorry, sir. We are thinking about going up to see the seals. Are they still there?" I asked. And I have never received a more indignant answer.

"They never leave!" he grimaced.

"And they are worth seeing?" I hesitated.

"Have you ever seen a seal colony before?" he asked.

"No, we haven't," Torgeir said.

"Then you should go. Be prepared for a noise and a smell out of this world. They never leave!" he exclaimed.

It turned out that he was also part owner in a fishery. The seals were hated creatures, eating a lot of fish, damaging his business. "They never leave!" seemed to be a part of his regular Tourette Syndrome routine. We drove north. We wanted to see these creatures for ourselves.

200,000 or so seals had occupied several kilometers of coastline. And made more noise than teenage girls outside Justin Bieber's hotel. The seals give birth just before Christmas, and there were loads of small and cute and smelly seal puppies when we visited in January. They are just centimeters from the elevated pathways that had been built to allow visitors to come close to the animals. Very fascinating! But the smell stuck to our hair and clothes, and long and thorough showers were needed to again achieve a semi-normal body odor.

Swaziland

Swaziland, the little country squeezed in between South Africa and Mozambique has the highest penetration of AIDS in the world. Over a fourth of the adults here have the illness. King Mswati the Third rules the million people, and does so rather harshly. As he has done since he became the youngest monarch in the world at the age of 18 back in 1986. The man has at least 15 wives, many of them much younger than himself.

Kjersti and I drove into the country from South Africa in our Fiat. We rented a room in a hostel were zebra was served for dinner. My sister went to bed early, as usual. I decided to remain by the fire and ended up staying up late, as usual.

Relebohile worked in the hostel and also sat by the fire. It turned out that she knew one of the wives of the queen. This particular wife was South African and in her 20's. She was, needless to say, beautiful. All his wives apparently share that particular characteristic. Relebohile however claimed that her friend was highly intelligent too. I asked why she would then voluntarily be one of 15 wives in Swaziland. Relebohile laughed.

"The king has given her her own credit cards and she spends most of her time traveling the world and shopping. She is only needed by the king every once in a while. The rest of the time, she enjoys life. At some point in time she will decide to just leave him and start her own real family."

It didn't sound too bad. As long as one of the world's four absolute monarchs does not discover the cunning plan. When a king has unlimited, centralized and absolute power and sovereignty, the fate shared by most wives of Henry VIII probably isn't far away.

Relebohile went on to tell me how important the 21st birthday is in many African countries. "It is very symbolic. That day you get a key. It's a key to your freedom, a key to get married, and a key to have kids. Do you have kids?" she asked out of the blue.

"No, I am a virgin," I joked.

"Seriously? Get your key, man!" she laughed.

Botswana

Kjersti took three months of her medical studies in Botswana. She assisted at several hospitals and clinics where the main challenge was the extreme spread of HIV and AIDS. Botswana is often considered a successful and wealthy African country, but the government must take its share of responsibility for the epidemics that have hit its citizens so hard. A couple, whether married or not, will be placed at random locations in the country upon finished education for their first assignments. Botswana is big and transport possibilities are limited, which means that the couple might end up seeing each other only a few times a year. Temptation often arises in the meantime, and some will not be able to resist a little quality time with a colleague or a friend. Which means that the AIDS virus may suddenly be introduced into the relationship, and yet again passed on to the lovers of the partner on the other side of the country.

One of Kjersti's tasks was to teach how to use contraceptives. For her, it became very important to show that condoms are the only type of contraceptive that actually reduces the spread of STDs and that only taking the pill does not. This may be common knowledge in the Western world, but not in Botswana. Some people had realized the dangers of rubber-free sex, just not many enough.

"I had visited a 40 year old woman, and I talked to her about HIV and AIDS and how important it is to use a condom during intercourse. She wasn't particularly interested, though, and maintained that this didn't apply to her. "Come on, I only have five steady bed partners," she explained. "And they are all good neighbors, so I am absolutely certain that they don't have no AIDS."

TIA. Do the math. If each and every one of them had five sexual partners, the neighborhood would be in major trouble in no time. And we might also want to take into consideration that this particular lady thought that five partners was way below average.

No wonder that Kjersti was mentally exhausted after work and needed something else to focus on. She played for the Norwegian national rugby team for years, and was usually voted the woman of the match or tournament despite her 153 centimeters and 49 kilos. She plays offense, not defense. When she was asked by the local newspaper back home why she was so good, she seized the opportunity.

"I have four older brothers that have always tormented me. Or toughened me, as they like to put it," she was quoted in the paper. We weren't even allowed to comment against the horrible allegations. Which, to be fair, weren't totally unfounded.

There were no rugby teams in rural Botswana, at least not for women. So Kjersti ended up playing football instead for the men's team in little Maun, a popular destination for participants of luxurious safaris in the middle of the country. We had just finished our little roundtrip in Southern Africa, and I joined to watch her play. She was by far the smallest person on the field, but still did particularly well. Kjersti was faster than most, although her passes didn't reach quite as far as her team mates. It was strange to see my blond little sister on a football pitch with 21 big and black lads. And it made me particularly proud, too.

It was time to leave her. We had visited eight countries by Fiat. She had one month left in Maun, and must have had a hell of a time. Africa certainly intrigued her enough to return a few years later, then to Uganda to study tropical medicine. She now works as a medical doctor in Førde, and is the only one to have followed in the footsteps of our dad. Two, Øystein and Torunn, have followed our mom, and become teachers.

Uganda

I visited Uganda before my sister traveled there as a student. Together with Semiha, a Turkish photographer I had first met in Istanbul. None of my friends from back home were interested in a small Uganda trip, so I asked for Turkish assistance. Semiha had never been to Africa before, and none of her friends had even heard about Uganda or Burundi. She had many warnings before departure, but returned with memories for a lifetime.

We had walked in from Rwanda on a muddy road. Quite a few car owners on the Ugandan side were trying to make a few extra dollars by driving people to more urban areas of the country. We paid for a ride to Kisoro. Where it was time for lunch. We purchased boiled eggs and fried chicken legs from a woman in a wooden stall on the side of the road. Lunch usually tastes the best outdoors; we consumed ours in some sort of a park, a narrow stretch of grass and a few trees in the middle of the village.

We decided to share a taxi to Kabale with two gentlemen. One was a tailor and one an accountant. Judging by the size of the guys, it was the tailor who made the most money, by far. He was naturally also better dressed than anyone else in the car. Being rather selfish, we let him have the passenger seat.

The night would be spent by Lake Bunyonyi outside Kabale. We checked into a hostel, and our own bungalow with a lake view and went for a mandatory canoe ride.

Dinner, goat and chicken, was served on an outdoor terrace by the lobby. An elderly British lady sat next to us. She had clearly discovered the meaning of life - to teach Ugandan 20 year olds good business etiquette. To ignore the conversation was impossible given the loud instructions, and the almost whispered replies.

"I can of course give you money or a couple of pigs, but I need to know that you can set up a viable business. You tell me that you want to be a pig farmer, and then you have to prove to me that you mean business. I want you to write me a business plan," she urged.

"OK, madam," he whispered.

"I am not being difficult, but I must see and feel your dedication. I need several pages and a budget. If it looks good I will lend you the money for a stake in your pig farm. Is that clear?"

"Yes, madam," he whispered.

"I will of course be happy to help you with the business plan, but you have to deliver. You have to show dedication and hard work. Understand?" She continued.

"Yes, madam," he whispered again.

Too much. We moved to a table further away. The monologue was monotonous and didn't seem likely to change character anytime soon. They shook hands half an hour later. I was curious if he would have patience to actually run the pig farm, or if he would soon have had too much of the women with white hair and huge glasses. Definitely British.

Kabale is not a big place. We found out the hard way when trying to leave. We entered a bus bound for Kampala, the capital. This was a 50-seater, and we both knew what that meant. It would have to fill up completely before departure. My non-existent patience was long gone when the driver finally started the engine. It had taken five hours to fill up. It didn't exactly start moving fast, either. The bus often stopped to pick up people or to let passengers leave. It was at any given time full or totally stuffed. Two passengers transported live chickens in a plastic bag, another guy had two piglets in a cardboard box.

We were relieved to see some sort of a shopping center with four floors in Kampala, maybe we could find an internet café. The temperature was over 30 degrees, and Semiha wasn't feeling great. After having updated our necessary statuses online, we walked down from the top floor. She fainted and fell down the last few steps, luckily landing on her tummy without hitting her head. I lifted her into the nearest restaurant and put her in the recovery position. She came back to her senses after less than a minute, by that time we had an audience of 12-15 people.

"What happened?" she asked weakly.

"I have no idea! You fainted. Are you OK?"

"My leg hurts!" she complained.

She had twisted her ankle and couldn't walk on it. Luckily, she had taken my hint and traveled with hand luggage only. I put one backpack over each shoulder and carried her to the nearest taxi, a black Datsun. The model hasn't been produced for years, as if anyone in Kampala cares.

Room service in a decent hotel provided dinner and an ice pack on Semiha's ankle. It helped enough for her to be able to hobble here and there the next day. We visited Burundi together too.

Guinea-Bissau

I took a bush taxi from Ziguinchor in Senegal to Guinea-Bissau. Obviously in a French Peugeot 504. The roads are macabre, and not at all recommended if you are in a hurry. Frequent police checks must be taken into account too. And to make sure that you won't just speed past the police, they block the entire road with seriously thick chains, stretched between big trees on opposite sides of the road. The checkpoints are effortless as long as the visa in your passport is valid, but they certainly take some time.

TIA.

I got talking to Mike the fisherman in the port in Bissau, the capital. He was hanging out by a rusty old wreck that had gone down just next to the pier. A third of it was above water. Mike complained about a lack of jobs.

"Huge fishing boats from the EU just come down here and fish everything. There is nothing left for us small local guys," he told me.

"But how can they do this?"

"Our politicians are corrupt. They get a lot of money from the European companies, and give them all the licenses. The fishing boats destroy our living. They take our fish, our jobs, and our money. I hate the politicians here. And I hate the EU. The EU even has the nerve to come here and take credit for giving us aid money and for partly financing airports and roads. But what they take away from us is much higher than what they give back. Hypocrites!"

Mike was well-spoken and well-informed for an unemployed fisherman in Guinea-Bissau.

"You are not from the EU, are you?"

"No, from Norway."

"Really? Are you a fisherman too?" the curious fellow asked.

I do not know how much of Mike's story is completely accurate, but it was obvious that the EU wanted everyone in the country to know which projects they support. Big metal signs that inform the public about financial support from the Union have been put up by many roads and public buildings.

Guinea-Bissau isn't the only country suffering from such problems either. Senegal suffered from over-fishing by factory trawlers for years. In 2012, their government finally told the EU to fish elsewhere. They had eventually realized that such industrial fishing destroyed the livelihood of local fishermen. That particular decision has proved successful; there are again a lot of fishermen on the Senegal coast. This creates jobs, boosts local economies and provides people with unsubsidized food from the EU and the US. The practice will hopefully be copied by Guinea-Bissau and other African countries as well.

PLANES, TRAINS AND AUTOMOBILES

198 countries - unaccountable traveled stretches and itineraries - a few legs of transport, to put it lightly. A lot of them have been undertaken by plane, which is usually problem-free. It isn't until I resort to cargo vessels, trains, buses, taxies, donkeys, rental cars, bikes and other modes of transport that problems arise more frequently. It is then that you really start getting to know a place and a country when you sit squeezed between local people, when you share a bus with several kinds of animals, and when you discover that the trip takes twice as long as you anticipated. The view is also better, or at least more detailed, than from 35,000 feet.

Not to mention that you escape all those annoying security controls. And a severe lack of food options.

El Salvador

I had one goal when I landed in El Salvador, in addition to actually see the country. I wanted to visit Honduras and Guatemala too. The bus system in this part of the world is very limited, especially when traveling from an airport, then onwards to the nearest bus station and further afield to other countries on roads less traveled. I opted for a rental car. I found several rentals stalls immediately after the passport control. I picked a local company. The man behind the counter was my age and looked rather friendly.

"What car would you like?" he enquired.

"Just the smallest and cheapest one you've got. How much for three days?"

"150 USD," he offered.

"And I can drive to Honduras and Guatemala as well?"

"Of course you can. There are roads there as well," he joked.

"Hehehe...and insurance and all is ok?" I completed my inquiry.

"My friend, do not worry. This is Central America," he assured me.

Trustworthy, indeed.

"But I do not have a small car. I will give you a little bigger one for the same price. Is it ok?"

I have never seen such a huge pickup, and I have lived both in the Midwest and the Norwegian middle of nowhere. I signed the papers and got in. I now know what a truck driver perspective is.

El Salvador is surfers' paradise, and you don't have to go far from the airport to experience it. I didn't drive far in my huge vehicle before reaching a surf camp on the beach. My bungalow was 50 meters from the shore, but the sounds of the waves battering the sand every few seconds was still deafening. Thor would have been envious of the sound. Luckily, I always carry earplugs while on the road, and they sure came to good use here. Despite originally being intended for noisy neighborhoods, horny room neigbors or hotels near mosques, and not for surf camps - they were essential to manage to get any sleep at all. I nevertheless dreamt about being at war- with frequent bomb explosions.

I took full advantage of both beach and waves the next day. I tried surfing on a rented board, but I had to acknowledge that I lacked a lot of basic skills to even dream about semi-mastering the giant waves. Øystein tried to teach me a few tricks months later in Stad on the Norwegian West Coast. He failed miserably, but I sure noticed that the water temperature there was far lower for sure.

Honduras

I drove into Honduras from El Salvador at dusk. A tourist with a rental car would normally have a fair amount of paperwork at the border. Then again, of course no tourist would drive a huge *truck*. The border police believed that I was an expat living there and just waved me across. Being relatively shy with bureaucracy, I did not hesitate to follow their orders.

I was soon in Octopeque, an intersection of a town that actually had a dozen or so hotels all of very different standards. A range of truck drivers from countries in Central America were taking advantage of the offerings. But I had planned to drive a little further to see the pyramids of Copan. The weather gods didn't agree with me on that account. I had to cross a mountain to get there, and I have never been as surprised by fog as I was then. At first, I could see about 20 meters in front of me, eventually only one or two. I could at times not even see where the pavement ended on the side of the road. I had no option but to turnaround.

Octopeque again. I checked out several of the hotels and was offered the cheapest room I have ever seen. The scruffy skinny guy with a thin moustache demanded two dollars. It actually didn't look too bad, but the other guests did. I declined the offer and checked into a hotel across the street. It was 150% more expensive, but I had five dollars to spare-and, my monster truck got its own safe spot in the backyard! If there are places where cars are stolen or stripped for everything including wheels, I had a feeling Octopeque would be among them.

I woke up early the next day. The fog was gone, and I decided to try to cross the mountain again. The weather was nice, the temperature too. I drove without shoes on. A policeman stopped me just outside town. There was no way in hell that the pickup could ever speed; and it turned out to be only a routine check point. The police officer didn't find anything wrong. But he dropped my driver's license on the floor of the car when giving it back. I opened the door to fetch it, and he could see that I drove barefoot.

"No shoes? Illegal. Now, I can fine you," he triumphed in what was actually English. I had to laugh.

"Seriously? Please show me the law I have broken, sir." I encouraged politely.

He kept demanding his fine; I kept smiling and eventually asked for a receipt. He just shook his head and signalled that I should continue. Nice try, if nothing else.

The pickup took me to Copan and a short pitstop before heading to Guatemala. I would objectively argue that the pyramids in Giza are more impressive, but I should probably not compare different types of architecture or building styles.

Mexico

There are pyramids in Mexico too. The big country comes with a lot more than what most people realize. More than cactus, tacos and tequila. Of course, when you finally visit a country you think you know relatively well, there are things that must be tested. Such as real Mexican tacos. It tastes better there. I found proof in a tiny local café.

The country often ends up in the shadow of its more famous neighbor to the north, the USA. Deserved or not, there is a lot about Mexico most people do not realize. The official name of Mexico is in fact very similar to that of the USA; Estados Únidos Mexicanos (United States of Mexico).

Mexico's flag contains three vertical stripes. The green stripe to the left symbolizes hope; the white in the middle represents innocence while the red to the right stands for the blood of the Mexican people. There is an eagle in the middle with some sort of snake in its beak. An Aztec legend says that the gods instructed the people to build a city where they saw an eagle eat a snake. An eagle must have done so once in Mexico City, the current capital in the country with more Spanish speaking people than anywhere else in the world.

The country is interesting, animal wise as well. The volcano rabbit is among the rarest animals in the country. It naturally lives in and near the volcanoes. While the smallest dog in the world comes from and is named after a state called Chihuahua. The scorpion is still much smaller, but a hell of a lot more fearsome. It is responsible for a thousand deaths every year.

I only had one day in Mexico City. My visit happened before I imposed the rule of nothing but hand luggage, so I carried both a backpack and a big suitcase. Both came with me downtown where I was able to store them in a hotel reception area. The receptionist thought that I had stayed there, and I didn't correct her. I could roam freely around one of the biggest cities in the world.

I managed to see the cathedral and to walk around and enjoy the Spanish inspired architecture in the old town. Plus a trip to Zocalo square, the world's third largest. Only the Red Square in Moscow and Tiananmen Square in Beijing are bigger. I was also surprised to see a Liverpool shopping center in an Art Deco building from the 1920's. I would personally have preferred a Tottenham house.

And that is what I had time for before finding the nearest metro station to return to the airport. To go by taxi is boring and impersonal besides the usual rush hour traffic. Which, it turned out, also exists in the underground. I just missed a super crowded train, which meant I was among the first in line for the next one. By the time it arrived, a few minutes later, the platform was heaving. I was luckily standing by the tracks, holding tight to my 20 kilos worth of suitcase. My backpack weighed half as much. When the doors opened, 30 kilos of luggage and me were lifted up and into the car as a result of everyone pushing onto this particular train. My feet hadn't touched the ground but I was all of a sudden standing, although totally squeezed, in the middle of the car. Traveling with a lot of luggage is not a problem as long as other people carry it for you.

Burundi

Bujumbura in Burundi is a chaotic little capital in a tiny country that is depending very much on coffee export. The trip was a part of a bigger trip in the region with Turkish Semiha who had also joined Uganda. To travel with someone who had never been to Africa before is interesting. The prejudices were apparent, but she soon got used to everyday life in Africa with street sellers everywhere, beggars on every corner, buses that do not leave until they are full; people that stare, and, insect crisps.

Semiha was ready to be introduced to pretty much anything. Lake Tanganyika is near Bujumbura, and we took a taxi to the beach. We were almost ambushed by kids who wanted to be photographed. Semiha always travels with a professional camera, so she was sort of asking for it. Eventually even youngsters and adults worked up the courage to ask for the same after a few beers at Black & White, the local beach bar.

But why the urge to be photographed? They would never see the photos anyway, let alone get copies of them. I asked the youngsters.

"It's cool knowing that you're inside the camera, and that someone in another country will look at us later and remember us on this beautiful day. It is happiness captured!"

Wise words from 19 year old, Walter.

We spoke with him and the other 10-12 youths. The group consisted of two couples and individuals that would most likely become couples by the end of the weekend.

The bus that would take us to Kingali was called "Yahoo!". It had nothing to do with the internet giant; the owner might just have been a fan. The bus had originally been yellow, big Yahoo! logos were now on all sides. We sat by the bus for two hours until it was full, and we could finally start the journey.

We got talking to several of the other passengers. They just could not get their heads around why "rich" people like us traveled by bus. We could afford to fly, surely.

"But then we wouldn't have met you," Semiha responded.

A charming approach and the same tactic I had used in São Tomé and Príncipe. Still valid.

Two fellow passengers, brothers, got us barbequed goat meat when we stopped for a rest. A couple and an adult daughter did the cooking in the shed of a restaurant halfway to the capital in Rwanda. The goat had been on wooden skewers over the glowing coals, and was served in brown paper bags with plenty of salt and pepper on the side.

"For dipping," the grill master explained.

Western road kitchens will never be the same.

Slovenia

I have never traveled to an airport just to find out that the plane I was supposed to be on would not, in fact, fly. Except in Slovenia. The Jat Airways flight from Ljubljana to Skopje was not listed on the departure screens that showed the remaining flights that day. I checked my ticket. The time and date was as I remembered. I tried to find an English speaker from Jat or the airport unsuccessfully. There were no Jat planes on the tarmac either. I had no choice but to return to the town center.

Where I went straight to jail.

An old prison has been converted to a youth hostel, and the cells have had much more comfortable beds installed than was the case when prisoners slept there.

Slovenia is a green country with half the area consisting of forests. This is also the case in Ljubljana with its many parks and woods surrounding River Ljubljanica. The town has been chemically cleansed for sights, but can still offer a variety of cozy and good restaurants, coffee shops and bars. And the prison-gone-hostel is in the Metelkova district, almost a free town where artists, musicians and young fans enjoy hanging out. A little like Christiania in Copenhagen, just a little less rough around the edges.

Jat Airways' office in town wouldn't open until the next day. I spent the evening walking around Metelkova where Janko and I got talking. He sat outside one of the coffee shops smoking a pipe. Not necessarily unusual, except that he was in his early 20's.

"How is it going?" he asked, while inhaling from the pipe.

"How do you know that I am not a local?" I asked.

"Look at you! No local would dress like you," he exclaimed.

"Oh, it's that bad, is it?" I asked with a smile.

"It was meant as a compliment, actually."

I sat down next to him and asked if he knew anything about Jat Airways.

"Their name is not by chance. They can't afford jet engines, so they made a name that sounds like they do. And they are renowned for awful service."

I was already looking forward to the next day. With good reason, it turned out.

I was outside Jat's entrance at the scheduled opening time. An overweight, or should I say obese, woman with unruly dark hair and over-dimensioned glasses opened the door ten minutes later. I smiled. I don't think she had ever learned how to.

"I had a ticket for your flight to Skopje yesterday." I stated.

"We had no flight to Skopje yesterday."

"I noticed. Why did you cancel it without informing passengers?"

"I don't know what you mean."

"So, do you have a flight to Skopje today?"

"We don't fly to Skopje anymore."

"So, how do I get to Skopje?"

"You can take the bus."

"But I have a ticket with your company."

"But we don't fly there."

"So how do I get a refund?"

"We don't do refunds."

Janko had been right and the talk-to-the-hand tactics worked. I decided to consider what I had paid for the ticket as lost cost, put the airline on my *no fly* list and found an internet café. The Internet told me that the fastest way to get where I was going was to go by train to Zagreb before flying to Skopje.

I did what the Internet told me to do.

Djibouti

It was a Thursday afternoon and I was in little Djibouti on the Horn of Africa. I received a message about Bjarne Andre's stag night that would take place only two days later. The best man had clearly prepared everything well. So well that he had decided to not only not tell the groom to be, he had kept it a secret from all Bjarne's friends too. I am relatively impulsive, but to travel from Djibouti to the outskirts of Oslo on very short notice turned out to be somewhat of a problem. Even though I had a flexible plane ticket home via Addis Abeba, Rome and London. My primary challenge turned out to be on the first leg. The number of planes leaving Djibouti is probably as low as you might think. But I decided to give it a shot. I packed my bag and took a cab to the airport. It is only five kilometers from the center. The pleasant guy in the Ethiopian Airlines office turned out to be quite positive when I approached him.

"It is an emergency, you say?"

"Yes, it's the funeral of a friend of mine. Or former friend, I guess," I lied. It sounded a little bit more plausible to have to leave for a funeral on very short notice, rather than to have to join a stag night.

"Oh, please accept my condolences. We have two free seats, sir," he offered.

But I soon discovered that a long weekend in Addis is much more attractive than a weekend in Djibouti. Both remaining seats were snapped up just twenty minutes before departure by passengers paying a lot more for their tickets than I had done for mine.

"Please try again tomorrow. When is the funeral?"

"Ehe...Saturday," I fumbled.

"No problem, we will still get you there in time."

I returned to Djibouti and checked into a new hotel. I might as well test out several of them, while I was at it.

"Do you have hot water?" I asked the receptionist.

"Of course, sir. This is a hot country," he smiled.

He had a point, and giggled over his witty answer. I checked in, showered in the sun heated water and went back out to hit town.

"Was your hot water hot enough?" he shouted after me, in triumph. The hotel didn't come with a concierge service or a door man.

I had learnt my way around the center after many kilometers by foot there the last couple of days. A French restaurant had become my locale. There was a pool table there, which a lot of the French soldiers stationed in the country seemed to take advantage of pretty close to 24/7. They were always eager to play new people, at least until they were beaten. I played far better than I normally did and beat one after one. That made them all turn sour, and none of them wanted a rematch.

I was soon in a restaurant surrounded by French guys that didn't only seem moody, they were actually moody too. Worse so than in France! The sole Norwegian in Djibouti was no longer welcome. I ordered an onion soup before I took the hint and took a hike.

I explored even larger parts of the peninsula the next day, before yet again returning to the airport. I was lucky; I got my boarding card in hand and was shown to security. Boarding in five minutes, it looked like I would make it to the stag night, after all.

"Mr. Garfors, please proceed to the gate," I heard through the noise of the very analogue speaker system. Fully paying passengers had yet again showed up last minute, and I would yet again have to return to town. There was no way in hell that I would be able to get to Norway in time for the party, and I gave up. Not even a brand new ticket via other destinations all the way home would work. I checked into my third hotel, this time without a stand-up comedian at the front desk.

And it was, after all, Friday night in Djibouti. It seemed like all the French soldiers were taking advantage of it, the streets were heaving. And where there are a lot of male soldiers, there are inevitably also a lot of women. I guess it is all due to the uniform.

I had a few beers and played a couple of pool matches. I recognized no one from last night; they were probably at base practicing their snooker skills. My winner's luck was anyhow over, and I decided to explore the nightlife instead. I walked to what seemed like a popular nightclub. The girl behind the bar looked straight at me with her big brown eyes when I entered. She was exceptionally beautiful.

"What can I get you, handsome?"

"A Cuba Libre, please."

She mixed the drink with three limes and three year old Havana Club. Perfect! No awful Captain Morgan, which tastes like asphalt. Whoever calls that rum should have the captain force them walk the plank.

"One Euro, please."

Very cheap! I picked out money from my pocket. She grabbed my arm and looked me straight into my irises. Her eyes were shining and looked pitch black in the dim light of the bar. Her make-up was perfect too.

"For one Euro more you will get me too!" she smiled and blinked.

I paid for my drink.

"Sorry, miss. Not interested. Thanks for the drink!" I found myself apologizing. Despite of the many women forced or threatened into the slavery of prostitution.

Montenegro

What used to be a relatively unknown country by the Mediterranean was first visited on a triple date. Nicole and I had rented a house outside the coastal town of Herceg Novi together with Øystein and Benedicte plus our friends Øystein Djupvik and his girlfriend at the time Lee-Heidi Lauritzen. The house was nicely located next to the sea, and even came with its own little pier. But the landlord turned out to be a sleazy and tight guy in his late 40's with a comb over and a thin porn star moustache. He was very soon given a nickname, "the horse-fly". He wasn't only sneaking around all the time, if we were stupid enough to start talking to the guy; we never got rid of him. A sad and probably lonely man. The wife beater shirt didn't do his image any good either. Such shirts rarely do.

It turned out to be quite a nice holiday, although *couple* trips have never really been my thing. This time there were three couples; which meant we needed two cars that we put to use in various constellations. Either a boys' car and a girls' car or one couple in one and two in the other. There was even a possibility to split a couple should anyone be sulking. Most nights were spent exchanging money through poker games, or exchanging stories.

I was back alone a few years later to visit the impressive Ostrog Monastery. It was been built in a gorge of an otherwise vertical mountain wall and almost looks like Tiger's Nest in Bhutan - only much more touristy. Not a place I'd stay in for long. I headed towards the only fjord in the country, and discovered that I could either take the motorway via Podgorica, or a short cut over a mountain. I opted for the latter. I have rarely driven on more narrow and curved roads. The idyllic villages, farmyards and mountain views still so made up for it.

I arrived at the point of an accident an hour and a half later. Two cars had crashed. They blocked the entire road; which didn't take much, really. There was a rock blocking the one side of the road, a fence the other. I could of course wait, but there were no signs of anything happening anytime soon. And none of the unfortunate accident participants spoke a word of English. I had two choices: to drive all the way back and drive on the motorway; or, to find an optional route somewhere in the mountains. Google Maps came in handy. I spotted some sort of a detour. I should have known better the moment I turned off from the paved road. The detour was a dirt road, if that. But whoever doesn't dare surely won't succeed. One of the hills was covered by pebble rocks, and there was no way the small rental car could climb it. A shepherd was looking after his cattle. He just shook his head.

So did I. But I refused to surrender without a fight. A shortcut is a shortcut. The solution was to reverse the car. The engine in the front would put weight on the aft wheels and contribute to an easier ascent. I even had some training, having managed to get up steep snow covered hills back home by reversing. Pebbles too had to give in for a reversing Ford Ka. The shepherd still kept shaking his head. But I was back on track, at least pavement, three kilometers later. And soon, in the middle age town of Kotor, where I found a hotel and an ace restaurant. The car paint was miraculously without a scratch following the close encounter of pebbles.

Bosnia and Hercegovina

The first part of "Bosnia and Hercegovina" derives from the Indo-European word "bosana" which means water. Which there is a lot of in the country, it has an overabundance of beautiful lakes, rivers and waterfalls. Not to forget the 24.5 kilometer long coastline, a little piece of land that cuts Croatia in two. I have been to Bosnia and Hercegovina several times, but never for long. But long enough for some lunches and walks. In a country where you still pay by mark - not German ones, but nevertheless.

My first visit was during the triple date trip to neighboring Montenegro. Herceg Novi didn't offer the great selection of activities, and no one protested a trip on a narrow mountain road to Bosnia.

"As long as we keep it a day trip," the girls agreed. They were a little skeptical following a lot of negative media on Bosnia. Øystein, DJ and myself were keen on exploring somewhat more, but we stopped at lunch in Trebinje. Thanks to the girls' veto power.

Before we visited tourist Mecca number one in Croatia, Dubrovnik. Shopping there and a walk about in the old town were allegedly compensations for the "dangerous" Bosnian trip.

I ended up astray on my second visit to Bosnia and Hercegovina. Just outside Trebinje, where I had been before. The orthodox monastery, Gračanica, lies on a hill overlooking the entire town. But the road to the top goes all the way around the hill. It was only too tempting to go straight up, through a forest. It turned out it wasn't easy, and a very steep cliff had to be climbed before reaching the top. The very alternative choice of route didn't exactly impress the policeman who stopped me on my way to the monastery. He luckily spoke no English, so I was only given a lecture in Bosnian, Serbian or Croatian. They are all official languages in the country and all very similar; I could not determine which one he spoke. I am still reasonably certain that his tirade included glossary not suitable to print.

Panama

Which fridge magnet I would bring back from Panama left no one surprised. The country is known for the canal, and nothing else. I checked into a youth hostel and got talking to two guys from Canada. They were also visiting to see the Panama Canal. We decided to all chip in for a taxi the next day.

The canal is 77 kilometers long. It connects the Pacific Ocean to the Caribbean Sea, hence the Atlantic Ocean too. The alternative is to fare all the way around South America - which takes time, costs money and can include a considerable weather risk. The storms of Cape Horn have sunk many a ship. The canal finally opened in 1914. It had taken 33 years to build. France started the work, but gave up in the end, and the US took over the giant task. A thousand ships used the canal every year following the grand opening. Fifteen times more use it these days. A bigger canal has been planned for quite some time in order to accommodate for bigger ships than those nicknamed Panamax, capable of carrying only 5,000 containers each. The new canal will be able to transport ships that can carry 13,000 containers. The new nickname? New Panamax ships, of course.

To watch a ship go through a couple of locks is exactly as non-exciting as it sounds. I have seen plenty of ships around the world. It is still fascinating to witness huge cargo ships displacing hundreds of thousands of tons slowly but surely being lifted up by something as common as water.

It is in any case not free to use the infrastructure. The luxurious cruise liner Norwegian Pearl did, according to USA Today, pay the highest price to date.

Going between the oceans reportedly cost 375,600 dollars. American Richard Halliburton paid a little bit less. He swam through the canal in 1928. That set him back 36 cents.

We are talking about one of the biggest and most complicated building projects ever undertaken. US based American Society of Civil Engineers has even voted the Panama Canal one of the world's seven modern wonders. Worth a visit and a fridge magnet, I'd say.

Brunei

Boats are commonly used to and from Brunei too. I traveled there on one from Kota Kinabalu in Malaysia. The advertisement said *speed* boat. If I'd known who in Malysia accepts complaints for misleading advertising, I would have been knocking at their door.

The sultan of Brunei has been a man surrounded by myths, for as long as I can remember. And with a name like his, he is begging for attention. I usually introduce myself relatively fast.

"Hello, I am Gunnar Garfors."

He spends a little longer.

"Hello, I am Kebawah Duli Yang Maha Mulia Paduka Seri Baginda Sultan Haji Hassanal Bolkiah Mu'izzaddin Waddaulah ibni Al-Marhum Sultan Haji Omar 'Ali Saifuddien Sa'adul Khairi Waddien, Sultan dan Yang Di-Pertuan Negara Brunei Darussalam. You can call me Hassan."

The man has a lot of everything, not only names. His official residence is called Istana Nurul Iman; it is 200,000 square meters big and comes with 1,888 rooms and 290 bathrooms. A wealthy chap. He still doesn't waste much compared to the notorious playboy Prince Jefri. His younger brother also had access to oil money - especially during his 12 years as Minister of Finance. The Prince is still considered the person who has spent the most money on himself. Or how about having 2,000 luxury cars; the yacht Tits with tenders Nipple 1 and Nipple 2; a range of hotels the world over; and, pieces of art by Manet, Degas and Renoir? Mike Tyson doesn't even reach his little left toe nail when it comes to personal spending.

There were no buses waiting at the harbor, so I had to catch a cab to Bandar Seri Begawan, the capital. Buses are not a common sight in this country, but who needs them when gasoline is heavily subsidized? Hassan's palace is well hidden and unfortunately not open for visitors, even though I suspect he might have a room to spare. The number of other sights in the Muslim sultan's country is limited too. Sharia law is partially practiced, so do not even think about finding alcohol serving bars - unless you know Jefri or Hassan, of course. If you don't, you will have to settle for a few mosques or the village of Kampong Ayer which is certainly worth a visit. It looks like it floats on the water. The houses and the roads between them are built on stilts.

There was no way I would take the not so speedy boat back to Malaysia after my sightseeing. So I opted for the plane option and one of the shortest international flights available. The plane from Royal Brunei Airlines had taxied to the end of the runway and were just about to take off when the pilot got on the speaker.

"We are missing two passengers," he announced.

An unusual message. I assumed that the airline didn't have a sophisticated computer system to keep track of their passengers. But it turned out that we were not talking about just anyone. Two black armored Mercedes sedans drove up to the side of the aircraft. One of those mobile stairways on the back of a car followed suit. The plane door was opened and two men came on board and were shown to their seats.

"It's the prince," someone behind me whispered. Whether it was Jefri or not, I don't know, but whoever it was had good enough connections to demand a seat on the plane at the very last minute.

Sierra Leone

Such is unlikely to happen in Sierra Leone. First of all, it's one of the world's youngest democracies. Second of all, the airport is way too far from the capital. You should not be afraid of water, if you want to go there from Freetown because you will have to board a boat to get to or from Kungi, the airport, in a reasonable amount of time. The question is whether it is even worthwhile to visit this country as a tourist when even getting from the airport is such a hassle. The answer is relatively straight forward.

Definitely.

The Hilton hotel chain has realized that too. And when Hilton comes, so will others. A lot of others. They are building their property on the Lumley beach, Sierra Leone's version of the beach promenades in Nice and Cannes, with restaurants, nightclubs, bars, other hotels and the mandatory golf course. But there are other beaches too. The 4,000 kilometer long coastline comes with some of the most beautiful, cleanest and most isolated beaches in the world. Even the climate is friendly to western bodies. The mercury in the thermometer rarely has to move below 24 or above 30 degrees.

Sierra Leone translates as the land of the mountain lion. It sounds beautiful and it is. It sounds scary, but it isn't. The country has for a long time been considered less than suited for tourists, but this is about to change. The civil war ended in 2002. Both the government and private investors are now investing in infrastructure and sustainable tourism. They are certainly doing a lot right, but it will be a while until Sierra Leone is mentioned in the same breath as Dominican Republic and Mauritius. And luckily so.

The country can offer so much more with its unique scenery, wild mountains, lakes and waterfalls. Traditional luxury is rare. But amazing nature experiences and genuine peace have still not become unfashionable. Sierra Leone is, simply put, a fantastic country with locals that do know the meaning of hospitality. An added bonus is their language. They speak English after their years as a British colony. That also explains some area names. Waterloo, Hastings, Man of War Bay, Pirate Bay, White Man's Bay, New England and Destruction Bay can all be found around Freetown.

The capital city has a huge street market and a range of embassies. In addition to a second hand shop selling "Quality Junks" - you might also experience begging, but less than in many other African countries. And those that beg might do so more elegantly than what we are used to. A seven year old boy tried his luck.

"I like the way you walk!" he said and held his hand towards me. A reward was clearly expected for such a compliment. He didn't get one. I do never, on principle, give to beggars – and especially not to children. I refuse to contribute to an understanding that begging can be considered a way of life. It only leads to parents keeping their children out of school, that they grow old knowing nothing but the life of a beggar and then they have their own kids. The vicious circle is complete.

I had four realistic choices in order to get back to the airport from Freetown. All included the risk of transforming yesterday's food into today's fish feed. The Atlantic can be pretty rough around here. The hovercraft creatively named Hovercraft, the white plastic Sea Coach boats (one of them is reassuringly named "Good Luck") or the local car ferry which will set you back less than a dollar to cross. But, of course the latter won't leave until it's full. Which can take 5-10 hours on a bad day. TIA. Provided you have a wealthy uncle, there is in theory a helicopter service too, but it is often unavailable due to a lack of spare parts. It also turned out that both Hovercraft and Sea Coach had cancelled their services the day of my departure. The car ferry had furthermore actually just left and none of my uncles are rich.

I started asking around, and discovered a fifth option - boat taxi. There are no official ones, but I asked around and found someone who knew someone who knew someone with a boat. Not a recommended option. The quality and seaworthiness of the boat wasn't exactly anywhere near world class. But the price was.

The boat taxi man of course knew I had no options. I was in an awful negotiation position. The horse-fly originally asked for 200 dollars, but I managed to talk it down to 130 dollars. And even that was closer to the full value of the boat than the service I ended up paying for. They didn't even serve cocktails on board.

TIA.

I got across relatively dry 45 minutes later. The boat had its living daylight kicked out of it though, and I was on more than a dozen occasions happy that I had once learned how to swim. I quietly thanked my swimming teacher from grade school.

EASY IS BORING

Some countries are harder than others to visit. Due to wars, visa related trouble or a lack of transportation there. With a little bit of guts, you can still visit most of them, although it might take annoyingly long to succeed in some cases.

That's when it is particularly important to remember that easy is boring. To wait in case of a monopoly situation, where there are no options as in passport control, is far better than abusing and wasting your energy on annoyance.

Angola

The former Portuguese colony Angola has a lot of money these days. Europe does not. The money in Angola is however divided in an unfair manner, and very unevenly. The new situation has in any case totally changed how you enter the country, particularly thanks to the combination of the financial crisis in the western world. It suddenly meant that Angolan immigration officers saw more and more unemployed Europeans trying their luck in newly rich Angola. The border police did not like the development, and getting a visa got very, very difficult all of a sudden.

I discovered.

I first tried official ways. To Norwegians, that means the embassy in Stockholm. I filled out all the necessary forms that were listed on the website, there were a few. I sent them, my passport and the required money to Sweden with one of my passports. They called me a few weeks later.

"We need more supporting documents."

"Really? But I have sent you everything you asked for on your website."

"The website has not been updated since 2003."

"Well, that isn't my fault, is it?"

At first, they refused to take any part of the blame, secondly they refused to send my passport back. Four phone calls later, all made by me, finally resulted in one of the embassy staff actually returning my passport. Without a visa in it. We don't frequent the same parties.

The trip to Angola was postponed. Until I tried again in Angola's embassy in Johannesburg. They were far more service minded, even polite there, but they were unable to issue me a visa since I didn't have employment in South Africa. I decided for a change in tactics. Guerilla style. In Brazzaville in Congo I booked a flight to Johannesburg, via Luanda, the Angolan capital. I hoped to be able to talk my way in during my 13 hour stay. I have, after all, taken a course in influential leadership at the Norwegian School of Management. I also brought a print out from the website of the Johannesburg embassy.

"The transit visa can be exceptionally granted at the border post to a foreign citizen who, in a continuous journey is forced to interrupt it to make a compulsory stop-over by the means of transport utilized."

The first police officer I encountered on the border surely has a grandfather in Germany. There was no way in hell that he would let me in, he even confiscated my passport.

"You will get it back when you leave," he said with a triumphing smile.

He enjoyed utilizing the little amount of power he had. Luckily I traveled with both my passports, and I noticed that a change of guards was about to take place. I waited for the new police officers to get into their routine before I approached one of them, a woman in her 30's. She let me leave the airport and enter the country. Hallelujah!

It was just after dawn, and I tried to find a taxi to take me to the beachfront of Luanda.

"So, it's your first time here?" a driver said and smiled, some laughed even.

The traffic was closer to going backwards than standing still. I took the hint and walked instead. Quatro de Fevereiro Airport is virtually in the middle of town, and I found a café on de Janeiro Street. I was starving and it was time for breakfast. It had been a few hours since my last meal in Brazzaville. Some other early risers were eating in the well named establishment Happy Hour Cafe Restaurant and Bar Take-Away. I took that as a sign of quality, despite the slightly ubiquitous name, and I asked if I could pay in US dollars. The waiter nodded, and I ordered bread, cheese, an omelet and coffee at the bar before sitting down at a tall table circled by stools. The bar crossed most of the side of the room, a big plasma screen occupied most of the wall space behind it, only disturbed by whiskey, rum and vodka bottles. I guessed they knew their happy hour, after all.

Soft porn started showing on TV just before my breakfast was served.

"Interesting choice of TV channel," I commented to the waiter who brought my breakfast.

"You mean the porn?"

"Yeah."

"It creates regular customers and makes most of you other guys stay longer too," he grinned.

"Would you like a Sex on the Beach?" he asked and blinked. I politely declined. There were no women, the dozen or so guests were all middle aged men. Why was I not surprised? The marketing certainly seemed to do its trick.

No surprise then that I was slightly aroused when I was back at the airport a couple of hours later. I prayed that the over ambitious policeman really had gone off duty. He had. The female police officer greeted me with a little smile when I returned after having gone through a very thorough security check, as well as checked in. Her smile disappeared when I asked to get my other passport back.

She luckily did not seem to understand that she had been sort of conned, and I got it back with a slight frown on her forehead.

Before I was allowed into the departure hall on the first floor, I had to stand in queue. One person at a time was let into a room, and the door shut. Whatever they did in there took about two minutes per person.

It was finally my turn.

"Any money?" a grim looking customs officer asked.

"Only dollars," I said and showed him a handful worth of American currency.

"No kwanza?"

"Nope, I haven't been here for long."

"Good! Enjoy your flight," the man behind the sterile desk said, and waved me out again. I had a few local kwanza, the change from Happy Hour, but I would like to keep them as souvenirs. It is clearly both illegal and difficult to smuggle their currency out of the country.

Saudi-Arabia

The country I always figured would be the worst to enter, turned out to be an easy match, thanks to a tiny loophole. I was going to travel from Khartoum in Sudan to a conference in Toronto, Canada. But if I flew via Riyadh, I suddenly qualified for a transit visa. There was of course no travel logic for me to go from Sudan to Toronto via Saudi, but the embassy didn't seem to mind. All that mattered was that I flew from one country into Saudi and then on to another, and that I stayed under 72 hours in their country. Tourist visas are only occasionally issued. The option was to convert to Islam, a slightly drastic measure, but a last resort nevertheless. Muslims are in theory required to visit Mecca on pilgrimage at least once in their lifetime.

Women can only visit Saudi-Arabia with a male family member, or on a business visa. We are, after all, talking about the only country in the world where women are not allowed to drive a car. That means that they are pretty much barred from working too. To walk to work in the desert heat is not an option. And that she will make enough to afford a private driver is unrealistic to most. What might sound like a relatively innocent rule has big consequences for equal rights.

I got through passport control in Riyadh with relative ease. Ali Al Aligi waited for me outside. I had never met him before, but he is a friend of Nina Lükke, who I know from back home. She had told him that a friend would visit, and he had without hesitation insisted on picking me up and showing me around.

Ali is one of the friendliest, most hospitable and smiling people I have met. He had even checked out the hotel I was to stay in the day before my arrival. And not only websites and reviews, he had visited in person and even insisted on seeing my room. The huge room had passed his high standards. And of course he had taken time off work to drive me from the airport to the hotel.

"My friends do not take taxis."

End of story. He dropped me off at the preapproved accommodation and went back to work. Before coming to get me in the evening to show me the national museum and Kingdom Center, a 300 meter high building that looks like a bottle opener. Before we finished the night with 20 courses sitting on a hand woven carpet on the floor of a traditional Saudi-Arabian restaurant. The perfect atmosphere for exchanging stories from all over the world.

I would explore the city on my own the next day, and I was ordered under no circumstances to talk to any women in the shopping centers. I would anyhow not meet females outside, it is just too hot for anyone with their minds in the right place to spend more than the required minute between the car and the parking place. If the religion police thought that our conversation was too intimate, that I was standing a little bit too close to a girl or that I just uttered anything deemed inappropriate it wouldn't take them a calorie to send me straight to jail. Where I would have to stay until the first Friday. I would then be put on public display on a square. They would lay me on the ground, have a hundred goats walk over me in order to make me nice and tender before I'd be whipped to the delight of everyone watching. The number of whip strokes would correlate to the seriousness of my crime towards the woman in question.

I decided to avoid anything that might look like picking up any girls in Riyadh.

My trip to the mall was rather uneventful, and I avoided anyone that could pass for a girl. The afternoon had been set aside for a desert safari. Ali picked up me and a mate of his, filled up the SUV with camping gear and a lot of food before we sped off towards the sand dunes. The 4WD had no problems surfing the sand. An hour of fun later, and we found a suitable camp site. The two locals started rigging a tent and a metal grill. We were enjoying ourselves with meat skewers, tea and shisha in no time.

"This is what we do on the weekends here in Riyadh. We have no beach, so we go into the desert for recreation."

Another 4WD approached only 50 meters away, before it got stuck in the sand. Four women were inside, and Ali walked over to offer his assistance. He was shouted at in return. Men are just not supposed to in any way deal with any women not related to them, unless her husband is there and initiates or approves of the discussion. The women were stuck in the sand for two hours. It was already dark by the time two males arrived in a huge SUV and pulled them to safety. The men were presumably relatives by at least one of the women.

"Sometimes it is too extreme," Ali said.

"What if this had been in the middle of the day at 50 degrees and they had run out of gas?" I wondered.

"They would still have refused to be helped. We would have had to wait until they passed out from the heat," Ali explained.

One of the richest countries in the world can thank oil for its wealth. The country is still very poor when it comes to relations between people. Thanks to rules inspired by super conservative interpretation of religion.

Nigeria

The most populous country in Africa is rich in natural resources too. Which means money, corruption and conflicts. The jihadist group Boko Haram does additionally create fear in the northern part of the country through terror and mass killings. The group fights for what they call a true Islamic state with sharia law. Western customs, rules and people are hated, and kidnappings take place regularly. Not exactly tourism friendly.

I flew into Kano, a city just south of Niger. My goal was N'Djamena in Chad, via Cameroon. Which meant that I had many hours of various modes of land-based transport to look forward to. I had no choice but to divide the journey into legs. I first took a minibus to Maiduguri. The city is nicknamed "the peace home", the irony is obvious. This is where Muslim extremist had a field day following the Danish cartoons of Muhammad back in 2006, 15 people were killed in demonstrations and 12 churches were destroyed. In 2009, the year before my visit, 700 people were killed by Boko Haram. And since then, many more. Peace, my ass.

The accommodation offered wouldn't even impress a homeless man in Siberia. I have admittedly stayed in many shady hotels around the world, but this was award-winning bad. My taxi driver was a rather patient fellow, until he started displaying psychotic behavior when I turned down his hotel suggestion number four.

"OK, I will take you to the best hotel in town."

I wasn't expecting Marriott, and I wasn't surprised. The hotel came with its own mosque, coincidentally just outside my door. I would not need an alarm clock. If I could ever manage to fall asleep. The cockroaches in my room were the size of bananas, and I performed mass extinction of the tough creatures by my shoe before I was sufficiently at ease to manage to sleep under the relatively clean bed linens. My room actually came with an ensuite bathroom, but the shower didn't work. The toilet itself was actually connected, but not the cistern. I had to carry water from the tiny sink in a dirty plastic cup to the dustbin which I eventually emptied into the toilet to make it flush.

There was a television set in the room, too. A 14 inch screen was somehow mounted on the wall. The content on it was less impressive, nothing but locally produced soap operas. Nigeria has one of the world's biggest film and television industries. Nollywood is Nigeria's and Africa's take on Holly- and Bollywood.

No breakfast was served following the mosque concert in the morning.
Zero stars.

Yemen

The New Year's Eve celebration in Yemen achieved the same rating. They did
not celebrate the occasion there, at least not back in 2009. The restaurant of my
choice for the night had four other guests, including a screaming baby. Nightlife
is non-existent in the strictly Muslim country, and fireworks are only available to
the army.

Khat is *the shit* it in Yemen, as in Somalia. Almost every man chews it regularly,
I even spotted several boys aged five or six who not only chewed khat, they
smoked shisha too. At the same time. Proper hardliners are created early.

The extensive use of khat is a huge problem in dry Yemen. The plant requires
vast amounts of water, not ideal in a country with a strictly limited supply. The
problem has only escalated the last few years, with increased demand domestically
as well as abroad. The consequence? Hardly any water at all in Yemen. Not
surprising, maybe. Khat chewing isn't a new hobby; it has been around for
thousands of years.

Did Jesus chew khat, or did he stick exclusively to wine?

The old town capital Sanaa is truly fantastic and cannot justifiably be left out of
a trip to the Middle East. The architecture is truly unique; it actually looks like a
giant gingerbread town. To visit is like traveling in time. Far back in time. The
ancient buildings create narrow streets and alleyways, and old men and women
sell everything needed for a household from small stalls scattered around in every
thinkable spot where there is a square meter to spare. Expect to see food
ingredients, vegetables, spices, stone pans, tools and the type of clothes that are
worn locally. Jeans and T-shirts were nowhere to be seen, and I stood out like a
live and kicking crocodile in a Michelin star restaurant. Enough so that an
educated Muslim man employed in a mosque to take notice. The nice old man
came over to me and asked what I was up to. When he noticed me again an hour
later, he invited me to his mosque. "Why not?" I said.

While inside, I would be converted. Or so was his plan. The iman himself
welcomed me into his office, actually a modern place with a brand new laptop
and western adjustable leather chairs with wheels.

He asked me about my religion and what I knew about Islam. Before he
condemned Islamic extremists and insisted that his faith was truly peaceful, and
the only right one. I was finally given a paperback version of the Koran.

"Please spend some time reading and reflecting on our holy book. Then come
back to us. Our door is always open."

Call me less than adventurous, but the book is still standing in my
bookshelf in Oslo. Unopened.

Syria

I had no problems entering Syria, but I also did so before the start of the civil war there. The Mercedes that took me there had probably done several hundred thousand kilometers on the clock; the odometer only had five figures. The owner of it had a red beard and mustache. He was around 40 years of age and drove a long distance taxi between Beirut and Damascus. That meant filling the car with four passengers and driving them from door to door. I was not informed of best taxi practices in Lebanon, and my patience was put to the test when I realized that he would pick up two other passengers from very different addresses in Beirut before making the trip across the mountain, or hill rather. The height difference isn't exactly significant. I couldn't ask him what he was doing or register a complaint either. The man wasn't the talking kind. Especially not when it came to any other language than Arabic.

I indicated that I would like to get off in the middle of Damascus, and the driver stopped in an instant. I had not booked a hotel room; I assumed that getting off in a central looking area would work. It did, although I soon discovered that the standard of available hotels was lower than I had hoped for, although higher than what I had feared.

There were two things I especially wanted to see in Damascus. The old covered market street Al-Hamidiyah Souq, which is over 400 meters long. It is packed with small shops that sell anything you can think of. And so it smells. Myrrah, fruit, tobacco, spices, leather. Then add the never ending haggling in the background. To enter, you have to walk between columns from an old Roman temple. There are ruins from a fortress wall on the other side. Pieces of evidence from a violent past.

My other destination was the old town. Labyrinths and labyrinths of narrow streets, alleys, ancient walls and doors that hid apartments, workshops and courtyards. It felt like being in another time, almost in another dimension. The authenticity was disrupted from time to time by other travelers and tourist groups. And now, a lot of this has been destroyed. By bloody war. As has been the case way too often throughout history.

I remained for two days in what is known to be the oldest city in the world with a continuous settlement. Damascus was founded between 10,000 and 12,000 years ago. The city had a reputation for being one of the best places for shopping in the Middle East, up until the start of the long lasting civil war. Everything wasn't genuine, of course, but still.

I started walking south. Towards Jordan. Towards Amman. Luckily, it took less than a kilometer before a friendly man decided to pick up the pale hitchhiker.

The Philippines

I have been to Asia a lot, but I have only made two trips to Syria's continent colleague Philippines. It is the 11th most populated country in the world, and the last one with more than 100 million inhabitants.

The most eye-catching aspect of the country is all the colorful and creatively decorated old minibuses that you can see pretty much everywhere. They are called "jeepneys" and will get you from any place to any other place, although changes of buses are often required. The jeepneys are well sought after as targets for foreign camera lenses, and have almost become symbols of the Philippines. To ride one is dirt cheap; just don't count on getting one with intact windows. The owners cannot afford air-conditioning, and the vehicles would have become way too hot and humid without the natural flow of air.

There are therefore not too many foreigners on board. The jeepneys are too slow, noisy and uncomfortable for more than a short trip; or so most spoiled visitors seem to think. But do not despair. There are plenty of western people in the country. Particularly in Manila, and maybe even more noticeably in Cebu City. And they do stand out, those old men. As in white, pale, foreign, semi-bald men with a severe lack of non-grey locks of hair. Most of them walk around with a cute local girl at a maximum of half his age. Quite often she is closer to being a third or even a fourth as old as her partner.

I try to understand.

In the Philippines, money and financial stability seems to be far more important than what we traditionally look upon as love in the western world. Just being there as a male foreign visitor is like advertising that I am there for one reason, and one reason only. Not that there is necessarily anything wrong with it. People look at it as very natural that I am seemingly there to pick up a girl. Or girls.

I often walk from hotel to hotel before deciding where to stay. I want to know the price and find out a thing or two about standards, facilities and how much noise there is from outside. In two of the hotels I surveyed in Cebu City, the receptionist came with me to show me the room I was considering renting. The first receptionist was a middle-aged man, the second a young woman. Both of them said pretty much the same thing when giving me the short hotel tour.

"See, it is very big. You have plenty of space for the girls you will bring back."

"Oh, so that is what you think I am here for? The girls?"

"Of course, sir! Everybody is."

A fair amount of it is probably prostitution, but in most cases it seems as if the women are looking for a regular long-term partner. Judging by the number of couples on the street and in bars, restaurants and nightclubs, a lot of them are successful. You may also notice it in a different way in the hotels. I may check-in all by myself, but I still always got two keys and breakfast coupons for two people. I should start selling my extra breakfasts on Craig's list.

The practice of finding rich old men comes with some side effects. 60 year old guys who are out on the town with 20 year-olds can never really rock the dance floor. However hard they try. I am sorry. And the guys will soon be fed up with going out as soon as they have impregnated the girl, or put a ring on her finger. The girls will then miss out on a lot of their youth. Which will be traded for a flat, a sofa, a car and nice curtains. A comfortable life. But perhaps not so rewarding or exciting.

I have certainly seen the same in other countries too. Older guys from the western middle class come to find a young and pretty girl. But in Cebu I noticed something I have never observed before. I was sitting on a sofa in the lobby area of the hotel, the only place where I could get WiFi. 8-10 of the men who came and went didn't walk next to a woman.

They walked next to two.

Whether it is all due to an old dream of having a threesome, that they can actually afford it, or whether it is in fact a genuine desire to help two families instead of just one, I do not know. Do note that I am not in any way trying to judge anyone. It is great that people get together, as long as both - or all three - are happy with it and find good reasons to do so. The way we have tried to define and organize love in the West is not necessarily the right one. I do still have one thing to ask. That the Filipino girls at least insist that the older guys change the way they dress. Shapeless T shirts, square glasses from the 80's, beige shorts and the awful backpack like things that you have around your waist - neither goes well with long white socks and black leather shoes.

Of course, looks aren't everything. To think ahead matters too. The young girls that opt in for a much older dude usually get a father to their kids thrown in for free. A dad that doesn't speak the language of his own kids. And a father that will die much earlier than they will. Which means single motherhood. And a dad no longer there for the celebration of the son's 10th or the daughter's 12th year birthday.

Then again, that might very well be exactly the point; to find a much older person that dies relatively soon and leaves a nice lump of money behind. Which enables them to finally go for their real love. The childhood sweetheart that makes 10 dollars a month selling cigarettes on the street or driving a jeepney. Fingers crossed that they will inherit some money to finance the lifestyle the foreign partner made them grow accustomed to. Selling cigarettes or driving a minibus won't do the trick. The problem may of course be that the western guys already have kids at home, and that the inheritance isn't a given. They might suddenly have to attend a trial in Melbourne, Munich or Miami to try get their legitimate share.

I had a coffee with Rävèn, a 29 year old nurse from Cebu. She claims that the underlying reason for the widespread "use" of old western men is poverty and the hope for a better life and better living standards.

"The girls are mostly uneducated, and they feel that it is the easiest way to get a better life and to get out of poverty here. They have seen other girls who have married foreign men and who are living abroad. Seemingly happily so. But most of the fat, old and ugly foreign guys that show up here are quite pathetic. The girls must be desperate," she said. I could sense pity in her voice. Or maybe it was empathy.

To find a girl for a foreign man in the Philippines is often done in a matter of hours, or minutes. Especially during weekends, when foreign guys occupy a majority of the tables outside the bars in Cebu. Most of the time, there is one man per table. And a spare seat or two. The lads are scouting and waiting. They are usually successful, or at least with female company, before midnight.

But no one approached me. Maybe I was too young to be attractive or maybe I seemed rather penniless and unable to take care of and raise a family. A Breitling watch, Prada shoes and an Armani suit might have worked as a compensation for young age. Then again, it wouldn't quite fit in with my semi-scruffy traveler image.Designer outfits and backpacks are rarely worn together.

Haiti

A backpack is the suitable travel companion in poverty stricken Haiti too. It is in many ways a forgotten country among so many more glamorous ones in the Caribbean; a playground for the relatively wealthy Europeans and North Americans. The country has had its share of bad luck, natural disasters and incompetent leaders. And a fair share of them too. In just over 100 years, between 1804 and 1915, the country struggled with 70 dictators. Jean-Bertrand Aristide came to power much later, although it didn't seem that way. The radical politician introduced Voodoo as the state religion next to Catholicism in his second presidential term.

The name of the country goes way back. Haiti was originally the home to Indians from the Taíno tribe. The name means "the good people". They called their country "Ayiti" which means "the mountain land." It eventually evolved into "Haiti". And the country righteously carries it name having more mountains than any other Caribbean country. The highest, Pic la Selle, is 2,680 meters high.

Gambling is popular here, and a lot of people believe that the gods will decide on who will win, for instance, the lottery. They therefore usually pray for signs that can give them the winning numbers. It rarely helps. Cock fights might be an option. They are popular as a traditional sport in Haiti. The birds are fed raw meat and chili peppers marinated in rum to make them even more fearless and aggressive. The effects of alcohol are clearly not exclusive to humans. The owner of the winning rooster will get over a month's pay as his prize.

To arrive in Haiti two years after the earth quake of 2010 was a strong experience. Despite the relatively long time since the quake, virtually nothing had happened in terms of improvements. Thousands of people still lived in tent camps in the middle of Port-Au-Prince. The capital was founded in 1749, but it has nothing to do with kings, princes or formerly known American singers. The name comes from a French ship that was once anchored in the bay of the new town.

I was met by awful sanitary conditions and smelly overflowing portable lavatories in plastic. The garden of the presidential palace was blocked off. Both the palace and most of the center were badly damaged, and will have to be rebuilt from scratch. But despite horrible conditions, there are many smiles to see, a lot of laughter to be heard. More than in Oslo, London and Seoul. Strange, isn't it?

I had taken the bus from the Dominican Republic. The contrast between the two are enormous. And there are vast differences internally in Haiti too. I had found a room at a couple's house, on Couchsurfing, and I stayed my first night in a middle class house, not far from the slums on the hills away from the town center. I walked for hours through the slums the next day. There wasn't much to be envious of. There is no sewage. Urine and feces were flowing in some sort of an open canal system running between the shacks, cabins and tents. Almost none of the kids had shoes, and the availability of medicine and food is severely limited. There are virtually no schools and the HIV and AIDS rates are higher than anywhere else in America.

It hurts to see how bad people have it. To visit Haiti and see, feel and smell up close for yourself decreases the indifference that is hard to escape by living in the bubble that a western country in many ways is. The conditions might tempt many to omit Haiti as a destination, just remember that tourism will contribute to people who really need an income. Given that you steer clear of all-inclusive resorts, at least. Direct alternative aid, in the shape of stimulating local businesses and local economies works the best, by far. As Dambisa Moyo said it in "Dead Aid".

ISLAND HOPPING

To travel from island country to island country sounds paradise like. And it can be. But many of the island states around the world struggle with poverty, a bad economy, a lack of fresh water and a threat from potentially increasing ocean levels. There aren't only palms, beaches and sun. Not only umbrella drinks and swimming pools, either. Although that is what most of us, as tourists, come to see. Or expect to see, even.

In one of these countries I saw two locals in their early 40's sitting by a table in an outdoor bar near a rough beach. Charles and Graham. It was lunch time, and I had walked many kilometers under a frying hot sun. I was sweating, thirsty and not hard to convince when I was invited to join their table. We exchanged the normal formalities, or small talk, before we got to the more important things in life.

Charles' phone suddenly rang; he looked on the display and grunted. Before picking up. It turned into a strange monologue. We could only hear what he said.

"Hello, babe! How is it going?"

"Yes, of course I will go get groceries."

"What, the dog ran away?"

"He always comes back, don't worry. Give him a couple of hours. He's just horny."

"I love you too! Bye, bye," he finished with a voice smooth as silk and hung up.

"Fucking hell, that bitch always manages to destroy my time in the sun! Awful! Are you married, Gunnar?" Charles shouted.

"No."

"Good! And I will give you one piece of advice, and one piece of advice only. Make sure it stays that way! Never, ever, ever get married! She will show the best side of herself, stay slim, wear sexy clothes, make you dinner and even shave her pussy. And then, when you are hitched. Kaboom! No more. Make your own food, do this, do that, give me money, give me more money, you ain't getting nothing tonight. You get the idea. Just do not get married!"

I really had to concentrate not to laugh out loud.

"Well, I've got no such plans, mate. Cheers!"

We toasted. And started talking about liquor. Charles took up half a bottle of Johnny Walker. It seemed just normal, although something wasn't quite right. Graham took a sip of his beer and smiled. He knew what was coming.

"I provide the entire region with this," he proudly announced.

"You import Johnny Walker? Well done!" I praised.

"No, no, no. Have a closer look," he insisted and pointed to the label of the bottle.

I examined the bottle. Johnny walked the wrong direction. And the whiskey wasn't called Johnny Walker, but Johnny Walkar. I laughed.

"You mean you are ripping them off?"

"Absolutely not. It's a totally different brand. But the locals don't know. And I benefit from the real ads on TV," Charles boasted.

"Hahaha, priceless! And how does it taste?"

"Well, Johnny Walker isn't exactly a premium brand anyway, is it?"

He avoided my question, quite a politician! We toasted again and finished what was left in our cans of beer. I walked over to the bar to buy another round. And quite right. The shelves behind the bar came with Bacardi, Gordon's and Johnny Walkar. I grinned.

"Hey, Charles! You want your own Johnny?" I shouted to him.

"Hell, no! I don't drink that shit, I only sell it. Give me a beer, man."

And that's pretty much how we passed the next hour. Until Charles' phone rang again. Followed by a loud sigh.

"Hello darling! Did the dog come back?"

"Good!"

"Of course I can pick up the kids, take them home, cook them dinner and take them to soccer practice."

"No problem, I will."

"Yes, yes, I love you too!"

He pressed the red button on his old phone. Hard. Smartphones had not yet come to the island.

"That fucking bitch is making my life so miserable. I fucking hate her guts! You wanna get me a Johnny, after all?"

I got him one. He swallowed it in one gulp. Before walking to the restroom. I decided to take the opportunity to get some background information on this strange relationship.

"What is the real story, Graham? He cannot be very happy with his wife."

"He certainly is not!"

"But why doesn't he just divorce her?"

Graham started laughing big time, he laughed so hard he was shaking.

"Oh, he can't. He married the wrong girl. She's the daughter of our president," he said, and made a distinct sigh while shaking his head.

Tuvalu

I could feel it even before the plane landed. The atmosphere. It was different. Different than in Fiji, Tonga and the Marshall Islands. Tuvalu is a unique country. Funafuti, the main island and capital, is a society in miniature. Just about. Everything has been built around the runway. The lifeline. Where a propeller plane from Fiji Airways lands twice a week with supplies, local people, some foreigners working at NGOs and the odd tourist that doesn't know better.

There is no smaller international terminal building anywhere. There can't be. The plane carries fewer than 50 people, and it was only half full. The passport control area, or should I say room, held less than ten people. The rest of us had to stand outside in the rain to wait for it to be our turn to have our passports stamped. What a liberating feeling! Totally informal, everyone spoke to everyone. People were friendly, accommodating, genuinely interested and helpful. Everything seemed to be real and transparent. I wasn't even allowed to walk the 1,500 meters to the flat I had rented. I was driven by a motorbike too. Later, several random people stopped and invited me for a ride on their motorbikes. Although it was never far to my destination. It couldn't be. Funafuti is only 2.4 square kilometers big, yet accounts for 9 percent of the country's area. Half the population lives there.

The third to the last country I visited will always be number one when it comes to hospitality. Tuvalu will be the first country to disappear for good should ocean levels raise much. Or at all.

An old fellow in a bar got in touch, one evening. He asked me where I was from.

"Norway."

"What? Nowhere?"

"Nor-way," I said. Slowly. The badly aged guy still looked confused.

"It's in Scandinavia. It's in Europe. Northern Europe."

It didn't seem to have made an impression. He drank a large sip of his canned beer. Before raising his voice.

"We are sinking. We are sinking because of you!"

He was clearly mad, furious even. He lifted his right hand and pointed at me.

"Because of me?" I asked. My voice trembled. I didn't feel that I could take all the responsibility alone, despite the occasional flight. I hardly eat steak, even. Or own pets. I looked around for escape routes.

"We are sinking because of pollution from Europe."

Countries and islands might sink, or drown, relatively soon, and the likelihood is that pollution from western countries can be blamed as the number one cause. Most scientists seem to agree that the ocean levels will rise. Politicians will have to fight over why, but it still doesn't hurt to take part in Earth Hour and other initiatives that are far more important. Perhaps it may help people in Tuvalu and elsewhere in the Pacific to remain living on their beloved islands. The threat of more water in the oceans does in any case make the old guy and many others like him nervous. Where will they and their grandchildren live in the future?

The lagoon by Funafuti is fantastic for swimming, snorkeling and diving. Just bring your own equipment, not many hire it out. I dove into the water from a little stone pier that goes a hundred meters into the sea, just outside the office of the prime minister. Four 12 year olds followed my example a few minutes later. They beat me in an impulsive swimming contest and made water bombs by jumping from the pier. The water temperature was just perfect. They explained that their uncle owned one of the boats that was moored next to a buoy a couple of stone throws away, and asked me if I could swim out to it. A challenge is a challenge. I swam out and climbed on board.

"You can do it too!" I shouted to them. The three boys managed to swim out and climb into the 12 foot big yellow boat within a matter of minutes. The girl was unable to do the same; I had to pull her by her arms to make sure that she could join in as well.

"Wow, so cool, she said."

Little pleasures! The kids were shouted home for dinner twenty minutes later. Their mom stood outside their little house by the water, hitting on a metal pan to make sure she caught their attention. I waved to her; she waved back and put on a broad, white smile while the kids all ran home.

The same night I went for a walk north on the narrow atoll. I walked straight into an acoustical experiment by the point, where it is at its narrowest. The waves hit the shore from both sides, but at different intensities and at different intervals. Waves in asynchronous stereo! So simple, yet so fantastic. I had an instant goose bumps attack.

Two days passed and it was time to leave the big little island nation. Big in terms of hospitality, little in area and number of people.

Seeing the country disappear from the plane window was melancholic. There isn't much room for each person, especially not with the runway taking up so much space. Despite being used only twice a week. For plane traffic, that is. The 1,524 meter long strip is used for yoga, drag racing, jogging, football, rugby or merely as a playground for kids or dogs the rest of the time.

Do not forget cash if you ever visit this fascinating country. You mean you have a black AmEx card? Platinum Visa? Superduper Mega MasterCard Diamond Plus? It just doesn't matter. This is one of a very few countries in the world where no credit cards are accepted. Bring Australian dollars. Or a begging cup.

Saint Kitts and Nevis

Saint Kitts and Nevis is primarily a cruise destination, and can boast about traditional beaches, eminent seafood and good drinks. It is a holiday paradise for many. But the authorities have been clever enough to find another income. By establishing a university that targets American students. The tuition fees are as high as in the US, but students save money on cheaper living.

"Reading here, beats reading in Minne-fucking-sota."

Greg doesn't have any filters between his brain and his mouth. The American was tired of snow and freezing temperatures, and he was not going back. I met him at a beach restaurant on the outskirt of the main island. He had his own motorbike and moved around with ease.

"But can you really concentrate here? With the amazing weather, beach parties and girls?"

"Well, I might use one year longer than at home, but it is so worth it!"

It was uncertain whether his liver agreed.

I stayed in a little hotel in Basseterre, the capital. Breakfast was served on the first floor terrace. English breakfast, except for sausages and bacon. That didn't really matter to me, British sausages taste awful anyway. But it made me curious. English breakfast without meat? I got the full picture when I noticed the little sign that was posted by the potted plants that circled the terrace.

"Be nice to the plants. They have feelings too, just like the rest of us!"

Saint Lucia

I have rarely been threatened by ass kicking, but that is exactly what happened in Castries, the small town capital of Saint Lucia in the Caribbean. I had decided to explore the few streets late at night. I ended up in a rough neighborhood, and soon had company. A very fit and presumably strong dude in a T-shirt and a pair of jeans with the waistline way too high walked over to me, stopped 20 centimeters away and looked me straight in the eyes. I don't think he had ever heard about toothpaste.

"Are you lost, white boy? This is my hood!" he shouted, even screamed.

Three of his crew and a couple of kids without shoes made a half a circle around us. They assumed some quality entertainment was just about to take place.

"Oh, I am sorry about intruding. I'll leave you guys to it," I answered, turned around on my heel and walked away.

"You scared, now, hey? You fucking scared?" the pleasant guy shouted after me. Someone was picking a fight. I kept walking at a very calm speed. I wouldn't benefit much by making him even more cross. A woman was selling barbequed chicken in a stall on the pavement by the bay, a few hundred meters away. She had made up the grill with an iron grid on some bricks over coal. It smelled amazing, and I stopped. My appetite was back, following the near trouble experience just up the street.

"Rough neighborhood around here, hey?" I asked nonchalantly.

"Oh, you didn't go up there, did you?"

She suddenly seemed worried.

"Well, not really. I just said hi to one of the guys there."

"Seems like you lived to tell the tale. I wouldn't go back if I were you, though," she adviced.

I took her word for it. While finishing the delicious chicken.

I have flown to or from over 300 airports. The best of them all is next to Castries. The terminal building is only 10 meters from a white beach. I checked in for my flight early in the morning and received my boarding card before I walked across the road to the beach, undressed and took a long swim.

Before drying up with my compact travel towel and getting dressed. A little hair salt never hurt anybody. I walked to airport security, and had to remove my shoes yet again. Before boarding and departure. Luxury! That the selection in the duty-free shop was particularly poor didn't matter a bit.

Saint Vincent and the Grenadines

Saint Vincent and the Grenadines isn't the most famous country in the Caribbean. Not the second most famous either. Not many know about the pristine islands of the country, with the odd exception of some cruise ship tourists and the occasional yacht enthusiast. And of course everyone who watched Pirates of the Caribbean, starring Johnny Depp. Most of the movies were shot here on the amazing islands. This was naturally exploited by tourist bosses in the country. Tourism income naturally increased a bit, but bananas still contribute by far as the main source of income.

I flew into Saint Vincent. The airport is walking distance from the capital Kingstown, and can only accommodate propeller planes. The janitor of the hotel where I had booked a room waited for me at arrivals. We reached the hotel, located on a very steep hill overlooking the Caribbean Sea five minutes later. I have never been a fan of exploring hotel rooms or emptying minibars, and I was on my way out again in less than two minutes to have a look around the local area instead. The walk to the center of Kingstown was a little odd. I picked a route that took me through the nice and expensive villa-hood with precision cut lawns before, only a few hundred meters later, I walked past small slum shacks where shoeless kids in dirty and shabby shorts in 80's style ran around playing between odd pieces of garbage. Kingstown is an interesting mix of such neighborhoods.

I walked through the market. Colorful, noisy and with a range of contradictory smells. No other westerners were in sight. It was clearly targeting a clientele primarily living in neighborhood number two. The sun was on the hot side, and I escaped into a hotel bar. The air conditioner was working overtime and I actually ordered a coffee with milk. Contrasts. A guy from Arizona came over to me within minutes.

"How's it going?" he asked.

"Not too bad, how are you?"

"Where are you from? I'm from Arizona."

"Norway."

"Norway? Is that upstate?"

He had probably come in on a cruise ship, probably not even knowing which country he was in.

"Are you staying in this hotel too?"

"No, I am staying on the other side of town."

The American was close to 30. He was wearing a baseball shirt and sagging jeans. His feet came with over dimensioned basketball shoes. A girl suddenly entered from the door to the lobby. She looked similar, but had slightly better taste in fashion. Not that it would take much.

"Hey, this is my sister. Her name is Trudy."

She sort of smiled, and reached out her hand. I took it and said hi. Shaking her hand was like trying to grab cold smoke. There was no resistance, no firmness whatsoever.

"Hey, I'm Trudy."

"Do you like her?" the brother spoke again.

"Yeah, you're cool, Trudy. What do you do?" I answered her directly. That was completely ignored. The brother continued.

"Do you want her?"

That's when I got it. The white trash brother was trying it on as a pimp. For his own sister. I politely and firmly declined, paid for my coffee and left.

I decided to opt for a different route back in the dark. The street lights were far apart. Most of the lights that helped me find my way came from the houses and street stall selling beer, soda, water and skewers along the road. There was a street party up on the hill and a lot of shouting, singing and dancing. It didn't feel entirely safe to walk there, but I kept a straight face and walked in the general direction of my hotel. A white car all of a sudden stopped next to me. The driver, a lonesome girl my age, rolled down the window.

"Do you want a ride?"

"Sure. Do you know where Bay Hill Apartments are?"

"Jump in, mate. This town ain't that big."

I got into the passenger seat.

"Thank you! This is really nice of you. But isn't it a little risky to pick up a random guy on the street like this?" I challenged her.

She put on a big grin. The white smile was pretty much the only thing I could see of the dark black girl in the darkness.

"I ain't no fool, man! I've got a black belt in Karate. If you try any shit, you'll be sorry for the rest of your short-assed life."

Presumably inspired by Pulp Fiction. I laughed.

"I like your attitude!"

"And don't you dare try to pick me up!"

"Hahaha...I don't think you would be interested."

We laughed together.

"Here's your hotel, man."

I said thank you yet again and jumped out. She would have done well in an American gangster flick.

Samoa

"The green island" Samoa would work just great as a location for a lot of other film genres. Both the diving and the snorkeling there are unreal. And the sashimi is amazingly fresh, even though the portions are smaller than in the Marshall Islands. I came straight from there, and I was experiencing withdrawal symptoms after eating so much fresh tuna. Samoa helped me lower my intake at a sensible speed.

I still never quite liked the ambiance there. It was too American, too shallow, too fake. The scenery is incredible, and I truly enjoyed driving around the island in a rental, but there was just something about the people I couldn't quite put my finger on.

Saturday night soon arrived, and I was served exquisite fish soup and lobster. Before barely being able to move to the combined pub and nightclub next door. Puppy fat Australian girls at backpacker age were ready for the meat market. I was luckily not among their targets this evening where I sat with my freshly squeezed pineapple juice at an outside table. I was just observing, and enjoying it. Abruptly, a black guy with dreadlocks suddenly came over to my table and sat down. Two white friends of his doubled the number of occupied chairs a few seconds later. I was not surprised that he wanted to know where I was from.

"Norway? That's fucking cold country! What are you doing here?"

"Just traveling. I came back from driving around your country a couple of hours ago."

The Rasta man wasn't interested in that kind of irrelevant info.

"I hear you Norwegians can drink."

I know what Doctor Vodka would have done. Can I call a friend?

"We're not too bad, I guess. We're Vikings, after all."

"Hey, listen! I really dig this Australian girl upstairs. But she told me to beat it until I could show myself as a real man and drink a foreigner under the table. And you're the only male foreigner here right now," he explained.

I smiled. One of the girls I had noticed a little earlier had momentarily actually blocked the move of a local hero. Priceless! There was no doubt in my mind what Doctor Vodka would have done, but I will never reach to his Achilles when it comes to drinking.

"Sorry, mate. I'm leaving early tomorrow. There will be other foreigners showing up soon, for sure."

"Fuck off back to Scandinavia, then!" he said, got up and walked over to the bar. His silent mates followed suit. I did not.

Palau

Palau is a Republic. It has presidential elections every four years. On the Tuesday after the first Monday in November. Coincidentally the same day as the US. The world's attention is, in other words, more centered around Washington D.C. than Ngerulmud or Koror. To count the votes from the 21,000 inhabitants takes almost a week, usually far slower than counting the votes of the country of 312 million people. Unless the Supreme Court needs to get involved.

To travel all the way to Palau to play football on a concrete indoor field is pushing it. Of course, that was not my reason to go in the first place, but I couldn't resist joining when I was asked by the local lads who were playing. They were unfortunately running out of time, so I only managed a few touches and a shot just off target. Close, but no cigar, in other words. In Koror, the biggest town in the country, with less than 13,000 people. Number two is the capital Ngerulmud with 381. That makes it the smallest capital in the world. The nearest competitor is the Vatican.

The Pacific state is well known among Asian divers for eminent conditions around the 300 or so islands. Some of them are unique cliff islands, tall rock formations with vegetation on top. I have not seen anything similar anywhere, but Thailand claims to have the same.

Drop Off Bar & Grill became base camp the few days I stayed in the country. The restaurant is five meters from the sea, and divers often come by boat for a burger and some beers following an action packed day at sea. I met a group of South Koreans. One of them, Kelvin, could not praise the diving experience highly enough.

The 30 year old had studied in Houston in the US and spoke with a broad Texas accent. With American enthusiasm. A"reef hook" is a line that has been attached to a rock or a reef. You hang on to it in areas with strong currents. That gives you the sensation of weightlessness keeping you in one position over time, something that makes it easier to observe fish and sharks.

"The sharks, man! I was hanging on to the reef hook and I almost stroked the backs of two sharks. Can you believe it? It was amazing. Amazing! I just can't believe it. I feel honored and privileged."

His enthusiasm was very real, for sure.

Sri Lanka

Sri Lanka is among Øystein's absolute favorite countries. Despite a relatively monotonous diet. You get rice and curry for breakfast, lunch and dinner. Just add chili sauce instead of ketchup. That doesn't scare Øystein though, not after living in India where spicy food is the rule, not the exception. He told me about extreme hospitality and a scenery that surpasses what can be seen most other places. There are a lot of mountains, rivers, and waterfalls there, and then also a lot of hydropower plants. Most of the power is produced environmentally friendly, just like at home.

The country came praised and recommended, but I was still positively surprised. I walked past a restaurant on the beach in Colombo. There was clearly a party being thrown there, and I walked over to the terrace in front of the restaurant, with barefeet and in shorts, to see what was happening.

"What is going on?" I asked two men in suits. They were standing in the sand smoking, a couple of meters from the terrace where a range of other well-dressed people stood with a drink each.

"It's a wedding," they responded, only semi-interested. I wasn't exactly dressed to their level. Their lack of interest disappeared immediately following their standard "Where are you from?" question.

"Norway?" they responded simultaneously, unnaturally fast. "Dinesh! This guy is from Norway!" one of them yelled. Another wedding-dressed man came over and reached out his hand.

"Hei, jeg heter Dinesh. Jeg har gått på folkehøyskole i Norge," he said. Which translates to "Hi, I am Dinesh. I attended folk college in Norway."

And that was pretty much what the 40 year old remembered in Norwegian. In addition to "skål", of course. Norwegian for "cheers". Dinesh was the best man, and he invited me to join the party. Despite my lack of shoes, tie and pretty much everything else. It was a little awkward to be the only one without any connection to the couple of honor, especially being dressed the way that I was.

I left two drinks later, when I had said hello to and congratulated the happy couple, and said goodbye to Dinesh, the party guest headhunter.

I found it a lot more comfortable to have dinner in another beach restaurant a few hundred meters away. Where I had a view of an improvised beach volley ball net. Cricket may be an important sport in Sri Lanka, but nothing beats volleyball, the national sport.

Vanuatu

Vanuatu is the last country in the world where cannibalism has been practiced. The last known case of the "eating disorder" happened in 1969. Not very recent, but recent enough for some people to freak out about it sufficiently to never visit the place.

It was never explained to me how humans were prepared for consumption, but journalist Nick Squires of The Telegraph newspaper had the pleasure back in 2008.[1] His article inspired me to go visit Vanuatu.

---

[1] telegraph.co.uk/travel/748417/Vanuatu-where-only-the-menu-has-changed.html

"First, our ancestors would dig a hole in the ground. They'd put hot stones in the hole, then cut up the person into pieces and put those on top. They'd add in some yams and taro, put in some more hot rocks, and cover it all over with banana leaves to keep the steam in," villager Berna Kambai told Squires. It took between three and five hours before the human delicacy was done. The size of the victim was closely related to preparation time, so small people were dangerously closer to becoming a dish if cannibals were hungry. The village chief always got to eat the head.

"We'd kill and eat people who stole our women or came to fight us, but we don't do that anymore. We feel very sorry for those people now," Berna giggled when he further explained to the British journalist.

I had flown in from Brisbane to Vanuatu, and the plane food had been of a different character. The cabin crew served breakfast on the morning flight; I sat next to a big Indian man. So big, that I was very happy that the middle seat was indeed free. He still almost touched me with his side. The big guy was clearly hungry and had looked forward to breakfast. Then it was our turn and the air hostess came to our row. I had seen the menu and knew that there was a choice between omelet and sandwich.

"What would you like, sir?"

She produced a tired smile. No surprise, the plane was almost full. I had been lucky with the empty seat next to me.

"I want chicken, the large man said."

"I am sorry sir, but we don't have chicken. You have a choice of an omelette and a sandwich."

"But I want chicken!"

The man couldn't possibly have flown a lot. He was eventually given the omelette and took off the aluminium foil on the top of the hot dish. He was not impressed.

"I am a big man. I need real food. This is not chicken. This is chicken baby! I want the mother of this!"

The man had a point. Although chickens don't lay eggs.

I checked into a cabin in a camping site on the outskirts of Port Vila and walked downtown. I spent the day exploring and finally discovered a bar with a pool table. I was soon challenged by a local taxi driver not on duty. He spoke no English, but such a game demands no language.

At least not until controversies arise. Or until one of the players turns out to be an exceptionally bad loser. And to be fair, I do not claim to usually lose in style, but still slightly better so than the driver. I won our first game without a doubt, and credit to him, he didn't complain much. He still demanded a rematch and a possible revenge. It was a closer call the second time around; I beat him on a technical knock-out. We had one ball each, in addition to the black one. He had called his half into one of the corners, and it went straight in. But so did the black, in one of the mid pockets. Via a couple of walls. I may have cheered a little too loud and a little too much. The result was anyhow that my opponent became so furious that he hit his cue on the table so that it broke. He surely achieved stopping my cheering. I didn't think it would improve the situation much to thank him for the game, and I walked away while he settled the cue bill with the bartender.

Fiji

Fiji is not very far to the east from Vanuatu. A paradise for a lot of backpackers. And you will find excellent diving conditions, cheap drinks and warm weather, just be aware of the overdose of tourists in parts of the country. To me, that makes the country vastly overrated, although there are possibilities to get away for it all on some smaller remote island, or even on the main one. I had to spend more time than I would have liked thanks to their non-corresponding flights to and from other island states. I visited the charming capital of Suva and touristy Nadi, where the main airport is located.

I took the bus from the airport to the center of Suva, and got talking to Michael, the man next to me. He told me he was a bureaucrat in the Ministry of Defense. I had not booked a hotel, and he insisted on finding a place "of acceptable standard" as he put it. My limit is much lower than most. That's just the way it goes after taking advantage of a variety of exceptionally bad accommodations, in places where just finding something resembling a roof is quite an accomplishment.

I was, needless to say, rather pleased with Michael's choice. He had found a yellow apartment hotel with a very gay receptionist who insisted on showing me my flat. I have rarely, if ever, experienced anyone spending more time demonstrating how to switch on and off the television set, how to change channels, how to close the curtains, how to turn on and off the shower and where the escape route was in case of a fire. The flat was on the ground floor. I think that he may have been interested. I thanked him for the thorough instructions, locked the door and walked to town.

I later ended up in Nadi, via Tuvalu. A little trick to get tourists to stay longer is to offer authentic activities. Drinking kava is one way to do so. Kava is a plant that if consumed has a mildly relaxing effect, but allegedly without reducing mental capacity. A cup or two will make your face go numb; more cups tend to make you sleepy. It isn't particularly good, it tastes like dirty mud water. Or so I seem to recall from childhood. The plant cannot be legally imported to Europe due to the danger of liver damage, but it is vastly popular in Fiji. At night, the locals gather to music and kava drinking, a tradition picked up by a number of the youth hostels around Nadi. The kava is served from a pot in the middle, while cups are passed around to visitors. The male employees of the hostel that play the guitar, sing and serve kava - pick up girls with ease. It turned out.

Sex, drugs and rock and roll. Just in the reverse order.

Most people are said to drink kava most days. It might help explain their attitude about time. The concept "Fiji time" is well known, and is used as an excuse when something is slow. Pretty much like TIA and hakuna matata.

There are also some innovative people working at the Fiji museum. Cannibalism was not unusual in earlier times, something missionary Thomas Baker was the last unlucky person to experience. Since he was eaten, there is nothing left of him to exhibit in the museum. Except for the shoes he wore when he was captured. They are still on display.

The Comoros

The Comoros never had problems with cannibals. The country is located between Madagascar and continental Africa. Only 800,000 people live on the island nation which is the world's largest manufacturer of *ylang-ylang*, an oil that is used in perfume. The world smells worse without the Comoros.

Public transport is scarce in the country. As in non-existent. You either hitchhike or you get on a privately-owned minibus. Even using your thumb isn't usually totally free of charge. You are expected to pay a little, especially as a foreign traveler. I got from the airport to Moroni on my second attempt.

There are different markets in the capital where they sell everything from morning fresh fish to fruits. Via beauty treatments. The latter comes in the form of a white cream that you smear on your face. Women everywhere wear it whether they go to the market or sell something there. Let me just note that the beauty mask is not particularly effective while in use.

I passed some youngsters while searching for a hotel. They played "fussball", a football game mounted on a cement table next to the harbor. There was obviously no point in asking them about hotels, they lived there and had probably never seen the inside of a local one. As is the case with most people in their hometowns. At least I was asked to play a match. A very short one. I was crushed in a matter of seconds. These lads could surely handle the metal ball that was being used to score goals.

I eventually found a hotel not too far from there. The standard was decent enough, and the receptionist bragged about the hotel restaurant. She was a little biased, of course, but I decided to have a glimpse, at least. Chef Laurent was a pleasant and smiling chap; he showed me one of the tables in the courtyard. It was time for lunch, and two of the other tables were occupied too. By locals. Usually a good sign. The club sandwich was top.

"But just wait for dinner. We will be getting some super fresh fish and lobster. Should I reserve you a table?"

I politely rejected the offer. But he didn't give up that easily.

"How about if I invite some friends of mine to join?"

"Do they speak English?" I wondered.

"Yes, of course!"

Fresh lobster is never wrong, and I might even pick up some good tips on what to do and see by his friends who I assumed lived there too. I hesitantly agreed to eat dinner there, after all. Five hours of exploration later saw me back, and a proud Laurent showed me to the same table. A girl aged 20 already sat there.

"Meet Vanessa!" he proudly said, or rather shouted.

I shook the hand of the stunning, but shy girl. She spoke no English whatsoever. And plural had become singular. "Friends" Laurent? But she was there, and we were both hungry. I ordered the lobster I had been craving since lunch. Vanessa ordered a burger with French fries. I tried to communicate in my non-existent French, and to understand enough to piece together that she studied something. And the conversation pretty much stopped there. Although Laurent certainly knew what he was doing in the kitchen. The lobster, the pepper sauce and the complementary tomato, onion and coriander salad were all exceptionally delicious!

But enough was enough, after a while. The non-conversation with Vanessa led nowhere. There weren't enough language skills around the table for uncomfortable silence to occur. I was about to say "bonjour" and leave. But just when I stood up, she grabbed my arm, made a kiss with her lips, blinked with her right eye and nodded towards the hotel rooms.

Laurent had set me up with a prostitute.

There was clearly a thing or two I didn't quite get when it came to communication in the Comoros. Friends were not plural but singular and Vanessa was working and not keen on being my friend for free.

I walked into the kitchen. Laurent stood by the counter, preparing something together with two assistants. I told him straight that I was not interested and that he would have to let the girl know.

"Why the hell did you get me a hooker?" I demanded.

Laurent got it that he had misunderstood and just shook his head.

"I will still pay for her dinner, but you will have to let her know that I am not a customer, that I never intended to be. I am not interested. OK?"

He nodded. I ate at other restaurants the remainder of my stay.

Federated States of Micronesia

At least there had been a choice of restaurants in the Comoros. In the Federated States of Micronesia, the selection was rather disappointing. But the people on the island state, located to the north east in the Pacific, more than compensated in terms of friendliness. The airport in Kolonia, the biggest town on Pohnpei Island

and in the country, is walking distance from the town center. Just do not believe for a second that I was left walking in peace. The third car that passed me and then stopped was driven by a middle aged guy with a comb over.

"Welcome to Kolonia, northerner!" he greeted me and insisted on driving me to my destination, Cliff Hotel. His wife and him even waited outside to see that I would get a room before they drove off.

Micronesia is the name of thousands of islands under American control, or belonging to one of five Pacific states: Palau, Marshall Islands, Kiribati, Nauru and Federated States of Micronesia. The latter consists of 600 islands, totaling as little as 700 square kilometers. The islands are rather spread out, though, covering an area the size of Kazakhstan. Yes, you know, Borat country. And the world's 9th biggest.

That, the prototype of a Pacific island, would be my home for two days. Way too little, of course. Time is indeed a luxury. My first dinner was consumed in Sei, a restaurant that in any other country would have passed as a fast food joint. In Kolonia, it was considered fine dining. The best in town, even. There is actually a surf camp on Pohnpei, and the restaurant there is allegedly much closer to western standards with a menu and all, but it is located out of town. You do not travel to Federated States of Micronesia to revel in Michelin stars. You go there to dive, swim and to enjoy islands you only thought existed inside the heads of cartoonists. Some people would call it paradise. Others would call it hell to get to. I am not among those people with an aversion for complicated itineraries, but you ought to have a particular interest in aviation to travel there by plane. It took me seven flights from Oslo. But there is always a yacht or a cargo ship, for those with the privilege of time.

Solomon Islands

There are still many more yachts a little further south, in the Solomon Islands. The half million people there have never made much fuss about their 900 or so islands. But why should they? They live in an island paradise that includes Morova, the world's biggest salt water lagoon.

At the yacht club in the capital of Honiara, you will meet a lot of local and foreign boat owners. And it is often possible to hitch a ride to other islands or other countries in the vicinity. I had a plane ticket, but I still visited the club. I had been told it was a good place to get info on activities and happenings in Honiara and the Solomon Islands overall.

In the bar I met Zach, an Australian businessman. He told me he ran a shop on one of the nearby streets.

"What are you doing here, stranger?" the man in the colorful shorts asked.

"Not much. The question is rather what I should be doing here."

"Not much. That's the beauty of the Solomons. You go on your boat, sail a bit, anchor it up and fish for your dinner. Then have your wife prepare it and eat it while sharing a bottle of wine. Life is good here!"

"I can tell. Where's your boat?"

"It's the Pelican 2, moored over there," he said and pointed.

"And your wife?"

"She left a couple of years ago. Now she's sailing the Caribbean with my ex-mate."

"Oh, I'm sorry!"

"No worries, mate. She was a bloody awful cook anyway. I make my own dinners now. And occasionally bring a local woman with me. They are always impressed when I do the cooking. That makes them spread their legs faster than you can say Na fata fooala i Fiu kira fooa dani firi ma ofodani fainia saulafi i luma aabu."

"What?"

He giggled and took a sip of the canned beer. It had been stored in some sort of a foam thermos to keep cold.

"It's Kwara'ae, the biggest local language. It's the name of an old Christian psalm book. It means something like evensongs, psalms and hymns. It's the only thing I can say in Kwara'ae."

It never seizes to amaze me what kind of people you meet in the most remote places of the world. Then again, what do they think about me?

As in the next morning. I walked down to the little but busy fish market in the harbor a stone's throw from the yacht club. I was looking for breakfast options. My hotel had offered dry baguettes with spreadable cheese way past its due date. On my stroll towards the center I was overcome by a sashimi urge. I picked up some soy sauce and wasabi in a small shop along the road, and then hit the fish market. I purchased two fish filets of acceptable size, one from each of two stalls. I got one tuna filet and one white fish I still do not know the name of. I asked the lady in the second stall to cut both filets to pieces, using her giant knife on the foldable and somewhat shaky table. She did as I asked, but with visible question marks on her forehead. I thanked her, and sat down in a set of stairs made by concrete. They lead down to a rusty wreck that was half sunk just by the harbor. An orginal breakfast view. I was fresh out of forks, so I used a wooden tooth pick to eat the extremely fresh sashimi. A dozen locals had surrounded me within five minutes to stare at this alternative fish eater. Déjà vu from China, ten years earlier.

Tonga

I visited the other side of the Pacific three years later. I was 37 years old and rented a scooter for the first time in my life from the tourist information shop in the capital Nuku'alofa. Having no experience with such, I didn't even stop to ponder over the fact that the helmet I was given was a bike helmet, not a motorbike one. A fact I didn't realize until a colleague pointed it out when seeing the photos of me on the scooter weeks later. That particular mode of transport is however without a doubt among the better to explore the tiny state.

The yellow bike took me to the impressive blow holes in the North West. Small tunnels in the rock formations go from the sea, and quite a few meters onto the shore. Every time the waves bang towards the island, the water is led into the tunnels and then there are fascinating geyser effects on land. Certainly worth a visit. Before the scooter took me on a dirt road further east. It led to an almost abandoned hotel by what must be the nicest beach I have ever been to. A coral reef just outside protected it and produced an amazing audiovisual theatre every time the waves hit it and the splash went high up into the air. The accompanying sound was equally dramatic.

The hotel is located on a cliff just above the beach. The rooms may not live up to western standards, but that would almost have ruined the charm of it anyway. I met the couple that runs the hotel; they were sitting on the terrace overlooking the sea. They welcomed me and gave me fresh coconut milk. I was there off-season, and they had no guests. Which meant that they could sit and enjoy the mild breeze, the waves and the swell which they could see from a bird's perspective.

"It's quiet this time of year. But we can live here on the view and the sounds alone. Best place in the world!"

None of them had ever been outside Tonga, but I'd say they were not far from the truth.

I will return to Keleti International Resort. Only with a girlfriend.

FIVE CONTINENTS IN ONE DAY

You do sometimes get the odd strange idea, I am sure. My idiotic ideas are frequent. Luckily, they are not all executed, but some of them are so wild, groundbreaking or unusual that they demand to be taken from the idea stage to the experimental stage.

I was one of fifteen passengers in a white minibus crossing the Bosporus Bridge in Istanbul when one such idea came to me in May of 2010.

The bus traveled from Europe to Asia. In two minutes. None of the mothers, kids, or men going home from work seemed to realize how fantastic that was. They probably did it twice a day, hundreds of times a year. But to an obsessed traveler, this was Christmas Eve and my birthday combined.

"How many continents can I visit in one day?" I wondered.

Hundreds of Internet searches for plane tickets later, I learned I could manage five continents in one day using scheduled transport only. My private jet was being serviced.

But again, theory is theory. Sorry, Einstein. I had to actually try this. And film it.

At first I thought it might work as a half-hour travel program, but I was too broke from all my other travels to rent a TV crew. So, what to do?

Adrian!

The choice was not an obvious one. He runs his own television production company, and would definitely be able to direct, shoot, do the sound and edit the whole thing together. But Adrian Butterworth was the least traveled guy I knew. The least traveled person, animal, or living creature, in fact. My mom's plants have traveled more than Adrian, and they are from a greenhouse on the outskirts of Naustdal.

Adrian and I studied together at university in Falmouth, and have remained best friends ever since. Well, it was all charity from my side, really. The poor bugger has no real friends. No surprise, really. He is an obnoxious fucker.

But so am I.

We fit very well together, and usually pass the time by slagging each other off. And he occasionally has something resembling a good idea.

I picked up the phone. "Ade!" I said. "I know you are fine, so I won't bother with the boring formalities."

"Hahaha, you're an impolite bastard anyway. What do you want?" he asked.

The tone between us never changes. It's cheeky, sarcastic, or outright rude. Quite often a combination of all three.

"Do you want to go traveling with me?" I asked. "All expenses paid. We'll visit five continents in one day."

There was no need to explain in detail, Adrian is sharp as hell.

"What?"

Or so I had thought. I explained the concept. I would travel; he would record it all through a documentary. We'd share the world record.

"Bloody mental!" he exclaimed when I was finished. "I'm in."

Fools are never hard to convince.

But Adrian is married. Surprisingly to a lovely and beautiful woman. Nels is from Romania and they live with their little daughter, Chloe, in Bournemouth. I refused to accept his participation until he had discussed it all at home with Nels. I know her well. When she and Adrian got married, I even drove her and his father to church. In a Saab convertible.

"I'll call you in two days, mate," I told him before ringing off.

I never got around to it, because Adrian called me the next day. Nels loved the idea, and he had already looked into what extra gear he would need to do the job. We would, after all, have to manage with hand luggage only.

I booked tickets for the madness. We would leave six weeks later, on June 18, 2012. I don't know when I last planned that far ahead for a trip.

The stunt would be performed on a Monday. It was the only day of the week we could actually do the trip if we were going to avoid Passport Control Hell on Earth, the United States of America. There you never know how long you will have to stand in line. I have gone through in less than a minute, and I have spent more than two hours in a queue. I was not going to let such an uncertainty jeopardize our idiotic plan.

We would start in Asia, and fly from there to Africa. We *could* visit both Europe and Asia in Turkey, but that would be too easy, I thought.

Easy is boring.

We had to do it all via commercial airports. From Africa we would go to Europe, before flying to North America and finalizing the madness in South America.

Turkey (Asia)

We started in Asia for one simple reason: availability of flights. In particular, a *very* early morning flight (1 AM) to our next continent, which was essential to completing our mission on time.

We decided to focus on just the Asian part of Istanbul.

"There's nothing worth seeing there!" my friends from the western and European side of town said. But I was soon introduced to their eastern friends when I stubbornly insisted and explained the concept.

As it turns out, eastern Istanbul is ace - just more traditional, and with a more tranquil atmosphere than the western side.

While we were there, waiting for it to be time for our madcap journey to begin, we came across some old guys who were playing some sort of card game and drinking tea. They agreed to let us film them, as long as the program would not air in Turkey.

"Then our wives would find out what we are really up to all day," one of the old guys said with a smile, before buying us tea.

A lot of westerners believe that the eastern side of Istanbul is much more conservative than the western side. In some ways it is, perhaps, but not when it comes to nightlife - it totally rocks on the Asian side!

We met Ebru, who showed us around and took us out for a traditional meal. She looked good on camera and had a lot to say - off camera - when I asked her about her country's old-fashioned views on sex and relationships.

"Here, everybody fucks everybody," she assured us.

I tried to get her to repeat that on camera, but to no avail.

As our flight time approached, we took a taxi to Sabiha Gökçen International Airport on the Asian side of Istanbul. We checked in just after midnight, and then did my on-camera bit outside the airport.

Our flight was scheduled to leave at 1:10 AM, but it took off nineteen minutes late. Not a good start, since we obviously had very limited time on each continent to begin with.

My Air Arabia debut was slightly surprising. For the first time on any flight I have been on, the flight deck crew started off their usual safety spiel with a travel prayer in Arabic.

I guess it worked. Despite the pilots' speeding to make up for lost time, we didn't crash. And our arrival in Africa was only seven minutes late.

Morocco (Africa)

We arrived in Casablanca just after four o'clock in the morning, where we were picked up at the airport by our guide, Nawal. She drove fast, almost furious. Red lights were ignored as a rule, and given our time constraints, I was delighted. Adrian was not. There were no seatbelts in the back seat.

But we got to the great mosque on time, and in one piece. Too bad Adrian's shots from the car weren't exactly steady. And that wasn't even due to alcohol consumption aboard the plane. Air Arabia doesn't serve alcohol. I guess he was just losing it.

The Hassan II Mosque, one of Casablanca's main attractions, is the tallest and the third biggest mosque in the world. Setting up equipment for an interview in front of it at 4:45 AM may not have been the most clever of plans. The mosque police were not impressed.

We were asked to leave the sacred ground in front of the mosque, so we conducted the interview just outside it. That was seen by the police as us "loopholing," and our interview was interrupted after a few minutes. There was no doubt that we would have to leave, fast, unless we wanted the opportunity to film the inside of an African police station. So we moved to sites with lower police presence to finish the interview.

The ride back to the airport was slightly slower than our trip out to the mosque had been.

"The police have woken up now," Nawal explained.

Air France was up next. Their 7:35 AM flight to Paris stays overnight in Casablanca, so we were fairly confident there would be no delays. The French did not disappoint, and took off seven minutes early.

France (Europe)

Europe was our Achilles heel. We had one hour and fifty-five minutes between flights, and needed to change terminals in the meantime. We also had to meet our local contact, get footage, and do a piece on camera in that short period of time.

Air France gave us two additional minutes, though. Yeah, I counted *minutes* on this trip. But then they added an hour by delaying their departure to our fourth continent, North America.

At least that meant we had plenty of time, and we even managed to relax a little. Coffee and croissants for everyone!

Then Øystein called. He had agreed to be our spokesman for the project. We would, after all, be on planes most of the time. I had sent him a message after we boarded in Casablanca, so he knew that we would most likely manage it all, and he had sent out a news release to the Norwegian press that morning.

"This is fucked up! You guys are all over the media!" he told us. "The two biggest newspapers and Norwegian Broadcasting Corporation have called, and some local newspapers have picked up on it from the big ones as well."

Nothing triggers media interest so well as a possible world record in the making.

There was still nothing from the British media, though. At least not yet.

Dominican Republic (North America)

The delay from Paris gave us less time in Punta Cana than we had anticipated, and robbed me of a swim with dolphins that we had arranged with a trainer at a marine park there. At least we still had time for some relaxation on a beach twenty minutes from the airport.

Although the islanders see themselves as Caribbeans, the Dominican Republic is actually one of twenty-three countries in North America. It is still refreshingly free from white tennis shoes.

The locals there love their boats. When they are finished with them for the day, they drive them at full speed up onto the snow white beaches, then calmly leave them and go order a cold beer from whatever bar they have "parked" next to.

Unfortunately, Adrian didn't manage to catch this on camera. How the hell could we have known about such madness in advance?

We got back to the airport on time, but still almost missed our departure from Punta Cana. The bloody airline decided to start boarding thirty minutes early.

Ade had to leave the luxury, pimped up, super-sized burger he had bought in order to be allowed on board. He was not particularly happy with the airline for departing before schedule.

I didn't really care. We were on board, safe and sound. Only pilot error, a hijacking, or the Venezuelan police stood between us and the strangest of world records.

Venezuela (South America)

Gol Transportes Aéreos did indeed land safely in Caracas. There we had to fill in three different forms before we were eventually allowed to enter the country at 10:15 p.m.

It was still June 18. The world record was ours! I have never felt better getting a stamp in my passport.

Our guide, Angie Velazco, met us at the airport - with four friends.

"Wow, a welcome committee," I said. Surprised.

"Congratulations!" Angie exclaimed, before giving me a big hug. Her four friends - three of them stunning girls - joined in the hug-fest. Adrian has never ever before hated so much to be the one *behind* the camera.

Angie drove us from the airport to Caracas, an hour away. To our surprise, she ran almost every red light.

"It's due to car jackings," she explained. I could feel Adrian squirm a bit in the back seat. I hadn't told him that Caracas was the murder capital of the world. I knew that would have freaked him out. Then again, I knew he would also be furious if I didn't tell him in advance, so I put it in the script for my piece to camera. A script I knew he wouldn't bother to read. He's a journalist, after all. Lazy bugger.

In Caracas, we headed straight to Juan Sebastian Bar. The celebration was on!

We had just experienced our longest Monday ever. But we were still working - sort of. So, sort of interview-style, I asked Angie about the rumor that Venezuela has the most beautiful girls in the world.

"Oh yes, it is certainly true!" she said with a big smile.

"And how about the guys? Are they equally handsome?" I asked, a natural follow-up question.

"No!" she replied. "And it is so unfair!"

Angie laughed. She is certainly one of the stunning women of Venezuela. So were her three friends who had come along for the impromptu celebration.

Adrian and I were too tired to sleep, anyway. And the night was still young.

Now that we had finished our journey and secured a world record, the bigger media outlets wanted to get in on the story. CNN called. And Adrian was interviewed on BBC. Luckily on BBC radio. He's got such a radio face. Media frenzy followed, and we were featured in newspapers and on websites, TV and radio in over 30 countries around the world. The idea really caught interest. Five continents in one day. Possibly madness, but a creative variant. That readers enjoyed. I received a fair amount of messages from impressed girls in Brazil and Bulgaria. And from a lot of intrigued guys in India. Possibly the three best countries for new friendships, although I think I might go for the two first ones.

A Guinness World Record

I received an email from London 21 months later, on March 14.

"Your record application has been approved."

The record text followed a little further down in the mail and was a bit more substantial.

"Gunnar Garfors (Norway) and Adrian Butterworth (UK) visited five continents in one calendar day, taking scheduled transport between the east side of Istanbul in Turkey (Asia), Casablanca in Morocco (Africa), Paris in France (Europe), Punta Cana in the Dominican Republic (North America) and Caracas in Venezuela (South America) on 18 May 2012. The entire trip took 28 hr 25 min, but the changing time zones ensured that Garfors and documentary filmmaker Butterworth cleared customs in each country in the same calendar day."

I was, coincidentally, in Amsterdam with friends on Pi day. We celebrated the Guinness World Record. Times 3.14.

THE END

I had invited friends and family to come along with me to my last country. After all, any goal of a certain size or importance must be celebrated. Or so my motto goes.

I hurried out of the passport control, following the uneasy look of the policeman behind the counter. And I was there! Cape Verde. I stepped from the airport terminal into the dark, into the salty air, into the smell of celebration, smiles and laughs. And soon long and warm hugs from my brother Øystein, his wife Benedicte, my youngest brother Håkon, my youngest sister Torunn and my good friend Doctor Vodka. Those that had been closest to me the last few years and who knew how big a thing this was to me. How much it had cost.

How many gadgets, designer clothes or sport cars I could have purchased. But oh, was I happy to have managed visiting every country in the world. With my mind and body pretty much intact.

The party was about to start.

In the westernmost African country just off the coast of continental Africa and an hour by plane south of the Canary Islands in Spain. The island nation is incredibly diverse, made up of 10 volcanic, yet very different islands. They are all beautiful, peaceful and with a high standard of living.

There were more people too. I had never thought that as many as 12 people would join in on the party. I must admit that I had expected that my brother Øystein and my mates Doctor Vodka, Andreas, Thomas and Ola would show up. They were all there, with the exception of Ola. And he had a valid excuse, his wife was due. Expectations or not, it made me incredibly thankful, humble and happy to see all of them there.

My sister Torunn and I had never traveled abroad together before, with the exception of family trips to Sweden and the UK when we were kids. She is a teacher and lives with her boyfriend Torgeir and two cats that are given much more attention than average kids.

The last five were a good mixture. Jørn doesn't need much of an introduction. He was our pensioner alibi. He was actually never the first in bed, but always the first up in the morning. The 58 year old impressively kept up with us. And certainly contributed to the party. He is an old musician and played on both spoons and mouth harps for us.

Frode Nordeide was there, too. He is the only person that I have met in both North Korea and Cape Verde. We are probably the only two people in world history that have hung out together in those two countries. How about a coffee back home in Norway? It's on me.

Charlotte Lievens from Belgium was the only non-Norwegian present. All official communication was therefore performed in English. We had met only once before, when she visited Oslo together with a friend. She was studying to become a journalist and we immediately hit it off thanks to her extremely strange and very untraditional sense of humor. As friends. She is clever and beautiful. But twice my height.

Trond-Ole Hjorthaug is a teacher colleague of Øystein who was told about the celebration at work. The guy from the northern part of the Norwegian West Coast is a great guy, we have hung out together before and I was happy to see him there.

The last person was an outsider. Torgeir Halvorsen is a tuba playing colleague of Øystein. My brother called me in early 2013 and asked if Torgeir could join.

"He plays the tuba? Will there be any food left for the rest of us?" I asked.

"He is actually not big. He is a tall and skinny bastard. A great guy with an amazing sense of humor. I guarantee that you will get along," Øystein responded.

"Well, you know me relatively well. New blood ad new impulses in parties are always positive. As long as you vouch for him to be reasonably shady, it is cool."

Torgeir fit straight into the group. He was in fact the only one who came with a congratulatory card .With a teddy bear and a balloon on it. He had written "To Gunnar" on it. And nothing else.

"We haven't actually met before, so I wasn't expecting a long speech, but perhaps a little bit more?"

"Come on, I don't know you! If you were expecting a formal speech, you should have come up with something better than celebrating 198 countries. It isn't even a round number!"

He had a point. And you can say a lot about Torgeir, but the card was the exception that proved the rule. He is not a man of few words.

Norwegian press went crazy on Thursday, and I had to answer all sorts of questions via the phone. And I made the front page of Firda, the local newspaper which had started everything with its article about Kyrgyzstan. "Photo: Frode Nordeide." Of course.

The celebration itself was held in one of the best hotels in Santa Maria, the capital of Sal. Odjo d'Agua has an outdoor terrace, literally built above the Atlantic Ocean. The view is incredible; the same is true of the surround sound.

We had ordered a big table, in an otherwise empty part of the restaurant. We finished several cases of Super Boch, the Portuguese beer that comes in 0.2 liter bottles.

Touchingly enough, my mom also contributed with a speech. Via Torunn.

"Dear Gunnar, the oldest child, and older brother. Congratulations on mission well accomplished! This has cost you a lot of time and money, and we have shared you with "the world" for many years now. You have still prioritized your family, occasionally, and been there when you have been invited by family and friends. We appreciate that! We would like to see more of you the next few years, and we hope that you can find your calm in more home-y ways. Hugs from mom and the three siblings who could not make it today."

My mom is incredible. A little bit of criticism was to be expected after four figures of days on the road. I have not traveled abroad with two of my siblings since we were kids. Åsmund lives in Bergen with his wife Silje and their kids Frida, Andreas, David and Benjamin. My sister Åshild lives in a flat back home in Naustdal. She works in a rest home.

Torunn gave her own speech, as a representative for my siblings.

"Dear Gunnar. We have a strange relationship, according to mom. I tell you off and try to get you to understand what you do. She thinks it should have been the other way around. The truth is that Gunnar is just more polite than me. He actually waits until my relationships have ended before he tells me that he hated my ex-boyfriends. I have a theory for why I don't think anyone is good enough for you. We will have to go all the way back to when I was in the 7th grade, when we snuck into the secondary school where you were a substitute teacher. On the walls of the girls' restroom someone had written 'I love Gunnar' a hundred places. There was also a counting system. 18 girls had signed that they were in love with you. You look as good now as you did 15 years ago."

I had no idea, being the eldest; I had actually been a substitute teacher for all my siblings except for Øystein and Åsmund. Torunn is the youngest, but she rarely speaks anything but her mind. She also has a pretty bad temper. Poor cats!

Øystein was toastmaster in the last country, Cape Verde. He had to be, really. As a more frequent participant in my trips, than anyone else. He was, of course, not going to let the occasion pass without giving hell. He had created a quiz. About me. The others were divided into teams, while it was up to me to give the right answers. One of the questions was relatively straight forward. *"How many pushups can Gunnar do in one go?"*

I had not seen the questions before. And I knew what was coming; I immediately stopped drinking Super Bock. I had half an hour before having to go through the answers, and I ordered water. A lot of water. Before I had to give them the answer to the questions. Amongst cheering from 12 people and some random restaurant guests. I managed 109 pushups before collapsing on the cement floor.

Torgeir's team was the closest. They had guessed 90. Andreas's team had insulted me by guessing 40. The penalty was more Super Bock! They didn't seem to mind.

But they accumulated a fair amount of alcohol in their blood streams. Andreas was sporting one of the coolest suits that I have ever seen, with shorts, not trousers. His stylish dress code still didn't prevent him from ripping out the lobster meat from the carcass with his bare hands.

"It was bloody stuck," he giggled. Before eating the lobster in a few bites. He later owned the town, and had dozens of compliments on his suit. They should only have known about his lobster eating habits.

We finished the night on a roof terrace in Santa Maria. A bar celebrated Bob Marley who had died May 11, 1981. They certainly celebrated him in style. Or so it smelled.

Cape Verde's motto is rather concise.

"No stress."

Without an exclamation mark. It would have contributed to stress, we were told.

The motto can be seen on T-shirts, flags and in shop windows. You will also hear it throughout the day from locals in town, on the beach and at the airport. Every time something takes longer than expected. Which means often. We are talking about a local variant of hakuna matata, Fiji time and TIA.

A salesman of sunglasses came up to us on the beach where we were resting on Sunday.

"How long will you stay here?" he asked.

"We're leaving tonight," Benedicte replied.

"Good luck going back to your stress!"

He put it eloquently.

This was the best party I ever attended. Fearing that it cannot be topped, even by my own wedding, there might not be one. Although I have finally done sufficient research to know where I would go on my honeymoon.

EPILOGUE

"So, what now?" I am asked at least three times a week.

As if my life is now over. As if the only reason I had to live was to visit those 198 countries. Well, I have to disappoint them. I won't be going to space or the moon or to the deepest ocean in the world. I wouldn't mind any of those trips, of course. My wallet would.

I am still working with digital radio at Norwegian Broadcasting Corporation, although I now also have a thrice weekly travel competition on Norway's highest rated radio program Nitimen ("The Nine o'clock Hour"). They also air the occasional travel report by me. And I am often invited to conferences and events to speak about my experiences and my trips or to rank the best or worst countries of the world. My traveling has made me a semi-celeb. Who would have thought?

Some people are indeed intrigued by all my traveling, some people are impressed, and others are appalled by it all. They think that I pollute too much, that I don't travel the way that I should – usually like they do – or that I haven't spent enough time in their country.

"What is the best country in the world?" is another question regularly thrown at me. 10, 20 or 30 times a week. Of course I should know, they think. The guy who visited every country out there. The guy with stories to tell from every one of them.

But I can't tell them. There are too many truly incredible countries, people and places out there. I wouldn't have told them if I could either. Because who am I to say that country F is better than country S? And it would certainly depend on their preferences anyway. What kind of activities they prefer, temperatures, time of the year, amount of experienced stress at work or in their personal life, how long it takes them to get there, who they meet, what they eat, how sick they will get and whether they like, crave or demand luxury or not. And do they want gourmet food, nightlife extravaganza, sacred sessions, a quiet wilderness, beautiful beaches, magic mountains or a little bit of everything. Not to mention who you are traveling with, if anyone, and if you are looking for a couple's holiday, to spend time with kids or the possibility of finding someone to make a kid with.

There are too many variables.

A solution is to travel as much as possible, to experience, taste, feel, breathe and smell everything and talk to everyone. I certainly have, also since "finishing" my 198 mission in 2013. There have been countless trips to several dozens of countries. And there will be many more. I certainly have no plan of slowing down on my traveling. Why would I want to insult my brain?

And maybe most importantly – *the* important question – what have I learned from all my traveling?

I have realized that those of us fortunate enough to live in the bubble of western civilization are usually unwilling or unable to leave it, just for a moment, to see, experience, feel and understand that we are not the center of the planet. That we are not the most important people in the world. That other people depend on what we do and what we don't. And that we depend on them too. If, for no other reason than for being ancestors of the same forefather and foremother, for being part of the same hugely extended family. So maybe, just maybe, we shouldn't take ourselves that seriously. Each and every one of us, is after all, only a tiny cog in a gigantic machine. A machine that has many parallel cogs that will cover for you should you stop caring, taking part or even existing.

"The cemetery is full of indispensable people," a former Director-General of NRK once said.

And until you end up there, engage with those you meet on your journeys, be polite and laugh, smile and cheer a lot. Life is too short for western arrogance. You know, the way too common and overbearing pride inside that bubble. You know, of western civilization.

The good thing about being inside it is of course that you can afford to leave it. Those on the outside can't leave. Nor would you want them to.

The bubble would burst.

Another world record

I couldn't get my mind off those four people who visited 17 countries in 24 hours and set a world record. Especially not after having challenged it with Øystein Djupvik and Tay-young Pak in May 2014 and failed. Well, we actually equalled the feat. But sharing a world record isn't quite my cup of tea. The three of us decided to try again 4 months later, two days after this book was first published in Norway.

This time we carried with us the experience of failure. We still didn't change the formula too much. We used a combination of two commercial flights and three rental cars. But it turned out that the first car was not an Audi A6, as ordered, but a bloody run-down Ford Focus with 100,000 kilometers on the clock.

"I totally fucked up my neck driving that hunk of shit," Øystein later complained. He single-handedly did all the driving, and set a world record on his own for being the person having driven in the most countries in one day.

We started in Greece and ended up in Liechtenstein after 23 hours and 30 minutes, having clocked up 19 countries in the same day. And finally the world record was ours.

"You could call it the ultimate boys' trip, three lads visiting all these countries and having a bit of fun," I later told The Telegraph on the phone from Zurich on our way home. And it sure was. Not only did we have a fantastic trip and break a world-record, bookmaker ComeOn! even took bets on which country we would visit next too. That people back home put money on us, sure felt cool!

The British newspaper wasn't the only one showing interest, either. The news of our mad trip went viral, and reached media outlets on every continent. Except for one.

Antarctica

Of course, there is a continent to go, one without any countries, one not yet mentioned, one standing out from the other six. They all have a human history going back thousands and thousands of years. Except for the only uninhabited one. Antarctica was first discovered around 1820, and the South Pole wasn't visited until 1911 when my fellow countryman Roald Amundsen skied in. Antarctica is still hard and very costly to visit.

But. It. Is. Totally. Worth. It.

I felt the cold the moment I stepped out of the plane. The penetrating cold. The snow that surrounded the gravel airstrip didn't exactly help, either. It turned out it wasn't as much the temperature, it was the wind. It crept in through any little opening of my clothes. We had been told that there would be no showers during our two day visit, so I had decided to pack nothing. Well, except for a toothbrush. You know, one of those foldable ones that you get on airplanes, with a very tiny tube of toothpaste that somehow fit in the middle. And I had opted for jeans covering long underwear and four layers of wool and cotton on my upper body. Plus my windbreaker, a grey hat and some gloves.

There are several ways to visit as a traveler, but only during their summer which occurs late October-mid March. I first tried a so-called air cruise in November. I would take a cruise ship there from Ushuaia, the world's southernmost city in Argentina, and fly back five days later. But a military plane crash-landed on the Antarctica airstrip and closed it for over a week. My trip was cancelled, and I spent my holiday in Argentina. Easy is boring.

I returned to South America a month later. To Punta Arenas in Chile. This time I would fly both ways and spend two days in Antarctica. The third option is a full cruise. That will take 9-20 days, and you are not even guaranteed to set foot on land.

It turned out that my group flying to King George Island also counted two Russians and three Americans. Antarctica does not of course, have facilities for tourists, and I did not expect luxury or comfort. We had to walk from the airstrip to the nearest research base, a Russian one, where we were offered instant coffee and chocolate snacks. That would keep us going around the area to explore the sights on base. They included a Chilean naval command center, a Russian church, a modular post office that would have looked less out of place on the Moon, an Antarctic beach and not much else. Before we returned to the Russian base for "dinner." People on a gourmet mission should bring own food. I would have, had I only known. The decent Chilean red wine somehow compensated. We still didn't spend a lot of time eating.

Then Alejo showed up. Our very experienced guide from Santiago was 57 years old, but he looked more like 97. His rough, partly red skin had taken many years to build up. With a little beating by sun, wind, snow, extreme cold and the very dry air that often takes Antarctica visitors by surprise. He had spent most of his life on the continent, skied to the South Pole and climbed Mount Vinson, the highest mountain there 16 times. He would take us to the Uruguayan base over a small snow-covered and roadless mountain in a bright yellow carrier, some sort of a bus on belts. We should be in safe hands. But even Alejo got stuck in the demanding summer conditions with rotten snow and hidden water lagoons. Half an hour of shoveling didn't help either. Our guide picked up his ancient Nokia phone. In Antarctica, battery life beats functionality.

"Solidarity is very strong in Antarctica. This is like a UN in miniature, everybody helps everybody. The Uruguayans are on their way to pull us out," Alejo told us upon hanging up.

An identical carrier, only red, was with us within an hour to give us a ride to the Uruguayan base. We were invited into their common room with a kitchen, a television corner as well as pool and table tennis tables. Beer, wine and Uruguayan liquor were plentiful. And the latter was indeed served on the rocks. As in crystal clear ice from the nearest glacier. What I'd call a nice touch.

Our carrier was salvaged the next day, by 4 people who spent 4 hours shoveling snow, practically digging the carrier out.

But Antarctica is nothing without the penguins. The funny, charming and trusting birds that will give you photo and selfie possibilities of a lifetime. Thousands of penguins live on Ardley Island, but I also saw several groups of 2-3 on random beaches around King George Island. If they don't make you smile, giggle or laugh, nothing will. Just be sure to also observe them in the water. I have never seen more able swimmers. Or indecisive. They cut corners at high speeds and somehow manage 90 degree turns in an instant. I have never seen anything like it. And I am from Norway.

Where fish were practically invented.

ALPHABETICAL LIST OF COUNTRIES; FILL IN YOUR OWN

You can fill in where you have been and what you have done there on the following lists. I recommend that you add together the number with a pencil so that you can keep it updated. There are two empty rows where you can fill in special hobbies or activities undertaken in each country, or you can compare your own traveling to that of your partner, your children or a friend or two.

Europe

There are 47 countries in Europe. Two of them, Russia and Turkey, are also in Asia. I count Russia as European as Moscow, the capital and biggest city is located there. Most of Turkey is located in Asia, but the biggest city by far is primarily located in Europe, and I therefore count Turkey as European. Cyprus is geographically near Asia, but it is culturally relatively European and a member of the EU. I count Cyprus as European.

Country	Page	Been there		
Albania	201			
Andorra	173			
Austria	84			
Belarus	248			
Belgium	149			
Bosnia and Herzegovina	290			
Bulgaria	179			
Croatia	238			
Cyprus	143			
Czech Republic	172			
Denmark	54			
Estonia	148			
Finland	177			
France	327			
Germany	183			
Greece	130			
Hungary	85			
Iceland	175			
Ireland	51			
Italy	189			

Country	Page			
Kosovo	131			
Latvia	193			
Liechtenstein	83			
Lithuania	128			
Luxembourg	82			
Macedonia	132			
Malta	95			
Moldova	170			
Monaco	144			
Montenegro	289			
Netherlands	182			
Norway	45			
Poland	188			
Portugal	142			
Romania	159			
Russia	186			
San Marino	174			
Serbia	171			
Slovakia	205			
Slovenia	286			
Spain	141			
Sweden	176			
Switzerland	83			
Turkey	325			
Ukraine	254			
United Kingdom	52			
Vatican	71			
IN TOTAL				

Africa

There are 55 countries in Africa. No other continents can match that.

Country	Page	Been there		
Algeria	273			
Angola	296			
Benin	99			
Botswana	277			
Burkina Faso	103			
Burundi	285			

Cameroon	65			
Cape Verde	330			
Central African Republic	97			
Chad	66			
Comoros	319			
Congo, Democratic Republic of the	272			
Congo Brazzaville	168			
Djibouti	287			
Egypt	136			
Equatorial Guinea	114			
Eritrea	240			
Ethiopia	75			
Gabon	108			
Gambia	271			
Ghana	118			
Guinea	218			
Guinea-Bissau	280			
Ivory Coast	274			
Kenya	260			
Lesotho	194			
Liberia	270			
Libya	253			
Madagascar	76			
Malawi	262			
Mali	267			
Mauritania	161			
Mauritius	138			
Morocco	326			
Mozambique	196			
Namibia	275			
Niger	102			
Nigeria	300			
Rwanda	167			
São Tomé and Príncipe	111			
Senegal	199			
Seychelles	139			
Sierra Leone	293			
Somalia	120			

South Africa	154			
South Sudan	164			
Sudan	268			
Swaziland	276			
Tanzania	261			
Togo	266			
Tunisia	129			
Uganda	278			
Western Sahara	200			
Zambia	208			
Zimbabwe	224			
IN TOTAL				

Asia

You will find 47 countries in Asia too. I do not count Russia or Turkey as Asian, but the countries are still listed at the bottom in italic so that you can tick them off have you been in the Asian parts of those countries.

Country	Page	Been there		
Afghanistan	34			
Armenia	191			
Azerbaijan	249			
Bahrain	71			
Bangladesh	72			
Bhutan	78			
Brunei	292			
Cambodia	92			
China	155			
East Timor	252			
Georgia	119			
India	151			
Indonesia	93			
Iran	210			
Iraq	124			
Israel	106			
Japan	57			
Jordan	104			
Kazakhstan	17			
Korea, North	244			

Korea, South	216			
Kuwait	70			
Kyrgyzstan	20			
Laos	115			
Lebanon	158			
Malaysia	187			
Maldives	134			
Mongolia	222			
Myanmar (Burma)	74			
Nepal	90			
Oman	236			
Pakistan	43			
Palestine	62			
Philippines	303			
Qatar	72			
Saudi Arabia	298			
Singapore	227			
Sri Lanka	315			
Syria	302			
Tajikistan	30			
Taiwan	55			
Thailand	136			
Turkmenistan	39			
United Arab Emirates	212			
Uzbekistan	27			
Vietnam	230			
Yemen	301			
Russia	*186*			
Turkey	*325*			
IN TOTAL				

Oceania

There are 14 countries in Oceania. This is the smallest continent in terms of land area, but the island nations stretch across a vast area of the Pacific Ocean.

Country	Page	Been there		
Australia	191			
Federated States of Micronesia	320			
Fiji	318			
Kiribati	250			
Marshall Islands	147			
Nauru	88			
New Zealand	68			
Palau	315			
Papa New Guinea	59			
Samoa	314			
Solomon Islands	321			
Tonga	322			
Tuvalu	308			
Vanuatu	316			
IN TOTAL				

North America

There are 23 countries on this particular continent. Not only the US of A, contrary to popular belief.

Country	Page	Been there		
Antigua and Barbuda	145			
The Bahamas	198			
Barbados	146			
Belize	143			
Canada	234			
Costa Rica	220			
Cuba	76			
Dominica	160			
Dominican Republic	327			
El Salvador	282			
Grenada	228			
Guatemala	153			
Haiti	305			

Honduras	283			
Jamaica	87			
Mexico	284			
Nicaragua	169			
Panama	291			
Saint Kitts and Nevis	310			
Saint Lucia	309			
Saint Vincent and the Grenadines	311			
Trinidad and Tobago	180			
United States of America	47			
IN TOTAL				

South America

There are only 12 countries in South America. That makes it the continent with the fewest countries.

Country	Page	Been there		
Argentina	157			
Bolivia	107			
Brazil	78			
Chile	64			
Colombia	202			
Ecuador	161			
Guyana	226			
Paraguay	221			
Peru	232			
Surinam	94			
Uruguay	179			
Venezuela	328			
IN TOTAL				

Antarctica

There are no countries in Antarctica, but it counts as the seventh continent.

	Page	Been there		
Antarctica	336			
IN TOTAL				

In total

	Visited continents	Visited countries		
The European continent				
The African continent				
The Asian continent				
The Oceanian continent				
The North American continent				
The South American continent				
Antarctica				
IN TOTAL	/7	/198	/198	/198
PERCENTAGES				

P.S. To calculate your percentage, divide the number of countries you have been to with 198 and multiply by a hundred. Let's say you have been to 34 countries.

34 / 198 = 0.1717.

0.1717 x 100 = 17.17.

You have then been to just over 17 percent of the 198 countries.

198 THANKS TO THE FOLLOWING

Norwegian publisher Samlaget that first dared to print this book in September 2014.

My brother Øystein and tuba guru Torgeir Halvorsen who used their own holidays to join me in an African desert to help finalize this book and make sure it was readable to most. I am particularly grateful to Øystein who has supported me extraordinarily throughout the entire writing process. He has read versions of this book several times, and is now suffering the consequences in a special home with a tall fence around a relatively nice garden in rural Chad. I send him postcards bimonthly.

Cynthia Morris and Tove Lie who were fascinated by my stories and who based on their own writing experiences gave me very valuable feedback.

Sheila Awalt who undertook the inhuman task of proofreading the English version of this book.

Tanja Birkeland, Laila AlJasem and Lia Miternique who have slaughtered the book more than once, something which have undoubtedly helped improve the end result.

Vegard Skjefstad and Hans Olav Nome for invaluable basketball training much needed for the cover photo.

Scandinavian Airlines SAS and Star Alliance for providing transport - with proper service thrown in - to more than 100 countries. Their eminent lounges didn't hurt either.

BONUS: THE 25 LEAST VISITED COUNTRIES IN THE WORLD

I first wrote about the world's 25 least visited countries on garfors.com in 2013, and the post has has been read almost a million times, in addition to have been translated to several languages, republished in many countries, rewritten and plagerised. Two years passed, and in 2015 it was time for an update of what I consider the ultimate traveler's bucket list.

Perhaps narrowly beaten by visiting all 198 countries in the world.

Why countries are less visited varies, but location, travel related logistics, costs, visa availability, governements or lack thereof and degree of war usually matters. Figures on international visitors are often sparse for the least visited countries, quite a few of them lack tourism offices or governmental agencies that usually report such numbers. UNWTO, World Tourism Organization and the UN, have rather comprehensive overviews, but several countries have not contributed with official numbers. I have therefore, as in 2013, had to look elsewhere. I have used news reports, passenger numbers from airports and spoken to tourist agencies. Tourist numbers can in any case never be totally accurate as various countries count tourists differently. Some do for instance count tourists arriving by plane, others track those that stay in hotels. And there are always some people that claim to be tourists, simply to avoid the extra bureaucracy that may come with travelling on business. Do also note that not all figures are from the same year.

You may be surprised to learn that North Korea is no longer among the 25 countries, with approximately 270,000 international tourists a year (most of them are Chinese).

25. (tie) Dominica: 78,000 tourists

Why so few? A lack of tourists is one of the reasons why this is my favourite Caribbean country. The two airports here cannot take down anything bigger than commercial propeller aircraft, so most people will have to go to some transit trouble to get there. Unless they have a small private jet, of course.

Why still visit? You can't really go wrong visiting a place nicknamed "The Nature Island of the Caribbean". The diverse and fantastic flora and fauna are protected by a number of natural parks, all accessible to you. Do also expect volcanic peaks and Boiling Lake. It is the second-largest hot spring in the world, only beaten by Frying Pan Lake in New Zealand.

What else? Rumours have that the lack of mainstream tourism makes Dominica one of the favourite hot spots for a number of American celebrities. Don't be surprised if Brad Pitt says hi in Pagua Bay Bar & Grill. Then again, you might prefer to meet his wife instead. *(Source: UNWTO, 2013)*

25. (tie) East Timor: 78,000 tourists

Why so few? I bet you do not even know which continent it's in. East Timor is not very well connected to the rest of the world, and you have probably never even heard about any of the airlines that fly there.

Why still visit? The diving is absolutely world-class! And you can stay in luxury hotels elsewhere. I slept in a windowless shed. With a hyperactive rooster nearby.

What else? You will get your visa on arrival in the airport. Nice and easy. And do not miss out on the opportunity to go by mikrolet, or minibus, at least once. They are the veins of the country and go virtually everywhere. Just don't expect them to be on time. *(Source: UNWTO, 2013.)*

23. (tie) Central African Republic: 71,000

Why so few? There is a civil war going on, and religious cleansing has occured on numerous occasions the last few years. It doesn't help that the government, or what is left of it, is weak or that rebel groups are known to randomly attack the international airport in Bangui.

Why still visit? Pygmy communities are not found many places in the world, and here you are invited to stay in pygme villages. Combine that with a trip to Dzanga Sangha Special Reserve, complete with shy forest elephants, mountain gorillas and other wildlife, and you will have a trip of a lifetime.

What else? It is an advantage to speak French when visiting the landlocked country. And do not photograph large groups of angry people without asking permission (then again, which of the mad men do you approach to ask?). I did, and I was very nearly lynched. *(Source: UN, 2012)*

23. (tie) Saint Vincent and the Grenadines: 71,000

Why so few? It is the second longest country name in the world and most people can't even remember half of it. Then again, the country with the longest name is doing just fine, tourism wise. I proudly intorduce The United Kingdom of Great Britain and Northern Ireland. It is no surprise, then, that the countries share a colonial history.

Why still visit? Venture outside Kingstown, the capital, and you will experience a very green and diverse country. You ought to hurry, though. A new airport is being built, and tourism numbers are expected to rise.

What else? Do not forget Vincy Mas, the carnival in late June and early July. You should not be surprised to find yourself surrounded by a lot of partying people, given its slogan: "Hottest Carnival in Caribbean". And of course the *Pirates of the Caribbean* films, starring Johnny Depp, were primarily filmed here. I might also add that the country has a primarily banana based economy. It's not a republic though, so save your jokes. *(Source: UN, 2014)*

22. Djibouti: 63,000

Why so few? You mean you actually know where this country is? A lot of French soldiers certainly do. They are based in Djibouti and fill up the capital every weekend. Expect indecent proposals on town.

Why still visit? Albeit extremely dry, the three regions of the country are diverse and worth a visit. Go scuba diving from the coastal plain and enjoy trips to the volcanic plateaus in the central and southern parts of the country and the mountain ranges in the north.

What else? This is one hot part of the world. Bring sun protection! You might also want to go swimming just outside the entrance to the Red Sea to cool down or to visit Lake Assal which is 157 meters below sea level, and Africa's lowest point. The very dry country was used as "The Forbidden Zone" in *Planet of the Apes*. Djibouti is the easiest point from which to enter Somaliland, a state within Somalia.

(Source: UN, 2013)

21. Liechtenstein: 60,000

Why so few? There is a hell of a lot more action in both Austria and Switzerland, the two only neighbouring countries. Liechtenstein is tiny, and there is virtually nothing going on there at night.

Why still visit? The mountainous scenery is truly fantastic! This is, after all, in the Alps and we are talking about one of only two double landlocked countries in the world. Guess which one is the other. A hint? It is 2,806 times bigger.

What else? Liechtenstein is the world's biggest producer of false teeth. Didn't you always want to know? *(Source: UNWTO, 2013)*

20. Guinea: 56,000

Why so few? The infrastructure in this beautiful and lush country is not quite up to speed, although several international airlines actually fly to Conakry, the capital. Recent ebola outbreaks didn't exactly do the country any favours, either.

Why still visit? The sunset experienced on the beaches is second to none. You might in particular want to experience it on weekends when loads of locals enjoy barbequed fish or meat and big brown bottles of Guiluxe, the local beer.

What else? You are likely to experience heart-warming hospitality. Leave your shyness at home. Or drink a few Guiuluxe to combat it. People will approach and talk to you. Your expected response is a smile. *(Source: UN, 2013)*

19. Tonga: 45,000

Why so few? It is one of the very last absolute monarchies in the world. And very few people can neither spell Nuku'alofa, the capital, nor Fua'amotu, the international airport, so buying a ticket may be tricky. Opening a door may be too. To some people.

Why still visit? The people in the Pacific are renowned for their hospitality. That is of course great in itself, but even better when you know that the Tongans love their feasts with massive barbeques, drinking and dancing.

What else? One of the most unreal, secluded and beautiful beaches I have ever visited is in Tonga. Where exactly? Well, you might find out if you read the chapter on Tonga on page 321 in this book. *(Source: UN, 2013)*

18. Sierra Leone: 44,000

Why so few? There are three realistic options getting from the only international airport to Freetown, the capital. They all include a boat on rough seas, and the risk of transforming your breakfast into fish feed.

Why still visit? The Land of the Mountain Lions will appeal to all your senses with an incredible diversity and an unmatched scenery. The temperature is pretty perfect too, it is rarely below 24 or above 30 degrees Celcius.

What else? They speak English in Sierra Leone, so you will get by easily. Its colonial past helps explain place names such as Waterloo, Man of War Bay, Pirate Bay, New England and Destruction Bay. Do note that this is the second country on this list to have had recent ebola outbreaks. *(Source: UN, 2014)*

16. (tie) Federated States of Micronesia: 35,000

Why so few? The country is often confused with Micronesia - the subregion of Oceania which also includes Nauru, Kiribati, Marshall Islands and Palau. And only United's Island Hopper service and Nauru's Our Airline will fly you to the country.

Why still visit? Micronesia will blow your mind away when it comes to diving and surfing. There is a surfcamp in Pohnpei. Don't expect a crowd.

What else? The number of tourists seem rather low, but keep in mind just over 100,000 inhabitants live there. Visitors that count for 35 percent of the population is still a bit. Then again, there is enough mouth-watering seafood for everyone. *(Source: UN, 2014)*

16. (tie) Mauritania: 35,000

Why so few? 75 percent of the country is desert, and it's spreading. Sand is more interesting than most people think, but still.

Why still visit? This is photography heaven. Some people come to the country to photograph a famous ship graveyard to the north, others take the opportunity to ride one of the longest trains in the world transporting iron ore on 200 or so cars. Jumping onto one of them is usually ok, just don't wear white shorts.
What else? Credit cards are accepted vitually nowhere. I brought US dollars to pay for my goat meat in a small desert town.
(Source: UN, 2103, estimate based on tourism expenditure)

15. Solomon Islands: 24,400

Why so few? It is much less famous than neighboring Papa New-Guinea, Vanuatu, New Caledonia and of course Australia.
Why still visit? It shouldn't be less famous at all. Visit secluded beaches, rainforests with waterfalls, volcanoes and world-class lagoons where you can experience some of the least dived spots in the world. You should also go to the outdoor fish market in capital Honiara, buy a few kinds of super fresh fish and have one of the fish mongers cut them into pieces. You will then experience a truly incredible and unusual sashimi meal by the sea.
What else? Malaria is actually a real threat here. Act accordingly. And fauna lovers are obliged to visit. There are over 230 types of tropical flowers here. Just don't expect to find them all in one spot, the country consists of over 900 islands.
(Source: UNWTO, 2013)

14. Liberia: 24,000

Why so few? What positive news did you last hear from Liberia, again? Neither stories on civil wars or ebola outbreaks qualify. Ellen Johnson Sirleaf was however elected the first female president in Africa in 2006. She was reelected 5 years later, the same year she received the Nobel Peace Prize.
Why still visit? There are a lot of beaches around Monrovia, and the town of Robertsport has some of the best surfing in Africa. And do not forget to experience the ace music scene. One of the music styles is known as hip co. Expect a mixture of hip hop and Liberian English.
What else? Liberia was primarily founded by freed American slaves, and the capital Monrovia is named after James Monroe. The fifth president of the USA worked hard to help establish the new African country. It may not come as much of a surprise that there is a ban on any form of slavery in the constitution.
(Source: UN, 2012, estimate based on tourism expenditure)

13. Comoros: 21,000

Why so few? Only 800,000 people live on the island nation, which has experienced 20 coups or attempted coups since 1975. That's when the country gained independence from France.

Why still visit? How can you resist a country with an airline called Ewa Air? Ewa means "yes" in Shikomor (Comorian). The countries offer great trekking to volcanoes, diving and sailing. And do visit the colourful markets in Moroni.
What else? The African country is the world's largest manufacturer of ylang-ylang, an oil that is used in perfume. The world smells better thanks to the Comoros.
(Source: African Statistical Yearbook, 2014)

12. Afghanistan: 13,300

Why so few? Regular bombings, terrorist attacks and being the home turf of Taliban might have something to do with it. War zone tourism never really did catch on.
Why still visit? The wild mountains, the beautiful scenery, the incredible history and the amazing people. And why not take the opportunity to try on a real burqa in one of the burqa shops. That ought to make you sympathize a little bit with burqa wearing women world-wide.
What else? Just make sure that you have a visa to your next destination after Afghanistan. We did not and had to stand 13 times in extremelly long and demotivating queues outside the Iranian consulate in Herat before we finally secured our permit *out* again. It only took three days thanks to my outrageous queue jumping which made the entire visa seeking community in Herat less than happy. I do hereby apologize.
(Sources: New York Times, 2012, adjusted by UN tourism expenditure numbers, 2013)

11. São Tomé and Príncipe: 10,000

Why so few? It might take a while to get there. I spent 40 hours on a cargo vessel.
Why still visit? There is a reason for the country's slogan "A well kept secret!" - expect impressive Portugese colonial architecture, colourful slums on the outskirt of São Tomé, great fishing, undervalued whale watching, pristine beaches and ace trekking opportunities. And did I mention their heart-warming hospitality?
What else? The country used to be the biggest supplier of cocoa. I am not a chocolatier, but they claim to have the world's best dark chocolate, and may very well be right. Thanks to Claudio Corallo, aka. "The chocolate king of São Tomé". Be aware that you need a visa in advance to be let into the country, or find yourself returned on the same mode of transport that got you there. Another 40 hours on a boat would not have been very welcome, in my case. Luckily, you can now get a visa in advance from your living room. Via email.
(Source: African Statistical Yearbook, 2014)

10. Turkmenistan: 8,697

Why so few? This country isn't as mad as North Korea, but it plays in the same league. They both require a mandatory tourist guide.

Why still visit? "The Door to Hell" is my favourite tourist attraction in the whole wide world. There are no tourists nearby the burning hole in the desert, which is part of the point. Do stay there in a tent overnight, near the flames or regret forever. Just bring food and vodka. Capital Ashgabat also holds the world record for having the most marble-clad buildings. Very impressive, except that virtually no one works in them.

What else? Citizens get free electricity, water and natural gas. I guess the late dictator had to do something nice to stay in power without too many problems. Saparmurat Nijazov took the name "Turkmenbashi" which means Father of all Turkmens, and he had a great number of places in the country named after him. Imagine that you were to travel with Turkmenbashi (the man) from Turkmenbashi (the airport) to Turkmenbashi (the city) during Turkmenbashi (the month) to visit Turkmenbashi (the school) in Turkmenbashi (the street) to drink Turkmenbashi (the vodka)? Probably not what you should do in a school, but you get my point.

(Source: Statistical Yearbook of Turkmenistan, 2011)

9. Guinea-Bissau: 7,500

Why so few? Infrastructure is rubbish and few airlines fly there. TAP Portugal even suspended their flights to and from Bissau after local police forced the pilots to bring 74 Syrian refugees to Lisbon in 2013.

Why still visit? You just have to visit the Bijagos Archipelago of some twenty islands outside the capital. The oysters there are divine. Just do not expect any signs of modern life.

What else? Do not miss out on old Portugese architecture or cooking inspired by the former colonist. To get in fast and easy, pick up your visa at the consulate in Ziguinchor in Senegal, just across the border. The operation will set you back 5 minutes. You are then not far from Varela, a tiny coastal village in a national park to the very north of Guinea-Bissau. Expect close to zero tourists, despite an Italian hotel with food to match.

(Source: UN, 2012, estimate based on tourism expenditure)

8. Libya: 6,250

Why so few? Gaddafi may be gone, but his legacy lives on through embassy attacks and bombings. And it didn't help much that Tripoli International Airport closed down after bombings in 2014, either. All flights were suspended, and there are now only a handful of flights to and from smaller Mitiga International

Airport. You mean you wouldn't fly with Libyan Airlines, Afriqiyah Airways or Buraq Air? Well, neither will most tourists.

Why still visit? You can finally get a visa on arrival. And there is plenty on offer for curious travelers, although you may want to wait until the security situation improves.

What else? There is hope, or so the Libyan government believes. I mean, they actually do have a Minister of Tourism. Ms. Ikram Bash Imam must have one of the most challenging jobs in the world.

(Source: UN, 2010, estimate based on tourism expenditure and stipulated decline, 2014)

7. Kiribati: 6,000

Why so few? 1. Virtually no one has even heard about the Pacific paradise. 2. Fewer still knows how to pronounce the name of the country.

Why still visit? There are loads of possibilities to fly to Kiribati. You can take a plane from Nauru or Marshall Islands once every two weeks. Yeah, or from slightly more famous Fiji, which has two weekly departures to South Tawara, the capital. And you can of course visit Christmas Islands from Fiji or Hawaii. It is in theory 6 hours by plane between Christmas Island and South Tawara, but the islands are not connected by flight.

What else? The letter "s" does not exist in Kiribati, but the sound "s" does. So, to pronounce "s" you write "ti" or "tu". "Kiribati" is therefore pronounced "Kiribass". "T" followed by any other letter than "i" or "u" is pronounced "t" as normal. Piece of cake. *(Source: UNWTO, 2013)*

6. Equatorial Guinea: 5,700

Why so few? This is the worst country on this list to get a visa to, unless you are actually a US citizen. They are excempt. You mean you're not a US citizen? Do accept my apologies. You will have to go through agonizing bureaucratic pain. Or not ever get too see Equatorial Guinea.

Why still visit? Equatorial Guinea is without a doubt bucket list material. And there is very little tourism infrastructure here, so you will be snorkeling all by yourself from one of the nice beaches, given that you bring your own fins and mask.

What else? Do not take any photos, unless you fancy sleeping in a prison cell or bribing a police officer. The country is ruled by Dictator Teodoro Obiang Nguema Mbasogo, although he prefers President as his title. The distribution of the massive oil wealth is extremelly unequal, it has one of the world's worst human rights track records and is allegedly very involved in human trafficking.

(Source: Wikipedia, estimate based on airport arrivals, 2009, then stipulated, 2014)

5. South Sudan: 5,500

Why so few? There is a civil war in the newest country in the world, and tourists are not commonplace. James, the receptionist in my hotel, virtually died from excessive laughter when I told him I was in Juba as a tourist.

Why still visit? James is probably still laughing. And he is particularly generous, even in the hotel bar, when he is in a good mood.

What else? Photography is actually illegal in South Sudan. So, leave your phone in your pocket or excercise extreme caution when snapping those forbidden shots. Two huge police officers were less than impressed when I snapped a couple of photos in the capital, and I had to delete them under their careful supervision. "Consider yourself lucky you are Norwegian," they said. I assume that was a thank you given the large number of Norwegian NGOs that operate in South Sudan.

(Source: Logcluster, estimate based on number of flights, 2013)

4. Marshall Islands: 4,600

Why so few? Because you didn't know that the country actually exists. It is located in the middle of the Pacific, and includes the Bikini Atoll. So, at least you sort of heard about the country.

Why still visit? Divers unite. There are over 1,000 different kinds of fish and 250 types of coral around the islands. That makes this the fishiest country in the world. No pun intended. I also woke up between Laura and Rita every morning, and you can too! Laura in the west is the best beach on Majuro while Rita is an area on the other side of the atoll.

What else? The US performed 67 tests of nuclear bombs here between 1946 and 1958. That includes the biggest nuclear test ever performed, codenamed Castle Bravo, a dry fuel thermonuclear hydrogen bomb. The Atomic Energy Commission regarded Marshall Islands "by far the most contaminated place in the world" in 1956. *(Source: UN, 2012)*

3. Tuvalu: 1,200

Why so few? The propeller plane from Fiji Airways arrives twice a week and is the only fast way to get in or out. There is also the very occasional cargo slash passenger ship (with empashis on cargo) sailing between Fiji and Tuvalu.

Why still visit? This country is one of a kind. People are more genuine and more welcoming than in most other places and everything seems more authentic than what is the case in 'the real world'. The friendliness I experienced in Tuvalu is second to none, expect plenty of offers to ride on the back of random people's mopeds.

What else? Do not forget cash if you ever visit this fascinating country. You mean you have a Black AmEx card? Platinum Visa? Superduper Mega Diamond MasterCard Plus? It just doesn't matter. This is one of a very few countries in the world where no credit cards are accepted. Bring Australian dollars. Or a begging cup. (*Source: UN, 2013*)

2. Somalia: 400 visitors

Why so few? There is a reason why Mo Farah runs so fast.

Why still visit? Mogadishu is now considered *relatively* safe and a lot of businesses have opened or reopened. Several tour companies will sort you out the invitation needed to get a visa on arrival (and they all offer guides with armed guards).

What else? Terror group al-Shabab is doing its best to take over the country. The government has luckily made progress the last few years, and now several foreign airlines have put Mogadishu on its route maps. Somaliland in the north is formally a part of Somalia, and is the only way to visit the country unless you want your mom to never speak to you ever again (then again, this can be a bonus if the similar effect is achieved for your mother-in-law).

(*Source: Estimate based on interviews with Somalian tour companies, 2014*)

1. Nauru: 160 visitors

Why so few? When did you last see a guide book with Nauru on it? The country is tiny, and comes with less than 10,000 inhabitants on 21 square kilometers. Only Our Airline serves the country with its old Boeing 737.

Why still visit? It is the least visited country in the world! And you can run around it.

What else? There are only two hotels in the country, virtually no nightlife and a number of refugees that have been deported from Australia. The country doesn't even have a capital, although Yaren - the biggest village - acts like one. (*Source: Crikey, 2011*)

But what about the three countries that were on my former list? North Korea (270,000), Chad (100,000) and Bhutan (125,000) all report an increase in tourist numbers. Syria would presumably be a likely candidate for the list, but the country had over 5 million visitors in 2011 and tourism numbers have reportedly dropped "over 95 percent". A decline of 98% still means over 100,000 tourists in the war-struck and terrorist plagued country.

The least original countries to visit

The other end of the list provides us with no huge surprises compared to last time, although Spain has passed China and Germany has passed the UK. Russia and Thailand has also made the top ten by replacing Malaysia and Mexico.

1. France 84.7 million tourists
2. USA 69.8 million tourists
3. Spain 60.7 million tourists
4. China 55.7 million tourists
5. Italy 47.7 million tourists
6. Turkey 37.8 million tourists
7. Germany 31.5 million tourists
8. United Kingdom 31.2 million tourists
9. Russia 28.4 million tourists
10. Thailand 26.5 million tourists

Maybe France doesn't sound so tempting, after all?

CONNECT WITH THE AUTHOR

I am always happy to hear from readers or fellow travelers, to exchange experiences or try to answer any questions. Do not hesitate to get in touch.

Follow me on Twitter: @garfors
Find me on Facebook: facebook.com/garfors
See my photos on Instagram: instagram.com/garfors
Or visit my blog on travel and media: garfors.com

Lightning Source UK Ltd.
Milton Keynes UK
UKOW06f1617040416

271499UK00001B/131/P